BUSINESS STUDIES

Fourth Edition
Teachers' Guide

Dave Hall-Rob Jones-Carlo Raffo-Alain Anderton

Edited by Ian Chambers and Dave Gray

CP

Acknowledgements

Graphics by Kevin O'Brien
Cover design by Tim Button
Cover image provided by Shutterstock
Proof reading by Sue Oliver, Sheila Evans Pritchard, Jo Kemp and Heather Doyle.

British Library Cataloguing in Publication Data
A catalogue record of this book is available from the British Library

ISBN 978 1 4058 9232 2

Pearson Education
Edinburgh Gate
Harlow
Essex
CM20 2JE

Contribution © Dave Hall, Rob Jones , Carlo Raffo, Alain Anderton, Ian Chambers, Dave Gray
First edition 1995 reprinted three times
Second edition 2000 reprinted twice
Third edition 2005 reprinted twice
Fourth edition 2008
Second impression 2008

Design page origination and production by Caroline Waring-Collins, Waring Collins Ltd, www.waringcollins.com
Printed by Ashford Colour Press Ltd., Gosport.

Contents

Business Studies (Fourth Edition) Teachers' Guide contains suggested answers to questions and case studies in the students' book **Business Studies (Fourth Edition)**. In some cases there is likely to be a single answer, as perhaps in a calculation question. In other cases there are various answers that may be given and alternatives may be suggested. However, other answers from those included here can also be valid. This should be taken into account by teachers and lecturers when marking work or giving out information as 'model answers'. Marks have also been suggested for case studies. Again, these should be treated as suggestions, which can be varied. They are maximum marks per question. Teachers and lecturers may wish to allocate marks for particular answers given or alternatively mark the answer by a level of response, taking into account assessment objectives – knowledge, application, analysis and evaluation. Suggestions on using mark schemes when marking answers are available on **MyBusSpace.co.uk**. A grid is also provided showing where units from the students' book can be used with particular specifications.

MyBusSpace.co.uk

This is an essential, online support resource for use by teachers and students. It includes an online student book, an accurate graphing tool, questions from the student book that can be answered and marked online, links to key websites providing access to latest business and economic data and a regular updated news section and examination guidance.

For more details contact 0800 579579

1 The nature of business

Question 1

(a) Enterprise is one of the four factors of production. The entrepreneur develops a business idea and then hires and organises the other three factors of production to carry out the activity. Entrepreneurs also take risks because they will often use some personal money to help set up the business. If the business does not succeed the entrepreneur may lose some or all of that money. If the business is successful, any money left over will belong to the entrepreneur. This is called profit. In this case the entrepreneur is Gerry Ford. He set out to bring the continental coffee experience to Britain. He founded Caffè Nero in 1997 and floated it on the London Stock Exchange four years later. He and a partner then bought it back for a reported £225m. Ford hopes to take the Caffè Nero brand to northern Europe and the Middle East, building on the allure of Italian espresso coffee and deli-style food. He is also looking to expand in Britain from 300 to 450 shops by 2010. The company's profits have grown 77% a year from £1.6m in 2003 to £9.1m in 2006. Gerry Ford will be a major beneficiary of this profit.

(b) Caffè Nero will use quite a lot of land. It operates around 330 outlets around the UK and each café will occupy a site - a plot of land. The land may be owned or leased. Caffè Nero will also use natural resources that have been extracted from land. Its main product is coffee. It will have to buy coffee beans which are grown on land. Caffè Nero also serves other food products such as gourmet handmade sandwiches (including panini, focaccia, and wraps), traditional pastas, soups, pizza, salads, biscotti, fresh pastries, and cakes. Most of the ingredients used in the preparation of this food will have come from the land. The people employed in each of the 330 cafes represent the labour used by Caffè Nero. There are likely to be several thousand. The company may also have a head office where administrative staff are employed. A mixture of part time and full time labour is likely to be employed throughout the business. Finally, examples of capital used by Caffè Nero include the furniture, fixtures and fittings in all of the outlets, the buildings themselves, computerised tills, coffee makers and other kitchen equipment used in the preparation of food.

Question 2

(a) Business activity is affected by a number of external forces. These are beyond the control of the individual business. In some cases they constrain a firm's decisions and may prevent its growth and development. However, in others they may provide opportunities. In this case an external force has provided an opportunity for Barchester Healthcare. Barchester Healthcare will benefit in the future from the ageing population. In common with most other countries, the UK has an ageing population. The proportion of people aged 65 and over is projected to increase from 16 per cent in 2006 to 22 per cent by 2031. This is an inevitable consequence of the age structure of the population alive today, in particular the ageing of the large numbers of people born after the Second World War and during the 1960s baby boom. In the future Barchester will have a bigger market to serve which provides more scope for growth.

(b) Business activity is often classed by the type of production that takes place. Barchester Healthcare is a tertiary sector business. This means that it supplies a service. In this case, Barchester provides a healthcare service for the elderly. It runs care homes for over 10,000 residents in over 160 locations. Barchester has a reputation for quality care throughout the UK and focuses on residents' individual needs and providing them with a home from home environment. In 1994 Moreton Hill was awarded the Care Home Design Award.

Case study

(a) All businesses sell their goods and services into markets. In this case Cumbrian Seafoods Ltd sells its output to business customers. The company operates in the fresh fish and seafood market. It has some very high profile customer such as Tesco and Morrisons. Its products include reduced-fat prawn cocktail and oat-coated mackerel, sold under Morrisons' Eat Smart label.

(4 marks)

(b) Cumbrian Seafoods Ltd main business activity is processing fish and seafood. Its wide range of products include value added seafood lines such as Smoked Haddock with Cheese and Chive Melt and Cod in a Mornay Sauce, reduced-fat prawn cocktail and oat-coated mackerel, sold under Morrisons' Eat Smart label. It has a new state of the art factory in Seaham and also owns a number of seafood companies in Cumbria and Northumberland. Most of the company's business activity is therefore in the secondary sector. However, chairman Peter Vassallo has invested in an Icelandic cod and haddock fishery. This suggests that the company is also involved in primary production, where resources are extracted from the land. Fish farming is a primary business activity.

(6 marks)

(c) (i) Business activity involves a number of functions. A business is a system and it has parts that work together to achieve objectives. The functions are all part of the system. One important function of any business is finance. Cumbrian Seafoods Ltd is likely to have quite a big finance department - it made a profit of £6.3 million in 2006. The finance department is responsible for the control of money in a business. It has a number of important duties. This includes recording business transactions, producing documents to illustrate the performance of the business and its financial position and controlling the flow of money in the business.

(ii) Cumbrian Seafoods Ltd is also likely to have a well developed marketing department. Evidence of this is provided by the fact that it has two very high profile customers - Tesco and Morrisons. Marketing has become very important in recent years due to an increase in competition in business. It is concerned with identifying consumer needs and satisfying them, i.e. finding out exactly what companies like Tesco and Morrison want. Examples of marketing activities are market research, advertising, packaging, promotion, distribution and pricing.

(12 marks)

(d) Most businesses are influenced by external factors. These are forces from outside which businesses cannot control. They are likely to constrain the activities of a business but may also provide opportunities. One important external factor which Cumbrian Seafoods Ltd has to take into consideration is the environment. Environmental factors have had a major affect on businesses in recent years. In this case, the fishing industry has been a particular focus for attention from environmentalists. However, Cumbrian Seafood Ltd understand the importance of conservation of marine stocks. In recent years sustainability has become a very hot topic, with high profile protests from a number of environmental groups highlighting local and global concerns. Throughout the life of the company, it has pioneered a sustainable purchasing policy going back more than 20 years. It continues to source from suppliers who meet or exceed the requirements of this policy. Cumbrian Seafoods has a sustainable purchasing policy. For example, it promotes eco-friendly line-caught fishing for its selection of mature fish and minimal by-catch. It educates customers to avoid the use of species from the 36 most heavily depleted stocks on the Marine Conservation Society (MCS) black list. It has invested heavily in developing legitimate, sustainable aquaculture projects across a widening range of species, to meet continuing growth in consumer demands. And finally, it has full traceability back to vessels with evidence that catch falls within quota. To Cumbrian Seafoods, sustainability is not only just about how, where and when it was caught. It is about the impact it has on the community, the eco-system and environmental issues. The company recognises the work of the MCS and Marine Stewardship Council and remains aware of the concern held by some sections of the industry that where certain areas have been certified, this may lead to an intolerable strain on the resource. In addition, it also recognises that wild caught fish is limited to current world catch levels, so it has invested heavily in developing legitimate, sustainable aquaculture projects across a widening range of species to meet continuing growth in consumer demand.

In addition to its commitment to sustainable fishing, Cumbrian Seafoods has recognised the importance of the environment in other areas. For example, when building its new factory, both in the building and the fitting out of the factory, Cumbrian Seafoods worked hard to reduce its carbon footprint from practical measures, rather than subscribing to 'offsets'. It also got planning permission for 2 wind turbines on the site which has allowed it to reach a position where it will achieve energy neutrality in its first year of activity.

Another external factor that will have affected Cumbrian Seafoods is the growing popularity of seafood in the diet. An increasing number of consumers are keen to eat a healthier diet, of which fish and other seafood is an important component. This has led to a big increase in the demand for fish and seafood which will obviously benefit this company. It is clear from these two examples that Cumbrian Seafoods Ltd has been influenced to a significant extent by external factors.

(18 marks)

2 | Enterprise

Question 1

(a) Entrepreneurs are people who initially set up businesses and run them once they are set up. Setting up a business is usually risky due to the uncertainties of operating in an unknown environment. Many businesses fail in the first year due to these uncertainties. John Baker appears to have many of these characteristics associated with entrepreneurs. He set up his own business, Coin Co International, collecting and sorting coins from airline passengers, and changing them into currency. He ran the business, employing 110 people in 2001. He also took risks. Leaving his job working on an airline to set up himself was a risk. The conditions in which he operated were risky. At first he did well , but then the business struggled. When the business struggled he then took another risk, moving into another market, collecting from taxis.

(b) Opportunity cost is the benefit lost from the next best alternative. In John's case it is likely to have been the earnings from his job working for the airline. It could be argued that it might be another business venture if that would have gained him more rewards than his job.

(c) (i) One problem of passing on his business is that his children may not have the same characteristics as John, whose characteristics have helped to make the business successful. These might include drive, commitment, decision making skills, self-confidence and judgment.

(ii) One solution to this is to train his children so that they develop new skills or make use of agencies to help them. Another solution is to employ other people in the business. It could be argued that no matter how much training is given, or how much help, the characteristics of entrepreneurs can only be taught to some extent. His children may not have the same drive that made John so successful for example. If this was the case then taking on others, or perhaps allowing part ownership, may be his only solution.

Question 2

(a) Successful entrepreneurs have certain characteristics. Whether or not Joshua would be a successful entrepreneur might depend on how many and to what extent he possessed these characteristics. Entrepreneurs often feel they can earn more working for themselves. This is the case with Joshua. On the other hand the reason Joshua has had low earnings is because he has failed to meet sales targets. This could suggest that he does not have the drive or judgment to make a successful entrepreneur. Successful entrepreneurs are also able to spot an opportunity and take it. They show initiative. Joshua has seen that there is no print company in the next market town and feels this might allow him to set up a successful business. Joshua does have self-confidence, an important trait for people setting up new ventures. He can take knocks and has perseverance when things do not go well. But his timekeeping is poor. He also does not work out of hours and is perhaps not prepared to take risks. He only sees people who he is certain will give him work. He therefore may miss out on new opportunities. He also fails to pursue large contracts. In conclusion, it could be argued that Joshua has self-confidence and

perseverance and has shown some initiative. However, being a successful entrepreneur requires real commitment, which Joshua does not appear to have according to his manager. He also, perhaps, lacks the risk taking abilities required for being a successful entrepreneur.

Case study

(a) An entrepreneur is a person who sets up new businesses and run them. Annabel Karmel has set up a number of successful ventures. Her first was perhaps as an author, writing books. After writing her first book she has since written 14 books about feeding children. Another venture of hers is designing cookery ranges, like the one for Boots. A further successful business activity is the development of ready-prepared meals. All of these activities were risky to some extent, another feature of an entrepreneur. For example, she wrote her first book with little real knowledge about writing or typing. **(5 marks)**

(b) Opportunity cost is the benefit lost from the next best alternative. In Annabel's case it is possible that the opportunity cost of writing her first book might have been earnings from a job. This might have been working for a business or working at home when looking after her children. It might have also been some other activity that could have earned money. For example, she might have decided to produce ready-made meals first.

(5 marks)

(c) Successful entrepreneurs have many characteristics. Annabel Karmel is a successful entrepreneur and possesses many of these traits. She showed perseverance. Initially she was turned down by 15 publishers. But she took her book to the Frankfurt book show and eventually found a publisher. She also showed initiative in a number of areas. She identified the need for books about cooking for children. She also identified a gap in the market for ready-prepared children's meals, now stocked by supermarket chains. She has shown a great commitment to her business over many years. On her own admission she gave up her social life for a number of years. She works late to make sure that jobs get done. Further, she is a self-starter and shows self-confidence. She was prepared to set up her own meal operation despite being approached by many businesses.

(15 marks)

(d) The greater potential financial rewards that can be earned from setting up in business attract many people to become entrepreneurs. Annabel Karmel is likely to have been rewarded well as a successful entrepreneur. She has written 14 books. Her first book has sold more than 2 millions copies. She was also able to invest £350,000 in a range of ready-prepared meals. These factors might suggest that financial rewards were an influence on running her own business.

However, there are perhaps other factors that were also important. Her first book was written when her child was experiencing eating difficulties as a form of therapy. She also made the decision not to work with other businesses when setting up her ready-prepared meal operation. As she states, she 'wanted to be in control of what she was doing'. She may have earned larger rewards by working as a larger operation, but she appeared to sacrifice this for more control.

In conclusion, it could be argued that financial rewards are likely to have been motivating to some extent, as everyone needs to earn money to pay for expenses. But in Annabel Karmel's case other factors appear to be as important, if not more important, in running her own business.

(15 marks)

3 Business ideas

Question 1

(a) Entrepreneurs get the ideas for their businesses from many areas. Claire's idea came from the experience of people that she was working with and perhaps her own personal experience. She worked in the City and noticed that colleagues were so busy they did not have time to organise their everyday life. This might have included making payments or arranging travel. She set up BuyTime, a lifestyle service, where a personal assistant would carry out these tasks for the client.

(b) Business Link's criteria are:

• Experience and expertise. Claire had experienced first hand working in the City how time was precious. She is likely to understand the demands of clients.

• Market. There is a market either to individuals or to businesses who use the service for their top employees. In particular there appears to be a market to women who work as they are increasingly working the same hours as men, but also expected to take care of aspects of home life.

• Competitors. The article does not mention any competitors. It might be assumed that there were few if any, otherwise Claire may not have noticed the gap in the market.

• Special nature. The service offered by Claire's business appears to be fairly unique. It caters for specific needs of business people who are not really offered this service by others.

• Funding. There is no mention of funding in the article, although it might be a fairly low cost business to start, as little capital might be needed for equipment etc. The main cost is likely to be the 12 staff and any premises.

• Risks. There are always risks with new ventures. Claire was starting a business she had no real experience in running. However, the costs of exit might be low, so risk may be reduced.

Overall, it might be argued that Claire's business idea is a good one and meets many of the Business Link criteria.

Question 2

(a) A franchisor is a business that allows other businesses to use its business idea for a fee. A franchisee is a business that pays for the right to use the business idea of the franchisor.

(b) There are certain advantages to an entrepreneur in buying a Domino's Pizza franchise. The main advantage is the reduced risk involved. Setting up a new business is always risky. Many fail in the initial trading period. But a franchisee selling Domino's Pizzas is selling an established product with a brand name. People know the products and it may be less difficult to build up a client base. Further, training and support is provided by the franchisor. This includes help in finding premises. The franchisor also takes on the role of marketing. So it can mass market to many people, increasing the brand name and establishing brand loyalty. All these features should help a new franchisee, such as Anthony Tagliamonti, to reduce risk and perhaps cut costs, although there is still the fee to be paid to the franchisor.

(c) There are also advantages to businesses in using the franchise model to expand and grow their operations. Expanding rapidly into many markets, perhaps in other countries, can be difficult. Operating a franchise allows businesses such as the owners of Domino's Pizza in the US to expand fairly rapidly into many areas. The business does not need to raise funds from a bank, for example. The funds are provided by the franchisees which pay fees of over £240,000 + VAT for the franchise. The model also helps to ensure that the business is operated with well motivated staff. As Anthony says, he is never bored and is always looking for new ways to increase sales. Poor motivation is often a problem with large organisations and the franchise model may help the owners of Domino's Pizza to get around this difficulty.

Case study

(a) Products that are distinctive, with different features from other products, can often, although not always, be successful. Washa Ltd, has developed the Rolla Washa. It is a plastic container into which rollers, used by painters, are put for cleaning. The product is distinctive because it saves, time, effort and water compared to the usual way of cleaning rollers. This would be useful for busy decorators. It also makes it more environmentally-friendly.

Tim and Elaine Woodley's soap products also have certain distinctive features. They are made 'from scratch'. They do not include animal products and are not tested on animals. This makes them appealing to ethical consumers. One of their products, the Red Star Pony Polish, is the only horse shampoo on the market that is free from animal products. **(5 marks)**

(b) There is a number of ways in which business can check to see if there is in fact a market for a new, innovative product and whether a successful business venture could be made out of it. One way is to examine the current market. If there are other products on the market, such as soaps for animals, then this might indicate people are willing to buy. But making a product different might also be successful. So checking to see if there is a gap in the market that no other product is filling might indicate the chances of success. In both businesses, they appear to be selling products which are not currently available on the market.

Another method of checking might involve using some form of market research. For example, Washa Ltd might have contacted distributors to see if the business had products they were interested in and might be able to sell. They would have experience of selling other products and might be able to give advice. Tim and Elaine Woodley might have taken advice from Business Link about their venture. They might have given them advice on protecting their rights when developing the product. Both businesses may also have carried out research into the views of customers. For example, decorators might have been asked their views on the new cleaning equipment and customers might have been asked about the desire for cruelty free soaps. **(10 marks)**

(c) Intellectual property is a term often talked about when businesses are developing new products. Property is what a business owns. It might be a physical set of premises, an office or a factory. Property has value for a business. Intellectual property is something of value that a business owns, but it not a physical item. It includes the value associated with non-physical aspects of a product. These might be the brand name of the product or the logo used to market the product. These aspects have a value. This might include the goodwill that customers have to the product and the brand loyalty they show, so they keep returning to buy the product, leading to continued sales and extended life cycles of the product. Businesses can take legal steps to protect their intellectual property rights. This might involve taking out a patent or registering a trade mark so that others cannot copy their property in the same way that others cannot steal physical property which is owned. **(10 marks)**

(d) It is important that businesses protect their intellectual property rights. In the two businesses in the cases, they would need to take legal steps to ensure that the brand names of the products are not copied by other businesses. They would also need to ensure that the ways their products are made are not copied by others. It is vital that new business ideas are protected. Developing new products can be expensive. A business would need to spend money before it brings a product to the market. Only after it starts to sell will it recoup this money. But if others can copy a product, then the chances of being able to sell well and operate successfully are greatly reduced. If a large business was able to produce its own version of the product, then it might prevent the business idea from ever talking off. It is suggested, for example, that Washa would be worth £2.5 million if its Rolla Washa product took off. If another business was simply able to bring out its own version of the Rolla Washa, perhaps even calling it the same name, then the business is unlikely to achieve this valuation. In conclusion, it could be argued that for all businesses, not just those in the article, it is vital to protect intellectual property rights.

(15 marks)

4 | Business plans

Question 1

(a) There are certain advantages to writing a business plan for new entrepreneurs. It appears that Robert Crampton had not thought through many aspects of his operation. A business plan makes entrepreneurs consider if they have a competitive advantage over others. Robert had not considered this. He simply thought that he had a good idea, that would appeal to children and adults. But he had not considered whether it was different enough from other products or whether it would be attractive enough from what was already available. A plan can also be used to assess the need for finance or any borrowing. Robert did not know how much money would need initially to be put into the business to start it up and pay for equipment or labour. If Robert had drawn up an effective business plan he might have been able to consider his future finances and whether his business would be attractive enough from alternatives to be successful.

(b) It could be argued that writing a business plan would be a waste of time if, as in the case of Robert, an entrepreneur decides not to go ahead with a business idea. Robert decided to remain in journalism rather than take on the business venture. So writing a plan for something that did not materialise could be argued to be a waste of time and money.

On the other hand, writing a business plan could have helped Robert to identify all aspects of a business idea clearly. He may have used this information in a number of ways. It might simply have made up his mind that his current occupation is a better option for him and make him more motivated in his current job. He might find that in future, if he no longer has a job, he may return to the business idea. He may be made redundant or he may decide that eventually he does want to work for himself. In this case the time spent would not have been wasted.

Question 2

(a) Other items that might be included in a business plan for a new salon could be:
* the business idea, to set up a beauty salon offering a variety of treatments;
* the market for the business, such as the potential size of the market and the likely customer;
* the personnel required, such as the number of stylists and other staff;
* the premises needed, including how large and whether they are to be leased or bought;
* financial forecasts, for example the likely cash flow each month;
* the finance required to set up the business initially, including how much will be put in by Tahira and how much by others.

(b) The objectives of a business are the goals it plans to achieve. Listing the objectives in a business plan helps a business. It sets out what the business wants to achieve. It gives it a clear idea of its goals, often in measurable targets. This can motivate the business. It can also be used to assess how successful the business is in future. For example, setting out objectives might allow a business to see if its targets are realistic given the market it is operating in and the nature of its service.

Case study

(a) A business plan contains a number of items. It includes the name of the business, in this case AKC Home Support Services. It describes the business opportunity, to provide a care business. It also sets out the objectives of the business, its goals. AKC had financial goals and strategic, long-term goals that it wanted to achieve set out in its plan. The business plan also includes forecasts. AKC may have included cash flow, profit and loss accounts and balance sheets. This may have helped to identify that the business was likely to get into financial problems working in another county. Business plans also include the finance needed. AKC required a loan to buy a residential care home. It also received funds from ShellLiveWIRE. **(15 marks)**

(b) Outside organisations can be a great help to businesses when drawing up a business plan. AKC has help from a variety of sources. This might be organisations such as Business Link or small business advisors. Or it might be from other people such as family and friends. Organisations are likely to have a wealth of experience in drawing up plans. They will be able to spot problems that the business could experience when drawing up the plan. The plan could then be revised. They are also likely to be able to draw on their experience of similar plans in the industry which have been successful so that a business can benchmark against other businesses. These organisations are likely to be objective. They might point out that sales in plans are over-optimistic. But other people who might run their own business can also help. They may have drawn up their own plans and can give advice on the best way to do this. They may be able to point out missing items. **(10 marks)**

(c) Some people argue that writing a business plan is a waste of time. They see it as form filling, as was the case with AKC at first. It can take time to research and then write a plan. This may also cost money. AKC felt at first that the plan was more for others, such as a bank that might be approached for a loan. There might be some support for this argument. Writing a plan will take time if done correctly. This time might be better used starting a business. Waiting might give others time to enter a market or create products or services, so that when the business is ready to begin it has lost the opportunity.

On the other hand many new businesses fail. One of the major reasons is that they are badly prepared, overestimate the market or plan poorly so that cash flow problems occur. These difficulties might be avoided with a well thought out business plan. Although a business plan is not a guarantee of success, it can help a business to have a clear idea of its aims and objectives and how to achieve them. So it might be argued that even though delays can be a problem, all business ventures should have a business plan. The key is to make sure that it is suitable for the business and is done quickly and efficiently so the opportunity is not lost. **(15 marks)**

Question 1

(a) Businesses fail for a number of reasons. Chris Watkins' business may have failed because of relying on too small a market. He was selling mainly to smaller stores rather than supermarket chains. This would have restricted his sales. Another problem might have been costs rising. He hoped to borrow £100,000 as a business loan. In the end he had to remortgage his house, which was likely to have been at a higher rate of interest. Another problem was unforeseen shocks. Chris would not have expected his marketing campaign to fail so badly.

(b) Businesses often fail because of badly produced business plans. Chris did produce a business plan. The figures in the plan looked good. It showed that sales revenue was higher than costs even in the first year. But there appear to have been many problems with the plan. Chris may have overestimated the size of his market. His market research may have been limited. Simply contacting some local shops for feedback may not have given a representative sample. Just because they said they would buy the product does not mean that they actually would. And the plan did not take into account the higher costs that resulted.

On the other hand the failure of the marketing plan was unexpected. This would have severely affected sales. But any good business plan would take into account unforeseen changes in the market to some extent. Chris did not have enough capital to cover this unexpected shock. So, in conclusion, it could be argued that the weak business plan was the main reason for the failure of the business.

Case study

Note: in the first impression of the 4th edition there is a misprint. This has been corrected in reprints. The total salary was £50,000 a year at their garage job.

(a) Writing a business plan is important for new business start-ups. A business plan makes businesses consider if they have a competitive advantage over others. They would consider whether their product was different enough compared with other products or whether it would be attractive enough from what was already available. A business plan will also help a start-up to assess the need for finance or borrowing. Having enough capital is vital for any new business. Without adequate capital a business may have to cease trading if it experiences difficulties. A business plan can also help a new start-up to assess if its objectives are realistic. It can ask others to view the plan and comment. If the objectives are not realistic they can be revised. This gives a greater chance of success. **(10 marks)**

(b) Rosie and Dean Spencer took a number of risks when starting up their business. One risk would simply have been leaving their paid jobs. They were working for a garage as mechanics. They planned that the new business venture would pay them a salary of £20,000 each. This was less than the £25,000 each they were receiving in their current job. They would have taken a risk that they could live on this lower income.

Another risk they took was in setting up a similar business but offering a better quality service at lower prices. They would have planned that the better service would mean that increased demand would offset the lower prices, so that turnover was higher. A further risk was that there was existing competition in the area, which had operated for many years perhaps with a loyal set of clients.

A further risk was that they could cope with the demands of working for themselves. Any new business start-up is demanding. Many people work longer hours than if they were working for another business. They found that the first year of operation was hectic. They may not have had the skills to run parts of the business, which would have been carried out by others in the garage in which they worked.

One important risk that they took was that they could obtain the finance for the operation. They needed both an overdraft and a bank loan to cover start-up costs. Without this, they may not have been able to set up. Further, if sales revenue of £200,000 had been less than this, they may not have been able to afford the repayments..
It could be argued that any business start-up is risky. New businesses can fail due to the demands placed upon them. But in Rosie and Dean's case they were operating a business in which they had previously had some experience of working. They may have been able to take some customers with them. This is likely to have reduced their risk to some extent. **(15 marks)**

(c) It could be argued that Rosie and Dean's business plan was poor. Many aspects of their plan did not materialise once they started trading. Demand was greater than anticipated. This meant that they had to take on one more employee than planned after 6 months, which would have raised labour costs. They also experienced financial difficulties. They exceeded their overdraft limit, mainly due to poor credit control. People were not paying their invoices and so the business was facing cash flow difficulties. They were only able to avert this crisis with business development agency funding. A further problem was that the rapid expansion was unforeseen. They had to move premises, but when these were vandalised work stopped. Customers had to wait for work. Some may have gone to other garages.

On the other hand there were some strong points of the plan. It seems to have been based on a good knowledge and research of the local market. They identified a need for a better service at lower prices. The fact that the business was so successful perhaps supports this. It also appears to have been realistic, with some growth anticipated. They had not anticipated taking out a great deal in drawings at the start, to give the business better chance of success.

The main problem appears to have been the unexpected circumstances that occurred. Greater demand would have led to more sales. These should have allowed the business to cope with the higher labour costs. But poor credit control meant that the business faced cash flow problems. It might be suggested that a good business plan should take into account unforeseen occurrences. But a business plan cannot cover everything, such as vandalism to the premises. In conclusion, it might be argued that the business plan was not actually poor. However, it was not as strong as it might have been and perhaps should have taken into account the possibilities of different situations. **(15 marks)**

6 | Stakeholders

Question 1

(a) (b) Possible stakeholders and their benefits include the following. The US airforce is the customer that is buying the tankers. It will benefit from gaining replacements for old tankers. EADS plants in France, Spain and Germany will provide the parts and the 6,000 people in Wales will be making the wings. They will be guaranteed work. Workers in Mobile will assemble the aircraft. 1,000 jobs will be created. People may gain employment in the area. They will have more money to spend in the city. Other British companies such as Cobham will be supplying parts. They will gain extra work. However, stakeholders at Boeing may suffer. The owners may suffer lower profits. There will be restructuring and some workers will lose jobs, such as those employed at the plant in Everett. Other workers and support staff will also lose their jobs. Suppliers of Boeing will lose orders.

Question 2

(a) NMG is a water supplier in the North East and South East of England. The objectives of customers might be to have clean water, provided securely and regularly, without problems or disruptions, at affordable prices. Investors might want the company to make profits so they can receive returns. The wider community may want the business to control any waste and minimise damage to the environment through its operations.

(b) It could be argued that stakeholders other than shareholders should have more influence in a water company than an engineering company. Water companies are providers of public services. These make use of natural resources which are necessities of life. In the past such operations have been controlled by government concerned about ensuring the operation of the business. It might be suggested that, given the importance of the service they provide, the public in its widest sense should have more control than shareholders, who are perhaps only interested in making profit.

On the other hand, water companies are businesses. They are in business to make money. People will only invest and buy shares for a return. Without shareholders the resources may not be provided unless the operations are taken into public ownership, at cost to the taxpayers. In this view it is the shareholders who are risking their own money in the business and should therefore have the major say in its operation.

Case study

(a) There is a variety of different stakeholders at The Body Shop. Stakeholders are likely to have their own particular objectives. It could be argued that given the large number of stakeholders in the company, inevitably there will be conflict between stakeholders.

Eighty per cent of customers, for example, shop at The Body Shop because of the values of the company. But the company has been taken over by L'Oreal which is 26 per cent owned by Nestlé. Nestlé has been criticised about its sale of baby milk in Third World countries. This might suggest that there are differences in approach between certain parts of the business organisation. Also, there might be a conflict between the views of customers and the owners of the business. Customers may take into account ethical considerations, but shareholders may be more concerned about profit.

There may also be conflict between suppliers and the business. The Body Shop works with suppliers. They are assessed annually to see if they conform to the supply standards set by the company. Suppliers have been encouraged to work with new natural ingredients and reduce alternatives to chemicals. This may cause the costs of suppliers to rise.

On the other hand The Body Shop states that it is committed to running a commercially successful, sustainable business. It does not believe that there is any conflict between commercial success and social and environmental responsibility. The Body Shop has been very successful in attracting customers to buy its products through its ethical stance. Eighty per cent shop with the business because of this. It could be argued therefore that it is in the interest of all stakeholders to make sure that they follow the ethical codes set down by the business. If they do so, then it will have been proved to be a successful business model and they will all benefit. Conflict may only result, therefore, if the model starts to become less successful.

(40 marks)

(b) Adopting a stakeholder approach for business involves giving less importance to the interests of owners and greater importance to the interests of others stakeholders than is usual for businesses in a competitive environment. Adopting such an approach by The Body Shop would mean that it would have to consider the views of all groups, including employees, customers, suppliers, franchisees, and even other companies.

There are likely to be major costs for this for the business. There will be costs involved in the communication and assimilation of all these views. This can be time consuming and expensive. It may delay key decisions, especially if there is a difference of opinion. If shareholders' views are marginalised they may take out their investment and the company may suffer as a result. For example, L'Oreal may decide to sell the business if it does not feel that it is being run to its liking.

On the other hand there are major advantages in taking a stakeholder approach. There are many different stakeholders in The Body Shop. If they feel their views are being taken into account, this can help to motivate them. This is especially important for franchisees, for example. It will also be motivating for the suppliers of products in developing economies who will feel that they are not simply being dictated to. Taking account of different views can benefit the business operations. Costs may be lowered and supply chain problems might be more easily solved. Customers might also be attracted to the business, resulting in increased sales.

In conclusion, it could be argued that taking a stakeholder approach is more important for a business like The Body Shop that stresses its corporate social responsibility. Taking such an approach may become a marketing tool for the business. If this is the case then the benefits are likely to outweigh the costs.

(40 marks)

Question 1

(a) One of the main disadvantages of operating as a sole trader is that the owner has unlimited liability. This means that if the business has debts, the owner is personally liable. In this case Joanna Carter could be forced to sell her personal and family possessions to meet these debts.

(b) One of the main advantages of operating as a sole trader is that Joanna will be able to keep all of the profit, after tax, made by the business. She does not have to share it with anyone else because she is the sole owner. Joanna will also benefit from the personal service she will be able to offer her customers. This is because sole traders tend to be small businesses. Joanna has a reputation for creative and thoughtful bouquets and arrangements. She may find that her clients prefer to deal directly with the owner of the business and pay a higher price for doing so. Sole traders like Joanna may also qualify for financial support. For example, she is in the process of applying for an Enterprising Woman grant run by Surrey University which will give her £350-worth of funding.

(c) Many new business owners seek help and support when they set up their businesses. Joanna has enjoyed help from her local Business Link - a free and impartial guide to business advice, resources and information. For example, she was able to book a place on an advanced bridal skills course with a highly respected London florist. The course costs £900 and half of the cost will be paid for through the Skills Development Team at Business Link. Joanna is also looking into a broadband grant so she can provide a slide show of her work for potential corporate customers and wedding bookings.

Question 2

(a) A deed of partnership is a legal document which outlines the partners' rights in the event of a dispute. For example, it covers the amount of capital each partner contributes and how the profits should be divided. If there is no deed of partnership then the arrangements between partners will be subject to the Partnership Act. According to this act profits will be divided equally between partners. Therefore, in this case, each partner will get £60,000 profit each (£180,000 ÷ 3).

(b) One of the main advantages of operating as a partnership is that the workload of and responsibility for running the business can be shared. For example, Gillian, Sarah and Maria will be able to cover for each other during illness, maternity leave and holidays. They can also exchange ideas and opinions when making key decisions. Partnerships are able to raise larger amounts of capital. In this case the three partners were able to contribute a total of £60,000. This amount may have been difficult for one person alone to find. The partners may also specialise and thus improve the efficiency of the business and offer a wider range of services. For example, Gillian may be specialising in cosmetic dental treatments.

(c) One of the main disadvantages of operating as a partnership is that the partners may disagree about the way the business should be run. In this case after three successful years in business together a disagreement did occur. Gillian wanted to develop the private work more aggressively. In particular she wanted to attract more patients requiring cosmetic work - this was generally very lucrative. However, Sarah and Maria were more committed to NHS work. They were not in it just for the money! It is possible in this case that the partnership may have to be dissolved because Gillian feels that the only way forward is for her to break away from the partnership.

Case study

(a) A partnership is defined in The Partnership Act 1890 as the 'relation which subsists between persons carrying on business with common view to profit'. In simple terms it means that a business has more than one owner. In this case there are two partners in the business - Hristo Petrov and Mark Watkins. These two joint owners will share responsibility for running the business and also share the profits.

(4 marks)

(b) Unincorporated businesses are those where there is no legal difference between the owners and the business. Everything is carried out in the name of the owners. In this case there is no legal difference between Oxford Vintage cars, the business, and Hristo Petrov and Mark Watkins, the owners. For example, if the business was sued the legal action would be directed at the two partners - Hristo and Mark - and not at Oxford Vintage Cars.

(6 marks)

(c) This case clearly highlights one of the most difficult problems faced by sole traders. This is the difficulty in raising finance. Sole traders often find that even if their businesses are successful, attracting new finance can be a problem. Small businesses are considered risky by money lenders and other capital providers. In this case Hristo Petrov has a particular problem because he has a poor credit rating due to the repossession of his house. This makes Hristo an even bigger risk and explains why he can't attract funding.

(6 marks)

(d) Hristo says that at first he did not want to enter into a partnership. This was probably because he had set up a successful and profitable business and did not want to share the future profits generated from his previous efforts. He may also have had reservations about sharing decision making. An equal partner has an equal say in the way the business should be run. Hristo may have been worried about the possibility of disagreements in the future.

(8 marks)

(e) One of the advantages of partnerships is that the owners can specialise in the different tasks required to run the business. This will improve efficiency and allow the business to provide customers with a wider range of services. It seems in this case that the partners will definitely specialise. For example, according to Hristo, Mark will be good on the restoration side and will be able to supervise the mechanics more effectively than himself. Also Hristo believes that his expertise is in the buying and selling of the cars so he will concentrate on that. This means that the business will benefit from the two partners concentrating on the different tasks that they are both good at. Specialisation will improve efficiency and therefore the business will make more profit. There is a lot of scope for specialisation here and you would expect Histro to exploit the opportunities as far as possible.

(12 marks)

Question 1

(a) It is evident that Gigasat Limited is a private limited company because it has the word 'Limited' in its name. There is also information in the case about the date the company was incorporated (16.10.2000) and its registered address in Leighton Buzzard. The registration number of the company is also given (04090608).

(b) (i) Limited companies have legal obligations. Some of these relate to shareholders. For example, shareholders in limited companies are entitled to attend the AGM. This means that Gigasat must inform all shareholders in writing of the date and venue for AGMs well in advance. Shareholders are also entitled to receive a copy of the annual report and accounts.

(ii) A private limited company also has legal obligations to the Registrar of Companies. Every year a copy of the accounts and annual reports must be filed with the registrar. Also, the registrar must be notified if there are any changes to the names of the directors.

(c) One of the main advantages of operating as a private limited company is that the owners have limited liability. This means that if the company collapses and ceases to trade, the owners will only lose the amount they originally invested in the company. For example, in this case Chris re-mortgaged his house to launch Gigasat. The money he raised by doing this is the most he can lose. He cannot be made to sell any further assets to meet business debts. Another advantage of operating as a private limited company is that more capital can be raised. Since there is no limit to the number of shareholders, Gigasat could invite more shareholders to contribute capital if they chose to. Also, control of the company cannot be lost to outsiders. This is because shares cannot be sold to new members without the consent of the existing shareholders.

Question 2

(a) Private equity companies are organisations that borrow money from banks, add a little of their own, and then use the cash to buy a business. In this case Duke Street Capital is a private equity company. They have bought Burton Foods, the UK's second largest biscuit producer, for £200 million.

(b) One of the key features of private equity companies is that they attempt to improve the efficiency of the businesses they buy. By doing this they will increase the profitability. Many say that they pursue efficiency ruthlessly. In this case, just two months after buying Burton Foods, it was announced that biscuit production would cease at its factory in the Wirral, with the loss of 660 jobs. The announcement of the job cuts sparked an angry reaction from unions. Tony Woodley, joint general secretary of the newly-created Unite union, said: 'We are not going to just roll over and accept this. We will be urgently consulting with our members about a strategy to keep the factory open and will meet management on Monday to hear their rationale for this body-blow to Merseyside manufacturing'. The factory in Moreton is the biggest employer in the Wirral after Vauxhall cars. Mr Woodley said the job losses would 'devastate the community'. Efficiency drives that result in job losses are said to be ruthless because of the effect they have on local communities, as illustrated in this case. However, Paul Kitchener, chief executive of Burton's Foods, said that while the company 'sincerely' regretted the loss of jobs, the changes were needed because of overcapacity in the biscuit market.

Case study

(a) One of the main reasons why a business becomes a public limited company is to raise finance. Public limited companies can raise large amounts of finance because there is no limit to the number of shares which can be sold and anyone is allowed to buy them. In this case, ImmuPharma has become a public limited company because it needed to raise money to help develop its drugs. According to the case, the main purpose of the float was to raise money to finance initial clinical trials on ImmuPharma's drugs for severe pain and MRSA-related infections.

(6 marks)

(b) The Alternative Investment Market (AIM) is a 'junior' stock market for smaller and often newly formed public limited companies. The main advantage to ImmuPharma of listing on AIM is that the high costs of obtaining a full listing on the London Stock Exchange are avoided. It is cheaper and easier to join AIM. However, ImmuPharma's shareholders will not have the same protection as those with 'fully' quoted shares.

(4 marks)

(c) The amount of money raised by the flotation is £28,815,000 (67.8 million × 42.5p).

(6 marks)

(d) One of the disadvantages of becoming a public limited company is the cost. Some of the floatation expenses include legal fees, publication and distribution of a prospectus, underwriting fees and administration costs. A good proportion of the £2.8 million raised by the floatation will be used to meet these costs. Other ongoing costs will be incurred to pay for compliance with company law and stock market regulations. Another problem is that since anyone can buy their shares, it is possible that the company may become the victim of a takeover. This means that outsiders could take control of the company. ImmuPharma will also have to disclose financial information to the Registrar of Companies. This means that anyone can view it and it may be useful to competitors. Some public limited companies become very large and are less effective at dealing with employees and customers at a personal level. They may be inflexible and find it difficult to cope with change. However, ImmuPharma are only a small plc so they should not suffer from such problems. Finally, there may be a divorce of ownership and control where the shareholders, because they are widely spread, lose effective control of the business to dominant executives. However, again, this is unlikely at the moment while ImmuPharma is so small.

(10 marks)

(e) At the moment the financial position of ImmuPharma does not look impressive. Its turnover is very small, just £44,818 in 2006, and it has made losses of around £2 million in both 2005 and 2006. However, this is quite typical for a pharmaceutical company whose activities focus on research and development. Revenues are expected to be low until clinical trials have been completed and the drugs can come to the market. ImmuPharma's main product is designed to treat Lupus, a chronic, potentially life-threatening disease. It is estimated that one million people worldwide have been diagnosed with the disease and there is currently no cure or specific treatment. Immupharma's drug, IPP-201101, has the potential to halt the progression of the disease in a substantial proportion of patients. According to a recent Datamonitor report, the currently unique ImmuPharma drug, has an 'achievable' peak market share of 50 per cent. The report also suggests that the drug could sell at a similar cost to interferon, the multiple sclerosis treatment - around $10,000 a year per patient. Also, Immupharma has stated that due to the nature of the disease and lack of treatments, the US Food and Drug Administration may permit a fast track development and approval process for Phase III once the Phase II study is finished. If approved, the drug could be available on the market as early as 2010. This seems a long way off but if the drug comes through the trials the revenue potential is enormous at $5,000 million per annum (50 per cent × 1,000,000 × $10,000). In the mean time, now that ImmuPharma is a plc, its profile will be raised and it will be easier to attract finance to fund further research and development if necessary. The future is uncertain because clinical trials can fail, but the potential is huge.

(14 marks)

9 | Legal structure - not-for-profit organisations

Question 1

(a) A worker co-operative is owned by the people who work in the business. Suma is a worker co-operative because the day-to-day work is carried out by self-managing teams of employees who are all paid the same wage, enjoy an equal voice and have an equal stake in the success of the business. Suma is a truly democratic business that does not operate with a hierarchical organisational structure. It uses an elected Management Committee to implement decisions and business plans. However, the decisions themselves are made at regular General Meetings with the consent of every cooperative member. There's no chief executive, no managing director and no company chairman.

(b) It is very likely that the staff working at Suma are well motivated. There may be a number of reasons for this. One important motivator is of a financial nature. Any trading surpluses generated by Suma are likely to be shared amongst the workforce. They have an equal stake in the business and are therefore entitled to equal shares in the financial benefits. Further, all workers are paid exactly the same wage. Consequently, the workforce is likely to be more united and there will be much less scope for conflict caused by pay differentials. Finally, all members are involved in decision making. They attend regular general meetings where their views can be expressed and ideas aired. This will make them more involved and they will feel that they have been recognised. This will also help to improve motivation.

Case study

(a) All charities have specialised aims. They exist to raise money for a specific 'good cause'. In this case Claire House raises money for a hospice that it runs for children with life threatening or life limiting conditions and their families from Merseyside, Cheshire, North Wales and the Isle of Man.

(6 marks)

(b) Claire House needs around £250,000 each month and has three main sources of income. The Hospice relies heavily on donations from the public. For example, it has a web site where donations can be made online. A proportion of income is generated by organising special fundraising events. Examples for 2007 include a beer festival, a golf tournament, a sponsored parachute jump, a charity ball and sponsored treks to Brazil and Nepal. The charity also runs around 20 charity shops in the region. The shops sell a range of second-hand items such as unwanted clothes, books, toys, DVDs/videos, ornaments etc. that have been donated by the general public.

(6 marks)

(c) In common with many charities Claire House enjoys the support of a number of local celebrities. For example, Claire House is supported by the actor and comedian Norman Wisdom, the Tranmere Rovers goalkeeper Eric Nixon and 60s pop legend Gerry Marsden. They help to raise the profile of the charity and play an important role in fundraising. For example, they are likely to attend the fundraising events and therefore help to attract more interest from the public. They might also give donations themselves and provide useful contacts for Claire House. They might also help to promote the charity by giving it a 'plug' when appearing on a television 'chat show' for example.

(8 marks)

(d) All charities face competition because they compete for funding. For example, Claire House relies on charitable donations from members of the public. However, there are large numbers of charities which people have to choose between when gifting money. The shops run by Claire House will also to have to compete for customers on the high street. There are likely to be other charity shops nearby and many of the second-hand products sold by charity shops can also be purchased at fetes, jumble sales, auctions and online. Claire House will also have to compete when organising special events. For example, on an evening when a charity ball is being held, there are many other leisure attractions which might discourage people from attending.

(8 marks)

(e) There are many similarities between Claire House and a profit-making organisation. Claire House provides a very important and highly valued care service. It runs a children's hospice which is dedicated to enhancing the quality of life, providing specialist respite, palliative, terminal and bereavement care. It employs staff such as nurses, carers, cleaners, therapists and counsellors. It has to buy resources such as medical supplies, food, bedding, insurance and utilities. It markets itself by promoting its charity on a web site and utilising the support given by local celebrities for example. Claire House is also likely to have financial targets and operate budgets. It will need to minimise costs and remain efficient. It has to operate within the law and may also be faced with competition when raising funds. Finally, it is also growing like a business. For example, it is trying to raise £2 million to build, equip and run the new teenager wing.

(12 marks)

Question 1

(a) The photograph shows a municipal/public park. The park is an example of a merit good. Merit goods are those which would be underprovided by the private sector. In the case of parks, it could be argued that the state should provide for such amenities and open them to any member of the public free at the point of entry.

(b) It is possible for the private sector to provide parks. Indeed, certain types of park such as safari parks and other theme parks, like Alton Towers, are provided successfully by the private sector. However, some people may not be able to afford to pay the entry charges for parks. Therefore, so those poorer members of society and children can have access to parks, a limited number of quite basic parks are provided by the state free of charge.

Question 2

(a) Executive agencies have become well established since their introduction in 1985. They are responsible for the supply of services previously provided by government departments. Executive agencies are operational bodies and do not get involved in policy making. They are headed by chief executives who are accountable to a government minister. Jobcentre Plus is one of the biggest executive agencies and employs around 100,000 people. It supports people of working age from welfare into work, and helps employers to fill their vacancies. It is part of the Department for Work and Pensions (DWP). Two of its key aims are to increase the supply of labour by helping unemployed and economically inactive people move into employment and to pay customers the correct benefit at the right time and protect the benefit system from fraud, error and abuse.

(b) One of the features of executive agencies is that they have tended to adopt business principles in their operations. The purpose of this is to improve efficiency. In this case, Jobcentre Plus sets targets to help improve efficiency. For example, targets are set for helping people into work, cutting fraud, helping employers to recruit workers and the time taken to process benefits. In 2006/7, the target for helping people into work was 13,500,000 points. The number of points actually scored was 9,986,476. This is about 81 per cent of the target. Monitoring performance in this way is something that most businesses would do.

Question 3

(a) The public sector is responsible for the provision of merit goods and public goods. Street lighting is an example of a public good. One of the features of public goods is non-rivalry. This means that consumption of the good by one individual does not reduce the amount available for others. Another feature is non-excludability. This means it is impossible to exclude others from benefiting from their use. Non-rivalry and non-excludability are both features of street lighting. If one person uses the light to see her way across the street, this does not 'use up' light for someone who wants to look at his watch. Also, it is impossible to stop using the light shining across the street. This means that it would be unlikely that people would pay directly for street lighting. If you paid £1 for light to cross the street, someone else could use it for free! If people will not pay, then businesses cannot make a profit and would not provide the service.

(b) PFI is one of a range of initiatives which fall under the Public Private Partnerships (PPP) umbrella. These involve private sector businesses such as Balfour Beatty in the provision of public services. The PFI is the most frequently used. Under a PFI contract, a capital project such as a school, hospital or housing estate has to be designed, built, financed and managed by a private consortium, under contracts that typically last for 30 years. The private consortium will be paid regularly from government funds according to its performance during that time period. If the consortium misses performance targets it will be paid less. One example of an area where PFI has been used extensively by the government is in the construction of hospitals. Balfour Beatty is a major builder of hospitals and schools through PFI contracts.

(c) Evidence in the case suggests that Balfour Beatty has been involved in quite a number of PFI contracts. Their involvement will benefit the government in a number of ways. For example, the government does not have to fund expensive one-off payments to build large-scale projects that may involve unpopular tax increases. The risk involved in funding large-scale projects is transferred to the private sector. For example, if Balfour Beatty goes out of business before a project is completed the government does not have to meet any extra costs that might accrue, they are borne by the company. Also, since the government is not funding the cost of projects the amount spent does not cause public borrowing to rise.

Case study

(a) Postal services in the UK have been provided by the public sector for many years. However, there has been a number of changes in the structure of the organisation during that time. In March 2001 the Post Office became a plc, but one wholly owned by the UK government. The change was brought about by the Postal Services Act 2000. It aimed to create a commercially focused company with a more strategic relationship with the government.. In the UK the business operates under three brands - Royal Mail, Post OfficeTM and Parcelforce Worldwide. Royal Mail provides postal services. The company has a statutory duty to provide a letter delivery service to every address in the UK.

(4 marks)

(b) In 2007 Royal Mail's total revenue was £6.86 billion. It generates revenue by charging for its services. Most of its revenue will come from the sale of stamps for letters and other items sent through the post. However, Royal Mail does provide other commercial services. For example, it provides business customers with a range of mail-related data tools to improve their marketing performance and increase the effectiveness of mail as a communication medium. Royal Mail has also developed an online shopping facility. This is estimated to reach 15% of retail sales by 2010 - a market worth over £40 billion. Over Christmas 2005 it delivered a record breaking 70 million items ordered online. Books, videos and DVDs remain the favourite low-ticket items, but bigger-ticket items are becoming more popular, such as clothing, which now accounts for 10% of total online sales. Finally, Royal Mail designs and produces the UK's stamps and philatelic products to celebrate anniversaries and momentous occasions. It also offers electronic stamps to use as a novel and eye-catching promotional aid for businesses. Stamps can be personalised with a favourite photo, to share with friends and family for invitations, birthday greetings and letters.

(8 marks)

(c) Royal Mail is facing difficult times. In 2007 its revenue was static. It also had to deal with trade union action when trying to cut costs and modernise its operations. Royal Mail faces a number of threats. The mail market in the UK is declining by around 2.5% per year. It is losing 40% of bulk business mail to rival postal operators. Overall this year, rivals will handle one in five of all letters posted in the UK. Rivals are 40% more efficient not because their people work harder but because they have already modernised and have much more technology and rivals pay their people 25% less than we do at Royal Mail.

Royal Mail needs to deal with the threat posed by competition. After the postal dispute was resolved the Royal Mail chief executive Adam Crozier, said: 'All along we have been clear that to become competitive we needed flexibility to modernise and we needed to reform our pension scheme because the costs were crippling the company'. 'Change is always difficult for everyone but it is vital if Royal Mail is to be able to thrive in the competitive market and build a successful future. I know that if we all work together we can achieve that success.' These comments show that the serious threats facing Royal Mail from competition have been recognised by the management.

(10 marks)

(d) In the last 30 years many public sector business activities have been privatised. At the moment Royal Mail is part of a very large plc that is completely state owned. However, some people have argued that the organisation should be privatised just like others such as British Gas and BT. If Royal Mail were organised there would be a number of impacts.

If Royal Mail operated in the private sector achieving a surplus or profit will become a more important objective. Most companies in the private sector pursue profit. This normally comes from shareholders' pressure.

In the private sector the prices charged by Royal Mail may change. If there is competition prices may come down like in telecommunications. However, in the absence of genuine competition prices may rise as they did in the rail and water industries. Some of the newly privatised businesses have cut back on staffing levels. For example, British Energy shed a quarter of its workforce just before privatisation. Royal Mail would probably cut its workforce if privatised. Evidence in the case suggests that 40,000 jobs would have been lost if Royal Mail management had been allowed to introduce some proposed costs cutting measures. Many companies increased investment following privatisation. For example, many of the water companies raised investment levels to fund new sewerage systems and purification plants. Immediately after privatisation, investment rose by about £1,000 million in the water industry. It is likely that Royal Mail would increase investment. Evidence in the case suggests that it needs to modernise. This is likely to involve some mechanisation at sorting offices for example.

Some of the companies have begun to offer new services and diversify since privatisation. Royal Mail has recently developed new services. For example, it now has an online service. New services like this are more likely to emerge in the private sector. Finally, there has been a number of mergers and takeovers involving newly privatised companies. For example, Hanson bought Eastern Electricity and an American railway company bought the British Rail freight service. North West Water and Norweb joined together to form United Utilities and Scottish Power bought Manweb. Once in the private sector Royal Mail may become a target for a takeover. It is likely that Royal Mail would be subject to a number of far reaching changes if it was privatised. The impact of such a move would be significant.

(18 marks)

11 The nature of marketing

Question 1

(a) (i) Levens Farm allows customers to 'pick your own'. This is an example of the farm selling to a consumer market because the berries go straight to the consumer.

(ii) Levens sells berries to retailers. This is an example of the Farm selling to a business to business retailer because the berries go to another business.

(b) (i) The article stresses the health benefits of berries and the evidence in the article suggests that it is this aspect of berries that is behind their increase in sales. This is an example of the identification of consumer requirements.

(ii) The article makes the link between berry eating and staving off cancer. It might be anticipated that as consumers become more aware of this alleged link that they will purchase more berries.

(iii) The article points to the huge growth in blackberry and raspberry sales. Knowledge of this might influence Levens Farm's production and contribute to higher profits.

Question 2

(a) Kitz-4-U is likely to be selling to a niche market because her products are highly specialised and aimed at relatively small groups of consumers.

(b) Operating as a niche market Kitz-4-U might attract competition. The main problem with this would be the capacity of the market to maintain more than one business. In addition, Kitz-4-U is vulnerable to swings in consumer spending. For example, the Golf Kit would be vulnerable to changes in the tastes and preferences of target golfers.

(c) It could be argued that there is the potential for Kitz-4-U to grow to become a mass marketing business. Whilst some of the kits, such as the Bowling Kit, are likely to remain as niche market others of the kits have the potential to become much larger in terms of sales volume. The Travel Kit, in particular, may have a very wide appeal amongst consumers.

Question 3

(a) The perceptual map produced by Mark and Tony shows the views of customers about different brands of guitar. The information could have been found by carrying out some form of conducted market research. They may have interviewed people on the street, done telephone interviews or held consumer panels or customer focus groups to ask questions. Alternatively they might have carried out a survey by sending out questionnaires in the post. They might even have considered using a website to gather views via e-mail questionnaires.

Alternatively, Mark and Tony may have used secondary data. They could have obtained prices from catalogues and researched magazines to find out whether the guitars were 'traditional' or 'modern'.

(b) Mark and Tony want to manufacture hand made guitars which incorporate the low noise pick-ups designed by Mark. The perceptual map might be useful to them in a number of ways. It will identify all the major competitors they face in the market and the views about price and style that customers perceive. This could given them an indication of the chances of success and the potential market share.

More interestingly it might help them examine the best place to position the product in the market. For instance, they want to sell hand made guitars, charging presumably a premium price. The map might indicate the level of competition at this end of the market. It might also help the business in its marketing, for example stressing the features of the product that it needs to promote at this end of the market, such as the noiseless pick-ups, which are different from those of other guitars. If the map shows that competition appears to be intense the business may decide to reposition the brand, although they may decide to leave the product in the position they first identified due to the extent of competition elsewhere in the market.

Case study

(a) House on the Hill is engaged in business to business marketing. Its products are sold to other businesses and not direct to consumers.

(3 marks)

(b) (i) House on the Hill could be described as selling to a niche market. This is because its main products are highly specialised and aimed at a particular market segment - businesses seeking to manage their help desks.

(3 marks)

(ii) By focusing upon businesses in the specific area in which they specialise House on the Hill are able to specifically focus upon meeting the needs of those businesses. In addition, because they are operating in such a specialised market, House on the Hill are less likely to attract competitor businesses.

(6 marks)

(c) The biggest change referred to in the article has been a gradual shift to what is termed relationship marketing. This is concerned with developing relationships with customers that last longer than the short term. There are likely to have been several factors that influenced this shift but essentially they can all be related to identifying, anticipating and satisfying consumer requirements. By forging strong relationships with actual and potential customers House on the Hill have been driven by a desire to satisfy these consumers; by getting to know their customers better the business is in a much stronger position to meet their needs. A driving force behind this shift is likely to have been the desire to make higher profits and to compete effectively with rival businesses.

(8 marks)

(d) The approach to marketing at House on the Hill as described in the article bears all of the hallmarks of effective marketing. Iain Broadhead describes how the business has come to 'understand what our customers want from our products'. This suggests a strong understanding of the basis of effective marketing where the needs of consumers are viewed as central to the business's operations. Their business philosophy could be said to be market orientated. Trudy Broadhead describes the importance of 'long standing relationships with our customers'. Here relationship marketing is placed at the centre of the business's activities. There is also a strong sense in the article of House on the Hill understanding that marketing is a process with no start and end. For example, the business makes 'every effort to adapt and amend' its products in response to changing consumer needs. The availability of a website with regular updates is evidence of this. House on the Hill is clearly a business that does not stand still. However, the article contains no hard information, for example in terms of sales or profits, about the performance of House on the Hill either in isolation or in relation to its competitors. Caution must therefore be exercised in drawing hard and fast conclusions from the data presented about the effectiveness of the business's marketing.

(10 marks)

12 | Market research

Question 1

(a) It would be an example of secondary research. This is because the Mintel report discovered by the health club on the Internet would already have been in existence.

(b) (i) The descriptive reasons the health club might use the report would be mainly concerned with what was happening in the health and fitness market. For example, it would be interested to know that 25 per cent of members see their health and fitness club as a place to meet people with similar interests.

(ii) The predictive reasons the health club might use the report would be concerned with predicting what is likely to happen in the future. For example, it would be interested to know Mintel's prediction that the market value for this sector was predicted to grow by 40 per cent at the time of writing.

(iii) The explanatory reasons the health club might use the report would be concerned with enabling the business to explain matters related to its marketing activities. For example, Mintel report that health and fitness clubs are more than just somewhere to get fit and healthy. This may help to explain why some members would like more social activities organised.

Question 2

(a) Test marketing involves the selling of a product in a limited area prior to its 'launch'. This allows a business to gauge the reaction of consumers and gives an indication of potential sales. Mistakes made on a national scale are likely to be far more costly than those made in a test market. By initially launching the new lunch bar in a test market, problems can be identified and rectified before a national launch is made. This might prevent future potential losses.

(b) (i) It is possible to argue that postal surveys would be of limited usefulness in this case. This is because it would not be necessary to cover a wide geographical area. The product is only being trialled in the South West. In addition, the relative cheapness of postal surveys would be offset by the need to send out samples of the new lunch bar with the survey itself. However, a postal survey is still likely to be significantly cheaper than the other two options under consideration. Finally, postal surveys tend to have a poor response rate.

(ii) The firm is seeking to gather information on initial consumer reactions to its products. Consumer panels may not be appropriate in this respect. This is because they are mainly used to gauge changes in consumer reaction over a period of time. However, it is possible that a one-off consumer panel could be set up to provide Vegran with the information they require, although this might still be expensive.

(iii) Personal interviews would allow Vegran to gain detailed information on consumer response to the new lunch bar. They need to be very careful about the people selected for interview or results could be misleading. It is also possible that personal interviews might be beyond the limited budget available. They are a time consuming and therefore an expensive method of collecting data.

(iv) There are two ways in which Vegran might use the Internet to collect marketing research information. First, it might attempt to gain primary data using a form of field research. It might set up a website providing information about Vegran's products with an attached questionnaire. This could be used to invite customers in the South West to comment on the bar. Second, it could make use of secondary data. It might search the websites of other businesses and organisations to seek information about the markets within which Vegran intends to operate. Alternatively it might look for general information on markets in which it is attempting to sell, such as sales of confectionery products in a particular year or over time.

Case study

(a) From the perspective of the owner of an independent pub, the research referred to in the article is secondary. This is because the research data is already in existence for the pub owner. The research referred to is based upon data external to the independent pub and was not commissioned by the pub owner.

(4 marks)

(b) There is a number of reasons why an independent pub owner might find the data useful. First, the research might help the pub owner to understand what is happening more widely in the beer and pub market. There are many descriptions in the research of trends in beer sales and these would be of great interest to any pub owner. Second, the data might help the pub owner to explain what is happening to his or her own business. For example, if the pub owner were experiencing falling sales of beer the data might help to explain this. Third, the research might help the pub owner to predict future eventualities. For example, the data reports the 'quiet revival' of sales of real ales. Were this to be sustained real ale sales would continue to grow in the future. Finally, the pub owner might find the data in the article useful because of its capacity to help him/her to explore possible future options for the pub. For example, the data reports a 7.5 per cent growth in the sales of regional beers. This might help the pub owner explore the possibility of stocking a wider selection of regional ales.

(6 marks)

(c) The pub owner might also wish to collect primary market research data. There are a number of options open to him/her in this respect. The pub owner could ask actual and/or potential customers to complete a short questionnaire on issues such as how satisfied they are with the current services and facilities available at the pub. This might include questions, for example, about the friendliness and hospitality of the bar staff. Complementary to this would be observing customers in the pub and gathering data about their behaviours in this setting. The pub owner might also interview customers about the service. It is likely in the context of a pub that these interviews would be relatively informal enabling information to be collected on relevant customer views and opinions. One variant upon this would be to form a small focus group of customers who might be invited to share their views collectively. Finally, the pub owner could make use of the Internet or the local press to find out how other pubs were changing and developing their services.

(10 marks)

(d) The data could prove very useful for the pub owner for the reasons outlined in response to (b) above. There are descriptive, analytical, exploratory and explanatory uses to which a pub owner could put this data. These might be immensely valuable to the pub owner in terms of enabling him/her to develop and change both the nature and level of services provided. For example, the pub owner might decide to stock more real ales, regional beers and wines and champagnes in line with some of the descriptive and explanatory trends identified in the research. Viewed from a different perspective the pub owner may be much more cautious about using this data. There are likely to be two main reasons for this. First, the data is very general in nature and only describes wider trends in beer sales. There is no data about how about how specific segments of the market, for example, are responding to these wider changes. This leads to the second reservation. This is about the extent to which the generalised data in the research relates to the consumption behaviours of the customers using the pub. For example, although it may be true that beer sales in general are falling this may not be the case for the particular groups of customers who use the pub owner's own establishment. There are many city and town centre bars and pubs that have experienced rapid increases in beer sales over the period mentioned in the article. This does not mean that the research shown in the article is wrong just that it does not necessarily apply to all pubs.

(10 marks)

13 | Sampling

Question 1

(a) The type of sampling method used was random sampling. This is where each member of a group or population is given an equal chance of being chosen. the sample is selected 'at random'.

(b) (i) Males alone were likely to have been interviewed as the target market was males rather than females. The pharmaceutical company that commissioned the research was interested in male health, perhaps to help it develop drugs to improve the health of men. In this case interviewing women would have been a waste of resources as they were not the target market.

(ii) Respondents from eight countries were interviewed rather than one as this would have given different data about male health. It could be that health varies from one country to another. So obtaining information from different countries may allow the business to develop products that meet a variety of needs, or different products for different needs.

(iii) The survey might have interviewed 20,000 people rather than 1,000 in order to gain a large amount of information about men's health, particularly if the pharmaceuticals company was aiming to develop products for a world market. The survey might have chosen 20,000 respondents rather than 500,000 in order to limit the costs of the survey, of telephone calls and web interviewing, and to keep control over the process, especially as second interviews took place.

(c) The statement 'random sampling meant that sample bias was eliminated' relates to bias or unrepresentative results that can result when only a proportion of the population is chosen to gauge its views, rather than the entire population. In this case 5 per cent of the 20,000 initial respondents were chosen for a second interview. They were chosen at random, using an algorithm. It is argued that selecting a sample at random goes some way towards eliminating bias. Choosing at random means that every person has an equal chance of being chosen. So the sample should be representative of all the people whose views the business wants to investigate.

Question 2

(a) A sample is part of the total population in which a business or survey is interested. Graham Hunter took a sample. He spoke to the Head buyer in each supermarket chain to gauge their opinions about what vegetables to grow. He would have wanted to know what vegetables to grow in the forthcoming year that consumers would buy. But he could not survey all consumers of these chains So he sought the opinion's of a sample - the three head buyers.

(b) One factor might have been cost. Graham is likely to have restricted funds for large scale market surveys. So he asked the opinions of buyers, rather than large numbers of customers buying from these chains. Another factor may have been the target market. He sells all of his produce to three supermarkets. He therefore chose to ask the views of the three head buyers for this market.

(c) It could be argued that taking a sample of three from all consumers in these three supermarket chains might be an unrepresentative sample. Three large chains may have many customers in the UK. On the other hand, Graham sells all his products only to the three supermarkets. They will have a good knowledge of the likely tastes of the buyers of his products. So it could be argued that the sample is quite representative of customers.

Question 3

(a) The phrase 'a 95 per cent confidence level was given for the responses' relates to the extent to which the result of a survey can be applied to the population. DPX carried out market research for a manufacturer of building materials to investigate the views of 30 smaller plumbers' and builders' merchants. The responses from this sample would be used for decision making. However, the manufacturer would want to know how representative these views were of all buyers of builders' materials, including chains such as Wickes and B&Q, before making decisions. In this case the responses were said to have a 95 per cent confidence level, so the manufacturer would know that in 95 out of 100 cases the the views of the sample would reflect the views of the population (all buyers of building materials).

(b) Confidence levels show the extent to which a business can be certain that the results obtained from a sample reflect the views of the population. In the case above the business would know that the results of the sample would be representative 95 times out of 100. To be more certain that the results can be applied to the population, the business must include a wider range of results. For example it could set a 99 per cent confidence level, which would include a wide range of results and the business could then be sure that in 99 cases out of 100 the views of the sample represent those of the population.

(c) Strategies are the plans used by a business to achieve its objectives. In this case the manufacturer of building materials has seen an unexpected fall in sales in the last 12 months. Its objective is therefore to reverse the decline in sales. The business might consider changing the 'product' element of the marketing mix on the basis of the information gained from market research which showed that it had lost competitiveness to a rival as a result of a fall in value for money. To improve the value for money offered by the business it might consider improving its services. This could include improving the reliability of products by improving quality assurance techniques or the standard of components and materials used. It might also consider offering a wider range of products to customers. Other elements of the marketing mix it might consider could include reducing price so that the price better reflects customers' view of value or changing distribution, for example improving on delivery times, or changes in promotion, such as offering discounts.

Case study

(a) (i) A sample is a part of the population that is selected to survey. A business or other organisation is interested in the views an opinions of this part of the total population because it feels that their views represent those of the total population. Is would be impossible to ask all people in a population for their views, so a sample is take,. The size of the sample is that number of people chosen for the sample from the total population.

(3 marks)

(ii) When attempting to find out the views of a sample, perhaps through a survey, a questionnaire is often used. It contains a series of questions designed to find out the views of the sample. It might include closed questions, with definite answers, or open questions, where respondents can provide their own answers. The results of the answers to questions in the questionnaire provide useful information about the views of the population and the market.

(3 marks)

(b) One reason why the research by Synovate was commissioned by the Competition Commission was to find out why people chose transport services, in this case the bus service provided by FirstGroup and the train service of Wessex Trains. Certain differences appeared in the findings. For example, a larger percentage of train passengers were heading for work than bus passengers. Certain features were considered more important. For buses, frequency of service was important, but for rains short journey time was said to be influential. But there were similarities, such as stopping at a convenient station being important or space for luggage as being least important. Another reason was to find out the reasons why people might change from one mode to another. This might be important for government, for example, in persuading the use of public transport. Bus users could find it easiest to change to train use, but train users would find it easiest to change to driving a car.

(6 marks)

(c) There is a variety of sampling methods that can be used when taking a survey of the total population. Synovate sampled 10,111 passengers who were train and bus users. The sample was taken by researchers boarding trains and buses between 7 am and 7.45 pm. Prepaid envelopes were given to those who could not complete the survey in time. The sample was divided between the two modes of transport, with 482 bus users and 529 train users. It also appears to have been divided according to age, gender and employment. It could be argued that this is an example of a stratified random sample. This is where a sample is taken at random from passengers. But the sample is divided into segments. In this case the segments are bus and train users. However, if the sample had targets for the number of people of a certain age or gender, then it might be that the sample was a quota sample. This is where a certain number of people that fall into these categories are surveyed. This is not clear from the information.

(8 marks)

(d) The owner of a taxi businesses in the South West of England might be interested in the data in the survey. It provides information about the views of bus and train users, such as the factors that are important in their choice of transport and what factors might persuade them to change the mode of transport. It also provides details of the characteristics or profile of the sample. The taxi driver might see that no more than half the users identify alternatives to bus or train as easy to change to. This could indicate that people tend to stick to the mode of transport they are used to. Bus users also indicate that cost is important. The survey shows that a larger proportion of those over 65 use buses than trains (14 per cent compared to 4 per cent). This is perhaps mainly due to free bus passes for pensioners. The taxi business may decide that this is not an important target market for the business. Therefore, the results of the survey might indicate the likely users of taxis and the extent to which they will be used, as well as the situations in which they might be used.

However, survey results must always be treated with caution. The taxi business would need to consider to what extent the survey results are representative of the population. For example, the survey deals with transport in the South West. But how representative is that of an area such as London for example? The research indicates. That few bus users use that mode of transport to get to work. But is this higher in London? Also, the sample does not include the views of people after 7.45 pm. That is the time when many people use taxis. So are the results representative of the taxi using public?

(10 marks)

14 | Market segmentation

Question 1

(a) There is a number of reasons why commercial radio might be a useful medium for businesses targeting ABC1s which might be suggested from the information in the article. First, 65% of ABC1s listen to commercial radio, compared to only 35% of C2DEs. This is a high proportion of people listening to commercial radio. It is even higher over a month, at 85%. This compares to ABC1s being only 48% of the total population and only 49% listening to all radio stations. So it could be argued that businesses potentially have a larger audience in this medium. Second, ABC1s tend to be 'light' viewers of commercial television and particularly avoid advertising on TV. Therefore they may be harder to reach via this medium. This makes the potential to reach them via commercial radio even more attractive for businesses aiming at this market segment. Further, ABC1s tend to listen to radio for extended periods of time. They also listen to only around 2 stations a week and even younger listeners stay loyal to one or two stations. Therefore a business which chooses a particular station might be more likely to reach its target market via an advertisement on commercial radio.

(b) A business wishing to appeal to ABC1s via commercial radio might effectively use this medium by identifying those radio stations favoured by ABC1s. The article states that ABC1s are loyal to their favourite stations and listen to them for extended periods. So it might look at listening figures on commercial stations to see which have the largest number of listeners. A business might also conpare the impact of local radio stations with national stations. For example, a business with a local service which is aiming to sell to ABC1s in a particular area might decide that an advertisement on a local station would have greater impact. The timing of commercials is also likely to be important. The article suggests times that might be most effective when targeting ABC1s. These might include advertising in the week rather than at weekends, when listening figures of this segment can be as low as 15%. It might include advertising at specific times, such as between 8-9 am when ABC1s are going to work and at 5-6 pm when they are going home. It might also include advertising generally in the morning rather than in the afternoon or evening.

Question 2

(a) The information in Table 4 is segmented by age, gender and type of sporting activity in England, so it would be on the basis of these three categories that a medium sized manufacturer of sports equipment might target particular segments of the market. Other than swimming, where the scope for sports equipment may be limited, it is health, fitness, gym or conditioning activities that are most popular. For women, such activities remain popular throughout the age ranges up to 64. For men, the popularity of such activities wanes more rapidly amongst 45-64 year olds. This would suggest the need to target health, fitness, gym and conditioning related equipment to a slightly younger age group for men than women.

In terms of recreational cycling there are much higher levels of participation amongst men than women suggesting the need to target male cyclists more intensively. Outdoor football, not surprisingly, is dominated by younger men at whom football equipment manufacturers might most usefully target their marketing efforts. Other than male golfers participation levels in all amongst the over 65s remains low, suggesting the need for marketing efforts to be targeted at younger participants.

Whilst the above response offers general guidelines to a manufacturer of sports equipment, the size of the business suggests that it may usefully seek to target some of the potential niche markets identified in the data. For example, 4 per cent of 16-24 year olds women play darts regularly. It may be that such darts players might usefully be targeted by the business. Likewise, although participation in keep fit, aerobics and dance exercise is dominated by women a small percentage of men regularly participate in such activities. This group might also be usefully targeted by a medium sized manufacturer of sports equipment.

Case study

(a) (i) Market segmentation is the process of breaking down a market into sub-groups with similar characteristics such as where they live or their lifestyles and opinions.

(3 marks)

(ii) Demographic segmentation is segmenting a market according to the demographic characteristics of different groups. Such demographic characteristics include age, gender, social class and income.

(3 marks)

(b) A small business offering financial services might benefit from market segmentation for a number of reasons. First, market segmentation should allow this business to know its consumers better. It might know as a result of market segmentation more about, for example, their age, social class, attitudes and religion. Second, market segmentation should enable the business to target particular market segments with different financial products. For example, younger customers might be introduced to the benefits of establishing a pension early in their careers and older customers might be enabled to invest their available income in tax efficient ways. In this way the financial products offered to consumers can be differentiated and tailored to meet their needs. Third, customers benefiting from the market segmentation developed by the financial services business may be pleased with the way the business has met their needs and may develop a sense of loyalty to that business. Overall, these benefits of market segmentation should enable the business to be placed in a stronger position in relation to developing a better relationship with its customers and consequently making increased profits.

(8 marks)

(c) Targeting Muslim customers would offer a number of benefits to a business marketing financial services. In particular this would include developing a much better understanding of the needs of Muslim customers and tailoring a range of financial products to meet the needs of Muslims. Overall, there would be the potential to develop a strong loyalty to the business from Muslim customers. However, there may also be downsides to this approach. In particular non-Muslim customers may come to view the business as mainly for Muslims and assume that it would not meet their needs. Consequently the business would need to be careful that it did not exclude non-Muslims.

(6 marks)

(d) For a small financial services business, selling to one market segment could be a very successful strategy. The business could really get to understand the needs of that one market segment and gear up its product range and approach to the needs of dealing with different individuals who were members of that particular market segment. In return the customers of the business in that particular market segment might have a strong sense of their needs being met and not only develop a loyalty to the business but also recommend the business to their friends and family.

The downside of such an approach would be the total reliance of this business upon one market segment. If the demand for financial services amongst members of this group declined, for example as a consequence of competitor businesses entering the same market, the business could find itself in difficulty. Another problem might be that the consumers in the targeted market segment might come to attach themselves increasingly less to this segment. So, for example, some British Muslims may increasingly come to prefer to be targeted according to other aspects of themselves than their religion. In this way, Muslim women in professional jobs may prefer to do business with a financial services business targeting other professional women rather than one targeting Muslims.

In conclusion, it could be argued that targeting one market segment can expose a small business to fragilities that a wider portfolio of customers would largely avoid.

(10 marks)

15 | Market size, share and growth

Question 1

(a) There is a number of factors in the article affecting the size and growth of the market for Ormskirk restaurants. The presence of a university with 17,000 students creates a large market for the restaurant's services. The building of a new road linking Ormskirk more effectively to the M58 may offer potential consumers easier access to the town as will the existing rail and bus services to Liverpool and Preston.

(b) The growth of this in market in the future is likely to depend upon a number of factors. These will include the future growth of Edge Hill University, the building, or not, of additional road and rail links and, more generally, the growth or decline of population in Ormskirk linked most likely to employment prospects in the town and surrounding areas.

Question 2

(a) (i) Radio 2 experienced a small increase in its share of radio listeners from 15.5% in 2006 to 15.8% in 2007.

(ii) Commercial radio saw its market share fall from 43.6% in 2006 to 43.3% in 2007. At the same time the BBC saw listeners rise from 54.2% to 54.5%.

(iii) Local commercial radio stations experienced a decline in market share from 32.6% of all listeners to 31.7% of all listeners

(b) There is a number of factors that can influence the share of the market of radio stations. Social changes, such as the number of people living on their own, can affect radio listening habits and benefit some radio stations at the expense of others. In addition, changes in legislation can affect different radio stations in divergent ways. For example, a loosening of the regulations around pirate radio stations would allow some smaller niche stations to gain market share. Further, personalities such as Johnny Vaughan and Terry Wogan can be particularly important in attracting listeners to one station at the expense of another.

Case study

(a) The main features of the market for British cheeses is that there is a distinction made between continental and British cheeses. The range of cheeses available to consumers is now extremely diverse, ranging from cheddar and variants upon traditional cheeses such as curry flavours through to luxury continental cheeses. A major trend has been the growth in regional and specialist British cheeses. The market for cheeses in Britain is large and growing and at the time of writing it was anticipated that it would continue to grow for the foreseeable future.

(4 marks)

(b) (i) In 2006 the market for British cheeses was worth £1.9 billion. This was an increase of 4% on 2004. Therefore the value of the market for cheese in 2004 was £1.824 billion. **(4 marks)**

(ii) The market value of continental cheeses fell 7% between 2004 and 2006 to £340 million. Therefore the value of the market for cheese in 2004 was £365.4 million. **(4 marks)**

(c) In the article the increase in the sales volume of regional and specialist British cheeses was attributed to a 'growing interest in environmental and ethical concerns' linked to an increasing interest in the 'origin of food'. This can be viewed as long-term social change as consumers in the UK take greater care over what they eat and where it comes from. To some extent this can be seen as reflecting wider economic changes as many groups have experienced higher incomes. This is reflected in the increasing tendency of many consumers to purchase foods based on factors other than price. **(8 marks)**

(d) Given that volume of sales of continental cheeses increased by an unspecified amount between 2004 and 2006 it might be anticipated that the value of these would also have increased. There are two main explanations for this. The first assumes that the prices charged by the manufacturers and distributors of continental cheeses remained much the same, the second that the prices charged by continental cheese manufacturers and distributors rose. The first explanation would be that the increase in the volume of sales was only small and that changes in variables such as exchange rates meant that the value of the cheeses actually fell. For example, if the exchange rate of the euro relative to sterling fell during this period then this would have the effect of depressing the sales value of continental cheeses during this period. The second explanation, for which there is some evidence in the article, would be that competitive pressures during this period forced down the prices charged by continental cheese manufacturers and distributors. This is the explanation offered by David Bird in the article. So although more cheese was sold the fall in the price of these cheeses meant that the total value of the cheeses declined. **(8 marks)**

(e) The size of the market for cheddar cheeses is likely to be determined by a number of factors. First, the economic fortunes of the UK. Although conventional economic wisdom would suggest that an increase in incomes would lead to more cheddar cheese being eaten this may not necessarily be the case. This is because as an already largely affluent nation a further increase in consumer incomes may not lead to consumption of higher levels of cheddar cheeses. Instead consumers may purchase more specialised and premium priced cheeses with a resulting decline in the demand for cheddar cheeses. Second, social changes may affect consumer attitudes and tastes. For example, a general shift towards eating more British and locally produced foods in general could be of benefit to cheddar cheese producers and lead to a growth in consumption. Conversely, a further shift in tastes towards continental and specialised cheeses could result in less cheddar cheese being purchased and a decline in market growth for this cheese. Third, legislative and technological changes could affect the growth in the market for cheddar cheeses. For example, the creation of new EU laws governing the production of dairy herds might force up the price of milk, raise the cost of cheddar production and lead to a fall off in demand. The creation of new technologies enabling good quality cheddar cheeses to be produced more cheaply would have the opposite effect with a further growth in the sales of this traditional cheese.

A note of caution must, however, be sounded in responding to this question because the future market for cheddar cheeses in the UK will be measured by sales volume and sales value. Depending upon a range of factors such as the level of inflation and the extent of competitive pressures in the UK cheese market, an increase in sales volume will not necessarily lead to an increase in sales value or vice versa. For example, if inflation was relatively high sales volume might decline but at the same time sales value might increase. **(8 marks)**

16 | The marketing mix

Question 1

(a) There is a number of elements of the marketing mix in the article about Biome Lifestyle. First, the products themselves are described, including hand made recycled teddy bears and eco shopper bags, Second, the price of the products; the recycled wrapping paper for example is £1.50 per sheet. Third, place is represented in terms of the website (www.biomelifestyle.com) from which the business's products are made available to consumers. Finally, promotion is mentioned in the form of on-line advertising.

(b) Both individually and collectively those elements of the marketing mix described in response to (a) above might help Biome Lifestyle to gain a competitive advantage. Individually, these elements of the marketing mix should be consistent with the needs and expectations of actual and potential customers so that they compare favourably with rival businesses. Collectively these elements of the marketing mix should be well balanced so that they support one another. Thus, for example, the pricing should be broadly consistent with the nature of the products and the promotional strategies employed.

Question 2

(a) There is a number of reasons why Jenny Bodey's shop has been so successful. It could be argued that she offers products which are targeted to the needs of her customers. She has concentrated on a specific product, catering for people in a local area. She has also chosen a product where profit margins are high as people are prepared to pay a high price for a special occasion. Dresses that are bought for just over £100 can be sold for three times that price. Further, her prices have been 'competitive', although still allowing her good margins. In addition, she has been prepared to offer discounts, including free accessories. However, at first she was perhaps offering discounts which were too generous. She has been prepared to revise her discount structure in order to reflect people's expectations. Another feature of her promotions has been advertising in a range of outlets, from regional wedding magazines to the local press. As she provides a local service her advertising needs to be aimed at the target group. Using local advertising is suited to these needs. However, using a range of adverts including brochures and magazine advertising means she has a better chance of reaching her customers. Another successful feature has been the places she sells the products. She has a shop in Bootle, Liverpool. This has relatively low rents which enables her to keep her costs down. However, she also makes use of other channels, such as wedding fairs which can also be relatively low cost operations.

Question 3

(a) There is a number of reasons why Jenny Bodey's shop has been so successful. It could be argued that she offers products which are targeted to the needs of her customers. She has concentrated on a specific product, catering for people in a local area. She has also chosen a product where profit margins are high as people are prepared to pay a high price for a special occasion. Dresses that are bought for just over £100 can be sold for three times that price. Further, her prices have been 'competitive', although still allowing her good margins. In addition, she has been prepared to offer discounts, including free accessories. However, at first she was perhaps offering discounts which were too generous. She has been prepared to revise her discount structure in order to reflect people's expectations. Another feature of her promotions has been advertising in a range of outlets, from regional wedding magazines to the local press. As she provides a local service her advertising needs to be aimed at the target group. Using local advertising is suited to these needs. However, using a range of adverts including brochures and magazine

advertising means she has a better chance of reaching her customers. Another successful feature has been the places she sells the products. She has a shop in Bootle, Liverpool. This has relatively low rents which enables her to keep her costs down. However, she also makes use of other channels, such as wedding fairs which can also be relatively low cost operations.

Case study

(a) The term marketing mix refers to the elements of a business's marketing. These are commonly referred to as the four Ps - product, promotion, price and place. For the marketing of services this is sometimes extended to include people, process and physical evidence. **(3 marks)**

(b) *Woman's Own's* unique selling point has changed over the years so that its USP could now be described as: Aimed at women in the over 35 age range, with a long tradition but changing with the times, and with a lively, bright and cheeky content.

(4 marks)

(c) There is a number of elements of the marketing mix of *Woman's Own* contained in the article. The price is 85p. The product has bold colours and clean, fresh lines. It was promoted via 'TV and billboard advertising'. There is no reference to place in the article but it is normal for women's magazines to be distributed via newsagents and supermarkets.

(6 marks)

(d) The factors influencing the marketing mix will have been as follows. The amount of finance available for the re-launch of Woman's Own will have affected the full range of the marketing mix. For example, the promotional budget will have been strongly influenced by this. Technological developments will have alerted and extended a range of possibilities not least in terms of the product itself. For example, the bolder colours available for the re-launch will have been linked to technological developments in terms of printing. The findings from the market research with consumers have clearly been highly influential in shaping the content of the magazine. For example, in the article reference is made to the use of focus groups in terms of the content and design of the magazine. The competitiveness of the market for women's magazine has also clearly been an influence upon the marketing mix. With so many competitors the price of the magazine will have been carefully calibrated to take account of this.

(10 marks)

(e) The article suggests a strong emphasis upon the nature of the product itself in the marketing of Woman's Own. Ultimately, whether or not this will have been the correct decision will be borne out in terms of sales levels; the customers will decide. There is much evidence in the article to suggest that the emphasis upon product would have been correct. In particular, the detailed feedback that the publishers of the magazine received from potential readers suggested a highly discerning readership who would be put off by weak or patronising copy. 'Weekly readers are an unforgiving lot' was the conclusion drawn from this and it suggests that any problems with the content of the magazine could be perilous for sales levels. It also suggests a lack of brand loyalty amongst potential customers and a willingness to opt for alternative publications. In addition, the fierce competition amongst publishers of women's magazines suggests the need for covers that stand out from rivals on news stand; hence the focus upon bold colours and 'cleaner, fresher' lines.

Nevertheless, there is some evidence that a greater emphasis upon promotion and price may be of value to the publishers. In particular, the tendency for 'repertoire buying' amongst women readers involving the selection of a range of titles does suggest less focus upon the detailed content of magazines and a more superficial browsing of content. Were this type of purchasing to become a stronger feature of magazine buying it is possible that IPC Connect might consider further emphasising the price of Womans' Own and heavily promoting the product so that it is on the 'repertoire buying' list of the vast majority of readers in the target age group.

(10 marks)

17 The product life cycle

Question 1

(a) A successful product which has been on the market for three years and with a four year development stage would match the diagram at the top of the page. a new car model could provide an approximate match. The product life cycle below may represent a product with a one year development stage, followed by a tremendous growth in sales during its first year on the market and an equally dramatic decline in sales 14-16 months after its introduction. A successful film or a popular music album could match the diagram's characteristics.

(b) There are two main reasons why some products have a very long life cycle. First, because of the successful use of product extension strategies which can breathe new life into otherwise jaded products on the verge of decline. For example, Heinz, has used a variety of methods to extend the life of baked beans and has been successful in maintaining them as a premium brand. Second, some products are not subject to the same swings in tastes and fashions as others. This is often because such products are timeless and difficult to improve upon and subsequent competitors have years of brand building to compete against. For example, the continued existence of Swan Vesta matches may be attributed more to the difficulty of producing matches better than those available 50 years ago than it is to the successful application of extension strategies.

(c) Timescales and sales levels are different for each product.

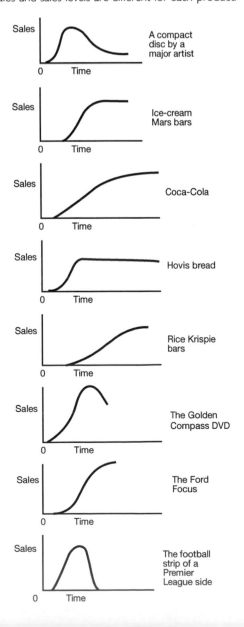

A compact disc by a major artist

Ice-cream Mars bars

Coca-Cola

Hovis bread

Rice Krispie bars

The Golden Compass DVD

The Ford Focus

The football strip of a Premier League side

Question 2

(a) (i) In 1984 it could be argued that the introduction of organic yoghurt was an example of a new product being brought to the market. Previously Rachel's had sold organic milk, followed by cream and butter. But 1984 saw 'the first commercial production of yoghurt'.
(ii) It could be argued that the introduction of organic fat-free yoghurt in 2001 was an extension strategy by the new owners of the business, Horizon Organic. Extension strategies are used by businesses as products reach maturity or decline stages in their product life cycle. They are designed to reinvigorate sales, by changing aspects of the product, such as ingredients or target markets. In this case yoghurt was changed so that it contained less fat than the traditional product, designed for customers wanting a lower fat product.

(b) Cash flow requirements vary at different stages of a product life cycle and in the operation of a business. In the case of Rachel's yoghurts before the new state-of-the-art dairy was built cash flow may have been low or even negative. Expenditure on such a large project would have required cash outflows for the business. Although it would have been earning positive cash flow from its existing products, it may have still faced cash flow problems due the the high level of spending needed on the dairy. Some of the negative cash flow would have been offset by borrowing, which would have provided a cash inflow. However, as the dairy became operational and the business started selling new products, helped for example by the large contract from the supermarket chain, cash inflows would have risen and eventually the negative cash flow would have turned into a positive cash flow, where cash inflows were greater than cash outflows.

Case study

(a)

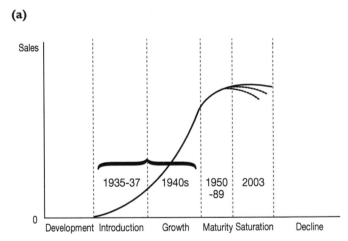

(3 marks)

(b) Significant periods in the product life cycle of the KitKat are as follows.
- Launched in 1935 as Rowntree's Chocolate Crisp.
- Became a national favourite in the 1940s.
- Sales decline in 2003.
- Variants on the KitKat introduced as Nestlé seek to extend the life of the product.

(6 marks)

(c) The article reveals a number of product extension strategies that have been used by Nestlé to extend the life span of this popular product. First there is evidence that Nestlé has sought to find new markets for the product. For example, there is a hot weather KitKat sold in Malaysia and flavours such as green tea geared up to the Japanese market. The range of KitKat products has been extensively increased not only in terms of meeting the needs of new markets but also in KitKat's existing markets. As such, there are now KitKat Chunkies, a dark chocolate KitKat and occasional variants upon the KitKat theme including a Halloween blood orange variety. In addition, the photographic evidence suggests that although the packaging of KitKat remains largely the same it has been subtly developed to reflect, for example, different celebrations as witnessed by the 'Happy Easter' image.

(8 marks)

(d) There are three main future changes that are likely to affect the product life cycle of the KitKat. First, the extent to which the extension strategies already employed by Nestlé are successful in preventing the KiKat from going into decline. If these strategies are successful then Nestlé will be able to continue producing at what is likely to be at or near full capacity. Second, the extent to which Nestlé needs to employ new extension strategies in order to maintain sales levels. A range of extension strategies as described in the article have already been employed by Nestlé, but it is quite possible that further strategies will be required. How successful these strategies are will affect the product life cycle of the KitKat. Unsuccessful strategies will lead to the eventual decline of the product. Third, will be a range of factors external to Nestlé. Foremost amongst these will be the extent of competition in a market which is described in the article as being 'cut throat'. Fierce and successful competition to the KitKat from rival confectionery manufacturers may well hasten the demise of this popular product.

(8 marks)

18 | New product development and product portfolio analysis

Question 1

(a) The total sales of all products over the period are shown in the table below.

2000	10,000
2001	14,000
2002	23,000
2003	30,000
2004	39,000
2005	42,000
2006	48,000
2007	52,000
2008	54,000

(b) A unique selling point of something is a feature of a product that differentiates it in markets from other products. It could be suggested that the patented tape measure has a USP. The patent of the product means that other businesses are prevented from copying its design or technology in the product and producing a copy-cat product for a period of time. Its unique feature is that it can measure irregular shapes and curves more accurately than other products. This may be attractive to customers, particularly those businesses and employees in the construction industry.

(c) There is some evidence of successful management of the product mix by Lokotronics. When product A reached its saturation stage in 2008, product D was continuing a period of steady growth and may have been entering maturity. This is classic product mix management. As one product reaches saturation another product, at or near its height of growth, arrives to take its place. Similarly, when product B began to decline in 2002, product C arrived on the market to take its place. In this way the decline in sales of product B was compensated for by the growth in sales of product C. This is shown in the table above. Over the period 2006 to 2008, sales of the four products grew from 48,000 to 52,000 to 54,000. One point of concern may be that product C appears to have reached saturation in 2008 and it is quite possible that it has entered a period of decline. Unless the company has launched new products onto the market to take its place, there may be problems in the future.

Question 2

(a) Two factors that will have influenced the development of the iPhone stand out in the article. One is the entrepreneurialism of Steve Jobs, the Chief Executive of Apple, who was instrumental in driving forward the iPhone project. The other is the development of technology that has enabled the creation of the touch screen aspects of the product.

(b) It is clear that the iPhone has experienced a high rate of market growth since its launch in 2007. Less clear is whether the iPhone will gain a large share of the market for mobile phones. Given the enormous size of the market for mobile phones and the relatively high cost of the iPhone it is possible that its market share will remain relatively small. In this case the iPhone will be a 'problem child' in terms of the Boston Matrix. If, however, the iPhone does, as Apple no doubt hope, gain a relatively large share of the market for mobile phones it will be categorised as a 'star'.

Case study

(a) The principal unique selling point of the Fusion Power Stealth is its high technology approach to shaving. The product presents itself as being at the cutting edge of technological development. Some of the specific features which contribute to this USP include the microchip to control vibrations, the five blades and a visually arresting orange and black handle.

(3 marks)

(b) One clear influence upon the development of the Fusion Power stealth has been a number of technological developments which have enabled Gillette, the manufacturers of this razor, to develop this product from its predecessor, the Fusion Power razor. These technological developments include a microchip to control vibrations and the use of additional blades to create an even closer shave.

(6 marks)

(c) It is possible to glean from the information provided some clues about the market position of the Fusion Power Stealth. The product is one of the main items in Gillette's range of products and Gillette has a 74 per cent share of the UK's market in razors. This suggests that the Fusion Power Stealth will have a high market share. In addition, the Stealth is the latest in a long line of Gillete razors all of which have successfully contributed to Gillette's current string position in the UK razor market. It might therefore be reasonably anticipated that the Fusion Power Stealth will also have a high market growth rate. This combination of high market share and high market growth rate would make the product a cash cow within the Boston Matrix. The decision that Gillette may have to face in relation to this product will be when to replace it with a new product. Gillette believe that their new product will probably only be the best shaving system for two years. This might mean replacing the Fusion Power Stealth within a relatively short time period even when it has acquired a position as a cash cow. This does make the razor market unusual in some respects as in many other markets businesses keep their cash cows going for many years. However, the information provided in the article points to a fast changing razor market in which products are replaced and/or upgraded at a rapid rate.

(8 marks)

(d) Given Gillette's strength in the market their decision to introduce the Fusion Power Stealth might seem rather odd. If the business is so successful why should it not stick with its existing product range? The principal response to this would be that keeping ahead of the market and constantly upgrading and replacing products has been the strategy that has enabled Gillette to be so successful in the UK razor market. According to this line of argument, were Gillette to stand still it might lose its position as the leading manufacturer of razors. There is evidence in the article to support this. When 9,000 consumers were asked to try the Fusion razor before it eventually replaced the Mach 3 the majority preferred this product, although 30 per cent did prefer the old product. It seems likely that Gillette's strategy of constantly introducing new technologies and offering consumers a fast-changing product has been successful.

(10 marks)

19 Price - influencing the market

Question 1

(a) A range of factors may have influenced the prices of the products shown in the photographs. Some examples of these factors are shown below:

- The flowers might be sold in a highly competitive market in which UK, Dutch and African based flower growers compete fiercely. This would mean that the price would be set largely by the market.
- The rings being sold at the jewellers might be priced partly in relation to the market segment they are aimed at. They might, for example, be aimed at young professionals and consequently be priced at a relatively high level to reflect the higher incomes of this market segment.
- The bottled water shown in the bottom left photograph might be priced according to largely what consumers think it is worth. Here the business marketing the product would pay attention to what consumers think about the value of the product.
- The petrol might be priced according to the costs of producing it. This would include the costs of buying the crude oil and of refining it and distributing it to petrol stations. In addition, the oil companies would also add on a mark-up for profits.

Question 2

(a) There are real benefits for Patel and Co of using a contribution as opposed to a cost plus pricing approach for their ladders. Contribution pricing allows Patel and Co much more flexibility when making their pricing decisions. With cost plus pricing each ladder would have been required to cover the full cost of producing it plus a markup for profit. With contribution pricing it is not even necessary for each ladder to cover its full costs of production. Consequently, Patel and Co are able to decide upon exactly which production costs they wish to include in the price of each individual product. They are also able to decide how much contribution to profits they wish each product to make. Overall, therefore, contribution pricing is a less crude method of pricing which allows Patel and Co to choose exactly the cost related price they wish for each of their products. It also allows market factors to be taken into account.

(b) From the information provided by the accountant it may be that the loft ladder is not a viable product for Patel and Co. The loft ladder only provides a £5 contribution to indirect costs and profit. It is quite likely that the actual indirect costs of producing each loft ladder are higher than £5. In this case not only is the loft ladder not covering its indirect costs, but it is also actually generating an overall loss for the firm. However, it could be that the direct costs of producing the loft ladder are high because it is a new product. If this were the case then in the longer term the loft ladder may become viable. Such a situation would justify Patel and Co's decision only to attach a small proportion of its indirect costs to the loft ladder.

Case study

(a) (i) Price discrimination is when the same product is sold to consumers at different prices. So, for example, the off peak fare for a return trip between Portsmouth and St Malo for two adults and two children is £300. The peak fare for the same journey could be twice this amount.

(3 marks)

(ii) Cost-plus pricing occurs when the price is calculated by calculating the average cost of production and adding a mark-up to calculate the price. So, for example, the £142 fare between Newhaven and Le Havre may have been calculated in this manner with average costs being £120 and a £22 mark-up added for profits.

(3 marks)

(b) The pricing strategy used by Brittany Ferries on the western routes seems to be very much market orientated with, possibly, a customer value pricing strategy. The evidence for this is that Brittany Ferry's strategy has been to go upmarket and get passengers to pay a premium 'floating hotel' services. Brittany Ferries may have chosen this strategy for two main reasons. First, because of a lack of competition; P&O pulled out of the western routes as is reported in the article. Second, because of market based focus in Brittany Ferries' pricing strategy.

(6 marks)

(c) One principal reason why prices might be higher on the western route than on the eastern route is the level of competition on these two routes. The article suggest a much higher level of competition on the eastern routes than on the western routes. Consequently Britanny Ferries dominates the western routes especially since P&O pulled out of this route. This lack of competition will offer Brittany Ferries more control over its pricing decisions and has given it the opportunity to use customer value pricing charging consumers what they are willing to pay. By contrast on the eastern routes there is a high level of competition with a range of businesses competing for the channel crossing market. In addition, on this eastern route the market is described as 'price sensitive'. Both factors are likely to bring down prices on this eastern route.

(8 marks)

(d) The article suggests that the cross-channel ferry operators are beginning to compete more effectively with the budget airlines through the use of more transparent pricing on their websites and through offering a service that is less prone to delays than those experienced by the passengers on budget airlines. There is a number of ways by which the budget airlines might wish to respond to this. First, they could ensure that their own websites also offer more transparent and clearer pricing. Second, they could work with the airports to ensure fewer delays. Third, they might wish to promote the benefits of flying as opposed to using cross channel ferries in a series of promotions. Finally, they could change their pricing on cross-channel routes to ensure that they remained competitive in relation to the ferry companies.

(10 marks)

Question 1

(a) (i) At £2 the quantity demanded is 800, so the total revenue is £1,600. At £3 the quantity demand is 600 so the total revenue is £1,800. The change in total revenue is therefore an increase of £200 (£1,600 to £1,800).

(ii) At £7 the quantity demanded is 300, so the total revenue is £2,100. At £10 the quantity demand is 200 so the total revenue is £2,000. The change in total revenue is therefore a fall of £100 (£2,100 to £2,000).

(iii) At £5 the quantity demanded is 400, so the total revenue is £2,000. At £3 the quantity demand is 600 so the total revenue is £1,800. The change in total revenue is therefore a fall of £200 (£2,000 to £1,800).

(b) The stationery shop might be reluctant to raise prices above £7 per pen because at the prices shown the revenue derived from the pens begins to decline. This any price increase above £7 would lead to a fall in revenue for the business. For example, raising price from £2 to £3 raises revenue from £1,600 (£2 × 800) to £1,800 (£3 × 600). Similarly, raising price from £5 to £6 raises revenue from £2,000 (£5 × 400) to £2,100 (£6 × 350). But raising price from £7 to £8 leads to a fall in revenue from £2,100 (£7 × 300) to £2,080 (£8 × 260).

Question 2

(a) The price change is from £200 to £240, an increase of £40. In percentage terms this price change can be calculated as follows.

Percentage change in price = (40 ÷ 200) × 100 = 20%

The change in demand resulting from this is from 800 to 600, a change of minus 200. In percentage terms this demand change can be calculated as follows.

Percentage change in quantity demanded
= (-200 ÷ 800) × 100 = -25%

So price elasticity of demand for Kaldor jukeboxes is:

Percentage change in quantity demanded ÷ percentage change in price = -25 ÷ 20 = (-)1.25.

This shows that demand is price elastic.

From the evidence given it would seem that the decision to raise the price of the jukeboxes was not a good one for the business. This is because demand is price elastic, which will lead to a decline in revenue resulting from the price change. At a price of £200 with sales of 800 the revenue was:

£200 × 800 = £160,000

However, at a price of £240 with sales of 600 the revenue was:

£240 × 600 = £144,00

Thus it can be seen that revenue has declined by £16,000 as a result of the price change.

Question 3

(a) Price elasticity is a measure of the responsiveness of quantity demanded to a change in the price of a product. The quantity demanded of a product can be said to be price elastic or inelastic. When the quantity demanded is highly price inelastic then the change in quantity demanded will be far less than the change in price. So, for example, price could increase a great deal and there would be a far smaller percentage reduction in the quantity demanded. A large reduction in price would bring about a far smaller percentage increase in quantity demanded.

(b) (i) It was expected that on the Millennium New Years' eve demand for taxi cab rides would rise. The demand for a service such as taxi cab rides can be influenced by many factors. A major influence might be seasonal factors, such as the time of year or seasonal celebrations. In this case people would have wanted to drink and party to celebrate the Millennium. Legislation prevents drinking and driving and so to get to their destinations for the Millennium eve party goers would have had to have taken a taxi ride. As it was a very special occasion demand may have been expected to have risen more than usual for a Saturday night or New Year's Eve.

(ii) It was expected that demand for taxi cab rides was going to rise and be relatively high on Millennium eve. Prices are one factor that could affect the demand for taxi cab rides. However, assuming that the price of a taxi cab ride did not change above its normal level and influence demand, then an increase in demand for cab rides could have severely reduced the chances of travellers getting a taxi cab ride on Millennium eve. There is only a limited number of taxis in any area. So supply is restricted or limited. If large numbers of travellers are demanding taxis then there is likely to be excess demand for taxis. Only some travellers will get taxi rides. Others will not be able to get a ride either to their party or back home. So some demand will be unsatisfied.

(c) Bill was 'disappointed with his takings' for the Millennium Eve night. He must have hoped that he would be at least as busy as on a normal Saturday night. If he had been, he would have been able to double his takings because the government had allowed London taxi drivers to double their prices. Price elasticity of demand would therefore have been 0. If demand is perfectly inelastic, a doubling of price leads to no change in quantity demanded. His costs would have been exactly the same as on a normal Saturday night. So the 100 per cent increase in revenue would have been all profit for Bill.

In fact, he was less busy than on a normal Saturday night. He transported 30 per cent fewer passengers. The price elasticity of supply was therefore -0.3 given that prices had increased by 100 per cent. However, with such inelastic demand, Bill Finch was still able to gain a significant increase in profit compared to a normal Saturday night. His takings were probably up by 40 per cent since he carried 70 per cent of his normal Saturday night passengers at twice the price. That 40 per cent will have been all extra profit because his petrol costs, if anything, will have fallen carrying fewer passengers.

These figures are approximate because the data do not state whether journeys were longer or shorter than on average, or whether the number of passengers carried equated with the number of journeys made.

Overall, Bill Finch will have made significantly more money by driving on the Millennium Eve compared to a normal busy Saturday night. If he hadn't driven, he would almost certainly have lost the most profitable night of the year on which to drive. So although he was disappointed that he did not make more money, he was probably still right to take the decision to drive. If he decided not to drive, the money lost would have been considerable.

Case study

(a)

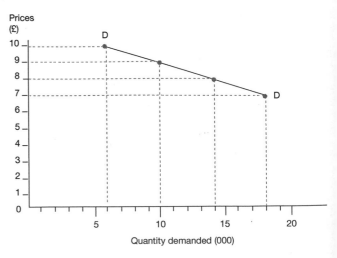

The relationship between price and demand for Californians is shown in the diagram above. As a general rule, as price falls the quantity demanded of Californians rises and as price rises the quantity demanded of Californians falls. This can be seen in the diagram. For example, if the price of Californians is £16 then 14,000 are demanded. If the price is reduced to £14 then 18,000 are demanded, a rise of 4,000. If the price is raised to £18 then 10,000 are purchased, a fall of 4,000. **(6 marks)**

(b) (i) The change in quantity demanded is from 10,000 to 14,000. Expressed in percentage terms this is:

(4,000 ÷ 10,000) × 100 = 40%

The change in price is from £18 to £16. Expressed in percentage terms this is:

(£2 ÷ £18) × 100 = (-) 11.11%

The price elasticity of demand for Californians for a reduction in price from £18 to £16 is therefore:

Percentage change in quantity demanded ÷ percentage change in price = 40 ÷ (-)11.11 = (-)3.6

(ii) The change in quantity demanded is from 14,000 to18,000. Expressed in percentage terms this is:

(4,000 ÷14,000) × 100 = 28.57%

The change in price is from £16 to £14. Expressed in percentage terms this is:

(£2 ÷ £16) × 100 = (-) 12.5%

The price elasticity of demand for Californians for a reduction in price from £16 to £14 is therefore:

Percentage change in quantity demanded ÷ percentage change in price = 28.57 ÷ (-)12.5 = (-) 2.29

(6 marks)

(c) The elasticity of demand shows the extent to which demand reacts to a change in price of a product. Generally as price rises, the quantity demanded of a product falls. As price falls, the quantity demanded rises. Elasticity of demand can illustrate the extent to which this change takes place. So, for example, if the price of Californians falls, the business might expect the quantity demanded to rise. A fall in price from £16 to £14 leads to a rise in quantity demanded from 14,000 to 18,000 Californians. However, the percentage change in quantity demanded is greater than the percentage change in price. The percentage change in quantity demanded is 29% compared to a percentage change in price of 12.5%. Demand for a product is said to be elastic when the percentage change in quantity demanded is greater than the percentage change in price. This is the case with the elasticity of demand for Californians. Elasticity can also be calculated using the formula:

Percentage change in quantity demanded ÷ percentage change in price

When the figure is greater than 1, demand is elastic. This is the case for Californians. For price falls from £18 to £16 and £16 to £14 the elasticity of demand is (-)3.6 and (-)2.29. Note that the minus signs are ignored. Only if the calculation was less than 1, ie 0.5, would demand be inelastic. **(6 marks)**

(d) The table shows how the demand for Californians changes in reaction to changes in the prices of competitors' products. The table clearly shows that as the prices of competitors' products fall the quantity demanded of Californians also falls. This occurs because the competitors' swimsuits are seen by consumers as acceptable substitutes for Californians. The cross elasticity of demand for Californians would, therefore, be found by calculating the percentage decline in the sales for Californians in relation to the percentage decrease in the price of competitors' products. Because competitor's swimsuits are substitutes for Californians the cross elasticity would be positive. The extent to which this would affect Bodyline would depend on the percentage changes. For example, a fall in price from £14 to £12, a 14 per cent fall in price, has led to a fall in sales of 3,600 for Bodyline. This is a 22 per cent fall, a proportionately greater fall in sales. **(10 marks)**

(e) The figures provided in answer to (b) indicate that Penny was right to suggest cutting the price of Californians. This is because for all of the price changes, demand for the Californian can be described as being price elastic. This means that any change in price will lead to a proportionally greater change in quantity demanded. Therefore, these price changes should lead to an increase in total revenue. Calculations of the total revenue generated by the Californian at the various price levels bear this out, as shown in the table below.

Price	Quantity demanded	Revenue
£14	18,000	£252,000
£16	14,000	£224,000
£18	10,000	£180,000
£20	6,000	£120,000

It can be seen from the above figures that each decrease in the price of the Californian leads to an increase in total revenue for Bodyline. Therefore, Penny may have been right to suggest a price decrease at the time she did.

(12 marks)

Question 1

(a) Trade fairs might be important to Anna's business for a number of reasons. First, they provide a regular alternative outlet to her normal retail activities. They therefore give her another method of increasing revenue. Second, they may give her the opportunity to test consumer reaction to her comics and consequently to make judgments about which comics to stock. Third, they may be a way of her gaining information about the activities of her competitors. She will be able to browse competitor stands and compare their activities with those of her own business. The nearest competitor to her own shop is 50 miles away. Fourth, she may be able to build up contacts and also develop relationships with a wider variety of customers. They may build up a loyalty to her business and return to the fairs each time they are held.

(b) Given the information in the article it could be argued that trade fairs will not be as successful as direct mailing in promoting comics, at least for a business of the same or a similar size to Anna's. There are advantages of trade fairs as explained in (a). But, as the article states, attending the trade fair at the NEC 'takes a lot of the time out of the week and does not always pay for itself'.

In contrast, direct mailing allows Anna to target particular groups of consumers in her local area. Such people are likely to represent the core of her customers and are the most likely to respond to promotional activities. Direct mailing is therefore likely to hit a wider target market. It might also attract some people who would not be willing to give up their time to visit the NEC for a trade fair.

Question 2

(a) There are two main promotional methods referred to in the article. Branding has been used by the publishers of newspapers in the UK as a means of enabling consumers to readily identify their products. The names of newspapers, such as the *Sun* and the *Daily Mirror* are very familiar brands to many UK consumers. Sales promotions in the form of free gifts have also been used to promote newspapers. For example, the *Daily Mail* gained readers largely, it is reported in the article, through free DVDs being given away.

(b) Both of the promotional methods identified in response to (a) above are below-the-line promotions. Above-the-line promotion refers to advertising, but below-the-line promotion is non-media promotion..

(c) It may be that a local newspaper could usefully offer free gifts in order to increase sales. Because most local newspapers have relatively small circulations it is likely that these gifts would need to be more modest than those offered by the big national newspapers. So, free DVDs of well known movies would be unlikely. Other gifts, for example, linked to local businesses would however be feasible. Local newspaper publishers also make strong use of branding to promote their products. Local newspapers are often strong brands in the localities at which they are aimed.

Question 3

(a) Below-the-line promotion is all promotional methods that do not make use of advertising media. There are many available to businesses. When deciding which to use, the business would need to take into account that its customers are other businesses. For example, it provides electrical wiring to businesses involved in the manufacture of railways infrastructure and conveyor systems. It could be argued that some below-the-line promotions may be more appropriate than others for Teepee. These are likely to be methods that reach business customers in the industry.

Sale promotions to businesses could be useful. For example, it may attract businesses through product endorsements from Subaru. This may be particularly useful in attracting other clients given that the product needs to be tested and quality is likely to be a major influence in any purchasing decision. The recommendation of a major rally car team could be influential. Another sales promotion could be offering special payment terms to buyers. For example, it might allow a business to take delivery now, but delay the payment period for 90 days if the current payment period is 30 days.

A certain amount of direct selling might also prove useful. Visiting other businesses and explaining the uses of the wire might help convince them of its quality. Further, direct mailing regularly in brochures to potential clients could help to attract customers. Direct emailing might also be used. Trade shows might also be important for this sector. Industrial products are often promoted at such shows and businesses visit the shows looking for new suppliers. Promotions in industry magazines and press releases aimed at the trade, stressing orders which have been won, might also attract the interest of new clients.

Case study

(a) There is a range of promotional methods referred to in the article. Most of these are above-the-line promotions. They include TV advertising campaigns, online advertising, cinema advertising and billboards. There are also references to below-the-line promotions including window displays, an example of merchandising, and branding.

(6 marks)

(b) This response will focus upon the TV advertising campaigns referred to in (a) above. These TV advertisements could be made informative by increasing consumer awareness of the products available. For example, the Marks and Spencer (M & S) advertisements could show a range of the clothes offered by this business. The advertisements could be made persuasive by making the businesses and products appear desirable to consumers. For example, by associating their products with a top Hollywood star Marks and Spencer will have increased the desirability of their products in the eyes of some of their consumers. Reassuring advertising would seek to reassure existing customers and demonstrate to them that they should continue using a particular product or brand. For example, the John Lewis advertisements might reassure existing customers by offering a stylish and intelligent advertisement that reinforces their already good image of this business.

(6 marks)

(c) There is likely to have been a number of factors influencing the choice of promotional methods for M & S and John Lewis. Both will have been concerned with the cost of the promotional methods shown, although as large retail businesses neither would find any major promotional methods beyond their means. The businesses will have been concerned with reaching the right audience through their promotions. For example, neither business will have been too interested in reaching an exclusively teenage audience because of the nature of the products they sell. Consequently they would be unlikely, for example, to advertise in teen magazines. Choosing a promotional method that best allowed each business to put across its chosen message would also be important. For example, John Lewis made use of cinema advertising no doubt, in part, because of the capacity of this form of advertising to project strong visual images. Finally both businesses would be careful to choose complementary promotional methods so that each medium used reinforced messages from other media. For example, the cinema advertising used by John Lewis would be likely to have been carefully co-ordinated to support their TV advertising.

(10 marks)

(d) A small independent fashion clothing business would have more restrictions on the promotional methods it could use than large businesses such as M & S and John Lewis. In particular, cost considerations in relation to the promotional methods chosen would be of paramount importance. Consequently it is highly unlikely that such a business could afford TV advertising or the use of billboards. However, advertising in local media and the use of a modest form of

Internet-based advertising would be possible. In terms of below-the-line promotions there would be many possibilities for such a business. Public relations, most especially in the form of press releases, perhaps linked to events such as fashion shows or fashion shoots, could play an important promotional role.

The business could also develop itself as a brand so that consumers recognised it more readily. This might involve the creation of a brand mark or design consistent with the image that the business wished to project. The business might wish to develop its merchandising by, for example, developing displays to be placed next to its clothes at clothing retailers.

Promotional offers in the form of sales promotions on particular lines of clothing might also be used by the business to encourage consumers to try its products. These might encourage consumers to sample some of the cheaper clothes in the range produced by the business.

Direct mailing might also be useful to the business, but only if it was able to ensure that the mailing list would enable the business to reach the intended target market of consumers.

Finally, direct selling would be likely to form an important part of the promotional mix chosen by the business. Talking in person to the owners, buyers and managers at a range of fashion retailers could be an important means of providing outlets in which the clothes could be sold. This promotional method would provide both a vital means of explaining their products to key individuals and offer a means of gaining feedback about the clothes produced by the business.

(12 marks)

Question 1

(a) (i) As a small operation KFM may have been affected by a number of factors. The size of the company, the technical nature of its product and the target market were all likely to have influenced the channel of distribution. A small company often has limited resources. It needs to keep costs down and so look for a cost efficient method of distribution. The fact that the product could be changed to meet specific needs of customers and the limited size of the target market at the time were likely to have contributed to the direct sales from producer to consumer, cutting out retailers, wholesalers or intermediaries. In some cases the business may even have sold 'online' via a download. This direct method is possible due to the technical nature of the product.

(ii) As it expands in the UK, KFM will want to distribute its products to a larger market. The product is likely to become more standardised to suit a wider range of customers and also to reduce the average cost of the business. The larger market may mean that the business would look for an intermediary such as a retail chain selling the product under its 'business and education section'.

(iii) Certain factors will be important in affecting the distribution channel of KFM if it expands abroad. One will be the size of the market. Selling to the USA, a large and diverse market, is likely to require some form of intermediary. It is possible to sell the product abroad as it does not deteriorate and should be more standardised. However, legal regulations may affect the business. KFM must make sure that its products conform with US specifications. It is also likely that the size of the company and its lack of knowledge of the US market means that an intermediary will be used.

(b) KFM has to make certain decisions about its channel of distribution as it expands. In the UK the use of a retail chain to distribute the product to customers seems appealing compared to distributing the product itself. Providing the product can be standardised to some extent the business is likely to reach a wider market, especially if it is growing.

KFM has three alternatives when expanding into the USA. It can use an agent to find a retail chain to stock the products, sell to a warehouse business or license the product to a US company. Given its lack of knowledge and the dispersed nature of the market it is likely to need to use some form of intermediary as explained above. Licensing the product to a manufacturer might give away too much control. Selling via a wholesaler may not be effective unless other support is given. Selling via an agent can be a relatively cheap way of entering a market. So using an agent might be a useful way to enter the market at first.

Question 2

(a) Two main channels of distribution are referred to in the article. The first is the distribution of CDs via retailers so the distribution channel is: manufacturer - retailer - consumer. The second is downloaded music from the Internet so the distribution channel here is similar: manufacturer - online retailer - consumer.

(b) A small UK based record shop/CD retailing business might take the view from this information that competing with downloaded music and the major retailers will be very difficult. Therefore such a business might wish to find a niche in the market from where it is better able to compete. This is likely to be a niche linked to particular music styles or music from particular eras and it might combine sales of second-hand CDs and albums with sales of new products.

Case study

(a) (i) The distribution channel currently used by Matrix Mobiles is: manufacturer - online retailer - consumer.

(3 marks)

(ii) The distribution channel under consideration by Matrix mobiles is:: manufacturer - retailer - consumer.

(3 marks)

(b) Finding the most suitable distribution channel for Matrix Mobiles is so important because their mobile phones need to be available to consumers in the right place if they are to maximise sales further, their mobile phones need to be available to consumers at the right time if they are to meet their consumers' needs.

(6 marks)

(c) There will be a number of factors influencing Matrix Mobiles' decision to open a shop. First, by opening a shop they will be able to reach consumers who are less inclined or unable to purchase their mobiles from a website. Second, they will be able to sell mobiles to consumers who want them straightaway. When selling products online there is always a time lag between the ordering of goods and the consumer actually receiving them. Third, Kamil Soud implies that opening a retail outlet will enable the business to compete on factors other than price. Opening a shop therefore might enable the business to stress aspects such as the quality of service to customers.

(8 marks)

(d) It is not clear from the evidence whether Matrix Mobiles (MM) should open its own shop in addition to its online retailing business. On the one hand, a shop might enable MM to reach consumers who do not choose to buy their phones on the Internet and as discussed in (c) above to stress aspects of their marketing other than price. On the other hand, a shop would add to their costs and, given the nature of their business, it is not clear in which location MM should actually open their shop. Brighton was ruled out and it was not clear what other suitable venues for a shop had been discussed. In addition, a shop would only enable their business to reach a relatively small number of consumers in a particular locality relative to their online business which can potentially reach millions.

Overall, it might therefore be argued that on balance MM should not open a shop and that they should concentrate upon their online business.

(10 marks)

23 | Branding

Question 1

(a) There have been no changes in the most valuable top 4 brands between 2006 and 2007. Beyond the top four brands the changes between 2006 and 2007 have been relatively small. Some of the more notable changes include Google's appearance in the top twenty in 2007 rising from 24 th in 2006, Intel's decline from 5th to 7th place and BMW's rise from 15th place in the top twenty to 13th place.

(b) There are two main reasons to account for the changes mentioned in response to (a). First, more successful branding and stronger brand positioning of those businesses that have moved up the table shown. This might be part of a wider marketing strategy employed by these businesses. Second, changes in the external environment in which these businesses operate. For example, the rapid expansion of the Chinese economy and BMW's success in targeting this market may account for their improvement. Intel's relative decline might similarly be explained by greater competitive forces in the markets in which they operate.

(c) There have been so few changes to the top ten ranked businesses because of the strength of the brands in this exalted market position. These top ten brands have all been built up over very long periods of time. This means that although their brand strength may ebb and flow over, for example, a ten year period, changes are likely to be minor from one year to another. This strength is in part derived from their global appeal. So if, for example, there was a loss of market position in one country this may be compensated for by gains in another.

Question 2

(a) A brand is a name, term, sign, symbol, design or any other feature which allows consumers to identify the products of a business and to differentiate them from those of other businesses. Rebranding therefore implies that a business, in this case Trigon, a Liverpool nut company, is trying to change one or more of these features. The business may have been trying to change its brand because its existing brand was not being identified sufficiently by customers or may not have have been differentiating its products effectively from those of its competitors.

(b) Certain factors may have influenced the choice of the new brand of the business. The brand name chosen by a business is vital. It must be instantly recognised and valued by customers. It must also say something to customers about the product and differentiate it clearly from rivals. The trade mark chosen by the business must carry out similar functions. It must be recognisable by customers, so that they do not buy other products. It must also convey something about the business to customers, so they retain brand loyalty and do not buy inferior quality, or in extreme cases copied, goods by other producers. The new brand chosen by the business must identify the USP of the product or the business itself. In the case of the Liverpool nut company, Trigon, this is likely to be that it manufactures high quality nuts, which are healthy, and have been manufactured over many years. The brand chosen must reach the target market. So, it must position itself in the market if it is to be successful. For example, a brand which was geared at people with nut allergies, people who did not like nuts, or at all food products, without identifying the target market of nut eaters, is likely to have been unsuccessful. Similarly choosing a brand name such as XTF or Motor city, which do not relate to the product, is also likely to miss the target market.

(c) If the company chose the first option, the MCN Food Company Limited, there is a number of advantages. The brand is not totally tied in to a particular product, and so will not restrict product development in future if the company wanted to diversify. It also makes use of warning on nuts (may contain nuts) in the name. The MCN logo is incorporated in a strong corporate logo which can be recognised. It also has humourous aspects which could be used in promotion. However, there is a danger that the MCN may not be recognised or may not be a strong enough brand for customers to remember. Using the phrase 'food company' may not be specific enough for the target market.

If the company chose the second option, Lightly Salted Food Company, this makes use of the current attention to foods with lower salt. It might attract customers who are interested in more healthy food options. Using food rather than snacks again implies a more healthy option compared to other foods such as crisps which may be perceived as less healthy. Using 'lightly salted' also relates to the previous business and may attract existing customers. The use of humour again in advertising might attract customers. Again, however, the use of 'food company' may not be specific enough for the target markets. And using salt at all in the title, even lightly salted, may put some people off.

If the company chose the third option, Elephant - the Big Snack Company, then a rather abstract solution is chosen. People have to relate to the fact that elephants eat nuts. However, the design, logo and advertising are likely to be memorable. The design will also reflect the history of the business, making it appear well established to clients. On the other hand, the brand may appear frivolous to some customers. Also they may have difficulty relating the fact that elephants eat nuts to the product.

The choice of brand is likely to depend on the type of approach and the view of the market taken by the company. For example, the business might want to retain some aspects of its previous operations in the name. It might be concerned to stress the healthy product aspect and it might want to relate the product to some aspect of the brand (ie nuts) and also introduce humour to promotion. Such an approach may lead it to choose the second option, especially as it might fear that the other two brands are too abstract.

(Note this evaluation is just one solution. other evaluations are equally applicable. So an answer which argues for options one or three is just as valid provided clear evaluation is shown.)

Case study

(a) (i) (ii) Manufacturer brands are brands created by producers of goods and services. The products that are sold then bear the names of the producers that have made them. In both cases, the products athat are sold by Hewlett-Packard and Burberry bear the manufacturers' brand name. So both Hewlett-Packard and Burberry could best be described as having manufacturer brands.

(4 marks)

(b) Both Burberry and Hewlett-Packard are seeking to re-position their brands so that they are viewed more favourably by targeted groups of consumers. Burberry are seeking to re-assert themselves as an exclusive high status brand, whilst Hewlett-Packard are trying to shed their past to some extent and to be associated with computers that match and support consumer's lifestyles. This should benefit Burberry by enabling them to focus once again upon their core market and Hewlett-Packard by allowing them to attract consumers turned off by their old, more functional image.

(6 marks)

(c) Hewlett-Packard suffered damage as a brand because their computers came to be seen by consumers as not meeting their needs. For example, their computers were not previously viewed as physically attractive and did not serve their needs by allowing email checks without 'booting up'. Burberry, a previously up market fashion brand came to be associated with down market trends amongst, for example, football supporters. Their existing customers therefore did not wish to be associated with this brand.

(10 marks)

(d) It seems highly likely that branding will be successful for both Hewlett-Packard and Burberry. Branding enables the products of these respective businesses to be differentiated from others in the market. For example, in the minds of consumers Hewlett-Packard's computers may be viewed by consumers very differently from those of Dell's. Branding creates loyalty amongst consumers. This gives businesses the scope to raise their prices above those of less recognised brands. This is the case for Burberry who are able to sell their products at far higher prices than those retailed by Primark, for example. Partly this is because businesses are able to develop an image for their products through branding so that consumers come to associate particular brands with particular qualities and attributes. However, although businesses such as Burberry and Hewlett-Packard do try to develop strong and positive brands consumers do not always respond to these efforts in the way that businesses anticipate. For example, an expensive promotional campaign designed to strengthen the Hewlett-Packard brand may be met with indifference by consumers. Similarly, Burberry's efforts to shrug off more 'down market' consumers might have little effect upon such groups who may continue to purchase and be visible in their attachment to this brand.

(12 marks)

24 The market

Question 1

(a) Two alternative presentations are shown below.

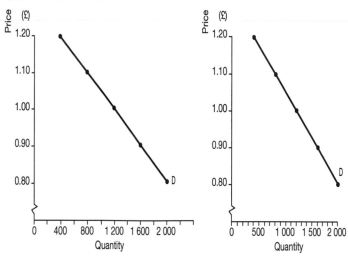

(b) The changes result in an extra 1,000 products being purchased at each price. Two alternative presentations of this change are shown below **(10 marks)**

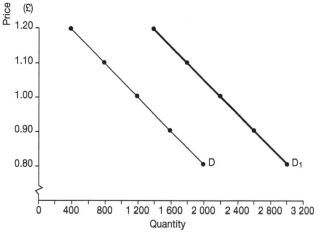

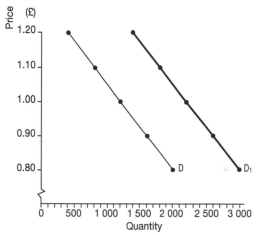

Question 2

(a) The equilibrium price of broccoli is £1.50 per kg. This is the point at which demand equals supply.

(b) (i)
- A reduction in average incomes of consumers purchasing organic vegetables, all things being equal, will lead to a fall in the equilibrium price of organic broccoli.
- Improved organic farming methods leading to a reduction in the costs of producing organic broccoli, all things being equal, will lead to a fall in the equilibrium price of organic broccoli.
- An increase in the popularity of organic vegetables, all things being equal, will lead to a rise in the equilibrium price of organic broccoli.
- A fall in the price of non-organic broccoli, all things being equal, will lead to a fall in the equilibrium price of organic broccoli.

(ii)
- A reduction in average incomes of consumers purchasing organic vegetables, all things being equal, will lead to a decrease in demand for organic broccoli.
- Improved organic farming methods leading to a reduction in the costs of producing organic broccoli, all things being equal, will lead to an increase in the supply of broccoli at any given price by businesses in the market.
- An increase in the popularity of organic vegetables, all things being equal, will lead to an increase in the demand for organic broccoli.
- A fall in the price of non-organic broccoli will lead to an increase in demand for non-organic vegetables, all things being equal. Purchasers will substitute their consumption of organic broccoli for non-organic broccoli. This means that there will be a decrease in the demand for organic broccoli.

Case study

(a) (i) The main demanders of oil are likely to be oil companies who refine the oil. This oil is used to produce petrol and other products, which firms then sell to the consumers. Once it has been converted to petrol or aviation fuel, the likely consumers will be car drivers, businesses who transport goods and airline companies. The oil may also be used in the production of plastics which will then be demanded by a number of business who use plastic as a raw material. Finally, homeowners may demand oil as a form of fuel to heat their homes.

(ii) The suppliers of oil are businesses who drill for oil in countries where oil is a natural resource for that country. OPEC countries are some of the principal suppliers of oil to markets and they operate a cartel where they can control the amount of oil being produced. Other countries who supply oil onto the world markets include Scotland, Russia and Norway. Many of the main suppliers of oil are those businesses who also sell petrol in the UK, including BP, Shell and Texaco to name a few. However, there are small firms who drill for oil and sell it to the larger petroleum companies. **(6 marks)**

(b) (i) There is a number of factors which are likely to affect the demand for oil in world markets.
- The price of oil - the cheaper the price of oil, the more will be demanded. However, even when the price of oil rises, demand does not fall by a large amount, due to it being relatively price inelastic in demand.
- The price of complementary goods - goods which use oil in their usage will affect the demand for oil. Air travel firms and car users are two the main buyers of oil. If the price of air travel was to rise, then the demand for air travel would fall and therefore so would the demand for oil.
- The incomes of the consumers in the world - the higher the levels of income earned the greater the demand for products using oil (ie cars/air travel) and therefore the greater the demand for oil. Also, as oil companies earn higher profit their demand for oil will rise as they seek to expand.
- Government legislation - increasingly, more developed countries are becoming aware of the environmental damage created through the use of oil in cars and production. As more countries introduce legislation to reduce the quantity of oil used, then demand will fall, as consumption falls.
- Weather - if countries experience extremely cold weather conditions, then this will cause the demand to rise in these areas.

(ii) There is a number of factors which will affect the supply of oil.

- The price of oil - the higher the price of oil the more oil companies will be prepared to produce to reap the higher profits.
- Discovery of new oil supplies - if countries discover more oil fields then they may begin to sell oil on the market, thus increasing the supply of oil.
- Political instability - Oil producing countries which experience political unrest or instability may reduce oil production to protect domestic reserves.
- Quotas - OPEC countries are the principal oil producers in the world. They set quotas of oil to be produced and sold, to maintain stable prices and outputs. If the quotas are increased then supply will rise and conversely, if the quotas are reduced, supply will fall.

(10 marks)

(c) (i) It can be seen from the data that the price of oil rose on a number of occasions. The rise in the price of oil occurs because of either an increase in the demand for oil or a decrease in the supply of oil.

- In 1995, the Nigerian oil workers went on strike. This led to a fall in the supply of oil due to the reduction in the amount of workers mining for oil, which in turn led to an increase in the price.
- In 1996 there was extremely cold weather in the US and Europe. This meant that more people needed fuel to heat their homes. This lead to an increase in the demand for oil and hence a rise in the price.
- In 1999 OPEC countries cut their production levels by 4.3m barrels per day, reducing the supply of oil onto the market, leading to the price increases in 2000.

(ii) The fall in the price of oil occurs because of an increase in the supply of oil or a decrease in the demand for oil.

- Between 1992 - 1994 the price of oil fell due to an increase in the production of oil by OPEC. The increase in supply led to a fall in the price of oil.
- Between 1997 - 1999 Iraq began exporting oil. This led to an increase in the amount of oil being supplied and led to a fall in the price level.
- 2002 saw a sharp fall in the price of oil. This was caused by two factors. First was economic recession in the USA, when the demand for oil fell as people's incomes had fallen. This led to a fall in the price. Coupled with this, there was an increase in the quantity of oil being produced by OPEC. This meant that the supply of oil increased, reducing the price of oil further.

(12 marks)

(d) The world market for oil is determined primarily by the demand and supply within the market. Therefore if the demand or supply for oil increases or decreases considerably, then a change in the price of oil would be expected. OPEC is a group of countries who operate as a cartel. This means that they collude together to set the price of the oil being produced. This is achieved through quotas, ie restricting the quantity of oil being supplied. OPEC have the ability to affect the price of oil considerably as they are the dominant suppliers of oil. However, there are other factors and other oil producing countries who can influence the price of oil within the market. If OPEC were to reduce the supply of oil to maintain higher prices and higher profits, then non-OPEC countries may fill the gap in oil production by increasing the quantity of oil supplied by themselves. As a result the world price of oil may not be affected.

Second, OPEC's strength in influencing the price of oil will depend upon the commitment of all countries within the cartel are prepared to offer. OPEC may decide to reduce supplies to keep the price of oil higher. However, there will always be the incentive to cheat as a member, and to sell the oil at a lower price. This will then reduce the ability of OPEC to affect the price. Also the level of stocks which oil suppliers already have will affect the power which OPEC countries have. If there are significant stocks held by particular companies then there will be less change in the price of oil, due to the reduced supply. Firms will be able to release their own stocks and not have to purchase these stocks from OPEC, thus offsetting the increased price caused by the fall in supply.

The price of oil is also determined by the demand for oil. If there is a sudden, unexpected increase in the demand for oil, as experienced during the cold weather, then this may lead to an increase in the price of oil. However, this will only affect the price of oil if the quantity supplied does not increase in reaction to the increased demand. Also, it will only have an impact on the price if the rise in demand for oil is unexpected. It will be more difficult to react to an unexpected change than it will be to respond to an expected change.

The state of the world economy will also have an impact on the price of oil. This may affect on both the supply and demand of oil. If there is a world recession, then the demand for oil will fall thus reducing the price of oil. Alongside this, the supply of oil may be falling due to uncertainty within the markets. This could raise price.

OPEC countries do have a considerable influence over the world price of oil as they have the ability to affect the supply of oil considerably. However, due to the nature of the product, they do not have total control over the price. Demand factors will have an impact and will lead to changes in the price of oil. The extent to which they do affect the price will depend upon the size of the changes in the demand for oil. It will also depend upon the action taken by other oil producing countries and their ability to increase or decrease supplies in reaction to OPEC's actions.

(12 marks)

25 | Competition and business

Question 1

(a) There is a number of factors that may influence the competition for the businesses shown in the photographs. The main factors are listed below:

- The number and size of other businesses in the same market. For example, there are many rival businesses producing potatoes and none large enough to dominate the market for this product. This makes the market for potatoes highly competitive in this respect.
- The extent of barriers to entry. For example, there are relatively few barriers to entry in terms of setting up a new café. Each year new cafes open up in many locations. This makes the market for small cafes relatively competitive in this respect. By way of contrast setting up a new bank is a major undertaking and there are many barriers to entry for new competitors wishing to enter this particular market
- The extent to which products can be differentiated. For a water supplier, differentiating its products from those of others may be difficult (although association with a place linked to clean fresh water such as the Peak District or the Alps can be helpful in this respect). In general this difficulty in differentiating its products will act to increase competition in the market for drinking water.
- The knowledge of buyers and sellers. Because of the complexity of banking and the general lack of knowledge about the banking system amongst many consumers it could be argued that a lack of knowledge about banking amongst consumers acts to limit competition in this market

Question 2

(a) The grocery industry is dominated by just a few large chains. There are thousands of independent grocery stores but they tend to be small and provide a local service only.

(b) The barriers to entry into the grocery industry include the cost of buying or renting space for stores, the potential difficulties associated with obtaining supply and the large costs of establishing a brand to compete with existing large retail chains. It is possible to buy an existing chain as Morrisons did when buying Safeway, but this costs billions of pounds, another barrier to entry.

(c) Supermarkets can attempt to differentiate their services in a number of ways. They can sell different products. They can charge relatively high prices or lower prices. They can promote in different ways. They can site their stores in different locations. They can provide services such as cafes or home delivery. They can open at different times. They can display products in different ways.

(d) It could be argued that knowledge about how to run a supermarket chain is available to all grocery store owners and supermarket owners. The Internet gives a variety of information on running businesses as do books. There are courses available on how to run businesses and certain organisations also provide advice. On the other hand it could be argued that the detailed knowledge and data required to run a business is guarded by the large supermarkets. Details of what prices work and how customers react to promotions are likely to be protected so that small rivals can not compete.

(e) If Tesco increases sales this may have one of two effects on Asda. It may have no effect if Tesco takes sales away from other grocers, such as smaller traders. On the other hand if sales are taken away from Asda, then the market share of Asda will fall.

Question 3

(a) The model of competition that best fits CyTA's position in the market before the entry of Telepassport Telecommunications into Cyprus is perhaps a monopoly. This is because CyTA was the only firm which existed in Cyprus and was government controlled. CyTA was a pure monopoly as according to the text, this was the only

telecommunications' firm operating within Cyprus and therefore would probably own 100 per cent of the market. The firm was also earning exceptionally high profits and this would support that the assertion the firm was exerting monopoly power.

(b) (i) The telecommunications industry in Cyprus is becoming more competitive. A new telecommunications firm is entering the industry, reducing the monopoly power which CyTA previously had. There will be more opportunities available for new firms to enter the industry and compete with the established firm. However, this may be very difficult, as CyTA has been established for a long time and will have strong brand loyalty. New firms may find it difficult to penetrate the market and may have to take large risks. The firms currently existing within the market, due to the entry of new competition, may find that their abnormal profits may begin to be eroded away, as new firms attract some of their previous customers. Also, if competitor firms charge a lower price, then this may lead to CyTA having to reduce its prices also, leading to a further fall in their profit levels.

(ii) Consumers are likely to benefit from the increased competition in the telecommunications market. Telepassport Telecommunications has suggested that CyTA is exploiting the customers with high prices. With greater competition, consumers will have a choice as to which firm they use, thus reducing prices and improving the service for the customers. However, this will only be successful if the new firms have sufficient financial resources to market their products effectively, to gain customers from an established firm and convince them to switch providers.

Case study

(a) (i) Competition is the rivalry between businesses offering products in the same market. It can take many forms. These include price competition, offering distinctive products, advertising and other promotion and distribution.

(3 marks)

(ii) A dominant player is a business with a strong position in a particular market. It may have a larger market share, for example. It is able to control variables in the market to some extent. For instance, it may be able to influence the price a product is set at. Other businesses tend to follow its lead.

(3 marks)

(b) In some ways the sandwich market could be described as corresponding to monopolistic competition. This is because there are few barriers to entry in this market and there are many small producers of sandwiches. However the presence in the sandwich market of big businesses such as Greggs, Marks and Spencer (M & S) and the large supermarket chains suggests oligopoly.

(6 marks)

(c) Two of the main factors influencing the competitiveness of the UK sandwich market are the extent to which sandwiches can be differentiated and the number and size of businesses in the sandwich market. In terms of the extent to which sandwiches can be differentiated there are some limits to this, but given the variety now available it seems that even within this relatively limited food type there are significant grounds for differentiation. Sandwiches available in many shops today have come a long way from the old ham and tomato and cheese and onion varieties. In terms of the number of competitors there are many in the market suggesting a high degree of competition, but some of these competitors are large and dominant businesses. Tesco and Sainsbury's, for example, are very large retailers of foodstuffs and their presence in the sandwich market could be argued to diminish competitive pressures in that market.

(6 marks)

(d) A small retailer might improve its competitiveness in the sandwich market by gaining a competitive advantage over its rivals. Given the presence in this market of large food chains this is unlikely to be competitive advantage in terms of lowering costs or competing on price. Instead a small firm's competitive advantage is more likely to be based upon differentiating its product from those of larger competitors and offering a quality product meeting consumer needs. For example, it might do this by selling its products to small and niche markets largely left untouched by larger retailers. Examples might be vegetarian sandwiches or organic sandwiches. It might also employ friendly and engaging staff who encourage customers to return to the shop. The training of new staff is likely to be very important in this respect.

(8 marks)

(e) In theory a small business could grow to dominate over 50 per cent of sandwich sales in the UK sandwich market. First, there are no barriers to entry in the sandwich market which would allow a new business to readily enter the market. Second, there is currently no one dominant player in this market that the small and growing business would need to displace.

However, there is a number of factors that make this highly unlikely. First, there are plenty of large and successful businesses such as M & S, Gregg's and Sainsbury's who are already well established in this market. Gaining a 50 per cent market share would mean taking market share from these businesses; an immensely difficult undertaking. Second, the data in the article reveals that a large share of the market for sandwiches is in the hands of other small, independent retailers. Again taking a 50 per cent share of the market would mean removing many of these competitors. Third, a business anticipating a 50 per cent share of the market would also need to be incredibly successful in attracting consumers. Given the nature of sandwiches as a product this would seem very unlikely. Finally, a business growing so dominant in the sandwich market would probably attract the attention of the Competition Commission, possibly causing it to restrict the market dominance of such a firm. Overall, it must therefore be concluded that the likelihood of such an eventuality was very slim indeed.

(10 marks)

26 | Marketing objectives

Question 1

(a) (i) An objective of Mars in the UK market for chocolate might be to increase its share of the market. At the time it had the third largest market share at 26%. It might want to grow its market share so that it overtakes Cadbury Schweppes, the current market leader with a 30% market share. Its short term objective, however, might be to overtake Nestlé, currently second in the market with 28%.

(ii) An objective of Cadbury Schweppes might be to maintain its share of the UK chocolate market and remain the business with the largest market share. At the time it was the market leader with 30% of the market. Its main competitors, Nestlé and Mars, follow fairly closely behind, with 28% and 26% respectively. Cadbury Schweppes might be concerned that such close competition could take its position as market leader.

(iii) Ferrero Rocher had just 2% market share of the UK market for chocolate at the time. Its objective might therefore have been to increase its share of the UK chocolate market. It would hope that in future it could erode the market share of the three main businesses and also take a share from 'others', which accounted for 12%.

(iv) At the time four main businesses appeared to be the major producers of chocolate products in Germany. These were Nestlé, Mars, Suchard and Ferrero Rocher which accounted for 64% of the market. Cadbury Schweppes is therefore likely to be part of the 'others' which accounted for 37% of the market. However, Cadbury Schweppes is likely to have had a percentage of the market which was less than 13% to be categorised within 'others'. Its objective might have been to increase its share so that it could be classed as one of the major producers.

Question 2

(a) (i) The internal factors in the marketing audit refer to the internal strengths and weaknesses of a business. The internal factors affecting the business could be:
- the organisation of the business;
- the nature of the product;
- production methods.

For Kodak internal strengths may include the widespread manufacturing capacity of Kodak, with plants all over the world and plans to expand into Asia, Latin America and Eastern Europe. In addition, expertise in the manufacture and marketing of cameras gained over a long period of involvement in the market as a leading business worldwide may be regarded as a strength. A further strength might be the brand name and image that the business has built up over the years. The internal weaknesses may include the need to shift production from traditional to digital photography following a long period during which the business specialised in non-digital photographic equipment, the presence of failed products on its list, including the Advanced Photo System cameras, and some technical specification difficulties with its digital cameras, including use of large amounts of battery power and poorer quality pictures.

(ii) The external factors affecting the marketing objectives of Kodak can be divided into external opportunities and threats. External factors that could affect the business might be:
- economic factors such as competition from other manufacturers and the growth of foreign markets;
- social factors such as the trend of not printing photos;
- technological factors such as the development of digital technology.

The external opportunities may include significant opportunities for growth in the market for digital cameras and digital camera equipment, further expansion in markets in Asia, Latin America and Eastern Europe and an anticipated continuation of the market for traditional photography built upon the existing market strengths of Kodak. The external threats may include the decline in the market for traditional photography and associated equipment, in particular, the ending of the production of 35mm cameras, the low proportion of shots printed from digital cameras and competition from other businesses engaged in the production of digital cameras and associated equipment.

Case study

(a) The target markets of Recovery Kitchens are those types of consumers which the business hopes will purchase the products and at which it aims its marketing. There are two types of consumer suggested in the article. The first is those consumers 'who are concerned about the environment'. They are likely to want products which minimise environmental damage in production. The second are consumers who want an 'old looking' kitchen. They might want recycled products so that kitchen styles fit in with the aged look of their houses or designs.

(4 marks)

(b) Objectives are the goals of the business. The marketing objectives of Recovery Kitchens are the marketing goals of the business. One objective could be production differentiation. This is where a business attempts to market a different product from those of its rivals to customers. The business manufactures kitchens only from reclaimed or recycled wood. A second objective could be consumer satisfaction. Businesses want to sell products that consumers want to buy. The business is trying to sell products that might appeal to ethically-orientated consumers. They are likely to be concerned about the environment and are attracted to products that take this into account.

(6 marks)

(c) The internal factors that might affect the business are factors within a business which affect its strengths and weaknesses. One internal factor is likely to be the availability of finance, for example, for any planned expansion following on from the use of managed wood. The way in which the business is organised is also likely to be important. The speed of decision making, for example, could be influenced by this and influence the capacity of the business to respond to external changes. A further internal factor might be the nature of the products sold by the business. For example, the business currently relies upon kitchens made from reclaimed wood. As suggested in the article, were the business to continue with this one source of wood for its kitchens it may be vulnerable to competition from other kitchen businesses using pine and other woods. The price of the business' products might also be an influence. Consumers may be willing to pay a higher price for recycled products, for example.

There are also external factors which could influence the opportunities and threats to the business. These are sometimes referred to as PESTLE factors. Political factors might include legislation, such as building regulations which determine kitchen products, or regulations regarding the replanting of trees. Economic factors might include changes in the economy. For example, changes in interest rates in future which are set to rise might affect borrowing and spending. They might also include the extent of competition. Social factors could include changing design tastes. For example, if design styles moved away from traditional kitchens to more modern styles, this could affect the sales of the business. Technology might also play some part. There is a tremendous amount of work involved in reclaiming wood for production of the kitchens. If technology advanced so that this was made easier and production costs may be reduced, this could help the business. A major external factor is the impact of green or environmental concerns. The business has been able to grow by attracting customers who are prepared to pay for reclaimed or recycled wood kitchens.

(12 marks)

(d) There is a number of possible objectives the business may have in moving to managed wood kitchens. The business may be concerned about holding on to its existing, albeit small, share of the market relative to its competitors. In particular it may be concerned about those local businesses offering cheaper pine products. These products can look very similar to reclaimed wood and may be sold at a cheaper price. Consequently it may have an objective of maintaining its share of the kitchen market for this type of product.

However, Recovery Kitchens Ltd is also concerned about the future sales levels of the business. Consequently it may have an objective to raise its sales levels. Further, it could be argued that the business is interested in introducing a new product. These are kitchens made from 'managed wood'. It would hope that such new products might attract new customers interested in this type of operation. It might also be suggested that, given the position in the market, it might be a profit satisficer rather than a profit maximiser.

(12 marks)

27 | Marketing budgets

Question 1

(a) The figures in Table 1 represent target sales. They are part of the marketing plan for two products of a pharmaceuticals company. A marketing plan shows what the business wants to achieve in future, target sales, rather than what it thinks it might achieve, forecast sales, or what it has achieved in the past, actual sales.

(b) Out of the two products Polix has been set higher targets for the number of sales, twice those of Lynix, and the market share, over one and a half times those of Lynix. Lynix has been set slightly higher sales value (turnover) targets, although it can charge higher prices. So it could be argued that Polix has the more ambitious sales targets.

Looking at the planned increases over the period Lynix is expected to increase its number of sales by 5.3% and Polix by 4.2%, Lynix is expected to increase sales value by 9.7% and Polix by 13.2%, and Lynix is expected to increase market share by 0.2% and Polix by 0.4%. Again it could be argued, from these figures, that Polix has slightly more ambitious sales targets.

Question 2

(a)

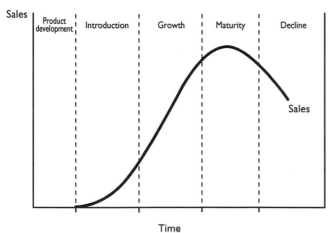

(i) Got Ya! is likely to be in the decline phase of the prouct life cycle above in the UK. The article says that 'sales have been declining for the past five years'.

(ii) Got Ya! is likely to be just before the introduction phase of the product life cycle above in China. The article says that 'TGP has decide to launch a Chinese version of Got Ya!' aiming for initial sales of 250,000 per month rising to 500,000 within three years in the introduction and then growth periods shown on the diagram.

(b) In the UK TPG is perhaps using sales-based budgeting. Sales based budgeting is where the level of expenditure on marketing is determined by sales. If sales are rising more is likely to be spent on marketing. If sales are not then spending in the marketing budget will be limited. In the UK, for example, TPG is unwilling to increase its marketing expenditure as it feels this will have 'little impact' on sales. However, in China it has allocated an extra £800,000 to the marketing budget for the six month period after the launch. At this time it expects sales to rise from 0 to 250,000 a month almost instantly. It could also be argued that it is using objective and task budgeting. Its objective is to break into the Chinese market and increase sales over a three year period. So it has allocated extra to the marketing budget to achieve this. The article also says it will review its marketing budget to see if further spending is needed to 'achieve its sales and profit goals'. This again suggests that objective and task budgeting may be being used.

Case study

(a) (i) £2.52m + £4.36m + £9.56m + 8.04m = £24.48m.
(ii) £16.6m + £20.4m + £46.2m + £44.6m = £127.8m.
(iii) Sales in 2004 would be £7.24 × 100 ÷ 20 = £36.2m.
(iv) The marketing budget for Vee in 2009 would be £46.2m × 20% = £9.24m.

(8 marks)

(b) The current method of setting marketing budgets used by Haffner plc is based on past sales figures. Budgets for the next period are based on 20 per cent of last year's sales. So, for example, in 2005 sales of Emme were £10.6m. Setting the budget would mean that the marketing budget allocated to Emme in 2006 would then be £10.6m × 20% = £2.12m. Similarly, the marketing budget for 2006 would be sales in 2006 of £10.8m × 20% = £2.16m. This method of allocating budgets can be useful for a business. Haffner bases the marketing budget on actual past performance. So if a product is doing well this method allocates a larger marketing budget next year. This is the case with Emme, the exclusive cosmetics range aimed at high income earners, for example. Each year sales increase and so each following year the sale budget increases. This is also the case with Cee, launched in 1990 as a product for the 20-40 year old office worker segment of the market. On the other hand the original range, Vee, and the budget range, Gee, have both seen sales fall over the period 2005-2008 and each following year their marketing budget allocation has fallen as a result.

Using a percentage of forecast sales to allocate budgets however may lead to different results. Taking Emme as an example, if marketing budgets this year were based on 20 per cent of forecast sales then in 2001, if forecast sales were £10.6m the marketing budget allocated would be £10.6m × 20% = £2.12m. This is the budget allocated currently for the following year. Each year the marketing budget allocated to Emme would be higher than it is currently. This would also be the case for Cee. In the case of those products which had falling sales, Vee and Gee, their marketing budgets would be lower than those figures currently shown in Table 2. Take 2005 for Gee. If sales were predicted to be £23.4m then the marketing budget allocated would be £23.4m × 20% = £4.68m. Currently it is £4.74m. So it the case of products with rising sales, marketing budgets allocated would be higher, but for products where sales were falling marketing budgets would be lower.

Of course this assumes that the predictions are correct and the predicted sales figures next year actually are those shown in Table 2. But they may not be. Take, for example, sales of Emme in 2005. Based on the existing method of allocating marketing budgets it would allocate £1.98m. Under the forecast system it would be allocated £2.12m expecting sales to rise. But they may not. If sales actually fell, then the business would have allocated a larger amount to the marketing budget for a product that was not doing as well as expected.

In conclusion, it could be argued that basing marketing expenditure on past sales is a safer method than using forecast sales. The predictions are based on actual sales in previous years. So the business has a firm basis on which to base its decisions. Using forecast figures makes assumptions that the forecasts are right, which they may not be. If a forecast is incorrect the business may be allocating too much to its marketing budget. On the other hand using forecast figures might be a better reflection of the market. For products where sales are rising more of the marketing budget is allocated than under the past sales system. For falling sales, less is allocated in the budget, which the business might see as the correct decision.

(12 marks)

(c) The current method of allocating budgets is a sales-based budgeting strategy. This is where budgets are based on past sales. This can be a fairly reliable method as it uses existing figures, but it does assume that past figures are a useful indication of future sales and that trends which are taking place will continue. As explained above, using sales-based strategy taking into account future sales can change the allocation of budgets. They may also change the amount of profit a business makes. For example, when sales are falling less is spent on marketing. So profits might rise as costs are cut compared to the existing system. This could be the case for a product such as Gee where sales are falling although they have been high in the past. When sales are rising costs increase. However, it could be argued that spending more when sales are rising will lead to even more sales than forecast. So the spending will be justified and revenue will rise even more than costs and so profit will rise. Of course, this again assumes that forecasts are correct. Taking Emme as an example, changing to forecast figures and greater spending on marketing could pay great dividends for the business. It is suggested that a significant minority of target customers do not know about the product. So increasing marketing expenditure on this product could lead to greater benefits.

Another strategy that the business might consider is to base marketing budgets on those of competitors. This has the advantage that it takes into account market forces. If other businesses are spending in particular areas then Haffner would need to decide whether to match this or to switch expenditure to other products. For example, it is suggested that Emme has an advertising:sales ratio which is half that of competitors. Yet this is a product with a growing market and has the highest profit margin of the four products in the product range. It has also been difficult to get this product into retail outlets. A greater effort to match the marketing expenditure of others in the industry might mean that profits increase. On the other hand the business must be careful that it can justify its marketing spending. It would have to be sure that raising marketing spending to levels of competitors would lead to increases in profit. Currently Emme has the lowest sales revenue of the four products, so the business would need to ensure that sales do rise so that profits can be made and spending is not wasted.

A further strategy that the business might use to allocate budgets is objective or task budgeting. This is where budgets are allocated according to the objectives of the business. For example, the business might decide that it wants to concentrate more on premium products and move away from its old image. If it did this then it might decide to allocate more of its marketing budget to Emme and Cee. Cee, for example, is regarded as a fairly exclusive premium brand. Although profit margins are average for the industry at present, greater promotion could lead to more sales. It is close to overtaking Vee, the original product as the main revenue earner for the business. Further promotion could help it to increase sales and profits. The business might decide to spend less on marketing Gee, for example, its budget range, and move its expenditure to Cee. It might also decide that, having won awards for its advertising, it will concentrate on this type of promotion rather than the sales force used for Vee. Cutting back on the sales force, where marketing spending has tended to be relatively high, will save costs and could again increase profits.

All of these methods suggest that the business could be able to increase its profitability by changing the methods by which it allocates its budget. But all have some form of risk. Moving to a future sales based allocation involves the need for accurate forecasting. Basing marketing on competitors can also be risky as matching the spending of rivals does not guarantee that sales will increase. If all rivals have the same spending and increase at the same time there may be nothing gained. Setting an objective to change the market or customers of the business can also be risky. Again there is no guarantee that new customers will be attracted and existing customers may be lost. Any change is likely to involve some risk. So the business should evaluate the possible gains in profit to be made against the risk of changing to another system.

(20 marks)

Question 1

(a) A marketing plan is a set of proposed marketing actions which if carried out should allow a business to achieve its marketing objectives. One feature of the marketing plan of a building society in this situation may have been the actions to be carried out. This would include the policies to attract ethnic minorities, such as leaflets on saving or mortgages. Another feature might be the responsibilities for the plan, including the people who would carry out the policies. For example a building society may employ people who speak Punjabi to deal directly with customers. A further feature may have been the target outcomes of the plan. For example, 9 per cent of England's population is made up of ethnic minorities. The plan may set a target of achieving 9 per cent of customers to be from ethnic minorities in the Birmingham area or perhaps even more than the 9 per cent national average, taking into account the percentage of the population that are from ethnic minorities in the West Midland area.

(b) It may be possible for the building society in the West Midlands to evaluate the plan in a number of ways.

It might evaluate the plan at the start. It might ask 'Does the plan fit in with the corporate strategy of the business?' For example, the plan to target ethnic minorities may fit in with an ethical stance taken by the building society to sell to a wider range of customers or to make its services more open to all people in the UK. It might also ask whether the plans are realistic. For example, would it be possible to provide services to 9 per cent of the West Midlands community, as this is the national average of people who are from ethnic minorities, or would a lower target or higher target be more appropriate?

The plan may also be evaluated in operation. For example the building society may consider whether the plan is actually working. How easy is it for people from ethnic minorities to find the material? Is it available in languages that are appropriate or are more languages needed? Do more people need to be recruited because the services are in demand? Are people who speak foreign languages always available for someone to talk to?

The plan may also be evaluated at the end. The business may consider whether it has achieved its target. If it has it might consider the plan to have been effective. Or it might evaluate that changes to the plan can be made to improve it. For example, many Sikh customers use services because their parents have told them about the building societies' plans. This may be a strategy the building society had not considered and could be made use of in future.

Question 2

(a) There is a number of advantages of marketing planning which Paul could have mentioned at the meeting. First, drawing up a marketing plan will provide SBC plc with the opportunity to reflect upon its marketing activities. This may involve the setting of marketing objectives and strategies to achieve them, for example, developing a new range of more efficient navigational instruments. Second, Paul could have mentioned that the setting of marketing objectives will allow clear targets to be drawn up. This will mean that the firm has criteria against which to judge its performance and, in addition, something tangible for managers and employees to aim at. Third, Paul could have mentioned that a marketing plan may result in improvements in employee motivation. Employees should have a clearer view of the direction in which the company is heading and would therefore feel more secure and prepared to act with increased confidence. Lastly, the plan can 'set the scene' for other plans (production of financial budgets, for example).

(b) From the comments made at the meeting, it is a fair guess that Paul may encounter a number of problems with marketing planning at SBC plc. The sales manager appears to confuse marketing with advertising. His comments, unfortunately, do not suggest a focus upon meeting the needs of the consumer. The production manager does not wish to be involved in marketing and clearly views it as being the responsibility of the marketing department. Such overriding concern with departmental loyalty might prevent SBC plc from properly considering the marketing issues which it faces. The senior accountant's remarks provide further confirmation of fears that marketing at SBC plc will be sidelined.

Case study

(a) Marketing planning might be useful for businesses in the games consoles market for a number of reasons.
- It allows businesses to reflect on marketing activities. For example, before the launch of XBox Microsoft recognised that it had to 'build demand for the product'. It would have been taking into account that it required a large marketing budget for promotion in order to break into a new market.
- It allows businesses to coordinate activities. For example, Microsoft was able to coordinate various aspects of its marketing mix, including introducing new products and setting prices that matched those of competitors.
- It allows businesses to make sure funds are available when needed. For example, Microsoft planned to spend $500m on the launch of XBox. The business will need to plan for these funds to be available.
- It allows businesses to set marketing targets to make sure their aims and objectives are taken into account. For example, Microsoft had the objective of moving beyond the PC market in its launch of XBox.
- It provides information which can be useful for stakeholders. Stakeholders of the business include shareholders, employees, customers and also related businesses. For example, developers of games for the XBox might have been interested to know the extent of marketing of the business. This could have influenced their own marketing and production plans.

(6 marks)

(b) A number of factors might affect the marketing of businesses in the game consoles market. Some of these are internal factors, within the business itself. One of these is the extent of funds available for marketing game consoles. Microsoft, for example, planned to spend $500m on the launch of XBox in 2001. This is a considerable sum, but an amount which might have been essential to break into the market. The business may have faced a reduced profit that year as a result of such a large expenditure or marketing funds might have had to be diverted from other areas of the business, such as the marketing of PCs. A second internal factor might be the ability to manufacture the product. Clearly a great deal of new technology is involved in the production of the XBox, the GameCube, the PS2, the PS3 and the Wii. The businesses would need to ensure that it was able to manufacture such products. This is likely to have required a great deal of resources devoted to new product development before their launch. Further, employees in the business would require the skills necessary to develop new technological products and manufacture them. This might require training or recruitment by the businesses.

A number of external or PESTLE factors might also be suggested. Political factors might have been obtaining patents on products or copyright for brand name registration. Economic factors are likely to include the actions of competitors in the market. For example, in 2003 in the USA the price of XBox was cut from $199 to $179 in response to a cut in price of Sony's PS2. Social factors might include trends in teenager purchase of computer games. It could be suggested that increasingly younger people are spending more on such games and less on other activities such as purchasing music. this might account for the growth in the market. The increasing awareness and access of younger people to the Internet might also be a social factor. Young people are now learning from a far earlier age to use computer technology and many homes now have computers. A further trend might be the attraction of 'non-core' purchasers. The Nintendo Wii appears to have gained a large increase in sales by selling to non-traditional gamers. These trends in leisure activities would all be encouraging for computer hardware and software manufacturers. Technological factors are the developments in new technology in the market. XBox, for example, offered online gaming. Also, developments in technology are likely to encourage more new product launches. Green factors might include the extent to which products can be recycled or reused after they are replaced by new products.

(10 marks)

(c)
Strengths

The XBox appears to have a number of strengths. It is manufactured by Microsoft. The company brand name is often cited as one of the most valuable brand images. It is respected and known for the manufacture of high quality technological products such as PCs. This is likely to be an advantage in launching new products in the same way as a brand name such as Virgin has been used in markets as diverse as the music industry, rail and air travel and financial services. It appeared to be particularly strong in the USA market, where its brand name might have made an impact. Further, it may be suggested that the XBox has certain features which give it an advantage over its rivals. At launch in 2001 it was argued that it would have three times the performance of the PS2. It also allowed Internet gaming without any extra items of equipment being required, unlike the PS2. Another strength could be the links developed with software manufacturers. In 2003, for example, it had 400 games including Star Wars and it acquired two companies to develop games exclusive to XBox. It also has strong links with retailers.

Weaknesses

There were perhaps a number of weaknesses in the position of the XBox over the period 2001-2004. At its launch in 2001 two of its major rivals, Sony's PS2 and Sega's Dreamcast, had already been on the market for a year. Being first into a new market often allows a business to develop a large market share quickly. People also develop brand loyalty which can be difficult to dislodge when new products come along. Further, its market share relative to those of rivals over the period seems to be relatively low. In particular it is suggested that it has found it difficult to break into the Japanese market, but has experienced difficulties in marketing to Asia in general. Perhaps more worrying for the business is the suggestion that it made a loss of $100 on every XBox sold in 2004 in these countries. A business often accepts that it will take time before it breaks even on new products and eventually makes a profit. Yet this is still likely to be a worry given the market share of XBox in certain areas of the e world.

Opportunities

Over the period there appear to have been opportunities for the business. Generally it could be argued that it is launching into a new, buoyant market, with growing sales and relatively only a few businesses in competition. It is sometimes easier to break into new markets when conditions are changing and sales are growing than mature markets with established businesses and sales patterns, especially if a business is prepared to spend on marketing. There was also a number of new opportunities within the market, such as the growth of online gaming. There is also the possibility of growth as the broadband market develops. In South Korea, for example, an area where broadband penetration is high, the business saw opportunities to develop market share a result of online gaming when XBox live was launched. Further, the demise of Sega Dreamcast and the move of that business into software development is likely to have given an opportunity for XBox to expand its market share, taking customers who would previously have bought Dreamcast. The global market share of XBox does seem to have increased, according to the information, from around 3% in 2002 to 15% in 2004. And it also appears to have achieved second place in the global market in 2003, despite the impact of price cutting increasing Nintendo's market share in the USA.

Threats

The major threat to the XBox appears to be the phenomenal success of the Nintendo Wii. It has broken sales records and revolutionised the gaming market, with its unique motion sensors, in the same way that the iPod has done with the music listening market. The Xbox and Sony PlayStation were tipped to be the market leaders but they are being massively outsold by the Wii.

(12 marks)

(d) On the one hand it could be argued that Microsoft's marketing planning has been effective. It planned to enter a new and growing market in a new product area. It recognised the need to spend a large amount on the launch and planned appropriately. Between launch and 2004 it had achieved a 15% worldwide market share and was arguably second in the market. It had also reacted to the actions of competitors, such as matching price changes. Further, it planned to offer a differentiated product from its competitors and developed strong links with retailers and software manufacturers. The success of game consoles is likely to be influenced to some extent by the amount of software available for the consoles. Buying companies to produce bespoke games is also likely to be good planning. Also, it planned to produce new versions of products in future, to take into account developments in technology.

On the other hand it might be suggested that the decision to launch after other competitors has led to problems. Sony initially gained a large and loyal customer base. Marketing of the XBox was relatively successful in the USA but less so in other areas of the world, such as Japan.

However, the major problem facing the XBox's marketing in 2007 and after was likely to be the major success of the Wii. It could be argued that no-one could have predicted its success on such a scale. In fact, many predicted that it would lag behind its rivals. Nintendo might hope that, like many other fashions, the desire for the Wii will decline in future. Nintendo also has more realistic games which may attract some customers, unless the Wiii can improve its graphics. When new models come out it may be able to introduce changes of its own to compete. In 2007-08 it seemed that the success of the Wii was likely to cause major marketing problems for the XBox.

(20 marks)

Question 1

(a) Market leaders are businesses which tend to dominate the market. In the article these businesses might be the 'travel giants' such as Thomas Cook or JMC. They are businesses with a large market share of the market for holidays, especially foreign holidays.

It might be argued that their decision to reduce prices to £150 on average was an attempt to defend their market position from attacks by other businesses, notably cut price operators. Previously they had not felt the need to reduce holiday prices, possibly content with their ability to influence the market. However, the actions of competitors may have forced them into this price reduction strategy. It might also be argued that it was an attempt to grow the market share that was lost to cut price operators recently in the past.

Market challengers are businesses which tend to want to eat into the market share of market leading businesses. They tend to use strategies which attack the market leader. In the past it is suggested that market leading businesses such as Thomas Cook and JMC had lost market share to low cost airlines, selling travel at reduced prices. It could be argued that this strategy is a direct attack on the market leading businesses, which forced them into retaliatory action. When low cost airlines first set up it might be suggested that they grew market share quickly by indirect attacks, targeting a particular section of the market - people who were willing to travel with 'no-frills' in exchange for low cost holidays. This is still true today, although the rapid growth in low cost airlines to so many destinations in Europe means that price reductions are today more likely to be a direct attack.

It might be suggested that some holiday operators are targeting niche markets. these could be geographical or some other form of differentiation. For example, some low cost airlines offer flights to destinations which previously may not have been thought of as major holiday resorts. These might include cities such as Basle and Seville. Also, some companies offer holidays targeted at specific needs, such as walking holidays or holidays for older people. Such niche marketing has been relatively successful. The article states that holidays outside the main travel destinations of countries such as Spain have done well.

Question 2

(a) A number of factors may have influenced Levis, leading to a change in strategy. The nature of the market is one influence. It is suggested that the market for fashion products like jeans is 'fast changing' and that Levis needs to react more quickly if it is to be competitive. Levis jeans appeared to be dated, looking very 1980's and 1990's products. The actions of competitors are also likely to have been an influence. The business faced intense competition both from cheaper end brands in supermarkets, own brand jeans such as Gap and more expensive designer jeans from companies such as Armani. The aims of the business and the views of key decision makers might have also had some effect. Levis decided to target a younger age group rather than the over 40s market. The business may have decided that this age group would pay a higher price for the product and turnover might increase more rapidly.

(b) It could be argued that Levis is in a position to make use of asset-based strategies. In the USA it is argued that 'everyone has heard of Levis'. Asset based marketing strategies are those which develop and market products which make use of the assets of the business. A strong brand name is an important asset as it can guarantee brand loyalty to some extent for new products. Customers will return to buy products with brand names they recognise. However, it is suggested in the article that 'instant brand recognition is not enough'. Some people might buy Levis because they recognise the quality associated with the brand. But to compete successfully Levis is likely to have to react quickly to changing tastes in the fashion

market by changing styles more quickly. Asset- based marketing is therefore a useful strategy for Levis, but in itself it may not guarantee success.

Question 3

(a) The strategy used by businesses in the article, sometimes referred to as viral or buzz marketing, involves known 'faces' using products in an attempt to advertise and promote them to potential customers. The aim is to create a 'buzz' about a product, so that people will want to be seen with the latest designs, knowing that they are also being used by customers who are relatively famous and who are admired by others. Another term for this type of marketing is viral marketing. This may be taken from the term virus. A health virus or a computer virus is an infection which is spread form one person or one computer to another. In analogy with a virus, here word of mouth spreads the promotion from one person to another. This generates a flow of promotion to many people, who convince each other to buy the product as it is the most fashionable thing to own.

(b) A number of factors might contribute to the success of such a strategy. One is the choice of the famous face or person to 'ignite the buzz'. The choice depends on the product. For example, choosing someone famous who is recognised by many people but is over 50 might not work for a product aimed at under 18s. The choice of a DJ to promote a Ford Focus might have been effective. But then so was the use of 'mom squads' from a religious background to promote hot dogs. To be effective, customers must identify with the people chosen to create a buzz.

Another factor might be the nature of the product itself. It might be argued that viral or buzz marketing would not work for some products. For example, it might be argued that it might be relatively easy to promote cars and food in this way. So might be the case with clothes or electrical goods. But creating a buzz for toilet roll, ironing boards or window cleaning fluid might be more difficult. On the other hand, some might suggest that it could be done as long as the people chosen are suitable.

Further factors might be geographical location, communication and how far the marketing will be effective. As it relies on word of mouth or other communication, people must be able to pass on the message to others for it to be effective. A DJ using a car in one area may have little effect on customers 500 miles away. This may require another DJ in another car. On the other hand, the use of the Internet today means that ideas can quickly move from one area to another. If the buzz generated in one area is very strong, it might quickly move to another as the message is passed to other people.

Case study

(a) (i) It is clear from the data presented in the case study that Coca-Cola is a market leader in the US soft drinks market. Consequently it will adopt market leader strategies including expanding the market so that, for example, greater product usage is encouraged and expanding their market share at the expense of competitors most particularly PepsiCo.

(ii) Because of Coca-Cola's strong market position other businesses in the US soft drinks market are more likely to use market challenger, market follower and market niche strategies. Their choice about which to use will depend upon the nature of the business seeking to compete. For example, relatively small soft drinks businesses may seek to employ market niche strategies seeking out groups of consumers overlooked by or too small for Coca-Cola to attend to. PepsiCo, however, may seek to directly compete with Coca-Cola by using market challenger strategies. This may involve direct attacks upon Coca-Cola, for example, through aggressive promotional campaigns and pricing policies.

(6 marks)

(b) The Ansoff Matrix would suggest that Coca-Cola are treating the domestic US market very differently from emerging markets in countries such as China, Russia and Nigeria. In the US market there is evidence of market penetration strategies with Coca-Cola seeking to achieve growth in a well-established market with existing products such as Coke Classic. There is also evidence here of product development with new products such as Coke Zero and Vault Red Blitz being introduced to this existing market. In Coca-Cola's emerging and new markets such as China there is evidence of market development with established Coca-Cola products such as Diet Coke being introduced, but also of diversification with new products, including Qoo being introduced in China.

(8 marks)

(c) There is a number of factors that may have influenced Coca-Cola's marketing strategy. First might be the objectives of Coca-Cola as a business. For example, Coca-Cola's attempts to win market share in countries such as South Africa and Nigeria is consistent with their global approach to business and their international marketing objectives. Second could be the strategies of competitor businesses, most particularly PepsiCo. For example, an aggressive marketing campaign by PepsiCo in one country is likely to influence Coca-Cola's strategy in that same country. Third could be the attitudes of senior managers. Marketing strategies at Coca-Cola are likely to be influenced by the extent to which, for example, their senior managers are willing to take risks. Greater risk taking is likely to see a greater turnover of products in the Coca-Cola range. Finally, Coca-Cola is the most valuable brand in the world at the time of writing and as such it is likely to utilise this position of strength taking advantage of this enormous strength in their marketing strategies.

(12 marks)

(d) There is a great deal of evidence to suggest that Coca-Cola's marketing strategies have been successful. Table 3 shows significant year on year increases in both revenue and gross profit from 2005 to 2007. In addition, their sales growth in 2007 was the best for seven years partly as a consequence of their marketing efforts in emerging markets such as Russia and Eastern Europe. However, there are also some signs that Coca-Cola's dominant position within the softs drink business is beginning to weaken. During the period 2000 to 2006 their share of the worldwide market declined and during the same period their share of the cola market slipped from 57% to 53%. As well as this, there is evidence that Coca-Cola are beginning to struggle in their domestic US market as increasingly health conscious consumers opt for different soft drinks. In conclusion therefore it can be said that the evidence about the success of Coca-Cola's marketing strategies is mixed and that further evidence would be required before a firm conclusion was arrived at.

(12 marks)

30 | International marketing

Question 1

(a) Foreign businesses appear to have entered the Indian coffee market in a number of ways. Caffè Nero are franchising their business in India. Lavazza have engaged in direct investment by buying out an Indian chain of coffee shops and others, unnamed in the article, are considering engaging in a joint venture with the Indian Landmark group.

(b) There are likely to be a range of factors influencing the success of foreign businesses in the Indian coffee market. Two, in particular stand out. First, the extent to which these businesses can adapt, amend and develop their business activities to suit the Indian market. Differences between the Indian coffee shop market and those in other countries and the capacity of the foreign businesses to deal with these will be of huge importance. Second, the extent to which India's coffee market continues to grow in line with forecasts. Large numbers of businesses are entering the Indian market and unless this market continues to grow quickly many of the new entrants may have their fingers burned.

Case study

(a) (i) Tesco entered the Chinese market through setting up a joint venture. It set this up with a Chinese business partner, Ting Hsing. Tesco perhaps had the option to set up its own foreign owned company. Instead it chose to enter the market with the co-operation of a Chinese business. **(4 marks)**

(ii) There are likely to have been two main attractions to the joint venture for Tesco. First, they can benefit from the local knowledge and experience of Ting Hsing. Second, their risk in entering the Chinese market is shared with this local business. **(4 marks)**

(b) Two differences between the Chinese and UK market in this area will be as follows. First, differences in legislation. This will affect factors such as food labelling and employment laws in relation to employees. Second, cultural differences. This would range from the obvious,

including language differences, through to the less obvious including the kinds of foods demanded by Chinese consumers. **(8 marks)**

(c) As a consequence of differences in the Chinese market such as those described in (b) Tesco would need to change and adapt its strategy to work successfully in that particular country. First, Tesco may need to adopt different business practices. For example, the same accounting techniques and conventions are unlikely to apply in both the UK and China. Second, Chinese consumers will be very different from UK consumers not only in terms of the different foods and drinks that they demand but also in terms of the in-store facilities that they expect. Third, Tesco will need to consider the political climate in China and adapt and develop its strategy in the light of any changes. **(8 marks)**

(d) There is evidence to suggest that Tesco's strategy in China was likely to prove successful after the £2 million profit in 2006. The market Tesco is aiming at is huge and growing very fast. It is a £135 billion market growing at 'double digit' pace. Tesco and its Chinese partner were planning to open 12 more hypermarkets at the time the article was written and the joint venture had the appearance of combining the benefits of Tesco's knowledge of running successful supermarkets with Ting Hsing's knowledge of the Chinese market. The UK influence on Hymail seemed to be very low profile. Customers do not appear to know that the business is foreign owned to some extent. This could be important in a country with a strong national identity. Unlike other chains Tesco is not building on its Western brands. It Happy Shopper stores still tend to look like traditional Chinese stores to some extent.

On the other hand, despite the high number of customers to their Hymail stores, spending per customer still remained low at less than £1 per visit reflecting the low level of wages received by Chinese consumers. In addition, and perhaps most importantly, Hymail stores clearly face a strong challenge from Hualian the domestic leader in this market. It is suggested that Tesco's position is a long way from its UK dominance for example and that it is unlikely to be a household name.

In conclusion, it could be argued that expanding into a new market in China would be a successful strategy. Tesco may feel that its expansion in existing markets is likely to be limited. However, if its aimed to achieve a market share similar to that of the UK this would be unlikely. Therefore it could be argued that its success would be limited. **(16 marks)**

31 E-commerce

Question 1

(a) Next.co.uk is an example of an E-tailer. This is because next.co.uk is the website where consumers can go to order Next clothes. It is online retailing.

(b) The prices of high street retailers might be cheaper online for two main reasons. First, to encourage consumers to shop online. Consumers are used to shopping on the High Street, but less familiar with E-tailing. The lower prices might encourage this form of purchasing. Second, to reflect the lower costs of E-tailing. Because High Street stores are expensive to run it is more expensive to sell clothing in this way than through websites. Therefore businesses may wish to pass on these E-tailing cost advantages to consumers in the form of lower prices.

Case study

(a) There are two main ways in which consumers can purchase music. First, downloading music in digital format to mobile phones, MP3 players and laptops. Second, purchasing music on CDs (and vinyl).

(4 marks)

(b) Sales of albums in CD format have been in decline since 2004 following a period of sporadic growth between 1997 and 2003. The pace of this decline has accelerated in recent years with 10.8 per cent fall in 2007.

(6 marks)

(c) The main reason why CD sales declined during 2007 appears to have been the growth in downloaded music. This form of purchasing music will of itself be damaging to CD sale. However, the fact that much downloaded music is purchased in the form of individual songs rather than albums appears to have exacerbated the decline of the CD.

(6 marks)

(d) Music businesses might adapt their marketing mixes in several ways to take account of declining CD sales. First, they might engage in strategies linked to the marketing and designed to arrest or slow down the rate of decline of CD sales. These might include pricing CDs more favourably, promoting their benefits and making them more widely available in a range if retail outlets. Second, music businesses might adapt their marketing mixes to reflect better the growth in digitally downloaded music. This might include, for example, promoting particular individual songs rather than albums on prime websites and other Internet based sites. They might also seek to ensure that all legal download sites include their music so that availability to consumers is assured. They might also consider pricing their downloaded music at prices attractive both to the download sites and to consumers.

(10 marks)

(e) There is likely to be a number of benefits for music businesses such as EMI associated with expanding the E-commerce aspects of their marketing. They will be able to reach a global market with their music much more easily than would have been the case through CD and vinyl sales, they can sell their music 24/7 rather than relying upon when music stores and other retail outlets are open and they can reduce their costs. For example, there is no longer the need to package CDs or even print the CDs themselves.

However, there will also be major costs of such a switch for the music businesses. There will be the costs of setting up online purchasing systems, although the business may already have these to some extent. There may be even more fierce competition from, for example, independent music producers. There are also the dangers of illegally downloaded music undermining sales of legally downloaded music and certain websites such as iTunes gaining a position of market dominance enabling them to drive down the price of the music provided by businesses.

In conclusion, it might be argued that music business have no choice but to expand the E-commerce aspects of their marketing, no matter what the costs. The purchasing of music is changing. The number of music retail shops is falling. Shops that sell CDs are now ending the sales of singles. If music business do not expand into this area it may suffer and its rivals that embrace the new technology may benefit.

(12 marks)

32 | Interpreting sample results

Question 1

(a) (i) Test product A $(0.3 \times £200,000) + (0.7 \times £50,000)$
$= £60,000 + £35,000$
$= £95,000$

Test product B $(0.5 \times £120,000) + (0.5 \times £30,000)$
$= £60,000 + £15,000$
$= £75,000$

(ii) Test product A £95,000 - £90,000 = £5,000 profit
Test product B £75,000 - £80,000 = £5,000 loss

(b) Based on the information in (a) the company should launch product A. It produces a profit of £5,000, whereas product B produces a loss of £5,000.

(c) Test product A £95,000 - £90,000 = £5,000 profit
Test product B £75,000 - £65,000 = £10,000 profit

If the cost of test product B fell to £65,000 then it would be more profitable to launch product B. It now makes, on average, a £10,000 profit for the business, whereas product A only makes a £5,000 profit.

Question 2

(a) (i) See figure below.
(ii) See figure below.

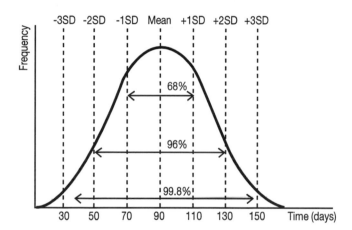

(b) (i) The percentage of people that might be expected to change their toothbrush after 70 days is everyone to the right of the -1SD line. This can be calculated by finding the value of 1SD and adding it to the 50 per cent of the population that lies to the right of the mean of 90. The value of one standard deviation is 0.3413 (taken from the table in the students' book). So the percentage of customers changing thier toothafter 70 days is:

0.3413 + 0.5 = 0.8413 or 84 per cent.

(ii) The percentage of people that might be expected to change their toothbrush after 130 days is everyone to the right of the 2SD line. This can be found by subtracting the percentage falling within 2SDs from the 50 per cent of the population that lies to the right of the mean of 90. The value of 2 SDs is 0.4772 (taken from the table in the students' book). So the percentage of customers changing their toothbrush after 130 days is:

0.5 - 0.4772 = 0.0228 or 2.28 per cent.

Question 3

(a) The range can be calculated by a mean of 35 inches plus or minus 3 standard deviations. The length measurements vary between:

35 inches + (3 x 0.5) = 35 + 1.5 = 36.5 inches
and
35 - (3 x 0.5) = 35 - 1.5 = 33.5 inches

(b) The figures below can be found in the table of standard numbers

in the students' book.

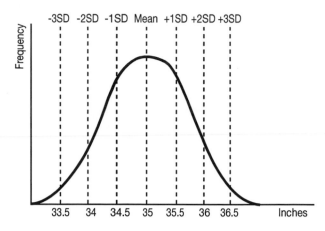

(i) 36.5 is 3 SDs from the mean. So the percentage above 36.5 inches would be:

0.5 - 3 SDs = 0.5 - 0.4987 = 0.0013 or 0.1 per cent.

This would normally be rounded down to zero.

(ii) 36 inches is 2 SDs from the mean. So the percentage between 35 and 36 inches would be:

2 SDs = 0.4772 or 48 per cent.

(iii) 35.8 inches is:

$$\frac{35.8 - 35}{0.5} = \frac{0.8}{0.5} = 1.6 \text{ SDs from the mean}$$

So the percentage between 35 and 35.8 inches would be:

1.6SDs = 0.4452 or 44.5 per cent

(iv) 34.2 inches is:

$$\frac{35 - 34.2}{0.5} = \frac{0.8}{0.5} = 1.6 \text{ SDs from the mean}$$

So the percentage below 34.2 inches would be:

0.5 - 1.6 SDs = 0.5 - 0.4452 = 0.0548 or 5.5 percent.

Case study

(a) (i) A mean is an average. So the mean number of responses is the average number of people responding. In the case of Heritage Cottages Ltd it is the average number of people replying to an advertisement for its brochure in weekly magazines. It calculated that the average number of responses to advertisements in all magazines was 1,500 a week, taking into account responses over a five year period. One method of calculating the average is the arithmetic mean. This is the total number of responses ÷ number of weeks. For example, if the business used a survey to find the average and took a survey of results over ten weeks, then the mean would have been calculated as:

$$\frac{15,000 \text{ (total responses)}}{10 \text{ (weeks)}} = 1,500$$

(ii) Customer enquiries are the requests by potential customers for brochures. Heritage Cottages was interested to know whether there would be a significant increase in enquiries if it changed its promotional strategy to advertising in Sunday newspapers rather than magazines. It hoped that there would be a major increase in the average number of enquiries per week as a result of the change. If so, the change in strategy could have been called successful. It would need to decide what it considered significant, ie whether it wanted a 5 per cent, 10 per cent or greater than 10 per cent increase as a result of the change. **(6 marks)**

(b) It could be argued that the results from a five year analysis of customer responses to magazine advertisements might have been normally distributed for a number of reasons.
- Over 5 years the company would expect to have enough responses to provide a large enough sample for it to be normally distributed.
- People will be responding independently and there is therefore no reason to expect a skewed response or significant variations from year to year.
- The company is using actual figures rather than estimates and therefore it is easier to check that the sample is normally distributed. **(8 marks)**

(c) (i)

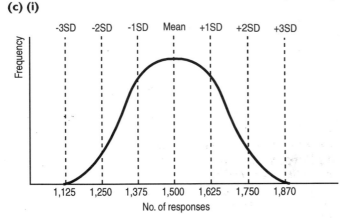

No. of responses

(6 marks)

(ii)   1,800 = 300   responses above the mean

$$300 = \frac{300}{125} \quad \text{SDs from mean}$$

= 2.4 SDs from mean.

(6 marks)

(d) Although the response of 1,800 was well above the mean, it was still below 3 SDs from the mean and therefore within the same possible range as the results over the last 5 years when magazine advertising was used.

Statistically, as 1,800 is 2.4SDs above the mean, then:
$$0.4918 + 0.5 = 0.9918 = 99\%$$
of responses lie below this figure. The company can therefore be 99 per cent certain that the 1,800 result shows an improved response, but it can't be 100 per cent certain. However, the business may conclude that 99 per cent is significant enough and decide that the switch in strategy has been successful using this technique.

Such quantitative techniques are useful for a business. They give measurable results, which can be compared and analysed. But is this sufficient for the business to conclude that the switch in strategy has been a success? The company would also need to consider issues such as:
- the relative costs of the advertising;
- the number of responses that lead to bookings. Was this higher with magazines?;
- how easy it is to target advertising using the large circulation newspapers;
- whether it might be losing 'loyal' customers who don't see the new adverts;
- is the uptake in response due to other factors, eg rising incomes or lower unemployment rather than changes in the media?

It could be argued that the business can only evaluate effectively the success of the changes in strategy by taking into account these other issues. A rise in the mean circulation would not necessarily be effective if costs increased significantly. Also, if a business gained increased responses but few turned into bookings, again the success might be deemed limited.

(14 marks)

33 | Forecasting and analysing markets

Question 1

(a)

										(£000)
Period	1	2	3	4	5	6	7	8	9	10
Sales	100	130	160	175	180	190	190	180	220	250
3 period	-	130	155	171.6	181.6	186.6	186.6	196.6	216.6	-
4 period	-	-	151.3	168.8	180	184.4	190	202.5	-	-

(b) 44v │141·25, 161·25, 176·25, 183·75,
MA 185 195 210.

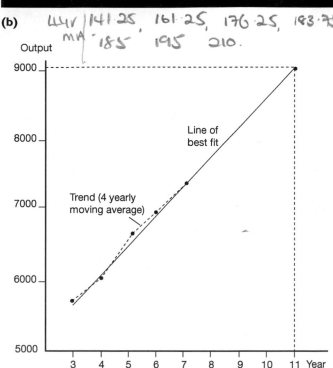

The trend (either the 3 period or 4 period moving average) is flatter than the actual sales figures when plotted onto a graph. Calculating a trend has the effect of 'evening out' the peaks and troughs which occur in actual figures over a period. This makes it easier to see the overall picture or trend taking place, and to predict what will happen in future.

Question 2

(a)

Year	Output	4 yearly moving total	8 yearly moving total	4 yearly moving average
1	5,000			
2	5,200			
3	5,800	22,000	44,800	5,600
4	6,000	22,800	47,400	5,925
5	5,800	24,600	51,600	6,450
6	7,000	27,000	55,400	6,925
7	8,200	28,400	58,600	7,325
8	7,400	30,200	61,800	7,725
9	7,600	31,600		
10	8,400			

(b)

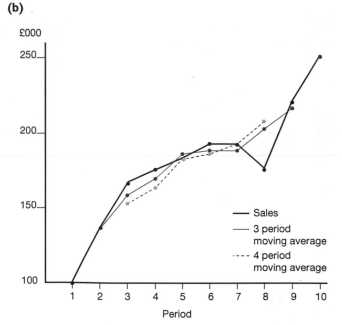

Predicted output in year 11 would be 9,050 units (plotted accurately on graph paper).

(c) (i)

Year	Output	Trend	Variation
3	5,800	5,600	+200
4	6,000	5,925	+75
5	5,800	6,450	-650
6	7,000	6,925	+75
7	8,200	7,325	+875
8	7,400	7,725	-325

(ii) The average cyclical variation is: $\dfrac{+250}{6} = 41.7$.

The predicted output figure in year 11 from the 4 yearly moving average is 9,050 units. However, this figure is unlikely to be totally accurate because it is based on a trend, and the trend is a smoother version of the actual figures. A more accurate prediction would be to add or subtract the average cyclical variation from the predicted output in year 11. This will 'add back on' or 'take away' the amount removed or added when the trend was smoothed out. So for year 11, output is 9,050 + 41.7 = 9,091.7 units.

Case study

(a) (i) A pattern which emerges from a series of data or figures, usually over a period of time is often referred to as a trend. A trend in sales figures is therefore the pattern of sales which emerges over a time period. They might be increasing, decreasing or remaining stable, and changing at different rates or similar rates.

(2 marks)

(ii) Finding an average from a number of figures over time together can be done by a method known as centring. This involves plotting or placing the average of the figures 'in the centre or middle' of the time period. A four period moving average therefore shows an average figure plotted in the centre of four periods, such as four quarters of a year, followed by another average plotted in the centre of the next four periods, and so on. Moving along from one average to the next and plotting these points together shows a trend. The pattern in the trend is easier to see than individual figures because fluctuations are removed.

(2 marks)

(b) (i)

					(£000)
Year	Quarter	Sales	4 qtr moving total	8 qtr moving total	4 qtr moving average
2006	3	100			
	4	180			
			480		
2007	1	140		1,040	130
			560		
	2	60		1,160	145
			600		
	3	180		1,240	155
			640		
	4	220		1,320	165
			680		
2008	1	180		1,400	175
			720		
	2	100		1,480	18
			760		
	3	220		1,560	195
			800		
	4	260		1,680	21
			880		
2009	1	220			
	2	180			

(10 marks)

(c) (i)

				(£000)
Year	Quarter	Sales	4 qtr moving average	Seasonal variation
2006	3	100		
	4	180		
2007	1	140	130	10
	2	60	145	-85
	3	180	155	25
	4	220	165	55
2008	1	180	17	55
	2	100	185	-85
	3	220	195	25
	4	260	210	50
2009	1	220		
	2	180		

(4 marks)

(ii) Centring is a technique used to calculate moving averages which have even numbers, ie a four quarter moving average. In a three period moving average, the average lies against the centre of three periods. For example, the centred moving average of quarters 2, 3 and 4 of 2007 for Jamesons is (£60,000 + £180,000 + £220,000) ÷ 3 = £153,333. This can be plotted against q3 of 2007. However, the central point of four figures lies between four figures. Plotting a point here would not give an accurate position on a graph. Centring allows this to be done. Calculating four quarter moving totals and eight quarter moving totals makes use of five different quarters of sales figures (ie q1-4 of 2007 and q1 of 2008). The average is then centred against the middle of these five periods (ie q3 of 2007). This gives an accurate position when plotted on a graph and a more accurate trend can therefore be shown.

(6 marks)

(ii) The average seasonal variation for the fourth quarter can be calculated from seasonal variation figures for the fourth quarters shown on the graph. There are two seasonal variation figures shown, the fourth quarter of 2007 (+£55,000) and the fourth quarter of 2008 (+£50,000). So the average seasonal variation for the fourth quarter is (£55,000 + £50,000) ÷ 2 = £52,500.

(4 marks)

(d) (See graph and answer over the page.)

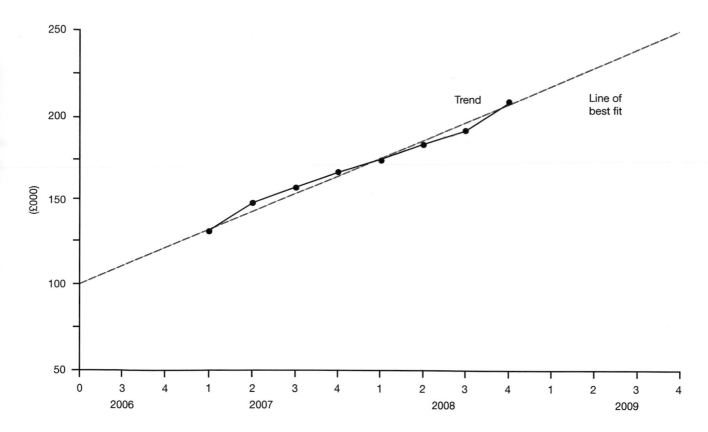

The sales in the fourth Quarter of 2009 can be forecast using the trend line in the diagram. the forecast is made by drawing a line of best fit through the points in the trend and then extending this line to the fourth quarter of 2009. The predicted sales in the fourth quarter of 2009 might therefore be £250,000 from the graph. (Using the mathematical method known as the sum of least squares the figure is actually £251,250 although this would not be required in an answer. Note also that in examinations, some leeway is often given to the predictions. So, for example, an answer between £240,000 and £260,000 might be accepted although an answer of £200,000 clearly wouldn't as the forecast would be fairly inaccurate given the trend line drawn.)

However, to more accurately forecast the figure in the fourth quarter of 2009, the fourth quarter seasonal variation needs to be taken into account. This shows the extent to which actual sales figures on average vary from the trend. This is £52,500. So the forecast in the fourth quarter of 2009 might be amended to give a forecast sales figure of £250,000 + £52,500 = £302,500.

When arriving at this forecast the business may have made certain assumptions. First, the business must assume that the information included in the backdata from sales figures is accurate. The figures may have been taken from past sales statistics. If so, the business may have to assume that these were correct figures. For example, if the figures were made up from totalled amounts of different products,

the totalling calculation should be accurate. A further problem with the figures may be the seasonal variation. It is based on just two amounts, the fourth quarters on 2007 and 2008, which totalled £52,500. But what if the seasonal variation for earlier years were negative figures? This may reduce the predicted figure below £250,000. The business may also assume that conditions in the fourth quarter of 2009 were not about to be significantly different to those in similar years or similar quarters. For example, the average seasonal variation for the fourth quarter of the previous two years had been more than £50,000. This suggests that the business does well in winter. But what if circumstances change? Competitors may introduce new products, taking a share of Jameson's sales in winter. Consumers may switch to other sports than winter activities. Holiday makers may cut down winter skiing trips. The business may even decide to launch even more summer products and find its sales pattern changes from winter to summer sales. All these changes may affect the sales of Jamesons for the fourth quarter of 2009.

So it could be argued that although the trend line gives a predicted value based on past information, and that taking into account the seasonal variation may give an even more accurate figure, care still needs to be taken when making forecasts and other factors may also need to be taken into account.

(12 marks)

34 | Sources of finance

Question 1

(a) Godwin's Ice Cream has managed to get a grant from a Rural Enterprise Scheme in Oxfordshire - indeed it is the first business to apply for one. The main advantage of this sort of funding is that usually grants do not have to be repaid. Consequently, the money given by the Rural Enterprise Scheme will not have to be given back. This will reduce the pressure on the business and not create a debt.

(b) It is common practice to write a business plan when applying for finance. Writing a detailed business plan helps to demonstrate to potential money lenders that those who are applying for finance are organised and have thought about what they are going to do with the finance. Money lenders will also be able to use the business plan to help decide whether the business is likely to be successful and how risky their loans might be. It is likely that the grant received by Godwin's Ice Cream would not have been approved without a business plan.

(c) (i) A bank overdraft is an external source of finance for Godwin's Ice Cream. This means that the money raised comes from outside the business. It comes from a bank. A business like Godwin's can only use external sources of finance to begin with because it is just starting out. Internal sources, such as profit, cannot be used until the business is established and generating income.

(ii) The main advantage of bank overdrafts is that they are flexible. This means that the money is only borrowed when it is actually needed at a particular point in time. For example, Godwin's might need to go overdrawn during the winter when sales of ice cream are likely to be lower. However, in the summer it may not need to go overdrawn at all. This means it will not incur any financing charges. Godwin's will only use the money if needs it. Also, the arrangement is flexible because Godwin's can borrow different amounts of money according to its needs - as long as it does not exceed its limit.

Question 2

(a) Texperts has raised £1.3 million. It plans to spend about £1 million on an advertising and marketing campaign. This is well above the £200,000 spent on marketing to date.

(b) Texperts was founded by Sarah McVittie and Thomas Roberts. Between them they own 30% of the company. They have about a 15% stake each. This appears to be quite a small proportion of the business. The rest is owned by Odey Asset Management (14%) and other investors such as the wealthy individuals who have already invested in the business.

(c) The most recent injection of capital has been provided by Odey Asset Management. They have put in £1.3 million. Odey Asset Management is an industrial specialist in the financial markets. Such organisations provide funds especially for business and commercial uses. They often invest in small and medium-sized businesses and frequently offer capital to businesses that have struggled to attract funding from other sources.

Texperts has also enjoyed funding from wealthy individuals. These can be described as business angels. Business angels may invest between £10,000 and £100,000, often in business start-ups or early stage expansions such as Texperts. Business angels often invest in companies like Texperts because they like the gamble involved, or being part of a new or developing business. They also get generous tax relief.

(d) One of the main problems with attracting funds from industrial specialists such as Odey Asset Management and business angels is that they take a stake in the company. For example, Odey Asset Management own 14% of Texperts and wealthy individuals (business angels) possibly owns around 50% between them. This means they are entitled to a share in the profit made by Texperts. They will also have a right to be involved in the decision making in the company. This could be a problem if the investors wanted the business to go in a different direction to the founders, Sarah McVittie and Thomas Roberts. There could be a conflict and the company could suffer as a result. However, the investors may be happy to sit back and leave the running of the business to Sarah and Thomas - especially if the company is doing well.

Case study

(a) At 30th April 2006, Gamingking had authorised share capital of £5 million and issued share capital of £2.907 million. Authorised share capital is the maximum amount of share capital a company can issue. In this case, Gamingking cannot issue more than £5 million worth of shares. Issued share capital is the amount of money the company has currently raised from the sale of shares. Gamingking has so far raised a total of £2.907 million of cash from the sale of shares.

(6 marks)

(b) Operating as a public limited company, Gamingking will have a wider variety of finance sources to choose from. The main advantage is that it will be able to raise money by selling shares to the general public. The company will also have a higher profile and more 'clout' when competing for funds. Gamingking may also have a higher 'credit rating' which means that banks will be more willing to lend. Generally, companies quoted on the stock market are in a better position to raise finance.

(8 marks)

(c) (i) At 30 April Gamingking had a loan of £800,000 from Barclays Bank. This loan was due to mature on 15th April 2010. A good proportion of the loan was used to buy Kelly's Eye (No.1) Ltd, the company's main competitor. After the acquisition, Gamingking became the leader in the provision of lotteries and game play products and services to the registered members' club marketplace. The Group now has a client base of 5,000 clubs in the UK.

(4 marks)

(ii) The loan from Barclays Bank was for £800,000. Taking out this loan would have an impact on the gearing for Gamingking. Gearing is the relationship between the loan capital and the share capital of a business. A company is said to be highly geared if it has a large proportion of loan capital. In this case, an increase in loan capital of £800,000 would raise Gamingking's gearing significantly. Its share capital was only £2.907 million in 2006. An extra £800,000 loan capital would raise gearing closer to 50%, assuming that loan capital was relatively low before the loan was taken out.

(8 marks)

(d) Retained profit is an internal source of finance. It is generated by the business. It is the single most important source of finance for established businesses. Around 65% of all business funding comes from retained profit. In 2006 and 2005 Gamingking retained all of its profit. The main advantage of this is that such finance is cheap. There are no financial charges such as interest, dividends or administration. However, there is an opportunity cost. The retained profit used by Gamingking cannot be returned to the owners. In this case it could lead to conflict between the people running the company and some of the owners such as Odey Asset Management and the business angels. One of the reasons why these investors provided capital in the first place was to get dividends. However, there is no evidence in the case to suggest that the investors are unhappy about all of the profit being retained. It is quite common for a business in the early stages of development to retain all of the profit.

(14 marks)

Question 1

(a) Costs which stay the same at all levels of output in the short run are called fixed costs. These costs remain the same whether a business produces nothing or is working at full capacity. In this case the fixed cost of the photocopier is the monthly hire fee of £100. It does not matter how many copies are made during the month, the hire cost is fixed at £100. Variable costs are those that increase when output goes up. In this case, the toner, paper and electricity (£1 for every 100 copies) are the variable costs of operating the photocopier. The more the photocopier is used, the higher the variable cost will be.

(b) The total annual cost of operating the photocopy if 68,000 copies are made is given by:

Total cost = fixed cost + variable cost
= (£100 × 12) + 68,000 ÷ 100 × £1)
= £1,200 + £680
= £1,880

(c) Indirect costs or overheads result from the whole business. It is not possible to associate these costs directly with particular products or processes. Indirect costs are usually fixed costs and direct costs variable costs, although in theory both direct and indirect costs can be fixed or variable. In this case, both the fixed cost and the variable cost associated with the photocopier are indirect. This is because the photocopier is not used directly in the production of online and video information films. The cost of the photocopier is a business overhead.

Question 2

(a) **(i)** Total fixed costs = £50 × 12 = £600
(ii) Total variable costs = £20 × 400 = £8000
(iii) Total cost = FC + VC = £600 + £8000 = £8600
(iv) Average cost = TC ÷ Q = £8600 ÷ 400 = £21.50
(v) Price = £21.50 + (50% × £21.50) = £21.50 + £10.75 = £32.25
(b) Total revenue if 250 are sold:
TR = P × Q = £32.25 × 250 = £8062.25

Case study

(a) Variable costs are those that increase when output is raised. Examples of variable costs that Wilkins might incur when manufacturing and supplying the conservatories include materials and components such as plastic, glass, metal fittings for the doors and windows, labour and any packaging used. **(4 marks)**

(b)

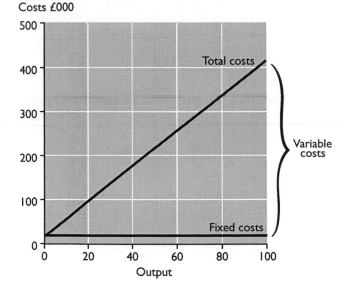

Costs £000

(c)

(12 marks)

(d) The profit that Wilkins will make on the contract is:

Profit = total revenue - total cost
= (£6,000 × 100) - (£20,000 + £400,000)
= £600,000 - £420,000
= £180,000

(8 marks)

(e) If fixed costs rose to £35,000 the effect on profit for the contract is given by:
Profit = total revenue - total cost
= (£6,000 × 100) - (£35,000 + £400,000)
= £600,000 - £435,000
= £165,000

(6 marks)

	0	10	20	30	40	50	60	70	80	90	£ 100
Fixed cost	20,000	20,000	20,000	20,000	20,000	20,000	20,000	20,000	20,000	20,000	20,000
Variable cost	0	40,000	80,000	120,000	160,000	200,000	240,000	280,000	320,000	360,000	400,000
Total cost	20,000	60,000	100,000	140,000	180,000	220,000	260,000	300,000	340,000	380,000	420,000

(10 marks)

36 | Contribution

Question 1

(a) Total contribution = total revenue - total variable cost
= £540 - 35p (15p + 10p + 10p) × 1,000
= £540 - £350
= £190

(b) Profit = total contribution - fixed costs
= £190 - £100
= £90

Question 2

(a) Contribution pricing involves setting a price for orders or individual products which exceeds the variable cost. This means that a particular order or product will always make a contribution when sold. This approach ignores fixed costs since a single order or product may not generate enough contribution to cover fixed costs. In this case Laura charges clients a price which more than covers her costs such as food, wine and other variable costs.

(b) *Note in the first impression of the 4th edition there is a printing error. This will be corrected in reprints. The parties should be labelled 1-4.*
Weekly profit = total contribution - fixed cost
= £435 - £100
= £335

	Price	Variable cost	Contribution
Party 1	240	155	85
Party 2	140	70	70
Party 3	320	180	140
Party 4	200	60	140
	900	**465**	**435**

(c) Contribution pricing needs to be used with caution. Obviously, to make a profit fixed costs have to be covered. It is possible that the contribution from a single order may not cover fixed costs. In this case two of Laura's dinner parties do not cover fixed costs (Party 1 and Party 2 both contribute less than £100). However, over the week, the total contribution easily covers fixed costs. Contribution pricing is most likely to be used when fixed costs are low or when a business knows through experience that fixed costs will be covered.

Case study

(a) Fixed costs are those that do not vary when output changes. Possible examples of fixed costs for Timmings Ltd might be machinery, depreciation, insurance, accountancy fees, advertising and office expenses. These are the general overheads of the business that will not vary according to output levels.

(3 marks)

(b) Unit contribution is the contribution a business receives from selling one unit of output. It is calculated by subtracting variable costs from the selling price. For the Butlers order the unit contribution is £1.40 (price of £8 - variable costs per unit of £6.60 [£2.20 + £3.40 + £1.00]). When more than one unit is sold it is possible to calculate the total contribution. This is the unit contribution multiplied by the number of units produced. For the Butlers order the total contribution will be £28,000 (£1.40 × 20,000). If this order was accepted by Timmings Ltd, the £28,000 would contribute to the fixed costs and profit for the order.

(6 marks)

(c) The total contribution for the four orders is:
Butlers (£8.00 - £6.60) × 20,000 = £28,000
A & P Ltd (£8.50 - £7.60) × 30,000 = £27,000
VC Singh (£7.00 - £5.70) × 25,000 = £32,500
VWD plc (£10.50 - £8.10) × 20,000 = £48,000.

(8 marks)

(d) (i) Timmings will accept the two orders that make the largest contribution. The calculations in (c) show that the VC Singh and VWD plc orders make the largest contributions.

(2 marks)

(ii) The profit made from accepting these orders is:
VC Singh profit = £32,500 - £5,000 = £27,500
VWD plc profit = £48,000 - £5,000 = £43,000
Therefore the total profit made from the two orders accepted is £70,500.

(6 marks)

(e) The approach to selecting orders used by Timmings Ltd will always ensure that the most lucrative orders are accepted. This will help to boost the financial performance of the company. However, there is a possible long-term drawback in using this approach. The customers who have their orders rejected may not return to Timmings Ltd again for another quote. This may be OK while Timmings is busy and demand for its products is high. But in the future, if demand falls, it may regret the orders it rejected.

(8 marks)

Question 1

(a) The number of rugs Jun Shan must sell to break even is given by:

$$BE = \frac{\text{Fixed cost}}{\text{Contribution}}$$

$$= \frac{£2,000}{£105 - £65}$$

$$= \frac{£2,000}{£40}$$

$$= 50 \text{ rugs}$$

(b) If 500 rugs are sold in a year the profit made is given by:

Profit = Total revenue - Total cost
= £105 × 500 - (£2,000 + £65 × 500)
= £52,500 - (£2,000 + £32,500)
= £52,500 - £34,500
= £18,000

(c) If the price is raised to £115 break-even output is given by:

$$BE = \frac{£2,000}{£115 - £65}$$

$$= \frac{£2,000}{£50}$$

$$= 40 \text{ rugs}$$

Question 2

(a) (i) £0.
(ii) £24,000.
(b) £4,000.
(c) (i) 10 guitars.
  (ii) £12,000.
(d) (i) 2 guitars.
  (ii) 10 guitars.
(e) (i) £18,000.
  (ii) £16,000.
  (iii) £2,000.
  (iv) £12,000.
  (v) £800.

Case study

(a) The contribution made by each batch of pies is given by:

Contribution = Selling price - variable cost
= 50p × 100 - £20
= £50 - £20
= £30

(4 marks)

(b) The number of batches Carl would need to sell in the first year to break-even is given by:

Break-even = Fixed costs/contribution
= £3,000 ÷ £30
= 100 batches

Therefore Carl would need to sell 10,000 (100 × 100) pies in a single year to break even. This appears to be quite a lot, however, it is only two batches every week.

(6 marks)

(c) The amount of profit made by Carl if he sold 55,000 pies in his first year would be given by:

Profit = TR - TC
= 50p × 55,000 - (£3,000 + 55,000/100 × £20)
= £27,500 - (£3,000 + £11,000)
= £27,500 - £14,000
= £13,500

(6 marks)

(d) The number of batches that Carl would need to produce and sell to break even at the new price and higher lease charge is given by:

$$BE = \frac{£5,000}{70p \times 100 - £20}$$

$$BE = \frac{£5,000}{£70 - £20}$$

$$BE = \frac{£5,000}{£50}$$

$$BE = 100 \text{ batches}$$

Consequently the changes in fixed cost and price have no effect on the break-even level of output. It is still 100 batches.

(6 marks)

(e) Break-even analysis is used in business as a tool to make decisions. A week before Carl signed a 12 month lease for the kitchen unit, he put some figures together to help him assess the possible profitability of the venture. These figures could have been used to find out how many pies he needed to sell to cover all of his costs, i.e. to break even. He may have done this before committing himself to the lease. Carl can also use break-even analysis to help answer 'what if' questions. For instance, he needed to look at the financial position of the business when the landlord raised the rent and what the effect would be if he also raised the price of his pies. He found that the break-even position did not alter after the changes in rent and price. Break-even analysis is also found in business plans. Carl might have included some break-even analysis in his business plan.

However, unfortunately break-even analysis does have some limitations. It is often regarded as too simplistic and some of its assumptions are unrealistic. It assumes that all output is sold, so that output equals sales, and no stocks are held. Many businesses hold stocks of finished goods to cope with changes in demand. There are also times when firms cannot sell what they produce and choose to stockpile their output to avoid laying off staff. Carl is not likely to keep stocks because his products are perishable. However, there is a chance he may not sell all he produces.

The break-even chart is drawn for a given set of conditions. It cannot cope with a sudden increase in wages and prices or changes in technology. The effectiveness of break-even analysis depends on the quality and accuracy of the data used to construct cost and revenue functions. If the data is poor and inaccurate, the conclusions drawn on the basis of the data are flawed. For example, if fixed costs are underestimated, the level of output required to break even will be higher than suggested by the break-even chart. However, in this case Carl's financial information does seem accurate.

It is assumed that the total revenue and total cost lines are linear or straight. This may not always be the case. For example, a business may have to offer discounts on large orders, so total revenues fall at high outputs. In this case the total revenue line would rise and then fall, and be curved. A business can lower costs by buying in bulk. So costs may fall at high outputs and the total cost function will be curved. This might be a problem for Carl in the future once his business is established and starts to grow.

When Carl is using break-even analysis he needs to be aware of these limitations. However, in the early stages of business development break-even may be helpful because the business is operating at a fairly simple level.

(18 marks)

Question 1

(a)

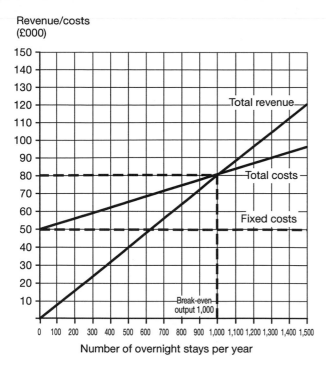

(b) (i) (ii)

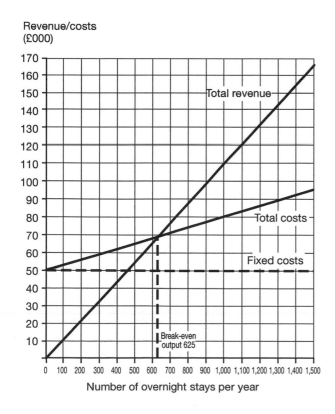

(c)

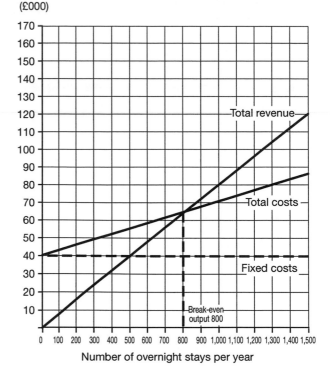

(d)

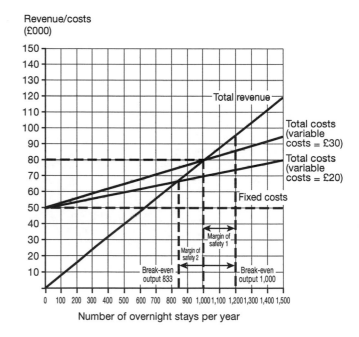

This assumes that variable costs are reduced to £20, but other answers may be given.

(i) A fall in variable cost will result in a fall in the break-even level of output. This is because a fall in variable costs with prices remaining the same means that each visit makes a greater contribution towards paying off fixed costs. Hence, fixed costs are paid off at a lower level of output. On a break-even diagram, lower variable costs are shown by a fall in the gradient of the total cost curve. In the diagram above, if variable cost falls from £30 to £20, the break-even level of output falls from 1,000 overnight stays to 833.

(ii) With the break-even level of output falling, the margin of safety at a level of 1,200 overnight stays will increase. In the diagram above, with the assumption that variable cost falls from £30 to £20, the margin of safety increases from 200 to 367.

Question 2

(a) The price Julia would need to receive in order to break-even is given by:

$$\text{Price} = \frac{\text{Total cost}}{\text{Output}}$$

$$= \frac{£6,000 + (60,000 \times £0.40)}{60,000}$$

$$= \frac{£6,000 + £24,000}{60,000}$$

$$= \frac{£30,000}{60,000}$$

Price = 50p.

This can be checked using the following calculation.
TR = 50p x 60,000 = £30,000
TC = £6,000 + 60,000 x £0.4 = £30,000

(b) (i) If the price Julia received was 48p per kilo, profit would be given by:

Profit = TR - TC
= (48p x 60,000) - (£6,000 + £0.4 x 60,000)
= £28,800 - £30,000
= -£1,200 (a loss)

(ii) If the price that Julia received was 51p per kilo profit would be given by:

Profit = 51p x 60,000 - (£6,000 + £0.4 x 60,000)
= £30,600 - £30,000
= £600

Case study

(a) A business breaks even when its total costs are exactly the same as total revenue. At this level of output the business makes neither a profit nor a loss. In this case, Amelia and Julia want to calculate how many hampers they need to sell in order for their new business to break even.

(4 marks)

(b) (i)

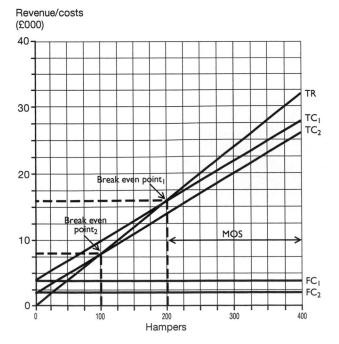

Revenue/costs
(£000)

Hampers

(10 marks)

(ii) Organic Hampers need to sell 200 hampers to break-even. This is the break-even point shown on the chart.

(2 marks)

(c) (i) See chart. The margin of safety is 200 hampers.

(2 marks)

(ii) According to the chart, the profit made if 400 hampers are sold will be £4,000. This is total revenue of £32,000 - fixed costs of £4,000 + total variable costs of £60 x 400 (£24,000) which is £32,000 - £28,000.

(2 marks)

(d) (i) The fixed costs are likely to fall in the second year because some of the fixed costs incurred in the first year would have been 'one-off' costs. It is common to incur 'one-off' costs when setting up a business. For example, in this case one of the start-up costs would have been setting up a web site. This cost would not be repeated in the second year.

(4 marks)

(ii) The break-even level of output is now 100 hampers. This is shown on the chart.

(2 marks)

(iii) If 500 hampers were sold in the second year, the amount of profit made is:

Profit = TR - TC
= 500 x £80 - (£2,000 + 500 x £60)
= £40,000 - (£2,000 + £30,000)
= £40,000 - £32,000
= £8,000

It is unlikely that both Amelia and Julia could afford to give up their factory jobs at the moment. Neither could live comfortably on £8,000. However, it might be possible for one of them to give up if she can use the extra time devoted to the business by increasing sales.

(6 marks)

(e) The break-even output can be lowered by decreasing costs or raising price. In this case the break-even output fell in the second year from 200 to 100 hampers when fixed costs fell from £4,000 to £2,000. The break-even output could be lowered further if variable costs were cut. This might be achieved by finding cheaper suppliers for the food or wicker baskets, for example. Alternatively the break-even output could be lowered if the price of the hampers was raised. However, the partners would have to consider the effect on demand if the price was increased. If the price was raised too much, demand may be insufficient to generate enough revenue to break-even. If this happened the business would make a loss.

(8 marks)

39 | Cash flow

Question 1

(a) (i) Total payments in June are expected to be £380. This is the total of all expected cash payments made to suppliers during the month of June. It includes vegetables, other ingredients, packaging and overheads such as fuel.

(ii) The net cash flow in June is calculated by subtracting the total payments from the total cash receipts. In June the total payments were expected to be £380, the total receipts were expected to be £400, therefore the net cash flow will be £20 (£400 - £380).

(iii) The closing balance in June is £160. This is calculated by adding the net cash flow for June to the opening cash balance. The opening cash balance for June is expected to be £140 and the net cash flow £20. Therefore the closing balance will be £160 (£20 + £140).

(b) The opening cash balance in May is zero. This is because the business has not begun trading yet. At the beginning of May there had been no cash receipts and no cash payments – therefore the opening cash balance must be zero.

(c) The expected cash position for Janet's business venture looks good. Over the nine month trading period the closing cash balance is expected to get bigger every single month. At the end of the nine month period the closing cash balance is expected to be £1,090. Janet is likely to be pleased with the forecast.

Question 2

Note: In the first impression of the 4th edition there is a misprint. This has been corrected in reprints. The opening balance figures should all be moved one column to the right.

(a) (i) The value of cash sales and total receipts for October is £5,000 (£5,270 - £270).

(ii) Total payments for August are £4,420 (£3,000 + £620 + £200 + £100 + £500).

(iii) The closing balance for November is -£180 (£580 - £760).

(iv) The opening balance for January is £900 (the same as the closing balance for December).

(b) Businesses draw up cash flow forecasts to help control and monitor cash flow in the business. Perhaps most important of all it will help Kieran to identify, in advance, the cash position of the business each month. The closing balances at the bottom of the forecast show how much cash he is expected to have at the end of each month. For example, Kieran knows in advance that his business will need some extra cash from somewhere in the first five months. He also knows that his cash position is likely to improve at the end of the time period. Preparing cash flow forecasts also helps to improve the overall planning of the business. Careful planning is important in business because it helps to clarify objectives and improve performance. Producing a cash flow forecast is part of the planning process because it deals with the future. Finally, it helps to monitor cash flow. At the end of the year Kieran can compare the figures in his forecast with the actual figures. By doing this he can find out where problems have occurred. Kieran might try to find reasons why certain figures are different. This will help to make future forecasts more accurate which means that they will be more useful.

(c) It is possible that the bank would grant Kieran the loan he is requesting. Kieran needs the money to buy some stock so that he can increase the range now that he has expanded. Kieran is only requesting a short term loan and is confident that he can repay it within nine months. According to his forecast the cash position of his business improves significantly over the time period. Indeed, the forecast even includes the repayments of the loan assuming it is granted. However, the bank may point out to Kieran that even with the loan the business is expected to go into debt in the first five months. It may be worried about this. It may ask him how he proposes to fund this cash deficit. However, on balance, bearing in mind the expected performance of the business, a loan may be granted.

Case study

(a) A cash flow forecast is a financial document, usually produced on a spreadsheet, which shows the likely receipts and payments of a business for a future time period. All expected payments and receipts are listed month by month and the expected cash balance is calculated at the end of each month. **(4 marks)**

(b) See table below.

	Apr	May	Jun	Jul	Aug	Sep	Oct	Nov	Dec £
Receipts									
Bank loan	3,000								
Own capital	2,000								
Cash receipts	2,000	2,100	2,000	2,500	2,500	2,000	1,000	500	0
Total cash receipts	7,000	2,100	2,000	2,500	2,500	2,000	1,000	500	0
Payments									
Van	2,000								
Tools & equipment	3,400								
Laptop	600								
Yellow pages		100							
General overheads	400	400	400	400	400	400	400	400	400
Advertising		100		100		100		100	
Drawings			800	800	800	800	800	800	800
Loan repayments		200	200	200	200	200	200	200	200
Total payments	6,600	800	1,400	1,500	1,400	1,500	1,400	1,500	1,400
Net cash flow	400	1,300	600	1,000	1,100	500	(400)	(1,000)	(1,400)
Opening balance	0	400	1,700	2,300	3,300	4,400	4,900	4,500	3,500
Closing balance	400	1,700	2,300	3,300	4,400	4,900	4,500	3,500	2,100

(12 marks)

(c) (i) The expected cash position for Kay Jones Garden Designs looks quite promising. In the first month of trading, when all the setting up costs are incurred, the business is still expected to have a positive cash balance at the end of the month. After that, the cash position improves every month up until September when it is expected to be £4,900. In the next few months the cash position worsens because revenue starts to decline. But even in December when there is no revenue, the closing cash position is still positive.

(4 marks)

(ii) The cash position of the business in early 2008 is expected to worsen. This is because revenue is likely to be zero for a few months. Garden design is likely to be affected by seasonal demand and people will not be thinking about a new garden until the growing season begins in the spring. If the cash payments stay at £1,400 each month and there is no more revenue, the cash position at the end of February will be -£700 (£2,100 - £2,800).

(4 marks)

(d) See table below.

(e) The amended cash flow for Kay Jones Garden Designs does not look so good. In April there will not be enough cash. The unexpected motor repairs mean that the cash position is -£800 at the end of April. In May the position is restored but in June, due to the cancelled order, the cash position is negative again. After this the cash position improves up until the end of the year. In December there is a negative balance again. Also, in early 2008, this negative balance will get much bigger because there will be no revenue coming in. Under these circumstances a bank may be reluctant to lend Kay £3,000. If she was granted a bank overdraft (in addition to the loan) she could survive the first few months of trading but would struggle again in early 2008. It is likely that a bank would ask Kay to put more money into the business herself and find ways of generating revenue during the winter months. She could also cut costs by reducing drawings, for example.

(10 marks)

	Apr	May	Jun	Jul	Aug	Sep	Oct	Nov	£ Dec
Receipts									
Bank loan	3,000								
Own capital	2,000								
Cash receipts	2,000	2,100	700	2,500	2,500	2,000	1,000	500	0
Total cash receipts	7,000	2,100	700	2,500	2,500	2,000	1,000	500	0
Payments									
Van	2,000								
Tools & equipment	3,400								
Laptop	600								
Yellow pages		100							
General overheads	400	400	400	400	400	400	400	400	400
Advertising	100		100		100		100		
Drawings			800	800	800	800	800	800	800
Loan repayments	200	200	200	200	200	200	200	200	200
Van repairs	1,200								
Total payments	7,800	800	1,400	1,500	1,400	1,500	1,400	1,500	1,400
Net cash flow	(800)	1,300	(700)	1,000	1,100	500	(400)	(1,000)	(1,400)
Opening balance	0	(800)	500	(200)	800	1,900	2,400	2,000	1,000
Closing balance	(800)	500	(200)	800	1,900	2,400	2,000	1000	(400)

(6 marks)

40 Improving cash flow

Question 1

(a) Cash is the life blood of a business. Without cash a business cannot operate. In this case Kwik Save ran out of cash. As a result the business collapsed in July 2007. Some new cash was injected into the business in February when it was bought by Mr Niklas. However, this was not enough and Kwik Save ran out of cash again. It could not pay its workers or suppliers and was taken into administration.

(b) (i) The employees of Kwik Save were hit badly. Just before the company collapsed 81 stores were closed and 700 people lost their jobs. A further 90 stores were closed on the day it collapsed with around 1,100 people being laid off. These people will have to find new jobs. However, it was hoped that some of the stores would be bought by other retailers and some people would be kept on. Also, many of the staff also worked for six weeks without pay. It is very unlikely that they will receive any money now that the business has collapsed.

(ii) Mr Niklas is likely to lose everything he put into the business. When a business goes into administration all the assets are sold for cash. The cash is used to pay creditors. If there is any left after all the creditors have been paid the owners, Mr Niklas in this case, can have the rest. However, it is very unlikely that Mr Niklas will receive anything. He will also have lost the cash that he injected in February when he bought the supermarket.

(c) One of the main problems faced by Kwik Save was intense competition from other supermarkets. They have suffered from a loss of trade due to price cutting by rivals such as Tesco and Asda. They have also lost business to foreign entrants into the market such as Aldi and Lidl. It is also suggested in the case that the business was badly managed. There are no details given, but there may have been mistakes such as choosing inappropriate product lines, using ineffective marketing strategies or poor organisation. It may also be the case that the business suffered from poor financial management. This is very likely since it ran out of cash and most of the sales in a supermarket would be for cash.

Question 2

(a) Adrian might improve his cash flow situation by considering aspects of the working capital equation - current assets and current liabilities. One way in which he could deal with a cash flow problem is to ensure that businesses which pay late make earlier payment. Businesses which buy garments from Adrian are debtors. They owe him money. Collecting payments more regularly, chasing payments and having overall a better credit control system, could help. Second, he could consider increasing his creditors. These are organisations that his business owes money to. For example, he could negotiate longer payment terms with his suppliers of materials used to make the garments. Changing payments from say 30 to 90 days will leave his business with cash for longer periods. Third, he could try to reduce the amount of stock of raw materials that he holds. By reducing stock, he could release cash into the business.

Case study

(a) A cash flow problem occurs when a business does not have enough cash. In this case Hotel Condor needs at least £15,000 to pay for work needed on the kitchen. The business only has £9,200 in the bank. This is a cash flow problem because there is not enough cash to meet the needs of the business. Unless the hotel owners can generate some cash, the business might have to close down. **(4 marks)**

(b) A wide range of factors can influence the cash flow of a business. Some of these are likely to be external which means they are beyond the control of the business. They result from events occurring outside the business. In this case, one of the reasons why trade has been declining at the Hotel Condor is because of the strong exchange rate between the pound and the dollar. The strong pound means that Americans have to pay more when travelling and staying in Britain. This has resulted in a fall in the number of American guests staying at the hotel and a fall in cash flowing to the business.

The hotel's cash flow problem was also the result of its forced closure in April. The hotel's failure to comply with health and safety legislation, which is determined by the government, means that it will have to upgrade hygiene standards in the kitchen. This is expected to cost £15,000 which the business currently does not have. Also, while the hotel is shut it will not be generating any revenue. Unforeseen expenditure like this is a common cause of cash flow problems. In this case it has been the result of an external factor. **(12 marks)**

(c) One way in which a business can improve cash flow is to attract fresh capital. In this case the owners of Hotel Condor, Ashraf and Asif Hussain, have invited a relative of theirs to contribute £50,000 in return for a share in the business. Whether this relative should accept depends on number of factors. Perhaps the most important one is whether the business is likely to be successful in the future. At the moment it is in trouble. It has a cash flow problem and without a cash injection it is likely to collapse. However, with the extra cash, the necessary improvements can be made to the kitchen and the hotel reopened. The business has negotiated what seems to be an attractive contract with a British company. They have booked 25 rooms for three months and plan to make regular use of the conference facilities. This looks like good business for the hotel. However, before this contract the hotel was struggling. A relaunch of the restaurant has failed and not very much extra business had resulted from a listing in some accommodation directories. It also sounds as though the hotel might be a little run down if its hygiene standards are not up to scratch.

The relative would also have to consider what assets the business has and what share of the business was being released for the £50,000 capital. As a sleeping partner there would be no involvement in the day to day running of the business - the role of a sleeping partner is to invest. To conclude, the investment would be a risk. There is evidence of decline and a serious cash crisis does exist at the moment. Unless the partner's capital was covered adequately by equity in the hotel property, I would suggest that the invitation should not be accepted. **(14 marks)**

(d) There are many ways to improve cash flow in a business. However, the methods will not be suitable for all businesses. For example, in this case, the hotel cannot generate sales for cash. The hotel has to shut down for a period and cannot take any bookings for two weeks. It might be able to attract advance bookings if they discount room rates but they would only collect deposits on bookings. They might also be subject to criticism from other guests who booked at the higher rates - particularly the British company that has just made a big block booking. Other unsuitable methods for Hotel Condor include selling off raw materials for cash, mounting a rigorous drive on overdue accounts, selling debts to a debt factor and selling off unwanted fixed assets. There is no evidence to suggest that these methods could be used.

Hotel Condor needs cash quickly. One good way would be to obtain a short-term loan or overdraft from a bank. They might be forced to use the hotel as security for new loans but at least they could get some cash and start trading again. They would obviously have to pay interest on loans and that would reduce the profitability of the business. In the short term this is probably the best way to improve cash flow for this business.

In the longer term, the business could get a huge injection of cash if it were to sell the hotel property and lease it back. This is a method used increasingly by businesses to generate cash. After the sale, the maintenance of the hotel property would be the responsibility of the leasing company. However, leasing in the long term is expensive and will reduce profits. The owners would have to consider carefully whether they would want to lose the main asset of the business. **(20 marks)**

41 | Setting budgets

Question 1

(a)

	JAN	FEB	MAR	APR	MAY	JUN £
Petrol sales	3,400	3,500	3,400	3,600	4,000	4,500
Grocery sales	650	650	700	700	750	800
Car accessories	450	500	500	550	550	600
Car sales	1,000	1,500	2,000	4,000	5,000	6,000
Servicing and repairs	4,300	4,800	5,000	4,500	4,000	3,500
MOTs	400	500	450	550	600	500
Total income	**10,200**	**11,450**	**12,050**	**13,900**	**14,900**	**15,900**

(b) One of the main purposes of setting budgets is to help monitor and control the finances of the business. Hannah and David Saunders do this by setting sales targets for each source of income. These sales targets will be shown in the income budget shown above. At the end of the financial period Hannah and David will be able to compare the actual sales with those set out in the budget. They will be able to see whether their targets have been met. If targets are not met they may carry out an investigation to find out why. Using an income budget in this way will help to monitor the performance of each part of the business.

(c) A profit budget shows the amount of profit a business is expected to make each month. It contains information on all income generated by the business and all expenditure. The information in this budget could be used in a profit budget because it shows the total income for the business in the given time period. Expenditure would be subtracted from the income totals to show profit for the business.

Question 2

(a)

	JAN	FEB	MAR	APR	MAY	JUN £
Sports Hall	1,400	1,600	1,700	1,700	1,500	1,300
Swimming pool	2,300	2,400	2,400	2,500	3,000	3,500
Games room	600	700	600	500	400	200
Fitness centre	3,200	3,500	3,600	3,600	3,400	3,200
Outdoor activities	500	400	500	600	800	1,000
Massage & beauty treatments	5,300	5,300	6,000	6,000	7,000	7,000
Administration	2,000	2,000	2,000	2,000	2,000	2,000
Café bar	3,200	3,500	3,700	4,000	5,000	7,000
Total expenditure	**18,500**	**19,400**	**20,500**	**20,900**	**23,100**	**25,200**

The total expenditure for the six month period is £127,600. This is found by adding the monthly totals together.

(b) Over the six month period the expenditure for the café bar has risen consistently from £3,200 in January to £7,000 in June. The most probable reason for this is that the café bar has got busier throughout the year and as a result more expenditure has been incurred. For example, more money would be spent on wages and supplies for the café bar if it was busier. It is also possible that Melanie has promoted the café bar more aggressively to encourage usage.

(c) Budgeting allows management to control the business. Melanie has probably set an expenditure budget to help keep control of costs in the leisure centre. The business is divided into departments and each department is responsible for its own spending. Setting an expenditure budget means that the person responsible for a particular department will not be able to spend more than the allocation shown in the budget. This keeps a 'lid' on spending. People who attempt to spend more than has been allocated will be held accountable and must explain their actions. In the absence of an expenditure budget, people in charge of a department may spend the firm's money carelessly.

Case study

(a) A budget is a financial plan which is agreed in advance. It must be a plan and not a forecast - a forecast is a prediction of what might happen in the future, whereas a budget is a planned outcome which the firm hopes to achieve. A budget can show a range of financial information. For example, it can show planned income, expenditure or profit. In this case the table shows an expenditure budget for the Agarka Mini Market. The budget shows how much each department in the store plans to spend over a six month period. Budgets are usually presented on a spreadsheet and financial information is listed in columns which represent a month. **(2 marks)**

(b)

	JUL	AUG	SEP	OCT	NOV	DEC £
Dairy						
Income	7,500	7,500	8,000	8,000	8,000	9,000
Expenditure	6,300	6,200	6,800	6,900	6,800	7,800
Profit	**1,200**	**1,300**	**1,200**	**1,100**	**1,200**	**1,200**

	JUL	AUG	SEP	OCT	NOV	DEC
Delicatessen						
Income	9,000	9,000	9,500	9,500	9,500	12,000
Expenditure	8,000	8,000	8,200	8,300	8,200	10,500
Profit	**1,000**	**1,000**	**1,300**	**1,200**	**1,300**	**1,500**

	JUL	AUG	SEP	OCT	NOV	DEC
Fresh produce						
Income	5,700	6,000	6,000	6,500	6,000	8,000
Expenditure	5,300	5,400	5,700	6,300	6,200	7,600
Profit	**400**	**600**	**300**	**200**	**(200)**	**400**

	JUL	AUG	SEP	OCT	NOV	DEC
Grocery						
Income	27,000	28,000	29,000	29,000	30,000	34,000
Expenditure	23,200	23,700	24,300	24,800	25,100	27,200
Profit	**3,800**	**4,300**	**4,700**	**4,200**	**4,900**	**6,800**

	JUL	AUG	SEP	OCT	NOV	DEC
Meat						
Income	8,000	8,000	8,500	8,500	9,000	12,000
Expenditure	6,500	6,400	6,500	6,900	7,000	9,200
Profit	**1,500**	**1,600**	**2,000**	**1,600**	**2,000**	**2,800**

	JUL	AUG	SEP	OCT	NOV	DEC
Liquor						
Income	3,000	4,000	5,000	6,000	8,000	17,000
Expenditure	2,300	2,700	3,700	4,200	6,100	11,200

700 1300 1300 1800 1900 **(18 marks)**

5800.

(c) (i) Over the six month time period the fresh produce department has the poorest profit record. It makes a lower profit in every single month than all other departments. Indeed, in November the department actually makes a loss of £200. **(4 marks)**

(ii) The poor profit made by the fresh produce department could be the result of a number of factors. The person responsible for the department may be running it badly. For example, produce might be being presented badly, there may be waste due to over-ordering, prices might be too high or costs might be too high. Another reason is the possible existence of strong competition in the area for fresh produce - farm shops for example. Alternatively there could be a drop in the demand for fresh produce generally - perhaps in favour of organic produce. **(4 marks)**

(d) (i) One of the purposes of budgets is to help motivate staff. Budgeting should act as a motivator to the workforce. It provides workers with targets and standards. Improving on the budget position is an indication of success for a department or group of workers. Fear of failing to reach budgeted targets may make workers work harder. In this case the people responsible for running departments are given bonuses related to the profit made by their department. This will motivate them to make more profit. **(6 marks)**

(ii) The person running the grocery department will get a bonus of £1,435 (£28,700 x 5 ÷ 100). **(4 marks)**

(e) The Agarka family might encounter a number of problems when setting budgets. For example, problems tend to arise because figures in budgets are not actual figures. The figures are plans, which could be based on historical data, forecasts or human judgment. The Agarka family might simply take historical data and add an arbitrary percentage to arrive at the budgeted value. The most important data in the preparation of nearly all budgets is sales data. If sales data are inaccurate, many of the store's budgets will be inexact. The accuracy of sales data might be improved if market research is used. However, it may be difficult to estimate sales of new products for a future period.

The setting of budgets may lead to conflict between departments or members of staff. For example, in this case heads of department get paid bonuses related to the profits made by their departments. This could lead to resentment if one department seems to make considerably more profit than others even if the effort put in by the heads is the same.

Another problem might be the cost of setting budgets. The time spent drawing up and evaluating budgets could have been spent on other tasks. For example, department heads could be improving the running of their departments by training staff. Time spent on paperwork and attending meetings in the grocery department means less time spent on grocery selling itself and increases in costs. **(12 marks)**

42 | Using budgets

Question 1

(a)

	JAN	FEB	MAR	APR	MAY	JUN	(£000) TOTAL
Budgeted income	1,200	1,300	1,400	1,400	1,500	1,600	8,400
Actual income	1,140	1,190	1,430	1,400	1,390	1,450	8,000
Variances	60A	110A	30F	0	110A	150A	400A

(b) In April there is no variance. This means that planned income was exactly the same as actual income. In April 2007 both planned and actual income was £1,400,000.

(c) Most of the monthly income variances are adverse for FT Office Supplies. This means that actual income has been lower than planned income. Over the whole six month period actual sales was £400,000 lower than planned sales. One possible reason for this is that demand has fallen for their products. New competition might have resulted in a loss of customers for FT Office Supplies, for example. Alternatively, the business may have changed its marketing strategy or stopped an advertising campaign. This could also lead to a fall in sales. Another possible reason is that the person(s) responsible for setting the budget, planned for unattainable levels of sales. It is possible that the planned income figures were too optimistic. The sales revenue budget planned for a 33% increase in sales over the period. This is demanding. Sales revenue did actually increase by 27% which is an impressive performance. Consequently, the owners of FT Office Supplies may not be too concerned about the adverse income variance.

Question 2

(a)

	JAN	FEB	MAR	APR	MAY	JUN	(£000) TOTAL
Direct cost variance	100F	50F	100F	50F	0	100F	400F
Overhead variance	10A	20A	10F	590A	450A	20A	1,080A
Total cost variance	90F	30F	110F	540A	450A	80F	680A

(b) The total cost variance for the six month period is £680,000A. This means that costs were £680,000 higher than planned. However, the total cost variance is influenced by the direct cost and the overheads variance. By looking at these other variances the reasons for the adverse total cost variance may become apparent. The direct cost variances are nearly all favourable, except for May when there was no variance. This means that direct costs were lower than planned. These favourable variances could be the result of lower material costs, lower direct labour costs or increased efficiency in production. The effect of these variances would be to reduce total costs. However, the overheads variance tells a different story. In most of the months shown the overheads variance is slightly adverse. But in April and May the actual overheads are considerably higher than those planned. The main reason for this is almost certainly the extra repair costs incurred to repair the worn out machinery. Without these very high unplanned overheads, the total cost variance would probably have been favourable due to the favourable direct cost variances. The overall effect of the total cost variance would be to

lower the profit for the period - by £680,000.

Question 3

(a) (i) The wage rate variance for Wallace & Co. between January and June is zero. This is because the budgeted wage rate of £5 per hour is exactly the same as the actual wage rate of £5 per hour.
(ii) The labour efficiency variance for Wallace & Co. between January and June is given by:

JAN	FEB	MAR	APR	MAY	JUN
(800-810) x £5	(800-820) x £5	(800-810) x £5	(800-200) x £5	(800-800) x £5	(800-810) x £5
£50 (A)	£100 (A)	£50 (A)	£3,000 (F)	0	£50 (A)

The labour efficiency variance for the whole budget period is £2,750 (F). This is calculated by:
£3,000 - (£50 + £100 + £50 + £50).
(iii) The direct labour variance is influenced by the wage rate variance and the labour efficiency variance. In this case the direct labour variances are the same as the labour efficiency variances. This is because the wage rate variances are zero. Thus, the total direct labour variance is £2,750 (F). This means that the direct wages bill for the six month period is £2,750 lower than expected.
(b) The favourable direct labour variance calculated in (a) arose mainly as a result of a sharp fall in the number of hours worked in April. The budgeted number of labour hours for April was 800, but only 200 hours were used. Such a sharp decrease suggests that the company experienced some unusual event in April. One possible explanation is that there was a strike for some reason. During a strike staff do not work and they are not paid. If production was held up for any other reason, such as a breakdown in machinery, it is likely that staff would still be paid. One other possibility is that some staff were laid off for the whole of April but still received a small payment.

Question 4

(a) (i) The sales margin price variance for Bromford Motors is:

Sales margin price variance = (actual price - budgeted price)
× actual sales

$$= (£9,325 - £9,500) \times 269$$

$$= -£175 \times 269$$

$$= £47,075 \text{ (A)}$$

(ii) The sales volume variance for Bromford Motors is given by:

Sales volume variance = (actual sales - budgeted sales)
× budgeted price

$$= (269 - 250) \times £9,500$$

$$= £180,500 \text{ (F)}$$

(iii) The sales margin variance can be calculated by combining the sales margin price variance and the sales volume variance. Therefore, the sales margin variance for Bromford Motors is £133,425 (F). This is calculated by £180,500 - £47,075.
(b) The sales margin price variance for Bromford Motors of £47,075 is adverse. This means that the average price of cars sold by the sales team is lower than budgeted price. There could be a number of reasons for this. One reason may be that the market has become very competitive and intense rivalry has forced prices in the car market down. Another reason may be that the sales team has chosen to cut prices in the salesroom in order to sell more cars. This may have been a calculated strategy aimed at raising turnover to maximise its budget-linked bonus.

The sales volume variance for Bromford Motors of £180,500 is favourable. Again there could be a number of reasons for this. One reason could be that the cars being sold are very appealing to consumers. Another could be that the sales team has been supported by an effective advertising campaign. Alternatively it could be the result of the price reductions being offered by the sales team. This may be the more likely scenario because the sales team's pay is linked to the value of sales.

Case study

(a) A variance is the difference between a budgeted value and an actual value. A favourable variance is one where the actual value is better than the budgeted value. In this case the profit variance for 2007 is £240,000F. This means that actual profit for the year was £240,000F higher than the budgeted profit.

(3 marks)

(b)

	2007	2006	(£000) 2005
Income variance	390F	210F	400F
Expenditure variance	150A	50A	300A
Profit variance	240F	160F	100F

(9 marks)

(c) The profit variance is arguably the most important variance of all. Profit is the key performance indicator for a business. Owners, managers and other stakeholders are likely to be very interested in the profit made by the business at the end of the year. The profit variance shows the difference between the planned profit and the actual profit for the year. The profit variance will show whether or not profit expectations have been realised.

(4 marks)

(d) In 2005 the profit variance was £100,000. It was a favourable variance and was caused by a £400,000 favourable income variance offset by a £300,000 adverse expenditure variance. These variances may have been caused by an increase in business. It is possible that Cynplex.com experienced an increase in orders. This would raise sales and increase the cost of sales. This would account for the favourable income variance and the adverse expenditure variance. Another possibility is that the Cynplex decided to increase marketing expenditure. Such action, if successful, would increase sales. This could also be responsible for the two variances.

In 2006, the profit variance was larger, it was £160,000 and favourable. However, both the income and expenditure variances were smaller. The expenditure variance fell to just £50,000 (A) and the income variance was £210,000 (F). The income variance may have been caused again by higher than expected sales. With more output an adverse expenditure variance would also be expected.

In 2007, the profit variance was even higher at £240,000 (F). Both the income and expenditure were larger than 2006 but not as large as 2005. It could be concluded that the speed in sales growth has made it difficult for the accountant at Cynplex to set accurate budgets. However, since the profit variance, the most important variance, is favourable, the company owners are not likely to be disappointed with the variances in this case.

(10 marks)

(e) Cynplex.com appears to be performing very well. The profit variances show that the company has exceeded profit expectations every single year since 2005. The profit variance was favourable in every single year. In 2005 it was £100,000F and by 2007 it had risen to £240,000F. According to the financial information shown in Table 6 Cynplex.com had planned to raise profit from £400,000 to £600,000. However, profit actually rose from £500,000 to £840,000. It is clear that the business is not only performing well but also better than expected.

This information should help Josh when deciding whether to float the company. Given these favourable profit variances Josh might decide that it is time to float the company. It is likely that the company would be well received on the stock market. Investors are likely to be interested in a company that consistently exceeds profit expectations. These profit variances would help Josh to be more confident about the success of a flotation.

(10 marks)

(f) Although using budgets can be very helpful when managing financial resources in a business, they do have some drawbacks. In some businesses, workers are left out of the planning process when budgets are set. If workers are not consulted about the budget, it will be more difficult to use that budget to motivate them. Budgets can be manipulated by managers. For example, the accountant in this case has great influence over the setting of the budgets. The accountant may be able to arrange a budget which is easy to achieve and makes Cynplex.com look successful. Some managers might be too focused on the current budget. They might take actions that undermine the future performance of the business just to meet current budget targets. For example, in this case, to achieve favourable profit variances in the current budget period the accountant might encourage others in the organisation to reduce staffing on customer service. This might save costs now but it could lead to customers drifting away over time due to poor service. Consequently the long term performance of the business would suffer.

However, in this case there is no real evidence to suggest that Cynplex.com is suffering from the drawbacks of using budgets. For example, profit variances have been favourable in three consecutive years and actual profits are still growing. There is no evidence of short termism. Neither is there any evidence of poor motivation among staff and nor is there evidence of the accountant manipulating the budgets. It is reasonably safe to draw the conclusion in this case that the financial management of the company is sound and that the problems of using budgets have not been experienced.

(14 marks)

43 | The role and objectives of accounting

Question 1

(a) Business activity involves purchasing resources, such as raw materials, labour and machinery and selling goods or services that have been produced using these resources. The purchase of resources from suppliers and the sale of products to customers are examples of business transactions. Examples of transactions in Isabel's business include:

- the payments she receives from bands when playing for them;
- the purchase of musical instruments from contacts in the USA;
- the sale of musical instruments to collectors and shops;
- resources that she buys, such as spare parts, to help renovate instruments;
- the payments she receives from students for music lessons;
- the purchase of music notation paper for her students;
- the purchase of other resources such as reeds, DVDs and videos to show playing techniques.

(b) Business owners have to keep a record of their business transactions. Every single transaction must be recorded. The records will be used to produce accounts which might be needed to see how well the business is doing, for example. Isabel runs a small business, therefore she is likely to keep her own records. She might record details of her purchases in a book. It is possible that Isabel will find it difficult to keep accurate records. This is mainly because a lot of his transactions will be for cash and she may not issue or receive receipts. Without receipts to verify transactions she might forget the details of some and they may go unrecorded. For example, she may buy some musical instruments from contacts who do not operate as businesses. These contacts are not likely to issue receipts. Also, she may receive payments from students and bands which are not verified by documents. Without documents to keep it is easy to forget that transactions ever took place and therefore her records will be incomplete.

Question 2

(a) (i) One group that use financial information regularly is the media. Business and commerce is often the subject of newspaper, TV, online and radio reports. For example, *the Financial Times* is a newspaper devoted almost entirely to business and financial reports. Also, BBC's Working Lunch provides daily updates on company news and the financial markets. The financial information in this case, about Next, would be used by the media. Next is a large, high profile fashion retailer. The media would be keen to report on its progress in their programmes, articles or reports. The information in this case has been extracted from Next Annual Report and Accounts. This gives details about the company's financial performance in 2007. Such information is reported regularly in the media.

(ii) Potential investors and financial analysts are likely to spend a lot of time assessing financial information relating to the performance of companies such as Next. The financial information in this case, such as revenue, profit and dividends per share for 2007, may be used by potential investors to help decide whether it is worth investing in Next. For example, pension funds, insurance companies and other institutional investors employ financial analysts to manage the money collected from pension contributions and insurance premiums. Much of this money is invested in shares. Analysts will analyse the financial information published by Next to determine whether Next shares are worth buying.

(b) Many investors want to buy shares in established companies that are financially sound, have a good financial history and also some future potential. In this case the information relating to the performance of Next is very positive. The first graph shows revenue

between 2003 and 2007. Revenue has increased by 50 per cent from £2.2 billion to £3.3 billion over the period. This shows that the company is large and that it has grown significantly. The second graph shows profit before tax. Profit has increased every single year from £301 million in 2003 to £478 million in 2007. This represents a 58.8 per cent increase and is very impressive. Finally, dividends per share have also increased by around 58 per cent from 31p in 2003 to 49p in 2007. The financial information presented here shows that Next has an impressive financial performance and might be an attractive proposition for a potential investor. However, it would be necessary to look at other information before making a final decision. For example, information relating to Next's share price would need to be analysed and the performance of competitors in the industry.

(c) Most companies make use of IT in their accounting process. A number of companies, such as Sage, provide fully integrated software packages which handle the whole accounting function. Such packages are very sophisticated and, provided details of all transactions are entered into the system, they are capable of numerous tasks. These might include keeping records of transactions with all customers showing up to date balances on all accounts, keeping records of transactions with all suppliers showing up to date balances on all accounts, producing daily, weekly, monthly or annual sales figures, producing an aged debtors list, producing an aged creditors list, producing trial balances, producing profit and loss accounts, producing balance sheets, calculating staff wages and producing wages slips and producing stock details. Next is likely to use IT in its accounts department and benefit from many of theses applications.

Case study

(a) easyJet is a very large plc and will have an accounts department employing a wide range of accounting and clerical staff. Accountants are responsible for supplying and using financial information. The accounts department will be responsible for recording all financial transactions undertaken by the company. They will also produce the final accounts. easyJet is likely to employ both financial and management accountants. The role of financial accountants is to make sure that a company's accounts are a 'true and fair' record of its transactions. They supervise the bookkeeping process, which involves recording the value of every single business transaction. From time to time they summarise these records and convert them into statements, which may be used by a wide range of groups. Financial accountants are concerned with the past. They need to know about accounting techniques, company law, auditing requirements and taxation law. The ability to work under quite severe time pressure with a variety of personnel, at all levels in the business, is also important.

(6 marks)

(b) One of the groups that may be interested in the financial information of a business is competitors. Other low cost airlines such as Flybe, Jet2.com and bmibaby may be interested in the financial information shown in the Figure and the Table. The information in the figure shows the revenue and profit generated by easyJet over a five year period. Rivals could use this information to make comparisons. They will be able to compare their own financial performance against that of easyJet. The information might also show whether easyJet is increasing its market share. Rivals will be concerned if easyJet is increasing market share at their expense. The significant increase in revenue generated by easyJet over the time period may be of some concern to other low cost airlines. However, it may not be a problem if the market is growing.

The Table, which shows the income statement for easyJet, will also be of interest to competitors. The statement gives information about the costs incurred by easyJet. The analysis of costs might also be useful. Competitors may be able to see whether easyJet is operating more or less efficiently than themselves, for example, by examining depreciation or operating costs. **(8 marks)**

(c) Much of the financial information produced by easyJet will be used internally. For example the information in the Table may be used for analysis and evaluation. It is possible to evaluate the performance of the company, make comparisons with competitors and keep a record of the firm's progress over a period of time. Financial information also helps the control of money flowing in and out of the business. This becomes more important as the firm grows and the amounts of money used increase. For example, easyJet's managers will be interested in the costs of the business business as shown in the table. They show that operating costs have risen over the period 2005-2006. It is important for the business to have cash reserves in case there is a sudden dip in trade caused by an external factor, for example.

One of the most important reasons why businesses need financial information is to help managers make decisions. Financial information is quantitative data which is very useful when making decisions. For example, managers might use cost information to help identify targets for cost cutting in the organisation. The analysis of costs in the table will be useful in this respect. For example, the total costs can be compared with budgeted costs. If actual costs have exceeded budgeted costs managers may decide that action needs to be taken. Problem areas can also be identified. For example, there has been a large rise in fuel costs. Other areas have seen a fall in costs, such as ground handling charges. Financial information is likely to be helpful when making a very wide range of business decisions.

(8 marks)

(d) An increasing number of businesses are concerned about social responsibility. In an effort to become better corporate citizens some businesses carry out a social audit. This is a way of measuring and reporting on a company's social and ethical performance. It is a move away from the traditional method of evaluating performance which measures accounting information such as revenue, profit or dividends. Businesses that undertake social audits are accountable to a wider range of stakeholders and are also committed to following the audits recommendations. Social accounting may look at the firm's impact on the environment, the workforce, suppliers or the wider community.

Information in the case suggests that easyJet carries out some social accounting. The data show extracts from easyJet's corporate and social responsibility report. For example, the bar chart in Figure 6 shows easyJet's contribution to CO_2 emissions. According to the graph easyJet has managed to reduce its emissions from 1 in 2000 to 0.824 in 2006. This may suggest that easyJet is committed to the reduction of environmental damage caused by aircraft.

Figure 7 also contains extracts from easyJet's Annual Report. Two sections are shown. Section E reflects easyJet's attitude towards health and safety. For example, the report states that 'safety is the number one priority for the business. easyJet aims to provide a safe and efficient work environment for all its people …'easyJet is committed to the development of an industry leading Fatigue Risk Management System (FRMS) for its pilots, as an integral part of the airline's safety management processes'. Section G comments on easyJet's ethical stance. For example, easyJet is committed to the highest standards of corporate behaviour from its Directors and employees. easyJet requires all of its people to perform their duties with efficiency and diligence and to always behave to customers and other people alike with courtesy and decorum'.

However, there is no evidence which suggests that easyJet has carried out an external social audit. Therefore it might be argued by some that the process is purely a PR exercise in order to improve corporate image. Indeed, many would argue that the increase in air traffic resulting from the expansion of easyJet's activities, has contributed to more environmental damage.

(10 marks)

(e) Most businesses today use IT in their accounting process. easyJet is likely to have invested very heavily in IT for accounting purposes. This is because of the significant advantages. Speed. Large numbers of transactions can be processed much more quickly in computerised than in manual systems. For example, easyJet conducts billions of transactions each year. If records of these transactions were stored in manual systems a huge quantity of resources would be required. In addition, access to information stored in a computer is very easy. From the billions of transactions that might be recorded, an operator can instantly call up details of one single transaction. Also because large volumes of data can be processed quickly, computer systems require a smaller workforce than manual systems. Therefore the cost of collecting and recording transactions can be reduced. Information can be input and accessed from different locations around the country or the world. Information from different easyJet sites eventually goes to one central processing unit where it is sorted and stored in the appropriate accounts. Information from every store can be retrieved and monitored from head office. Electronic data exchange may be used to transmit information in this way.

The design of accounting programs means that staff do not need a detailed knowledge of bookkeeping and accounts to be able to input and retrieve data. Consequently, training costs could be lower and a business might employ non-specialist staff in the accounts department to keep labour costs down. Computerised systems are more accurate than manual systems when processing data. Partly this is because computers do not become distracted or tired when performing large numbers of routine operations. By using a system of passwords, it is possible to restrict access. This prevents the unauthorised use of sensitive information. Intranets, which allow one computer to communicate with another like the larger Internet, may be also used by easyJet.

The widespread use of computerised accounting systems suggest that the benefits outweigh the drawbacks. However, easyJet may encounter certain problems. The cost of purchasing and then upgrading computer hardware and software can be expensive. Staff training costs can also be high. It is sometimes necessary to employ specialist IT staff to monitor the system. This adds to the cost. There is a wide range of computer systems and it is not always easy for a business to choose the most appropriate package. If an incorrect choice is made the mistake may be costly. Problems often arise when a new computer system is installed. It might not run smoothly because of 'bugs' in the system. Other difficulties arise if a 'virus' is downloaded from the Internet or via an email, or if inexperienced staff cause the system to crash. When this occurs, it can lead to problems and delays to staff, customers and suppliers.

The use of computerised systems may cause industrial relations problems. If staff see technology as a threat to their jobs or status, they might not cooperate with management when systems are installed. This can result in delays and friction between managers and employees. Although security can be increased by the use of passwords, employees or outsiders might be able to 'hack' into the system. This unauthorised access might be used by a disgruntled employee to sabotage the business, or by a competitor who hopes to gain an advantage. Finally, computer systems are only effective if data is inputted correctly. If inaccurate data is entered, the reports that are generated will also be inaccurate, misleading and of little use.

(16 marks)

44 | Balance sheets

Question 1

(a) (i) The Maltings is a care home so examples of fixtures and fittings might be the furniture in the care home such as beds, chairs, tables and settees; decoration; built in wardrobes; curtains; light fittings; carpets; bathroom and kitchen units and radiators.

(ii) Trade creditors are amounts owed to suppliers. In this case the business might owe money to suppliers of food for the care home, suppliers of fuel, utility providers such as water, electricity, gas and service providers such as transport for guests.

(b) (i) Net current assets = £16,900.
(ii) Net assets = £731,900.
(iii) Retained profit = £186,800.

(c) Net current assets in the balance sheet is the working capital of the business. In this case working capital is £16,900. Calculating working capital is important. Working capital is used to pay the day-to-day bills of the business. If this is inadequate the business may struggle to make important payments to key suppliers or to employees. In this case The Maltings appears to have sufficient working capital.

Question 2

(a) The value of most fixed assets will fall over time. This is due to depreciation. Accountants make an allowance for depreciation every year. They estimate this allowance and subtract it from the value of assets in the previous year to get a new value for fixed assets. In this case, Melanie's vehicle was valued at £5,000 in the balance sheet in 2007. In 2008 this had fallen to £4,000. This suggests that depreciation was £1,000.

Sometimes the value of fixed assets will fall if some have been sold off during the year. However, there is no evidence in this case that Melanie has sold any fixed assets.

(b) The opening capital in a sole trader balance sheet is the same as the closing capital in the previous year. In this case the opening capital for Melanie Cooper's business is £32,500 in 2008. This is the same as the amount for closing capital in 2007, ie £32,500.

(c) Drawings is the amount of money taken out of a business by the owner. The money is usually taken out for personal use. In this case, Melanie has increased her drawings from £26,000 in 2007 to £28,800 in 2008. One possible reason for this is that Melanie's living and other personal expenses were higher in 2008. This meant she had to take more money from the business. This is not an unusual action - drawings are likely to rise over time provided the business is successful.

(d) The balance sheet can be used to show the value of a business. The net assets provide a rough guide to the value of a business. In this case, Melanie's gift shop in Brighton is worth £33,300. This has increased from £32,500 in 2007. However, the balance sheet does not show any intangible assets such as goodwill. If Melanie's business is consistently successful there may be some goodwill. This means that net assets are likely to undervalue the business.

Case study

(a) Winters Timber Ltd has to produce a balance sheet by law because it is a limited company. All limited companies have to file a copy of their balance sheet with the Registrar of Companies every year. However, the balance sheet might also be produced to help stakeholders understand the financial position of the business. For example, it can be used by financial managers to assess the solvency of the business.

(4 marks)

(b) Fixed assets are important resources owned by the business. They are assets with a life span of more than one year. They are likely

to be used repeatedly for the life of the business or until they are no longer any use. In this case, there are two fixed assets listed in the balance sheet. The most valuable is equipment and machinery. In 2008 this was valued at £1,200,000. Winters Timber is likely to own machinery such as electrical saws, tools and computers. The company recently installed a panelmaster system for the manufacture of fence panels. The company also owns vehicles. These are listed at £340,000 in the balance sheet. This might include company cars for directors and vans or lorries used for delivery.

(4 marks)

(c) (i) The balance sheet shows that retained profit has increased from £600,000 in 2007 to £960,000 in 2008. This is because the profit retained in 2006 is added to the total of retained profit in 2007. Winters Timber Ltd must have retained £360,000 of its profit in 2008. If this is added to the total of retained profit in the 2005 balance sheet, the new total for retained profit becomes £960,000 (£360,000 + £600,000).

(ii) The value of vehicles in the balance sheet has increased from £310,000 in 2007 to £340,000 in 2008. Usually, the value of fixed assets in the balance sheet falls each year because an allowance is made for depreciation. In this case such an allowance will have been made. However, the increase in the value of vehicles has arisen because new vehicles must have been acquired. Either, newer and more expensive vehicles have been bought to replace worn out ones, or more vehicles have been added to the existing fleet.

(8 marks)

(d) Information in the balance sheet suggests that Winters Timber Ltd is in a fairly healthy financial state. The company's working capital has increased from £130,000 in 2007 to £235,000 in 2008. This means the business has more liquid resources available to meet immediate debts. The company has also increased its cash balance from £100,000 to £180,000. This is a significant percentage increase and suggests that the company has generated a good amount of cash during the year's trading. The company has also been able to retain £360,000 of its profit. This shows that the company made a healthy profit and was able to retain some for future investment such as the purchase of new machinery like the panelmaster. The company was also able to purchase new vehicles. These purchases of new fixed assets were achieved without going into any further debt. The mortgage stayed constant at £500,000 and there was little change in the amount of current liabilities. Finally, the value of the company did fall slightly from £1,340,000 to £1,275,000. However, there does not appear to be any increase in debt which could have caused this so there is no reason to worry. The company appears to be in good financial shape. **(8 marks)**

(e) The balance sheet has a number of uses for a business and Winters Timber Ltd may benefit from these. In general, it provides a summary and valuation of all business assets, capital and liabilities. More specifically, the balance sheet can be used to analyse the asset structure of a business. It can show interested stakeholders how the money raised by the business has been spent on different types of asset. For example, more than three quarters of Winters' capital has been spent on fixed assets. This is quite good since fixed assets are the productive assets for a company. The balance sheet can also be used to analyse the capital structure of a business. Winters Timber has raised funds from many different sources, such as shareholders' capital, retained profit and long term and short term sources. One of the key uses of a balance sheet is that it shows working capital. The working capital can indicate whether a firm is able to pay its everyday expenses or is likely to have problems. This is discussed in detail in (d). Finally, a balance sheet may provide a guide to a firm's value. Generally, the value of the business is represented by the value of net assets. In this case net assets are £1,275,000 in 2008, so Winters Timber is worth over a million pounds to the shareholders.

On the other hand there are also limitations to balance sheets. The value of many assets listed in the balance sheet may not reflect the amount of money the business would receive if they were sold. For example, fixed assets are listed at cost less an allowance for depreciation. However, the depreciation allowance is estimated by accountants. If estimates are inaccurate, the value of assets will also be inaccurate. Also, many balance sheets do not include intangible assets.

Assets such as goodwill, brand names and the skills of the workforce may be excluded because they are difficult to value or could change suddenly. If such assets are excluded, the value of the business may be understated. A balance sheet is a static statement. Many of the values for assets, capital and liabilities listed in the statement are only valid for the day the balance sheet was published. After another day's trading, many of the figures will have changed. This can restrict its usefulness. Finally, it could be argued that a balance sheet lacks detail. Many of the figures are totals and are not broken down. For example, the value of other reserves in 2008 was £115,000. This figure gives no information about the nature of these reserves. Therefore, when stakeholders are using the balance sheet these limitations need to be taken into account. **(16 marks)**

Question 1

(a) Short term assets which can be changed into cash within one year are called current assets. The table shows the current assets of Corbridge Engineering Ltd. The company has stocks of raw materials and stocks of finished goods. Stocks are classed as current assets because the business would hope to convert them into cash within twelve months.

Work-in-progress is also classified as stock. It represents partly finished goods, eg partly completed components or pressings. The business would hope to convert work-in-progress into cash within a year as well. Corbridge also has debtors. This is the amount of money owed by customers who have bought goods on trade credit. Related to debtors is prepayments. A prepayment is a sum, such as insurance, rent or uniform business rate, which is paid in advance. At the end of the financial year any service which has been paid for but not fully consumed is listed in the balance sheet as a prepayment. Finally, the business has some cash in hand and at bank. Cash is the most liquid asset.

(b) During 2006 Corbridge Engineering Ltd experienced cash flow difficulties. Table 1 provides some evidence of this. In 2006 the company only had £2,900 cash. The huge majority of its current assets were tied up in stock and debtors. At the beginning of 2007 some measures were taken to improve cash flow by addressing the stock and debtor problems. It seems that these measures had some effect. The amount of cash held by the business rose to £187,600 in 2007. This is a very big improvement. Much of the improvement is the result of a reduction in debtors. Debtors have been reduced from £438,000 to £289,600. Stocks have also been reduced but not on the same scale. For example, stocks of raw materials have only fallen by £1,600 from £135,600 to £134,000. Further reductions in stocks could improve cash flow even more.

Question 2

(a) FRD Ltd has a much higher proportion of its capital tied up in plant, machinery and equipment than Allens. FRD Ltd owns two articulated lorries and some specialist trailers. This will make up the bulk of the £55,000 tied up in this category of asset. In contrast Allens only has £6,000 of plant machinery and equipment, perhaps some computer equipment or electronic tills. Allens has more money invested in fixtures and fittings. The store will be fitted out with shelving and display units, for example. FRD Ltd has a small office which is likely to contain some office furniture for example. Both businesses have some money tied up in other fixed assets. However, there are no details as to what these might be.

Allens has a lot more money tied up in current assets than FRD. For example, it has stock of £58,000 compared to just £1,000 for FRD. This is to be expected because Allens is an electrical goods store and will naturally hold large stocks of electrical goods for resale. The stock belonging to FRD might be stocks of fuel for example. FRD has a much larger amount for debtors. The reason for this is because FRD probably offers its customers trade credit whereas Allens is a cash and carry where most customers pay cash for goods. Finally, Allens has more cash then FRD. The main reason for this is likely to be the fact that Allens' customers pay in cash whereas FRD offers trade credit and has more money tied up in debtors.

(b) Depreciation is the consumption or using up of fixed assets. Businesses make a provision for depreciation each year in their accounts. Depreciation is treated as a business cost. In this case, FRD Ltd will make the largest charge for depreciation. This is because it owns more fixed assets than Allens.

Case study

(a) Domino's Pizza Group Limited is a wholly owned subsidiary of Domino's Pizza UK and Irl plc and holds the master franchise licence to own, operate and franchise Domino's Pizza stores in England, Scotland, Wales and Ireland. A subsidiary is a business which is owned by another business. Such a business is classified as a subsidiary if the owner has at least 50 per cent of the shares. In this case Domino's Pizza Group Limited is a wholly owned subsidiary which means that 100 per cent of the shares are owned by Domino's Pizza UK and Irl plc. **(4 marks)**

(b) Tangible assets are the physical assets of a business. They can be touched. The most long term or the least liquid of these assets appear at the top of the list of fixed assets on the balance sheet. In this case, Domino's Pizza has three main categories of fixed asset. Table 2 shows that at the end of 2006 Domino's had a total of £13,780,000 of fixed assets. This total included freehold land and buildings, lease improvement and equipment. These are the most productive assets for Domino's Pizza and will be used repeatedly for a long period of time. **(4 marks)**

(c) During 2006 Domino's purchased £1,945,000 of equipment. This was to be expected because during the year Domino's opened another 46 new stores. These new stores would need new equipment such as ovens, kitchen equipment, display counters and electronic tills. It is also likely that new equipment was purchased for many of Domino's existing stores - to replace worn out equipment for example. **(4 marks)**

(d) Fixed assets are shown at their net book value in the balance sheet. The net book value is the historic cost minus depreciation. At the beginning of 2006 the historic cost of Domino's fixed assets was £19,215,000. During the year Domino's purchased £2,294,000 more fixed assets. However, during the same period the company sold £523,000 of assets. This means that the historic cost of all Domino's fixed assets was £20,986,000. To get the net book value it is necessary to subtract depreciation. The depreciation charge for 2006 was £1,671,000. This is added to the accumulated depreciation (£5,622,000) making a total of £7,206,000 (note there is an adjustment of -£87,000 for depreciation on disposed fixed assets). This total is then subtracted from the historic cost to give a net book value of £13,780,000 (£20,986,000 - £7,206,000). **(6 marks)**

(e) (i) Fixed assets are used again and again over a long period of time. For example, an oven might be used for many years to bake pizzas. During their operation fixed assets such as ovens are consumed and their value is 'used up'. This measure of consumption or any other reduction in the useful economic life of a fixed asset is known as depreciation. Accountants recognise this and make a provision for depreciation in the accounts. They estimate depreciation for the year and treat it as a cost in the profit and loss account or income statement. For example, in 2006 the depreciation charge for Domino's was £1,671,000. If accountants did not recognise depreciation, profit for the year would be overstated. **(6 marks)**

(ii) Domino's fixed assets might depreciate for a number of reasons. Machinery, tools and equipment all suffer wear and tear when they are used. They deteriorate, which can sometimes affect their operation or effectiveness. Eventually they will have to be replaced. Changing technology can often make assets obsolete. Although a machine such as a computer may still work, it may not be used because a new computer is more efficient. Capital goods which are hardly used or poorly maintained may depreciate quickly. The life of machinery can be prolonged if it is 'looked after'. Finally, the passing of time can also lead to depreciation. For example, if an asset is leased, the 'buyer' can use the asset for a period of time. As the expiry date gets close, the lease becomes worth less and less. **(6 marks)**

(f) In 2006, Domino's had £773,000 of goodwill shown in the balance sheet. Goodwill is an intangible asset. Over many years of trading companies such as Domino's Pizza build up goodwill. They may have gained a good reputation, which means that customers will use their services or purchase their products. Goodwill may be placed on the balance sheet. If it does not appear on the balance sheet, the value of the company will be understated. From an accountant's point of view, goodwill is equal to the amount by which the purchase price of a business exceeds the net assets (total assets - total liabilities). Accountants have to estimate goodwill on the balance sheet. It is also 'written off', over a period of time. The 'writing off' of goodwill means that the value of goodwill will fall over time.

However, if a business grows there is likely to be more goodwill. Consequently the value of goodwill will rise over time. Whether or not the value of Domino's goodwill rises or falls in the future depends on the rate at which it is written off and how fast the company grows. If Domino's Pizza grows and continues to enjoy a good reputation, goodwill may rise at a faster rate than it is 'written off'.

(10 marks)

Question 1

(a) (i) £10 000. Freehold property. Initial cost = £500 000. Life of 50 years. Depreciation in first year is £500 000 ÷ 50 = £10 000 a year.

(ii) £200 000. Paint plant. Initial cost = £2 000 000. Life of 10 years. Depreciation in first year is £2 000 000 ÷ 10 = £200 000 a year.
(iii) £20 000. Vehicles. Initial cost = £60 000. Life of 3 years. Depreciation in first year is £60 000 ÷ 3 = £20 000 a year.
(iv) £230 000. This is made up of £10 000 + £200 000 + £20 000 = £230 000.
(b) Freehold property £500 000 - £10 000 = £490 000. Paint plant £2 000 000 - £200 000 = £1 800 000. Vehicles £60 000 - £20 000 = £40 000.
(c) See table below.

	Freehold property		Paint book		Vehicles	
	Depreciation cost	Net book value	Depreciation cost	Net book value	Depreciation cost	Net book value
First purchased		500 000		2 000 000		60 000
First year	10 000	490 000	200 000	1 800 000	20 000	40 000
Second year	10 000	480 000	200 000	1 600 000	20 000	20 000
Third year	10 000	470 000	200 000	1 400 000	20 000	0
Fourth year	10 000	460 000	200 000	1 200 000		

£

Question 2

(a)

	Cutting machine		Freehold premises		Cutting machine	
	Depreciation cost	Net book value	Depreciation cost	Net book value	Depreciation cost	Net book value
2008	0	500 000	0	0	0	0
2009	100 000	400 000	0	800 000	0	0
2010	80 000	320 000	40 000	760 000	0	600 000
2011	64 000	256 000	38 000	722 000	120 000	480 000
2012	51 200	204 800	36 100	685 900	96 000	384 000
2013	40 960	163 840	34 295	651 605	76 800	307 200

£

Question 3

(a) (i) FIFO method

Date	Stock received and price	Stock issued and price	Stock valuation	
			Goods in stock	Total
1.7.08	50 @ £2		(50 @ £2 = £100)	£100
3.8.08	100 @ £2.20		(50 @ £2 = £100)	
			(100 @ £2.20 = £220)	£320
19.8.08		50 @ £2		
		50 @ £2.20	(50 @ £2.20 = £110)	£110
23.9.08	200 @ £2.30		(50 @ £2.20 = £110)	
			(200 @ £2.30 = £460)	£570
25.9.08		50 @ £2.20		
		100 @ £2.30	(100 @ £2.30 = £2.30)	£230

Thus, the value of closing stock using the FIFO method is £230.

(ii) LIFO method

Date	Stock received and price	Stock issued and price	Stock valuation	
			Goods in stock	Total
1.7.08	50 @ £2		(50 @ £2 = £100)	£100
3.8.08	100 @ £2.20		(50 @ £2 = £100)	
			(100 @ £2.20 = £220)	£320
19.8.08		100 @ £2.20	(50 @ £2 = £100)	£100
23.9.08	200 @ £2.30		(50 @ £2 = £100)	
			(200 @ £2.30 = £460)	£560
25.9.08		150 @ £2.20	(50 @ £2 = £100)	
			(50 @ £2.30 = £115)	£215

Thus, the value of closing stock using the LIFO method is £215.

(iii) Average cost method

Date	Stock received and price	Stock issued and price		Stock valuation	
1.7.08	50 @ £2		£2	(50 @ £2 = £100)	£100
3.8.08	100 @ £2.20		£2.13	(150 @ £2.13 = £319.50)	£319.50
19.8.08		100	£2.13	(50 @ £2.13 = £106.50)	£106.50
23.9.08	200 @ £2.30		£2.266	(250 @ £2.266 = £566.50)	£566.50
25.9.08		150	£2.266	(100 @ £2.266 = £226.60)	£226.60

Thus, the value of closing stock using the average cost method is £226.60.

(b) If the stock in the above transactions was perishable, the business should use the FIFO method to issue stock. Because perishable stock deteriorates quickly the business must always issue the oldest stock before it has time to perish. The FIFO method ensures that the oldest stock is issued first because it issues the stock which was first purchased by the business.

(c) In practice it is the FIFO method which is favoured by firms when stocks are valued. This method ensures that any stocks issued are priced at the cost of earlier stocks, while any remaining stock is valued much closer to the replacement cost. The LIFO method is least favoured because it involves valuing current stock at 'old' or 'out of date' prices. The replacement cost of stock could be quite different to the prices current stock is valued at. Also, in practice, stocks are more likely to be issued physically using the FIFO method for reasons discussed in (b).

Case study

(a)

Date	Stock received and price	Stock issued and price	Stock valuation	
			Goods in stock	Total
04.07.08	400,000 @ 100p		400,000 x 100p = £400,000	£400,000
07.07.08		350,000 @ 100p	50,000 x 100p = £50,000	£50,000
07.07.08	400,000 @ 100p		450,000 x 100p = £450,000	£450,000
12.07.08		410,000 @100p	40,000 x 100p = £40,000	£40,000
14.07.08	400,000 @ 100p		440,000 x 100p = £440,000	£440,000
18.07.08		360,000 @ 100p	80,000 x 100p = £80,000	£80,000
19.07.08	400,000 @ 105p		80,000 x 100p = £80,000	
			400,000 x 105p = £420,000	£500,000
23.07.08		80,000 @ 100p		
		380,000 @ 105p	20,000 x 105p = £21,000	£21,000
24.07.08	400,000 @105p		420,000 x 105p = £441,000	£441,000
28.07.08		410,000 @105p	10,000 x 105p = £10,500	£10,500

(8 marks)

(b)

Turnover			£2,133,000
Cost of sales	Opening stock	0	
	Purchases £2,040,000		
		£2,040,000	
Less closing stock		10,500	
		£2,029,500	
Gross profit			**£103,500**

NB Purchases can be found by:
400,000 x 100p + 400,000 x 100p + 400,000 x 100p + 400,000 x 105p + 400,000 x 105p.

(6 marks)

(c) (i)

Date	Stock received and price	Stock issued and price	Stock valuation	
			Goods in stock	Total
04.07.08	400,000 @ 100p		400,000 x 100p = £400,000	£400,000
07.07.08		350,000 @ 100p	50,000 x 100p = £50,000	£50,000
07.07.08	400,000 @ 100p		450,000 x 100p = £450,000	£450,000
12.07.08		410,000 @100p	40,000 x 100p = £40,000	£40,000
14.07.08	400,000 @ 100p		440,000 x 100p = £440,000	£440,000
18.07.08		360,000 @ 100p	80,000 x 100p = £80,000	£80,000
19.07.08	400,000 @ 105p		80,000 x 100p = £80,000	
			400,000 x 105p = £420,000	£500,000
23.07.08		60,000 @ 100p		
		400,000 @ 105p	20,000 x 100p = £20,000	£20,000
24.07.08	400,000 @ 105p		20,000 x 100p = £20,000	
			400,000 x 105p = £420,000	£440,000
28.07.08		400,000 @ 105p		
		10,000 @100p	10,000 x 100p = £10,000	£10,000

(8 marks)

(ii)

Turnover			£2,133,000
Cost of sales	Opening stock	0	
	Purchases £2,040,000		
		£2,040,000	
Less closing stock		10,000	
		£2,030,000	
Gross profit			**£103,000**

NB Purchases can be found by:
400,000 x 100p + 400,000 x 100p + 400,000 x 100p + 400,000 x 105p + 400,000 x 105p.

(4 marks)

(d) (i) Annual depreciation provision is given by:

$$\text{Depreciation} = \frac{\text{Cost - Residual value}}{\text{Expected life}}$$

$$= \frac{£30,000 - £4,000}{10}$$

$$= \frac{£26,000}{10}$$

$$= £2,600$$

(4 marks)

(ii)

Year	Depreciation allowance	Book value
1	£2,600	£27,400
2	£2,600	£24,800
3	£2,600	£22,200
4	£2,600	£19,600
5	£2,600	£17,000
6	£2,600	£14,400
7	£2,600	£11,800
8	£2,600	£9,200
9	£2,600	£6,600
10	£2,600	£4,000

(4 marks)

(e) If the breakdown truck was sold for £12,000 at the end of year 6, Stella will make a £2,400 loss on disposal. This is because the book value at the end of year 6 was £14,400. This is greater than the net realisable value (sale price of £12,000).

(6 marks)

Question 1

(a) Williams & Son is a property development company. Its working capital cycle will be lengthy. This is because some of the time lags between different stages in the cycle will be long. For example, it will take time for the business to find a suitable plot of land, gain planning permission, draw up plans and acquire the land. During this stage there will be many costs such as legal and professional but no revenue. Once the land is acquired it will also take a long time to construct the property. Again, during this time costs will be incurred such as wages for builders, raw materials and overheads. Some suppliers offer 60 days credit. This is helpful but the business will still not receive any revenue unless deposits have been paid for properties that have already been sold. Finally, when the properties are complete there might be another delay. Sometimes new properties are not sold until after they have been completed. This will delay cash coming into the business even further. In contrast, the working capital cycle for Tina's Taxi Service is very short. She provides a minibus service to the airport. All the fares are paid in cash at the end of the journey. Tina does not have to pay wages until the end of the week and the fuel is purchased on 30 days credit. This means that she has the cash before the bills have to be paid. This is a very sound position to be in and very different from that of the property developer.

Question 2

(a) Poor credit control is where a business fails to control debtors and fails to collect money owed from debtors in time. This appears to be the case at F&H Welding Products. It gave customers 45 days credit but none of the four large contractors, for example, paid on time. This may also have been the case with other companies the business dealt with. Overstocking is where a business holds too much stock for its requirements. In the case of F&H Welding Products the business anticipated an increase in orders and ordered stock appropriately. But orders fell by 20% due to competition from abroad.

(b) One way in which the company solved its difficulties was by improving its credit control. Frank Smith, the managing director, visited the four large contractors who were debtors of the business to explain the liquidity problems it was having and encouraged them to pay sooner. This worked for some businesses but not for all. Frank Smith also changed all debtors' payment periods to 30 days from the previous 45 day agreement. To encourage payment on time he offered a 5% discount which was paid for by slightly increasing prices. Refusing to accept further orders from late payers would also have helped to improve credit control as late payers may have feared the business would no longer supply them. Reducing the stocks of the business, whilst at the same time moving nearer to a form of just in time delivery, also helped to prevent money being tied up in stocks.

(c) A business has insufficient working capital when it has either too few current assets in relation to its current liabilities or its current liabilities are relatively too high. There may also be insufficient working capital if the business cannot convert its current assets into cash to pay its day to day bills, which is the function of working capital for a business. For example, the business had debtors and stocks. But it was unable to collect money from debtors quickly enough to pay bills that were due. Stocks were also lying idle and not being converted into cash because the business had over-stocked. The only way that F&H Welding Products could get around these difficulties at certain times was to call on its overdraft facility which would then increase the liabilities of the business, reducing working capital. Another working capital problem that the business faced was that it offered longer payment period terms to debtors than it had for its own creditors. This meant that it was paying back money it owed before it had received money from businesses that were its debtors. Again this would have led to working capital difficulties. For these reasons it could be argued that F&H Welding Products simply didn't have enough working capital. The changes made by the company, such as reducing payment times and cutting stocks, will have helped the working capital situation of the business. There is not enough evidence given in the data to say whether these changes completely solved the problem.

Case study

(a) Working capital (sometimes called circulating capital) is the amount of money needed to pay for the day to day trading of a business. Businesses like LED Ltd and Hopes Ltd needs working capital to pay expenses such as wages, stock, electricity and gas charges, and to buy components to make products. The working capital of a business is the amount left over after all current debts have been paid. It can be calculated by subtracting current liabilities from current assets. **(4 marks)**

(b) Sometimes businesses get a cash injection into their working capital cycle. Examples include loans, fresh capital, the proceeds from asset sales or non-operating income. In this case, in 2008, Hopes Ltd took out a short term loan to pay for the construction of a large greenhouse adjacent to the store. The loan, for investment in a greenhouse, will allow the company to grow and stock a wider range of plants and similar products. **(4 marks)**

(c) In 2008 LED Ltd had £10,000 of stocks while Hopes Ltd had £460,000. This is quite a difference for two businesses that are roughly the same size. One reason why Hopes has a much larger stock level is because it is a retailer. At any point in time Hopes will have large stocks of goods such as paint, wall coverings, tiles, bathroom units, kitchen units, kitchen appliances, tools, building materials, switches, sockets, etc. on display in the store. There may also be further stocks which are not on display. This is the nature of retailing. Businesses like Hopes display goods for customers to look at and buy.

In contrast, LED Ltd is a manufacturer. It does not need to carry such large quantities of stock. Also, LED Ltd is a JIT manufacturer. This approach to manufacturing involves production without holding stocks. Components and raw materials are delivered to the factory exactly when they are needed. All goods made are sent straight to customers. There are no stocks of finished goods. These are the two main reasons why Hopes has a much larger stock value than LED Ltd. **(8 marks)**

(d) LED Ltd might encounter two problems when operating with low levels of stock. If the company does not carry any stocks of raw materials or components, there could be a break in production if suppliers fail to turn up or deliver the wrong goods. This means that workers and machinery may be idle for a period of time. This could prove very expensive for LED Ltd. One of the problems with JIT manufacturing is that firms are heavily reliant on suppliers. Another problem is that LED Ltd may not be able to react quickly to a sharp increase in demand. Businesses that hold quantities of finished goods can meet unexpected orders more easily. LED Ltd might have to ask customers to wait while it steps up production. This might result in disgruntled or lost customers.
(6 marks)

(e) The working capital of a business can be calculated using the formula:

Working capital = current assets - current liabilities

For LED Ltd

Working capital = £738,000 - £486,000 = £252,000

For Hopes Ltd

Working capital = £695,000 - £745,000 = - £50,000
(6 marks)

(f) LED Ltd has a working capital of £252,000. It could be argued that this is an adequate level of working capital. This is because the textbook rule is that the typical business needs around twice the amount of current assets as current liabilities to operate safely. This means that its current ratio is between 1.5:1 and 2:1. In this case the value of LED's current assets is 1.52 the size of current liabilities. This means that LED Ltd just about falls into the acceptable range. LED Ltd also has a healthy cash balance of £343,000 and debtors, which is a fairly liquid asset, of £385,000.

In contrast, Hopes Ltd has a negative value for working capital. It is - £50,000. This means that current liabilities are higher than current assets. This might be interpreted as quite a worry for the business.

However, some businesses can operate effectively with very low levels of working capital, even negative. These are usually retailers or similar businesses that buy their goods on trade credit and sell them soon after for cash. In this case, Hopes Ltd is a DIY store and it buys in stock from manufacturers and wholesalers and, on average, does not pay them for at least 45 days. The stock though is sold quickly in the stores, often within days of delivery from suppliers. Most of Hopes customers pay cash. So Hopes, like most large retailers, can operate safely owing suppliers large amounts (£387,000 in this case), but having very few debtors (only £112,000 in this case). The result is negative working capital. **(12 marks)**

Question 1

(a) A trading account is used to calculate gross profit. Gross profit is the amount of profit made by the business after the cost of sales has been subtracted from turnover. The trading account may also show how the cost of sales is adjusted for stock. In this case, the trading account for Berry Ltd does show opening stock and closing stock.
(b) The opening stock for Berry Ltd is £65,300 (£554,600 - £489,300). The gross profit for Berry Ltd is £297,100 (£780,400 - £483,300).
(c) Business turnover must not include the value of VAT in an account. Indirect taxes such as VAT are added to the sale price of goods. It is paid by customers to businesses but then handed over to the government. Including VAT would overstate the turnover of Berry Ltd.

Question 2

(a) The profit and loss account in this case shows clearly the gross profit and the net profit. The gross profit is calculated by subtracting cost of sales from turnover. In 2007 this was £288,000 for the Frozen Food Centre. The net profit is the amount of profit after all business costs have been subtracted from turnover. It can be calculated by subtracting expenses from gross profit. In this case it is £195,700. Profit and loss accounts, such as those in this case, show clearly the difference between gross profit and net profit.
(b) One of the main differences between the profit and loss account of a sole trader and that of a private limited company is the amount of detail shown. The accounts of sole traders tend to show more detail. For example, in this case there is a complete list of expenses such as wages, motor expenses, telephone and electricity. In a private limited company profit and loss account expenses would be summarised.
(c) Turnover for the Frozen Food Centre has increased by a significant amount. It rose by 48.3 per cent between 2007 and 2008, from £529,700 to £785,600. The main reason for this was the heavy investment in advertising made by Imran. He believed that the store had the capacity to at least double turnover. According to the profit and loss the amount spent on advertising rose from just £400 in 2006 to a massive £15,800 in 2008. Clearly the adverts on local radio followed by the leaflet distribution had a very positive effect on sales.
(d) The performance of the Frozen Food Centre has improved significantly over the two years. Turnover has increased by 48.3 per cent, gross profit has gone up by 78.9 per cent and net profit by a staggering 158.8 per cent. Imran is likely to be very pleased with the performance of his business. His belief that the store could improve its performance was correct.

Question 3

(a) Administrative expenses are the general overheads incurred when running a business. Examples of administrative expenses for a company like Ultra Electronics might include the wages and salaries of administrators and office workers, office expenses such as heating and lighting, telephone, printing and stationery and depreciation.
(b) The term 'finance cost' in the income statement refers to the amount of interest paid when borrowing money. The interest on bank loans or overdrafts would be examples.
(c) New international accounting standards introduced in 2005 mean that a public limited company must distinguish between continuing operations and discontinued operations in its income statement. Continuing operations refer to business activities that are currently owned by the company. Discontinued operations are those businesses which were sold off during the financial year. Ultra Electronics does not have any discontinued operations on its income statement.
(d) The performance of Ultra Electronics appears to have improved over the two years. The value of revenue has increased by £34,630,000, a 10.1 per cent increase. Gross profit has increased by 11.2 per cent and net profit by 34.7 per cent. The shareholders of Ultra Electronics will be particularly pleased with the increase in net profit. This might mean that higher dividends will be paid. One of the reasons for the improvement in net profit performance is the rise in investment revenue and the fall in finance cost.

Case study

(a) (i) Revenue in 2008 = £2,300m (£920 million + £1,380 million).
(ii) Finance costs in 2007 = £30m (£420 million - £390 million).
(iii) Taxation in 2008 = £100m (£520 million - £420 million).
(6 marks)
(b) (i) Plc accounts show the earnings per share (EPS) at the bottom of the income statement. For Elgood earnings per share were 23.6p in 2008. This is calculated by dividing the profit after tax by the total number of issued shares. The earnings per share gives an indication of a company's performance. The higher it is the better. The EPS is always shown for the basic shareholding and the fully diluted shareholding (the diluted shareholding includes shares which may be purchased as a result of share option schemes the company has).
(ii) The cost of sales (£920m in 2008) is the direct costs incurred by the business. In this case examples of cost of sales might be the cost of construction materials such as sand, cement, timber, tiles, bricks, pipes, wire and glass. Direct labour such as a bricklayer's wages will also be an example. **(6 marks)**
(c) The income statement of Elgood Construction plc may be of interest to a number of stakeholders. The shareholders are likely to be interested to see how the company has performed. They will want to know how much profit the company has made. Managers of the company may be interested to see if their decisions during the year have benefited the company. For example, they may be interested to see how well overheads have been controlled during the year. Other stakeholders may also use the income statement. For example, workers may use it to argue for improvements in their pay and conditions of service. Banks are likely to ask to see the income statement if a business wishes to borrow money. Suppliers may check the income statement of a business to decide whether or not to give trade credit. Tax authorities use the income statement to calculate some taxes on businesses. **(8 marks)**
(d) The income statement for Elgood Construction plc provides evidence to suggest that the company is performing well and has also improved over the two years. The company is profitable and has increased profit. The company has also grown between 2007 and 2008. During this period revenue grew by 16.2 per cent from £1,980 million to £2,300 million. This is quite a fast rate of growth. All measures of profit for Elgood show an improvement. Gross profit rose by 17.9 per cent, operating profit by 30.9 per cent and profit after tax by an even larger 35.5 per cent. The big improvement in net profit shows that managers have been successful in keeping overheads down. This is because net profit grew faster than gross profit. Indeed, the income statement shows that administrative expenses such as office expenses, depreciation and accountancy fees, actually fell over the time period from £250 million to £230 million. The company shareholders will also be pleased that earnings per share have increased from 18.9p to 23.6p. **(10 marks)**
(e) The income statement can be used to evaluate the financial performance of a business. But using it for this purpose has limitations for a number of reasons. The income statement only gives data about revenue, costs, profit and how the profit is used. Much more financial data is needed to assess accurately the performance of a business. For example, the cash flow position of Elgood is a vital indicator of performance. So too is the amount of debt. The income statement gives data about the finances of a business. But it does not say anything about the environmental or social impact of the business and only indirectly gives information about new product development or efficiency of production. Financial data is only one source of data for evaluating the overall performance of a business. For example,

Elgood may have a poor environmental record. The income statement is a record of the past performance of a business. So it can be used as one piece of evidence to evaluate the performance of the business in the past. But it is not necessarily a good indication of present or future performance. Much can happen within six months or a year to a business. For example, the economy might go into recession. This could affect Elgood quite badly.

The income statement shown here only gives performance data for two years. This is of limited value when judging performance. It gives an indication of the profitability of the business but many more years of data would be required to carry out a more thorough evaluation. The income statement shown here lacks detail. Most of the figures are summaries. More detailed information, such as an analysis of administration expenses and cost of sales, would enable a more thorough evaluation. Some businesses 'window dress' their accounts. This means that the true financial circumstances are disguised. For example, there may be a temptation to minimise profit, for example, by not putting some revenue 'through the books' or exaggerating costs. This will distort the true picture. Finally, income statements can have special features which need to be noted in evaluating performance. Occasionally a business will change its tax year. Accounts might for a single period be presented for 9 months or 15 months, say, instead of the usual 12 months. An increase in profit would be expected if the accounts covered 15 months rather than 12 months. This makes it very difficult to judge performance over time from the income statement. Equally, the costs and revenue sources of these businesses are constantly changing. It becomes very difficult to judge from the income statement whether the operations of the business are being well managed because so much of the profit is coming from new parts of the business. Elgood needs to be aware of many of these factors when carrying out an evaluation of performance using the income statement. **(20 marks)**

49 | Measuring and increasing profit

Question 1

(a)

	Dover	Ashford	Canterbury £
Turnover	158,000	142,000	197,000
Cost of sales	102,000	101,000	146,000
Gross profit	56,000	41,000	51,000
Overheads	31,000	29,000	33,000
Net profit	25,000	12,000	18,000

(b) The net profit margins for the three shops are calculated as follows.

$$\text{Dover} = \frac{£25,000}{£158,000} \times 100 = 15.8\%$$

$$\text{Ashford} = \frac{£12,000}{£142,000} \times 100 = 8.5\%$$

$$\text{Canterbury} = \frac{£18,000}{£197,000} \times 100 = 9.1\%$$

(c) (i) The calculations in (b) show that Dover is the best performing shop in the butchers' chain. It has a net profit margin of 15.8 per cent compared with 9.1 per cent for Canterbury and 8.4 per cent for Ashford. In fact the performance of the Dover shop is nearly twice as good as the other two.

(ii) The net profit margins for the three shops provide some useful information for the financial management of the business. The margins show that Dover is by far the best performer. Goodalls will probably look closely for reasons why the Dover shop is performing so well compared with the other two. Hopefully, the good practice in place at the Dover shop can be transferred to the Ashford and Canterbury shops. Goodalls might also be alerted by the sluggish performance of the Canterbury shop which has the highest turnover. The shop only makes a profit of £18,000 on a turnover of £197,000. The net profit margins help financial managers to analyse more accurately the profit made by businesses.

Question 2

(a) The return on capital is method used to measure the profitability of a business. It is the amount of profit a business makes expressed as a proportion of the capital invested in it. The return on capital is expressed as a percentage.

(b) The return on capital for the three businesses is given by:

$$\text{For Leonard \& Co} = \frac{£245,000}{£2,340,000} \times 100 = 10.5\%$$

$$\text{For Simpsons plc} = \frac{£466,000}{£7,800,000} \times 100 = 6\%$$

$$\text{For Argo Ltd} = \frac{£156,000}{£1,400,000} \times 100 = 11.1\%$$

(c) According to the calculations in (b), Argo Ltd has the highest return on capital. Even though Simpsons plc made a much larger profit, Argo Ltd has performed more effectively. However, Argo Ltd has performed only slightly better than Leonard & Co. There is only a difference of 0.6 per cent between the two returns. One reason why the return on capital for Simpsons plc was relatively low, was because it took over a rival last year and incurred some high costs. This would reduce profit and therefore reduce the return on capital. The returns generated by Leonard & Co and Argo Ltd seem reasonable. Both returns (around 11 per cent) are higher than an investor would get leaving the money in the bank (6 per cent). However, when risk is taken into account there is not much difference!

(d) When comparing the rate of return of one business with that of others, it is important to compare 'like with like'. The returns on capital may vary from industry to industry and from business to business. Fair comparisons can only be made between businesses if they operate in the same industry and have the same characteristics. In this case all of the businesses are involved in the supply of glass-related products. However, their product lines and activities are different. For example, Leonard & Co make wine glasses and crystalware while Argo makes glass furniture. Also, Simpsons is a retailer while the other businesses are manufacturers. These companies do have different characteristics and therefore comparing their returns on capital may not be entirely meaningful.

Case study

(a)

	2004	2005	2006	2007
Net profit margin	9.60%	8.60%	7.70%	10.30%

(8 marks)

(b) The size of profit can be misleading when measuring the performance of a business. In this case the profit of Compton Foods gets larger every single year. It rises from £235,000 in 2004 to £331,000 in 2007. This suggests that its performance is improving every year. However, this is not the case. A number of other factors have to be taken into account. For example, how much profit was made in relation to turnover. Turnover has also risen over the time period. It is necessary to look at net profit margins which take into account both the rise in net profit, and the rise in turnover. The net profit margins calculated in (a) show clearly that performance declined between 2004 and 2006. The net profit margins fell from 9.6 per cent to 7.7 per cent. This shows that the size of profit can be misleading when measuring performance.

(8 marks)

(c) Between 2006 and 2007 there was a sharp increase in the net profit margin of Compton Foods. It rose from 7.7 per cent to 10.3 per cent. This represents a significant improvement in performance. The main reason for the improvement is the new investment in the business. In 2006, the company's shareholders injected some fresh capital. £300,000 was raised to pay for a computerised packing machine and the introduction of new shift patterns. Both of these measures would help to improve the efficiency of the business. The new technology would help to raise capital productivity while the new shift patterns would help to improve labour productivity. As a result costs would fall and profit rise.

(8 marks)

(d) It is important to recognise that profit is not the same as cash. At the end of 2007 Compton Foods had £378,000 in the bank, yet the company only made a profit of £331,000 during 2007. Differences between cash and profit can arise for a number of reasons. In this case the amount of cash is higher than the profit for the year. One main reason is that the owners injected some more capital into the business. They put another £300,000 into the business in 2007. Much of this would have been used up paying for the new machine and introducing the changes to the shift patterns. However, there may have been some left over. Another reason is that there was probably some cash already in the bank at the beginning of the financial year. The year's profit added to this would enhance the cash balance at the end of the year. There are other reasons but in this case these two are the main ones.

(8 marks)

(e)

	2004	2005	2006	2007
Return on capital	15.6%	16.1%	16.4%	18.4%

(8 marks)

(f) Compton Foods was probably concerned that its net profit margins were falling. This shows that the performance of the business was worsening. In order to improve the profit margins the business raised some more capital for investment. £300,000 was spent on a computerised packing machine and the introduction of new shift patterns. The effect of this investment was to raise the net profit margin from 7.7 per cent in 2006 to 10.3 per cent in 2007. There was also an increase in the return on capital. This rose from 16.4 per cent to 18.4 per cent. Consequently there have been some significant improvements in the performance of the business.

However, the investment resulted in seven staff being laid off since the new machinery and new shift patterns were more efficient and less labour was needed. This destroyed the harmony between the owners and the workers. The workers benefited financially from the new shift patterns but they were resentful about their colleagues being laid off. This was the first time in the history of the company that staff had been made redundant. A worker representative said 'Working here will never be the same. There used to be an atmosphere of a family company here, but that's all changed now. The company is dominated by the accountants'.

Unfortunately there are often implications for the business when measures are taken to improve performance. Not all stakeholders will benefit. In this case the shareholders have benefited from the improvements because there is more profit. The remaining workers have also benefited financially from the shift changes. However, seven workers have lost their jobs and industrial relations at the plant have become difficult. This might have a long term effect on the business. If relations remain difficult problems could arise in the future. However, given time, the redundancies may be forgotten and the workers may begin to appreciate their financial benefits. Good industrial relations might be restored and the company may continue to prosper, in which case the changes will have been worth it.

(12 marks)

50 | Financial data and performance

Case study

(a)

	2003	2004	2005	2006	2007
Sainsbury					
Revenue	18,144	18,239	16,573	17,317	18,518
Profit	695	675	254	267	380
Profit margin	3.83%	3.70%	1.53%	1.54%	2.05%
Tesco					
Revenue	26,004	30,814	33,974	39,454	42,641
Profit	1,401	1,708	2,029	2,277	2,545
Profit margin	5.39%	5.54%	5.97%	5.77%	5.97%

(10 marks)

(b) The information shown in the Table above can be used to make an inter-firm comparison over time. This involves comparing the financial data of the two supermarkets over a period of time. In this case, there is enough information to compare the performance of the two companies over a five year period. The comparison between these two companies is a meaningful one because they are rivals. They are both supermarket chains. **(4 marks)**

(c) (i) Looking at performance indicators for a single year is not very helpful. This is because one year's trading figures may not reflect what has been going on over a longer time period. A more thorough evaluation of a company's performance can be undertaken by looking at many years' figures. This is called trend analysis and involves looking at data over a long period of time and spotting patterns in data. In this case, financial data is given for a five year period. **(4 marks)**

(ii) Evidence in the Table above suggests that Tesco has performed the best over the five year period shown. Its revenue has increased by around 64 per cent from £26,004 million to £42,641 million. In contrast Sainsbury's revenue has remained fairly flat with a slight dip in 2005 and 2006. Tesco's profit has also risen impressively over the time period. In 2003 it was £1,401 million. By 2006 it had risen by

about 82 per cent to £2,545 million. Unfortunately Sainsbury saw its profit fall from £695 million in 2003 to £254 million in 2005. Since then it has recovered a little to £380 million in 2007. Tesco also has better profit margins. In 2003 its profit margin was 5.39 per cent compared to Sainsbury's of 3.83 per cent. Over the five year period Tesco has managed to increase its profit margin to 5.97 per cent. This does not appear to be very much but when turnover is so high (ie billions of pounds) a very small increase in the profit margin can have a significant effect on the size of profit. In contrast Sainsbury has seen its margin fall to 1.53 per cent in 2005 and then recover slightly to 2.05 per cent in 2007. To conclude, Tesco has performed better in all respects and is going from strength to strength. However, Sainsbury has always lagged behind and suffered a very poor spell between 2004 and 2006 - although it does seem to be making a recovery now. **(10 marks)**

(d) One of the reasons for producing accounts and compiling other forms of financial data is to help make business decisions. When choosing between different courses of action a business will want to gather as much relevant information as possible. Having relevant and accurate information is likely to help businesses make more informed decisions. It is also helpful to have a range of quantitative information because it is easier to analyse. Financial data falls into this category. Financial data will be used when acquisitions are made. Before a company takes over another business it needs to look very closely at the financial circumstances of the business. A wide range of financial data will be analysed before a bid can be made. The size of the bid is likely to depend on the results of this financial analysis. Tesco and Sainsbury may have used financial data in this way.

All businesses have to invest from time to time. Making an investment decision is fraught with uncertainty. Businesses are likely to use quantitative appraisal methods when choosing between different investment projects. For example, Tesco and Sainsbury will use financial data when deciding where to open new stores. A business will use financial data when deciding its corporate strategy. For example, if Tesco is considering whether to increase its operations in overseas markets, it will have to evaluate the impact such a venture would have on the financial position of the business.

Tesco and Sainsbury are continually developing their product range in stores. They have also tried new store formats. Such ventures are often risky. In order to minimise the risk the supermarkets will consider carefully the impact such moves would have on the financial standing of the business. A wide range of financial data might be analysed when making such decisions. **(12 marks)**

51 Accounting concepts

Question 1

(a) The going concept assumes that a business will carry on trading for the foreseeable future. In other words, it is not expected to be closed down or be sold. This concept affects the way that assets are valued. For a going concern, it is reasonable to value assets at their historical cost. In this case, the fixed assets shown in the balance sheet such as the van for £1,400 and the machinery for £1,700, will all be valued at historic cost. This is the price for which these assets were purchased.

(b) Emily is wondering whether to close her business down because trade has taken a downturn. She hopes to sell the assets to raise finance for another business venture. If a business is about to close down, assets should be valued at their net realisable value. This is the amount that they would sell for as second hand assets. Under most circumstances it is likely that the net realisable value of assets, like machinery and stock, will be lower than their historical cost. This is because they are quite specialised and may not be in high demand.

Question 2

(a) According to the materiality concept a business should not waste time trying to accurately record items of expenditure which are trivial. For example, in this case the buckets, mop and broom were all purchased for less then £10 each. These resources are not a 'material' items. Even though they are expected to be used for many years the purchases should be recorded once and treated as an expense in the year they were bought. No attempt should be made to 'write off' this expenditure over the period of time the resources are in use. This avoids cluttering up the balance sheet with trivial items. Only the van, computer and vacuum cleaner should be listed as fixed assets in the balance sheet.

(b) Unfortunately there is no law or formal guideline which governs materiality. Different firms may use a variety of arbitrary methods to determine which items of expenditure are material and which are not. The method of assessing materiality will be selected by accountants using their judgment. In this case, Lisa might decide that all items purchased under a certain amount, say £50, should be classified as revenue expenditure.

Question 3

(a) The business entity concept states that the financial affairs of a business should be completely separate from those of the owner. The business is treated as a separate entity. This means that personal transactions must not be confused with business transactions. Here, the financial transactions undertaken by Chaminda's employment agency must not be confused with his own personal transactions. In this case, the lap top computer purchased for £1,200 is used both for business and personal purposes. Consequently, only a proportion of the cost can be attributed to the business.

(b) The computer is used for business purposes for 40 hours per week (8hrs × 5). It is also used for personal reasons for 20 hours a week. Therefore it is used for 60 hours a week. Consequently, the cost attributable to the business is 40/60 × £1,200 = £800.

Case study

(a) Jon's accounts should reflect a 'true and fair' view of the financial position of the business. To achieve this accountants follow a set of rules or guidelines. They are known as accounting conventions or concepts. By using a set of agreed uniform concepts when recording, analysing and presenting financial information, accountants can avoid confusion. Without the use of accounting concepts there is likely to be inconsistency and inaccuracy. This would render the accounts almost useless. It would not be possible to draw meaningful conclusions from the information. Such conclusions would be unreliable. Business accounts are used by a wide range of groups and need to be as accurate as possible. For example, if Jon wanted to compare the performance of his business with that of another chiropractor, he would be confident that another company's accounts would be produced according to the same set of rules and principles.

(4 marks)

(b) As far as possible Jon's accounts should be based on verifiable evidence rather than on personal opinion. In other words they should be objective rather than subjective. So, for example, Jon's accountant should value a transaction on the basis of an invoice rather than his or her own personal opinion. This avoids bias. Consider what might happen if two accountants were asked their opinion on the value of a particular transaction, for example the purchase of new premises. They might disagree because value can be measured in many different ways. However, if they were asked to value the transaction according to the invoice, they would likely record exactly the same value.

(6 marks)

(c) All of Jon's transactions are recorded in money terms. This complies with the money measurement concept. The concept states that financial records, including the value of transactions, assets, liabilities and capital, should be expressed in monetary terms. There are two key reasons for recording financial information in this way. Most transactions have an agreed monetary value and are expressed in monetary terms. Few transactions are carried out by barter or 'swapping', ie with no money involved. The different values of products and assets can be more easily compared in money terms. For example, the relative value of two buildings that cost £300,000 and £950,000 is more clearly expressed in monetary terms than a descriptive term such as 'medium' price and 'high' price. However, the use of money to record financial information does have some limitations. One problem is that some information cannot be expressed in money terms. As a result it might be ignored. This is often the case for some intangible assets. **(6 marks)**

(d) Jon should treat the transactions as follows.

- Part of the £15,000 quarterly rent payment must be included in the current trading year as an expense. If the quarterly rent was due one month before the end of the trading year, then a third of the payment must be included in this year's accounts. Therefore, Jon should record £5,000 (£15,000 × 1/3) for this year. This practice conforms to the accruals or matching convention.
- Jon cannot record the overpayment as revenue. The money will have to be repaid to the client. Jon should record £210 as revenue and £20 as an overpayment. This also conforms to the accruals concept.
- The £150 transaction will have been recorded as revenue when the goods or services were exchanged. This is according to the realisation concept. It seems likely that the money owed will not be collected because the client cannot be traced. Therefore the £150 should be treated as a bad debt. This complies with the prudence concept. Accountants should always record costs as soon as they are known. Bad debts can be listed as an expense in the profit and loss account or income statement.
- According to the accruals concept transactions should be recorded when goods are exchanged even when payment is delayed. The £560 of stationery should be included as a purchase in the current trading year. It does not matter that payment will be delayed until the next year.
- According to the historical cost concept all assets are valued at their original cost not their current value. Therefore the equipment that Jon purchased during the year for £2,500 must be valued at £2,500. This should be the case even though now the same equipment could be bought for £1,500.
- According to the principle of separate entity, the cost of operating an asset that is used for both business and personal use should be divided between the owner and the business. In this case, Jon incurs a total motoring cost of £12,800 for the year. According to information in the case the number of miles used for business use is 8,000. This compares with 2,000 for personal use. Therefore, the cost to the business during the year is £10,240 (£12,800 × 8,000 ÷ 10,000).

(24 marks)

52 | Costing methods

Question 1

(a)

	Fury	Trialmaster	XL10
Direct labour	£250	£150	£200
Raw materials	£150	£120	£100
Components	£400	£300	£340
Other direct costs	£200	£130	£160
Total direct costs	£1,000	£700	£800

Total direct cost of producing 100 of each:

Fury $= 100 \times £1,000 = £100,000$

Trialmaster $= 100 \times £700 = £70,000$

XL10 $= 100 \times £800 = £80,000$

Total direct costs = £250,000

(b) Total indirect costs to be allocated = £600,000

Indirect cost of producing 100 of each:

Fury $= \dfrac{£100,000}{£250,000} \times £600,000 = £240,000$

Trialmaster $= \dfrac{£70,000}{£250,000} \times £600,000 = £168,000$

XL10 $= \dfrac{£80,000}{£250,000} \times £600,000 = £192,000$

(c) Full cost of producing 100 of each:

Fury $= £100,000 + £240,000 = £340,000$

Trialmaster $= £70,000 + £168,000 = £238,000$

XL10 $= £80,000 + £192,000 = £272,000$

Total = £850,000

Total = £850,000 made up of direct costs of £250,000 and indirect costs of £600.000

Question 2

(a) When businesses are using absorption costing they may decide to allocate indirect costs in an arbitrary way, as a proportion of direct costs for example. However, this could result in misleading costings because the allocation of indirect costs is not based on any actual indirect costs incurred. A better way is to apportion overheads or indirect costs. This involves allocating a certain percentage or proportion of indirect costs to each cost centre. A business must decide on what basis to apportion indirect costs. The basis depends on the nature of the indirect cost. In this case Renfrews needs to apportion rent and electricity and administration overheads. Rent and electricity could be apportioned according to the floor space used by each department in the store. This is because both rent charges and electricity usage are linked to the size of areas occupied by different parts of the business. For example, the bigger the department the more electricity it will use for heating and lighting. Administration costs could be apportioned according to the number of staff

employed in each department. This is because many administration costs are generated by employees, payroll and training for example.

(b) The full cost of operating each department at Renfrews is:

Food Hall
Direct costs	= £400,000
Rent & electricity 800 ÷ 2,600 × £300,000	= £92,308
Administration 12 ÷ 36 × £200,000	= £66,667
Full cost	= £558,975

Women's wear
Direct costs	= £200,000
Rent & electricity 600 ÷ 2,600 × £300,000	= £69,231
Administration 8 ÷ 36 × £200,000	= £44,444
Full cost	= £313,675

Men's wear
Direct costs	= £100,000
Rent & electricity 600 ÷ 2,600 × £300,000	= £69,231
Administration 4 ÷ 36 × £200,000	= £22,222
Full cost	= £191,453

Electrical goods
Direct costs	= £200,000
Rent & electricity 400 ÷ 2,600 × £300,000	= £46,154
Administration 6 ÷ 36 × £200,000	= £33,333
Full cost	= £279,487

Toys
Direct costs	= £100,000
Rent & electricity 200 ÷ 2,600 × £300,000	= £23,077
Administration 6 ÷ 36 × £200,000	= £33,333
Full cost	= £156,410

Question 3

(a) Standard costing helps businesses to monitor and control costs. A standard cost is a planned or 'target' cost. It is normally associated with a specific activity or a particular unit of production. In this case the standard cost of manufacturing the new toy is 505p. This includes all of the different costs associated with the production of one unit and means that the usual cost per toy is 505p. Standard costing involves calculating the usual or planned costs of an activity and then comparing these with the actual costs incurred. Both are shown below.

Description	Standard cost	Actual cost
Materials	65p	70p
Labour	180p	230p
Machinery	210p	205p
Overheads	50p	50p
Total	505p	555p

(b)(i) The difference between the standard cost and the actual cost is called a variance. In this case the total variance for the new toy 50p. This variance is adverse because the actual cost is 50p higher than the standard cost.

(ii) The adverse variance calculated here appears to be higher than expected labour costs. There is a 50p adverse labour cost variance which is quite significant. This means that either more labour time was needed to make the toy or the cost of labour rose - as a result of a wage increase perhaps. The most likely cause for the variance is that more labour was needed than expected. If the actual labour costs cannot be reduced and remain at 230p per unit, the standard cost will have to be adjusted.

(c) Blackburn Mouldings Ltd may enjoy a number of benefits from using standard costing. By comparing standard costs with actual costs a business can identify areas of weakness and inefficient practice. In this case, it has come to light that labour costs are higher than expected. The company will look into the reasons why and probably take some action. Standard costing is likely to be used as a means of controlling costs in a business. Staff at Blackburn Mouldings may be motivated if they achieve cost targets which they are involved in setting. In some cases staff might be rewarded financially if they reach or exceed targets. Finally, standard costs may represent the best estimate of what a product should cost to make. So, by using standard costs, estimates of costs for products and price quotations for orders are likely to be more reliable.

Case study

(a) Contribution = Price - Variable costs
= £250,000 - (£34,500 + £111,200 + £29,400 + £23,600)
= £250,000 - £198,700
= £51,300

(4 marks)

(b) Profit = Total contribution - Fixed costs
= 12 × £51,300 - £280,000
= £615,600 - £280,000
= £335,600

(4 marks)

(c) Contribution = Price - Variable costs
= £185,000 - (£26,400 + £98,500 + £32,000 + £22,500)
= £185,000 - £179,400
= £5,600

(4 marks)

(d) The order received from D L Jensholm is an unexpected order. It can be treated as a special order. The contribution made by the order is very low at £5,600. The contributions made by templates sold to Dave Shepherd's regular customer are considerably higher at £51,300. If all orders contributed as little as £5,600, the business would not make a profit because the overheads would not be covered. However, there are some sound reasons for accepting this special order.

From a financial point of view, at least the order makes a positive contribution. The £5,600 will contribute towards the overheads and the profit for the year, including the order, would rise by £5,600. Also, the business is not working at full capacity. So, by accepting the order the company's resources will be better employed. This will help to improve efficiency. It might also improve staff morale. They may feel more secure if they know that the company is winning new orders. Another reason for accepting the order is that it is providing the company with an exporting opportunity. Although the order from D L Jensholm is not profitable, there may be future orders which do

generate profit. Accepting this order might help to establish the company's name in Norway.

There is one other possible problem. If existing customers find out that products have been sold to others for lower prices this might cause resentment. It might damage the image of the company and lead to lost sales in the future. If they do decide to accept the order, Dave Shepherd Ltd should not broadcast the fact that they are doing work for a lower price. Finally, many businesses faced with this decision are likely to accept the order. It is a positive move.

(14 marks)

(e) Absorption costing is a popular method of costing. Its main principle is that all the overheads or indirect costs are 'absorbed' by cost centres. In other words, all overheads are included when calculating the cost of producing particular items. In this case it would involve calculating exactly how much it would cost to make a template. All costs, including overheads, would be included.

Dave Shepherd Ltd would enjoy a number of benefits if they adopted this method. It ensures that all costs are fully recovered. This means that that Dave Shepherd Ltd will cover all of their costs including overheads. Therefore if the business uses a cost-plus pricing policy, it knows that the prices charged will generate a profit. It is also fair provided overheads are not allocated in an arbitrary way. This is because costs are apportioned to those activities that actually incur them.

Finally, the method conforms to the accounting standard SSAP 9 Stocks and work-in-progress. This states that absorption costing should be used when valuing stocks in the final accounts. This is because absorption costing includes a share of the fixed costs. It therefore recognises these fixed costs in the same period as revenues, and so conforms to the 'matching' principle.

However, absorption costing does have some limitations. The cost information used by Dave Shepherd Ltd might be inaccurate. This is because the figures are generally based on historical data which may not reflect future costs or activity levels. As a result, businesses might underabsorb or overabsorb their overheads and could set prices that are too low or too high. In practice, absorption costing can be complex, time consuming and expensive to gather detailed information from different cost centres. This is particularly the case for small firms that do not employ specialist cost accountants. Finally, some costs are difficult to apportion exactly to a particular cost centre. For example, how can a business apportion electricity costs to different cost centres accurately if there is only one meter? If Dave Shepherd Ltd was seriously considering changing from marginal costing to absorption costing, they would have to evaluate these advantages and disadvantages.

(14 marks)

53 | Investment appraisal

Question 1

(a) The expected net cash flow is the amount of money the business expects to receive each year over the life of an investment project, less the estimated running costs. For example, in this case, Delrose expects to get £6,000 every year for six years if System A is purchased. This is £6,000 is after the running costs have been deducted.

(b) The payback periods for each system are given as follows.
• System A 4 years.
• System B 4 years 6 months.
• System C 3 years.
System C has the shortest payback period. Therefore Delrose would invest in System C.

(c) The payback method is a very simple method of investment appraisal. This is one of its advantages. However, one important reason why Delrose may have used the payback method in this case is because computer systems can become obsolete quite quickly. Computer technology moves very fast indeed and Delrose would be keen to get its money back as soon as possible. This is because Delrose might have to upgrade its computers again quite soon.

Question 2

(a) (i)

Investment project	Profit (£)	Profit pa (£)	ARR
R & D	8,000	1,333.33	13.89%
Marketing campaign	7,000	1,166.66	12.96%
New CNC machinery	4,200	700.00	8.97%

(ii) According to the ARR in the above table, the R & D project should be selected. However, it is only marginally better than the marketing campaign.

(b) The main advantage of the ARR method of investment appraisal to Hastings group is that it shows clearly the profitability of an investment project. For example, it is clear in this case that the R & D project generates the highest return. Also, not only does it allow a range of projects to be compared, the overall rate of return can be compared to other uses for investment funds. For example, if Hastings Group were to place funds in a bank deposit account, the rate of return in 2007 would be about 6%. The returns generated by all three investment projects are greater than this. However, if interest rates increased significantly, Hastings might decide to reconsider their position.

Question 3

(a) See table below.
(b) Machine A. £47,000.
Net present value = £87,000 + £114,000 + £132,000 + £171,000 + £100,000 + £43,000 - £600,000 = £647,000 - £600,000 = £47,000.
Machine B. £112,500.
Net present value = £174,000 + £228,000 + £132,000 + £85,500 + £50,000 + £43,000 - £600,000 = £712,500 - £600,000 = £112,500.
(c) Machine B would be chosen as it has a higher net present value. Both machines have an initial cost of £600,000. But after taking this away the cash flow from machine B is higher.

Case study

(a) Investment appraisal involves a business objectively evaluating an investment project to determine whether or not it is likely to be profitable. Investment appraisal also allows businesses to make comparisons between different investment projects. In this case Chambers plc is comparing two projects (automation and TQM) after eliminating another two using the payback method. There is a number of quantitative investment appraisal methods that a business might use when evaluating projects. However, they all involve comparing the capital cost of each project with the net cash flow.

(4 marks)

(b) The decision to invest by business is the most difficult it has to make because of the risk involved. There is no guarantee that an investment project will generate a profit. If all cost and revenue data upon which a decision would be based was accurate, there would not be such a problem. However, revenue information in particular comes from predictions. It may be based on forecasts of future demand and conditions in the economy. Even costs, which are perhaps easier to predict, can vary. In this case Chambers has to estimate the expected net cash flows of an automation project and the introduction of TQM. This is quite difficult. In the past, the people who ran Chambers plc were risk averse. This means they were reluctant to take the risk and invest. They were apprehensive about whether investment projects would generate a return. They were frightened of losing money. However, the new management team believes that the risk is necessary because the company has fallen behind its competitors.

(6 marks)

		0	1	2	3	4	5	6 £000
Machine A		(600)	100	150	200	300	200	100
		(600)	87	114	132	171	100	43
			(100 x 0.87)	(150 x 0.76)	(200 x 0.66)	(300 x 0.57)	(200 x 0.50)	(100 x 0.43)
Machine B		(600)	200	300	200	150	100	100
		(600)	174	228	132	85.5	50	43
			(200 x 0.87)	(300 x 0.76)	(200 x 0.66)	(150 x 0.57)	(100 x 0.50)	(100 x 0.43)

(c) (i) ARR

	Automation	TQM
		£
Capital cost	5,000,000	4,400,000
Total income	14,200,000	11,400,000
Profit	9,200,000	7,000,000
Profit pa	1,840,000	1,400,000
ARR	36.8%	31.8%

(6 marks)

(ii) NPV

	Automation		TQM	
	£m	£000	£m	£000
Yr 1	2.3 x £0.95 =	2,185	2.1 x £0.95 =	1,995
	2.6 x £0.90 =	2,340	2.1 x £0.90 =	1,890
	2.8 x £0.86 =	2,408	2.3 x £0.86 =	1,978
	3.3 x £0.82 =	2,706	2.4 x £0.82 =	1,968
	3.2 x £0.78 =	2,496	2.5 x £0.78 =	1,950
	PV =	12,135		9,781
Less	Capital cost	5,000		4,400
	NPV =	7,135		5,381

(8 marks)

(d) According to the calculations in (c), the automation appears to be the most favourable investment project. Both the ARR and the NPV are higher for the automation.

(2 marks)

(e) When businesses evaluate investment projects they may look at both quantitative factors and qualitative factors. The quantitative factors relate to costs and predicted net cash flows. In this case, on quantitative grounds, the automation project is likely to be selected. This is because it generates the highest returns according to the ARR and the NPV. However, the directors of Chambers may also consider qualitative factors - these are non-financial considerations. In this case there is a significant qualitative factor to consider. Both investment projects will have an impact on the workforce. If the automation programme is selected around 50 staff are certain to lose their jobs - possibly more. This could have an impact on the morale of the remaining workers. They may feel that in the future their jobs could be threatened as well. They may also resent their colleagues being made redundant. Involuntary redundancies are likely to lead to conflict and disruption. For example there may be strikes.

The introduction of TQM will also affect staff. According to an employee representative, 'The introduction of TQM will create pressure and stress for many of the lads here'...'Some of them just aren't up to it'. This may mean that staff would resist the introduction of TQM. However, faced with the choice between redundancies and retraining in TQM it is likely that the workers would prefer TQM. This means that the directors of Chambers have a difficult choice to make. Do they go for automation and risk industrial conflict, or invest in TQM and try to maintain good relations with workers? Arguably, they would opt for automation. This generates a much better ARR and NPV. So, although the key qualitative factor in this instance is significant, it is not likely to change the minds of the directors. The company is currently making a loss and therefore must improve financial performance. This means that quantitative factors are likely to carry more sway.

(14 marks)

54 | Selecting financial strategies

Question 1

(a) Oceanlinx is floating on AIM to raise £35 million. The money is needed because the company has just signed a commercial agreement to supply electricity generated by wave power off the coast of Cornwall. Oceanlinx plan to build six generators, as well as invest in research and development and hire new staff. The site, called Wave Hub, 10 miles out to sea, was given planning permission last month to begin operating. It is an area of 4km by 2km, in which wave power developers can set up plants and plug into the power grid through an undersea socket. It is expected to be operational in 2009 and will generate enough electricity for 7,500 homes.

(b) One of the advantages of raising money in this way is that very large amounts of money can be raised. By floating on AIM, Oceanlinx hope to raise £35 million. This is a very large amount of money and a flotation may be the only way Oceanlinx can raise such an amount. Another advantage is that the money raised will be permanent capital. It will not have to be repaid. However, there will be a long-term commitment from the company to pay dividends to shareholders. Finally, the flotation will help to raise the profile of the company. There is likely to be a lot of publicity surrounding the flotation - attention in the media for example. People will get to know about the company and this might benefit it in a number of ways. For example, it may be easier to sell the shares.

Question 2

(a) Sometimes established companies have to restructure their finances. This often means raising new finance and changing the emphasis of funding methods. In this case Frank O'Connell has had to restructure the funding of his bakeries. The entire finance of the business was restructured onto a loan with an agreement that the interest rate would be reviewed after 12 months. The existing commercial mortgage and overdraft facility were converted to a new mortgage over a longer term. This released cash back into the business and reduced the monthly repayment. A larger mortgage was possible because some of the property owned by the business was undervalued.

(b) The need for financial restructuring often arises when a company gets into difficulties. For example, a company might be pressured into handing over some of its equity in exchange for debt if it starts to experience trading difficulties. In this case Frank O'Connell's business was having trouble with the bank. The business was constantly exceeding its overdraft limit and cheques were being returned. This is an intolerable position because eventually suppliers would refuse to trade with Frank's business. Fortunately, he was able to solve the problem by restructuring the financing of the business. Also, if the company starts to improve, the interest rate on the loan will be reviewed.

Case study

(a) Ambercom plc appears to have a clear financial objective. It aims to increase shareholder value. This is stated in the first sentence in the company's mission statement - 'Building value for our shareholders is our goal'. Consequently Ambercom will need to increase profits so that higher dividends can be paid to shareholders. This will also help the share price rise, both of which will help to build shareholder value. **(4 marks)**

(b) One part of the financial strategy outlined in the case is to close down the Australian division. This is a downsizing exercise designed to cut costs. The Australian division is currently making a loss. In 2007 the division made a loss of £15.5 million. According to information in the case, there has been a growing resistance to the use of fertilisers and pesticides in Australia. The number of customers in the region

has fallen by 40 per cent in the last three years and there is no reason to believe that the decline is about to halt. Although the division is closing down, the remaining customers in the region will be served by the Indian plant. Although the company is committed to growth, it cannot afford to have a loss-making division in the organisation. Growth can be achieved by expanding activities in the other regions and by developing new products in the R & D centre. **(6 marks)**

(c) Ambercom plc uses profit centres to monitor the performance of each division. There is a number of advantages of this approach. Although it is important to measure the performance of the whole business, it is also helpful to monitor the progress of different divisions. Profit centres can be used to hold individual parts of the business accountable. Without profit centres an inefficient division might not be identified and held accountable for its poor performance. In this case the Australian division is performing badly. The use of profit centres has clearly identified this. To make decisions about different divisions at Ambercom, managers need financial information about each division. Profit centres help provide this information. In this case the financial information from each profit centre has helped the board to decide to close the Australian divisions. Profit centres can help to improve motivation in an organisation. The performance of profit centres may depend on the quality of work done by the people employed in them. It is possible to motivate staff in centres by offering them incentives to achieve goals or targets. For example, managers might be given financial incentives linked to the profit made by each centre. However, in this case the performance of the Australian division appears to have been hit by an external factor. Workers cannot really be blamed for the resistance to pesticides and fertilisers in Australia. **(8 marks)**

(d) (i) A rights issue is a method used by companies to raise finance. It involves selling shares to existing shareholders. New shares are sold at a discount to existing shareholders as an incentive to buy them. In this case, Ambercom hopes to raise £150 million from a rights issue. **(4 marks)**

(ii) The £150 million rights issue planned by Ambercom plc is to meet two key funding obligations. £100 million will be needed to fund the research and development centre. The rest of the money will help meet the costs of closing down the Australian division. For example, the staff will be entitled to redundancy payments. **(4 marks)**

(e) The main financial objective of Ambercom plc is to increase shareholder value. This means that the business must make more profit. The financial strategy outlined in the case comprises three elements. First of all the Australian division is going to be closed down. Unfortunately there has been a growing resistance to the use of fertilisers and pesticides in Australia. The number of customers in the region has fallen by 40 per cent in the last three years and there is no reason to believe that the decline is about to halt. This action should help to increase profits. Without the Australian division, the company would have made an extra £15.5 million profit in 2007. This is how much the Australian division lost. So once the division is closed these losses will not be incurred again and total company profits will rise.

The second element of the financial strategy involves investing £100 million in a new research and development centre. The main purpose of the centre will be to develop more environmentally friendly fertilisers and pesticides. This is a big investment for the company and involves quite a lot of risk. If the R & D centre becomes successful and starts to deliver a stream of new products, the company's future should be secure and profits are likely to rise. However, if the centre fails to deliver it could become a very costly venture leading to future losses.

The third part of the financial strategy involves raising £150 million through a rights issue. The money will be used to fund the new research and development centre and help pay for the closure of the Australian division. This is a good way of raising money for the company. It is permanent capital and does not have to be repaid. It will not burden the company with debt and the company's gearing should fall. This will improve the financial standing of the business. To conclude, the future plight of the company looks to hang on whether the new R & D centre will be successful. If it is, the company is likely to prosper and shareholder value will rise. Therefore the financial objective will be met. However, if it doesn't, the company could seriously struggle. **(10 marks)**

(f) Ambercom plc plans to spend £100 million on a new research centre. The pattern of capital expenditure for a business will often focus on the current needs of the business. The amount of money a business has for capital expenditure is often restricted and there may be multiple demands on the limited amount of money available. Consequently a business has to look at the current needs of a business and favour those which are more urgent. For example, Ambercom may have other investment projects which look attractive. However, the new research centre may represent the greatest need for the company. This may be because there is an urgent need to develop more environmentally friendly fertilisers and pesticides. Inevitably, when faced with a choice between alternative investment projects a business will prefer to invest in the project with the greatest return. Ambercom may have used a quantitative method of investment appraisal to measure the likely return on the R & D centre. A company like Ambercom is not likely to spend £100 million on an investment project without evaluating the possible returns.

Investment in capital expenditure is fraught with risk. This is because the return on an investment project is not certain. It is possible for an investment project to yield a negative return and even endanger the survival of a business. In this case the investment in an R & D centre is very risky. It could be many years before a new, environmentally friendly pesticide is developed. However, in this case the risk may be considered necessary.

The allocation of capital expenditure may be influenced by external factors. In this case this is quite an influential external factor. Ambercom has been forced to close its Australian division due to resistance to its products. There is also a growing trend globally for a more environmentally friendly approach to business. Consequently, Ambercom will come under increasing pressure to develop environmentally friendly pesticides and fertilisers. It could be argued that it is this factor that has had the most influence on the decision to invest in a new R & D centre. Failure to respond to environmental concerns could result in Ambercom losing its market to those companies that do.

(14 marks)

Question 1

(a) (i) and (ii)

	HR Owen		Bpi	
	2008	**2007**	**2008**	**2007**
Current ratio	1.16	0.96	1.76	1.58
Acid test ratio	0.37	0.36	0.89	0.85

(b) (i) According to the calculations in (a) bpi is the most liquid of the two companies. The current ratio in both years for bpi lies in the preferred range of 1.5 to 2. The acid test ratio in both years is just below 1. HR Owen's figures are significantly worse. The current ratios in both years are well below 1.5 and the acid test ratios are well below the preferred target of 1. Between 2007 and 2008 both companies have improved their liquidity position slightly. For example, the current ratios for both companies have increased.

(ii) There may be a plausible reason why HR Owen appears to have a poorer liquidity position than bpi. HR Owen is a specialist car retailer, it sells prestige cars from car showrooms. Consequently its main asset will be stock (the value of cars in the showroom). This would account for the low acid test ratios. It is also possible that HR Owen is paid immediately when a sale is made - it probably does not have to wait for customers to pay. Therefore it does not have to wait for cash. This means they can operate with much lower current and acid test ratios. Bpi is a manufacturer and probably allows its customers trade credit. This means they have to wait for cash and therefore need higher liquidity ratios to be safe.

Question 2

(a) (I)

$$\text{Debt collection period} = \frac{\text{Debtors}}{\text{Turnover}} \times 365$$

$$\text{For 2007 Debt collection period} = \frac{£15,600,000}{£98,433,000} \times 365 = 58 \text{ days}$$

$$\text{For 2008 Debt collection period} = \frac{£11,870}{£102,872,000} \times 365 = 42 \text{ days}$$

(ii)

$$\text{Creditor days} = \frac{\text{Creditors}}{\text{Cost of sales}} \times 365$$

$$\text{For 2007 Creditor days} = \frac{£11,800,000}{£98,433,000} \times 356 = 44 \text{ days}$$

$$\text{For 2008 Creditor days} = \frac{£14,300,000}{£102,872,000} \times 365 = 51 \text{ days}$$

(b) It is likely that the cash flow of Grantham Paints has improved. The measures it took seem to have worked. The extra resources devoted to debt collection seem to have had an impact. The debt collection period has fallen from 58 days to 42 days. This means that the company will get its cash quicker from customers. The new payment terms have also had a positive impact. The credit payment period has risen from 44 days to 51 days. This means that the company can hold on to its cash a little longer before paying suppliers. Both of these changes will help to improve cash flow.

(c) (i)

$$\text{Stock turnover} = \frac{\text{Stocks}}{\text{Cost of sales}} \times 365$$

$$\text{For 2007 Stock turnover} = \frac{£3,467,000}{£56,670,000} \times 365 = 22 \text{ days}$$

$$\text{For 2008 Stock turnover} = \frac{£3,889,000}{£58,981,000} \times 365 = 24 \text{ days}$$

(ii) The stock turnover for Grantham Paints is quite similar for the two years. In 2007 it was 24 days and in 2008 22 days. This is a very slight improvement. By speeding up stock turnover further the business will help to improve cash flow. This is because stock is converted into goods and sold more quickly. To improve stock control Grantham Paints need to operate with less stock. They could adopt JIT manufacturing perhaps or introduce a computerised stock control system.

Question 3

(a) (i) and (ii)

	Alum Resources	GTR plc	Aztec Mining
Dividends per share	6.9p	42.7p	23.9p
Dividend yield	2.3%	3.2%	1.8%

(b) According to the calculations in (a) Najia should invest in GTR plc. This mining company has the highest dividend yield.

(c) The information shown in the table is not really sufficient to help Najia decide in which company to invest. There are only one year's figures. These may not be reflective of the general trend for the company. For example, the 3.2 per cent yield made by GTR plc may be due to exceptional circumstances. Ideally, Najia would need to look at several years' dividend yields for each company. She may also want to use other ratios but cannot do so on the basis of the information shown.

Question 4

(a)

Ratio	2004	2005	2006	2007	2008
EPS	62.5p	69.5p	61p	57.6p	45.2p
P/E ratio	19.7	15.8	16.1	15.3	15.7
Return on equity	10.9%	12.0%	12.0%	11.2%	9.5%

(b) There is some evidence to suggest that Rockhampton's shareholders would be satisfied with the company's five year performance. The earnings per share have dropped from 62.5p to 45.2p. However, the EPS on its own does not say very much about the performance of the company. The P/E ratio, which uses the EPS, says a lot more. The P/E ratio of 15.7 in 2008 means that the market price of the share is 15.7 times higher than its current level of earnings. Assuming that nothing changes, it would take 15.7 years for these shares to earn their current market value. The P/E ratio for Rockhampton Quarries fell over the time period from 19.7 to 15.7. It might be argued that confidence in the company is beginning to wane. However, a P/E ratio of around 15 is generally considered to be positive.

The return on equity over the five year period is fairly solid just above 10%. If the interest rate in the economy is 5%, the return to shareholders is double (although risk has to be taken into account). The only worry is that it fell below 10% in 2008 and the general trend is for a slight decrease over the time period.

To conclude, shareholders are likely to be pleased with the five year performance of the company. It is fairly consistent and both the P/E ratio and returns to equity are at least satisfactory. However, there might be concerns that the company is about to experience a downturn in its fortunes - EPS and the returns to equity both fell in 2008. Finally, it would be useful to look at other shareholders' returns such as dividends per share and dividend yield before making a final judgement.

Case study

(a) Information in the accounts can show how well a business is performing. For example, in this case the accounts show that the profit made by easyJet has increased from £66.2m to £117.8m. However, ratio analysis provides a more rigorous and precise analysis. Financial ratios can be calculated by comparing two figures in the accounts which are related in some way. It may be one number expressed as a percentage of another or simply one number divided by another. For an accounting ratio to be useful the two figures must be connected, eg profit is arguably related to the amount of capital a firm uses. Ratios can be used to analyse profitability, liquidity, solvency, how efficiently the business uses assets and how well shareholders' investments have performed.

(4 marks)

(b) One important ratio for many business stakeholders is the gearing ratio. The gearing ratio can be used to analyse the capital structure of a business. It compares the amount of capital raised from ordinary shareholders with that raised in loans. This is important because the interest on loans is a fixed commitment, whereas the dividends for ordinary shareholders are not. Gearing ratios can assess whether or not a business is burdened by its loans. This is because highly geared companies must still pay their interest even when trading becomes difficult. In this case the gearing ratio for easyJet is 31 per cent. This is below 50 per cent and suggests that the company is

low geared. This means that easyJet is not likely to be burdened by its loans.

(6 marks)

(c)

	2006	2005
Net profit margin	7.3%	4.9%
ROCE	7.3%	5.4%
Current ratio	2.14	2.15
Asset turnover	1.65	1.55

(16 marks)

(d) Information in the case suggests that since easyJet was launched in 1995, it has grown from strength to strength. Much of the evidence provided by the ratios calculated in (c) tend to support this view. The net profit margin, which helps to show how well a business has controlled its costs, has increased between 2005 and 2006. It rose significantly from 4.9 per cent to 7.3 per cent. This is a big improvement and shows that the company has kept a firm control over its costs even though revenue has risen. The ROCE is one of the most important ratios which is used to measure the performance of a business. It is sometimes referred to as the primary ratio. It compares the profit, ie return, made by the business with the amount of money invested, ie its capital. The advantage of this ratio is that it relates profit to the size of the business. The ROCE for easyJet has increased significantly from 5.4 per cent to 7.3 per cent over the two years. This again is a significant improvement. It shows that the business has generated a bigger return in relation to the amount invested in the company. However, some might argue that a 7.3 per cent return is quite modest. This is because capital could be deposited in a bank and earn around 6 per cent in 2006 without risk.

The current ratio shows how much working capital a business has. It is a liquidity ratio. In both 2005 and 2006 the current ratio for easyJet was sound. The current ratio should roughly lie between 1.5 and 2. In this case it is just slightly above 2 in both years. This suggests that easyJet can pay its immediate debts quite comfortably. Finally, the asset turnover for easyJet has also improved. It has risen from 1.55 to 1.65. The asset turnover shows how productively the company is using its assets such as aircraft. The asset turnover varies in different industries. In retailing, where turnover is high and the value of fixed assets is relatively low, the asset turnover can be 3 or more. In contrast, in manufacturing, where there is often heavier investment in fixed assets, the ratio is generally lower. For example, it can be 1 or less. A comparison with another airline would show whether this ratio, and others, are an indication of good performance. However, on the basis of the evidence shown here, easyJet seems to be performing well.

(14 marks)

56 | The value and limitations of ratio analysis

Question 1

(a) (i) Managers at the business manipulated sales by pursuing a strategy which would increase sales disproportionately in the last financial month of the year, April. Bonuses were offered to staff to pursue energetic sales methods during April. Staff, for example, attempted to persuade customers to accept delivery of their cars before the 30 April rather than in early May so that sales were shown in the financial year to the end of April rather than in the following financial year.

(ii) Managers at the business manipulated costs in a number of ways which were designed to cut out unnecessary expense. Staff who left before the end of the year were not replaced so that wages costs were lower. Further, stocks were allowed to run down so that the costs of replacing used stock were not incurred.

(b) Manipulating sales so that orders were taken before the 30 April could have led to falling revenues in the following financial year. Sales that would normally have taken place in May were pulled forward by sales staff into the current financial year. If these sales were not made up in the next financial year then revenue may fall. On the other hand the business may recognise the possible fall in revenue and use promotional strategies to make up for the fall in revenue.

The attempts to manipulate costs may have led to reduced costs for the business in the current financial year. However, the reduced costs led to operating difficulties. For example, waiting times for a service increased on average by a day as the business may have been short staffed due to the failure to replace employees who had left. Services may also have been delayed because parts were not readily available on site and had to be ordered in. If this was the case then in the following financial year the business would have had to replace staff, incurring higher wage costs. It would also have had to replenish stocks that were allowed to run down.

It could be argued that the following year sales may fall, unless steps are taken to prevent this, and costs may rise. So profits in the financial year following may be expected to fall.

Case study

(a) Ratio analysis is used by CNV Plastics to help evaluate the performance of businesses. It has a number of distinct advantages. Ratios are easy to calculate. They are generally one number divided by another, using figures that can be taken directly from the accounts. Most ratios have a consistent formula and only a few (such as gearing) are subject to variation in definition by different users. This simplicity makes ratios easy to understand. For example, a net profit margin of 7 per cent is easily recognisable as being better than one of 4 per cent. Ratio analysis can be carried out very quickly. Once the CNV accounts have been prepared the financial situation of a company can be analysed very quickly indeed.

Ratios are ideal for making comparisons between companies, especially those in the same industry that operate under the same environmental conditions. CNV Plastics may compare its performance with another plastics manufacturer. Interfirm comparisons, comparisons over time and interfirm comparisons over time can all be made using ratio analysis. CNV Plastics might also use ratios to make internal comparisons. For example, it could compare the net profit margins for different products or the ROCE in different divisions. Finally, ratio analysis may be of use to decision makers at CNV Plastics. This is because ratio analysis can help to identify

strengths and weaknesses in the company. For example, if CNV discovers that its gross profit margins are very high but net margins are very low, managers may decide to undertake a cost minimisation strategy. **(8 marks)**

(b) Accounts must represent a 'true and fair record' of the financial affairs of a business. Legislation and financial reporting standards place limits on the different ways in which a business can present accounts. These limits are designed to prevent fraud and misrepresentation in the compilation and presentation of accounts. However, businesses can manipulate their accounts legally to present different financial pictures. This is known as window dressing. There is a number of ways in which accounts can be window dressed. One is to reduce profit by writing off some bad debts. **(4 marks)**

(c) Businesses may want to window dress their accounts for a variety of reasons. For example, managers of companies might want to put as good a financial picture forward as possible for shareholders and potential shareholders. Good financial results will attract praise and perhaps rewards. They might also prevent criticism from shareholders and the financial press. However, in this case CNV Plastics wants to attract some new funding. It wants to borrow £10 million. The chances of attracting new finance will be improved if the company looks good. However, if banks and other money lenders discover that the accounts have been window dressed, the credibility and reputation of the company could be damaged. Their credit rating might be reduced significantly. This could have a long term effect on the company. It may never be able to raise finance again. **(6 marks)**

(d) (i) One way in which CNV Plastics proposes to window dress the accounts is to change the way it calculates depreciation. By changing the method of calculation the net profit for the year will rise from £6 million to £8 million. This will affect both the net profit margin and the ROCE. These two ratios both use net profit in their calculation. When the net profit rises from £6 million to £8 million both the net profit margin and the ROCE will rise. This will suggest that the company has performed better than it really has. For example, with the higher profit the net margin has more than doubled from 2.4 per cent in 2007 to 5.4 per cent in 2008. **(8 marks)**

(ii) CNV's financial director also suggested selling the factory and leasing it back. Not only would this improve the performance of the company but it would also help to boost working capital since the company would receive some cash when selling it. The sale of the factory would increase the amount of cash held by CNV Plastics. This would increase the size of current assets which would then have an impact on the current ratio. The current ratio would increase with more current assets. Table 1 shows that the current ratio has improved from 1.1 in 2007 to 1.6 in 2008. This is quite a significant improvement and brings the current ratio into the 'ideal' range of 1.5 to 2.

Selling the factory and leasing it back would not affect the gearing ratio. This is because the gearing ratio is to do with the amount of loan capital and share capital the company has. The sale of the factory will not affect the amount of debt or the amount of share capital the company has. Although the gearing ratio has increased slightly from 41 per cent to 42 per cent over the two years, this has nothing to do with the sale of the factory. **(8 marks)**

(e) The sale of the factory will clearly boost working capital and improve the current ratio in the short term. This will benefit the company by providing some much needed cash and making it more attractive to money lenders. However, in the long term leasing a factory can be expensive. CNV Plastics will have to pay leasing charges indefinitely. This cost will reduce the profitability of the company every year. Consequently in the long term profits will be lower. CNV Plastics will also lose a valuable fixed asset on the balance sheet. In the future the company will have less collateral to use as security when borrowing money. This could be a problem. **(8 marks)**

57 | Constructing accounts

Question 1

Note: in the first impression of the 4th edition there is a misprint. This has been corrected in reprints. The figure for retained profit in 2007 should be £422,000 not £772,000.

(a)

Munro & Thompson Ltd
Balance sheet as at 31.12.08

	2008 £000s	2007 £000s
Fixed assets		
Equipment and machinery	4,450	3,600
Vehicles	120	140
	4,570	3,740
Current assets		
Stock & work-in-progress	145	122
Debtors	85	80
Cash at bank	30	20
	260	222
Creditors: amounts falling due in one year		
Trade creditors	87	65
Accruals	23	25
Taxation	50	40
	160	130
Net current assets	100	92
Creditors: amounts falling due after one year		
Mortgage	(200)	(300)
Other long term liabilities	(340)	(280)
Net assets	4,130	3,252
Capital and reserves		
Share capital	2,500	2,500
Other reserves	420	330
Retained profit	1,210	422
	4,130	3,252

(b) The financial position of the business appears to have improved over the two years. There are two key pieces of evidence which supports this view. The value of the company, according to the value of net assets, has increased from £3,552,000 to £4,130,000. This means that the company is worth more. Also, the value of retained profit rose from £422,000 to £1,210,000. This means that the company has made at least £788,000 (£1,210,000 - £422,000) profit in 2008. It may be more than this if dividends were paid to shareholders. Finally, the company has been able to invest in new equipment and machinery and long-term debt has been reduced slightly from £580,000 to £540,000.

Question 2

(a)

Maynard Ltd
Profit and loss account 31.3.08

	2008 £000s	2007 £000s
Turnover	7,800	5,700
Cost of sales	3,780	2,100
Gross profit	4,020	3,600
Admin expenses	1,560	1,800
Operating profit	2,460	1,800
Net interest payable	70	45
Profit before tax	2,390	1,755
Taxation	580	450
Profit after tax	1,810	1,305
Dividends	600	500
Retained profit	1,210	805

(b) The profit and loss account shows that the financial performance of Maynard has improved over the two year period. Sales revenue, profit and dividends have all increased. Turnover has risen from £5,700,000 to £7,800,000 - an increase of 36.8 per cent. Profit after tax has increased by the slightly higher amount of 38.7 per cent. Dividends have increased by 20 per cent from £500,000 to £600,000. The company's shareholders should be very pleased with this performance.

Case study

(a)

```
              Cutpricetours.com
          Balance sheet as at 31.3.08
```

	2008 £m	2007 £m
Fixed assets		
Computer equipment	14.0	16.0
Other fixed assets	5.3	4.2
	19.3	20.2
Current assets		
Stocks	2.11	1.95
Debtors and prepayments	4.33	3.87
Cash at bank	12.9	18.7
	19.34	24.52
Creditors: amounts falling due in one year		
Trade creditors	9.44	8.49
Other current liabilities	4.27	3.91
Taxation	2.55	1.76
	16.26	14.16
Net current assets	3.08	10.36
Creditors: amounts falling due after one year		
Bank loan	(8.5)	(4.5)
Other long term liabilities	(1.3)	(1.1)
	(9.8)	(5.6)
Net assets	12.58	24.96
Capital and reserves		
Share capital	5.0	5.0
Other reserves	3.1	6.0
Retained profit	4.48	13.96
	12.58	24.96

(18 marks)

(b) The balance sheet for Cutpricetours.com shows some very significant changes over the two years. The value of the company has dropped sharply from £24.96m to £12.58m. The main reason for this is the fall in retained profit. The company obviously made a loss in 2008. This was probably due to huge expenditure on advertising (around £10m). This expenditure was funded partly internally and partly from a bank loan. The balance sheet shows this clearly. The cash balance at the bank has fallen by around £6 million and the amount owed to the bank (long term loans) has increased by £4 million. As a result of this strategy the value of working capital has also fallen sharply by around £7 million. The company is generally in worse shape in 2008 than in 2007. However, it must be hoping that the huge investment in advertising will eventually pay off in the future when the company becomes recognised nationally. However, this will not be known for a few years. Finally, most other changes in the balance sheet are not significant. There has been a small investment in other fixed assets and the company has reduced other reserves during the year.

(10 marks)

(c)

```
              Cutpricetours.com
          Balance sheet as at 31.3.08
```

	2008 £m
Fixed assets	
Computer equipment	15.0
Other fixed assets	5.3
	20.3
Current assets	
Stocks	2.11
Debtors and prepayments	3.53
Cash at bank	12.7
	18.34
Creditors: amounts falling due in one year	
Trade creditors	10.44
Other current liabilities	4.27
Taxation	2.55
	17.26
Net current assets	1.08
Creditors: amounts falling due after one year	
Bank loan	7.5
Other long term liabilities	1.3
	8.8
Net assets	12.58
Capital and reserves	
Share capital	5.0
Other reserves	3.1
Retained profit	4.48
	12.58

(12 marks)

58 | The valuation of businesses

Question 1

(a) Market capitalisation = Share price × Number of shares

£7,4218m = 783p × Number of shares

$$\frac{£7,418m}{783p} = \text{Number of shares}$$

9,473,818,600 = Number of shares

Therefore the value of the S & N if the offer was accepted is given by:

Market capitalisation = 800p × 9,473,818,600

= £7,579 million

(b) One of the main reasons why the valuation of a company is necessary is if one company wishes to takeover another. In this case Carlsberg and Heineken want to takeover S & N. For the takeover to occur the shareholders have to accept an offer from the buyers. In this case, three months of negotiations took place before the directors of S & N recommended that an 800p a share offer should be accepted. The 800p a share offer values S & N at £7,579 million. This must have been the value agreed between the negotiators representing S & N and the buyers. This valuation would reflect the value of all the assets owned by S & N. Once this valuation was agreed it could be tabled to the S & N shareholders.

(c) After S & N recommended to shareholders to accept the 800p a share offer, the company warned that, after three months of negotiations, this may not be the end of the takeover battle. John Dunsmore, chief executive of S & N, said: 'We've retained our bid defence strategy intact'. S & N believes that the recent publication of its profit growth forecasts for Baltic Beverages Holding, its Russian joint venture with Carlsberg, may tempt other brewers to make rival offers. If other brewers do enter the bidding process the value of S & N is likely to rise. This is because rival bidders will have to offer more than the 800p a share offer. If a bidding war were to break out, where two or more brewers want to buy S & N, the value of the company could rise significantly.

Case study

(a) The value of Telecity fell sharply from around £1 billion, when it was first floated during the dot.com boom, to just £58 million in 2005. The main reason for this was because business dried up. Demand for its services fell and therefore Telecity struggled to generate sales and profit. However, it might also be argued that the company was overvalued during the dot.com boom. This was the case with many dot.com companies during the boom. Share prices in such companies went up sharply, driven mainly by exuberance and 'blind faith'. Like many companies, Telecity's share price fell when it was realised that sales and profits were not going to live up to expectations.

(4 marks)

(b) One of the reasons why a company valuation is necessary is to prepare for a flotation. Before a company can be floated on the stock exchange, the number of shares to be issued and the share price at flotation have to be determined. The value of the company will influence the share price. Obviously, if the company is worth a lot of money the share price will be higher. In this case the share price at flotation was set at 220p. This was based on a company valuation of £436 million.

(4 marks)

(c) (i) When Telecity was floated in October 2007 its market capitalisation was £436 million. However, in January 2008 the share price had risen to 251p. At this time the number of shares issued by Telecity was 198.092 million, therefore the market capitalisation was £497.211 million (251p × 198.092 million). This represents an increase in value of around £61 million.

(6 marks)

(ii) The calculations in (i) show a significant increase in the value of Telecity. An increase in value of £61 million represents a 14 per cent increase in around one year. This suggests that the shares are in demand because investors feel that the future of the company is bright. There is some information in the case which supports this view. For the whole of 2006, Telecity had annual underlying earnings of £13.2m. In the first half of this year, it had already made £10.3m on sales of £46.1m. Analysts say it should be able to hit earnings of £34m next year. The data hosting market has been taking off in recent years as the rapid take-up of broadband Internet access has boosted web usage among consumers, and increased regulation means companies have to retain their data for longer. This is all good news for Telecity and helps to explain why the market capitalisation of the company has increased.

(6 marks)

(d) (i) The value of net assets is given by:

Net assets = Total assets - Total liabilities
= (£149,887,000 + £35,055,000) + (£37,467,000 + £64,765,000)
= £184,942,000 - £102,232,000
= £82,701,000.

(4 marks)

(ii) One way of valuing a company is to look at the size of net assets. In this case the value of net assets is very different from the value of market capitalisation. Indeed the difference is enormous. Telecity's market capitalisation at the time of flotation was £436 million. One year before this the value of net assets was only £82.7 million. There is a difference of £353.3 million. This highlights some of the difficulties in valuing a business. When calculating the market capitalisation of a business the current share price is used. Sometimes the share price does not reflect accurately the performance of the business. Share prices can be influenced by external factors, such as interest rates and the actions of speculators. Also, the share price of a particular company may be a lot lower than one would expect because the company is 'out of favour' with the City. If share prices do not reflect the performance of the business the valuation will be inaccurate. For example, in the winter of 2007/08 share prices fell very sharply indeed. This was caused by the so called 'credit crunch' and other external factors and suggests that the 251p share price of Telecity underestimates the value of the company if using market capitalisation. This would make the difference between net assets and market capitalisation even bigger.

When using net assets to value a company, the true value of some assets may not appear on the balance sheet. These are intangible assets such as goodwill, brand names and copyrights. Therefore, if excluded, the value of the company would be understated. Many accountants choose not to include the value of intangible assets because they are difficult to value. Also, the value of intangible assets can change quite sharply and suddenly. In this case, Telecity may have some valuable intangible assets such as goodwill. For example, it has some very high profile customers such as the BBC, Sony and AOL. This would suggest that future income streams are fairly sound. It is likely in this case that the value of net assets is significantly understated.

Finally, the comparison made here between the market capitalisation and the value of net assets is not a good one. This is because the information being compared comes from two different time periods. The net assets are valued on 31.12.06 whilst the market capitalisation is stated for October 2007. There is 10 months difference between the figures. Consequently, it is not possible to draw meaningful conclusions. However, it is likely that the market capitalisation more accurately reflects the value of Telecity in 2007.

(16 marks)

Question 1

(a) The business sells into regional markets. The chart shows that it has a Marketing Manager for the North West region, the North East region and the Midlands region.

(b) The chain of command at a business shows the path through which orders are passed down the hierarchy. In the engineering company the decision about overall marketing strategy, for example, would be passed from the Chief Executive to the Marketing Director. This would then be passed down to the National Marketing Manager who would convey elements of this to his or her Regional Managers. The Regional Managers would then given instructions on how the strategy was to be carried out to Sales Representatives in the region.

(c) The span of control is the number of people for whom a manager or other employee is responsible. The span of control of the National Marketing Manager is three. He or she is responsible for the three Regional Marketing Managers.

(d) The National Marketing Manager is immediately subordinate to the Director of Marketing.

(e) Reducing the sales representatives from five to three could have certain effects on the Marketing Managers. On the one hand there would be fewer subordinates. This might make the co-ordination role of the Marketing Managers easier. On the other hand, if there are fewer Sales Representatives, the Marketing Managers may have to take on some of their responsibilities, which may increase their workloads.

Question 2

(a) (i) There are numerous possible effects on employees at BP if the changes are implemented. First, there would be substantially fewer employees required once the restructuring had been undertaken. In addition the company suggested that it is keen to listen more acutely to what front line employees have to say and make them more accountable. This suggests that perhaps employees may be delegated more responsibilities and empowered to undertake these responsibilities. There is also a suggestion that employees will need to be more flexible and be able to work in multi-skilled teams that focus on either production or exploration.

(ii) Changes are also likely to affect management. There will be fewer levels of management, suggesting that the company will be delayering, with shorter chains of command and a wider span of control. This suggests that managers will need to develop leadership skills that will lead to employee empowerment, including providing appropriate support and resources, developing improved planning and communication of what is required, giving employees authority and responsibility and allowing participation. In addition, they are likely to have to manage and co-ordinate specialist teams.

(iii) For clients, the changes are likely to mean more appropriate and quicker response from specialist teams to any particular enquires or support requirements. This is likely to lead to clients becoming more satisfied with services provided, which will result in repeat custom and enhanced reputation in the market.

(b) BP could experience considerable resistance from managers and employees. For both managers and employees there is every likelihood that some may be made redundant through the restructuring. Managers and employees will also need to develop new skills to work in new ways that may provoke anxiety and fear. This anxiety and fear will also affect morale in the short and medium term, which can be demotivating.

Question 3

(a) The leisure company wants the Manchester Film Association to develop an innovative mult-imedia training package. There is a number of staff in the business who each can bring specialist skills to the project. Examining the different forms of organisational structures there is evidence to suggest that certain forms may be better than others.

The hierarchical, bureaucratic or pyramid structure is not suitable as this tends to suit medium sized and large business where specialist functions can developed to respond to standard business activity. However, the leisure business has a particular project that needs developing. The independence structure is again unlikely to be suitable as this would rely on particular individuals undertaking the whole task and this would not be possible for Manchester Film Association as no one member of staff would have the skills to complete the project independently.

The entrepreneurial structure could work in this situation. Mike would be the decision maker and he would delegate particular tasks to Lisa and Shoaib. However, this would put a large onus of responsibility on Mike and given his lack of work experience this may not be appropriate. In addition, there would be little opportunity for sharing and pooling ideas.

The matrix form perhaps might be the most suitable as it would allow Lisa and Shoaib to work together as a specialist team with Mike to develop an appropriate package that would meet the requirements of the leisure business more fully.

Question 4

(a) The business has grown, taken on more designers, a new salesperson and also expanded into card production and supply. Clearly if all these new people work through Wesley there may come a point when the business becomes inefficient as too much of a load is placed on him to make decisions. For example, because communications and decisions about developments go through Wesley, designers may not be as responsive as the salesperson requires for new customers. This may result in potential lost markets and sales. Lead times for production and supply may alter because of unforeseen difficulties which may not be communicated to designers effectively via Wesley, thereby creating possible time lapses. Also selling designs in the USA may present new challenges to a business that was not familiar with this market previously. If Wesley takes responsibility for this, there will be a great deal of extra work. Alternatively he may wish to delegate to another person. Furthermore, the acquisition of a small printing business will require co-ordination between the design team and the manufacturer.

Because of these problems it could be argued that Wesley might reorganise the business into a more traditional bureaucratic structure, with department managers in sales, design, production and distribution meeting on a regular basis in order to deal with day to day business decisions. Clear responsibilities and clear communication lines could be developed via an organisational chart and new management styles would need to be created. Wesley may at times also use a matrix structure for the organisation so that teams of managers and designers work on a particular new project and there is a clear recognition about what needs to be done, and when. He could use this system for new projects and new customers and at the same time hold on to a more traditional approach for regular on-going custom. It is unlikely that he would use an independence structure as this would give power to individuals to make decisions without consultation. This could result in chaos as designers, the salesperson and the production and supply team all did their own thing, without communication or liaison.

Case study

(a) (i) A business hierarchy shows the vertical structure and organisation of a business. A business hierarchy has different levels, with owners, senior employees or directors at the top and manual, administrative staff or assistants at the bottom. The hierarchy also shows which employees have authority over employees below them in the hierarchy, their subordinates.

(3 marks)

(ii) A department is a part of an organisation which contains a group of people who do similar jobs. Many larger businesses are divided into departments, such as the marketing department, the human resources department, the accounting department or the production department. The employees in each department will have similar skills and knowledge. For example, people in the accounting department will have the skills to produce the accounts of the business, such as the profit and loss account, the balance sheet, cash flow forecasts and budgets. The employees in a snow safety department will have the skills to ensure skiers and members of the public are safe in snow conditions.

(3 marks)

(b) (i) Figure 4 shows the hierarchy of the Snow Safety Department. A span of control in a hierarchy shows the number of workers who report directly to a superior. This is the person directly above them in the hierarchy. The Snow Safety manager in Figure 4 has a span of control of 3 employees. They are the 3 Snow Safety Supervisors.

(3 marks)

(ii) Delegation is the passing down of authority in a hierarchy. Authority will be passed from a superior to a subordinate. The subordinate will then have the authority to make decisions or carry out a task. The Patrol Leader, one of the 3 Snow Safety Supervisors, could delegate authority to an immediate subordinate, such as one of the 4 Senior Avalanche Patrollers. However, a task may be delegated even further down the hierarchy, for example, to one of the 13 Patrollers.

(3 marks)

(c) Before the change in organisational structure in the 1980s, the avalanche control operation at Lake Louise Ski Area was organised into three separate departments. They were the Ski Patrol, Avalanche Crew and Trail Crew. Each department was responsible for a particular aspect of mountain safety. For example, the Ski Patrol looked after accidents to skiers, the Avalanche Crew monitored and controlled avalanches and the Trail Crew maintained the slopes. A problem that can exist with different departments is that, unless their areas of operation are clearly outlined, they can sometimes carry out the same task. This can lead to duplicated operations, the wrong department carrying out a particular operation or even conflict between departments. This occurred at the resort, as for example, when the Trail Crew, arriving first at an accident, carried out the job of the Ski Patrol. Many different departments can also be expensive

for an organisation. And each will have its own hierarchy. This makes decision making and communication difficult. For these reasons the operations were reorganised in the 1990s into one Snow Safety Department. This seemed to make sense. Departments are made up of people who carry out similar tasks and have similar skills. Staff numbers were reduced from 40 to 25 as there was clearly a duplication of tasks within each department. The new single department had a clear hierarchy of authority, with a Snow Safety Manager in charge who was answerable to the Ski Resort Area Manager. Below the Manager were Supervisors, Senior Avalanche Patrollers, Senior Patrollers and Patrollers. Each layer of the hierarchy had its own responsibilities. This single hierarchy would have prevented duplication of operations and meant that employees had a clear idea of their responsibilities and to whom they should report as their superiors. Superiors would also have a clear indication of subordinates and to whom they could delegate authority if necessary.

(8 marks)

(d) There are likely to be certain benefits in delegating authority and responsibility down the hierarchy. A major benefit is greater motivation. Delegation of decision making can motivate employees to work harder. They feel empowered to take decisions where they may be best suited. They feel as if their views are valued by superiors in the organisation. Further, in the situations faced by the snow safety team making decisions immediately could be vital to protect the safety of people. Giving subordinates the power to make decisions on the spot in an avalanche situation could save lives.

On the other hand delegating authority and responsibility could also be a problem. It is vital that people who make decisions have the right skills. Delegating decision making to patrollers without the skills or experience to make decisions could lead to difficulties and at worst accidents in such life-threatening situations. Delegating too much decision making could also lead to a lack of a co-ordinated and consistent strategy of the business. It may mean that, in the same situation, two different decisions are made.

In conclusion, it could be argued that given the difficult situations faced by the snow patrol, it is important that too much authority is not delegated. It may be important for immediate decisions to be made, but they could be made in communication with others if possible. Any decision making must be carefully considered and evaluated.

(10 marks)

60 | Business organisation

Question 1

(a) Wycombe Holdings is organised according to function. This is where a business divides its activities into a number of sections or departments according to the operation undertaken. In this case the business is first divided into three key functional areas. These include production, finance and marketing. However, there are further functional divisions. For example, the production department is made up of three other sections. These include design, manufacturing and finishing and packaging. Organising a business in this way means that each section or department can focus on just one specific business area. Specialisation will help the department to improve efficiency and become expert in that single function. For example, specialist staff can be employed who are likely to have superior knowledge and capabilities to general workers or non-specialists. This method of organisation can also improve accountability in the business. For example, each department is likely to have a manager who will be responsible for allocating resources, recruiting and leading staff and achieving departmental goals. In this case the design manager is likely to be accountable to the production manager. This puts pressure on the departmental manager to ensure that the department performs effectively. This method of organisation also makes it easier for individual members of staff to understand their role and position in the business structure. For example, staff in the Wycombe Holdings accounts department are likely to be trained in this department, will be familiar with their superiors and will know where to seek help and support. **(10 marks)**

Question 2

(a) Evidence in the case suggests that Unilever may use two methods of organisation. One method used is organisation by product or activity. The company produces a wide range of different food and home and personal care products. Examples of the different products produced by Unilever include food products such as meal replacements, ice cream, tea, spreads and other products such as deodorants, skin and hair products. It is also possible that Unilever is organised according to geographical area. Figure 2 shows that sales of Unilever's products are divided into three categories - Americas, Europe and Asia/Africa. **(6 marks)**

(b) One of the advantages to Unilever of organising the business according to product or activity is that focus is improved. If each section concentrates on the delivery of one specific product the needs of customers may be more effectively satisfied. This method of organisation also allows each division to operate as a profit centre. This will help the business to monitor the performance of each product group. Organisation by product may also encourage competition between departments. This could improve the overall performance of the business. It is also possible that co-operation in the business might improve. Because each division is pursuing the same goal, eg profit, it may be possible to share resources and expertise. For example, Unilever might use the same distribution system to deliver all of its products.

One of the advantages of organising a business by area is that local needs can be more effectively satisfied. This is particularly the case when companies sell in different global markets. For example, the needs of Unilever's European customers may differ from those of the Americas. Also, operating on a regional basis should help to improve communications. For example, one of Unilever's European managers may be more able to inform European customers of new product lines than general managers. Finally, it may be possible to encourage healthy competition between different areas in the company. For example, prizes may be awarded to those areas that provide the best customer service.

It could be argued that organising the business in two different ways might also benefit the organisation. For example, not only might a European manager be able to inform European customers about product lines, but a specialist manager in the area of personal care products might be able to provide more detailed information. Another benefit is that costs and profit centres might be more accurately targeted and so costs can be controlled more effectively. **(14 marks)**

Case study

(a) Organisation by function is one of the most common methods of organising a business. Ernie Anderson organised StarCars according to business function. StarCars had four functional areas - bookings and administration, car maintenance and preparation, finance and accounts and marketing and development. Organising the business in this way allows each functional area to specialise in one specific business activity. Specialisation will help the department to improve efficiency and become expert in that single function. For example, staff working on bookings and administration will, after time, develop the most efficient way to complete tasks. It is also possible to employ specialist staff when this method of organisation is used. For example, StarCars employed a car mechanic to take responsibility for the preparation and maintenance of the cars in the business. Finally, when the business was first set up other methods of organisation may not have been appropriate. For example, Geographical organisation would not have been appropriate because originally there was only one centre. **(6 marks)**

(b)

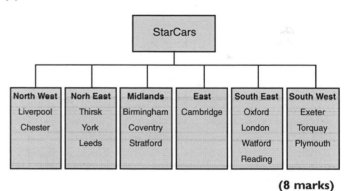

(8 marks)

(c) Some businesses organise their operations according to the different products they make. This means that each section focuses on the production of one specific product in the company's range. However, it is unlikely that StarCars would adopt this method. Dividing a business according to the different products is most suitable for companies that produce a wide range of different products. StarCars offers a single service. It provides a car hire service which is almost exactly the same in all branches. Consequently, there is no opportunity to divide the business according to different products. **(6 marks)**

(d) The reorganisation of StarCars is likely to improve accountability. When the company was organised according to function, evidence suggested that there was no real incentive for each centre to maximise performance. It could be argued that each centre lacked a leader. This was because Ernie was the only leader in the company and as the business expanded he was not really able to motivate each individual centre. Ernie was occupied with the development of the business and did not really have the time to ensure that each individual centre maximised its financial performance. There was a lack of accountability because employees at each centre did not really have any immediate supervisor or manager. However, after the reorganisation Ernie appointed six regional managers. Each manager was required to visit the centres regularly. For example, the manager in charge of the North Eastern region would have to visit all three centres in York, Thirsk and Leeds every day to ensure that everything was running smoothly. Also, staff at each centre would now have a line manager. All staff in the organisation would be accountable to a regional manager. Finally, the new regional managers were also under pressure to perform. A significant fraction of their earnings was to be related to capacity utilisation. If cars were hired out 80% of the time regional managers got a £10,000 bonus. This bonus increased by a further £17,000 if 95% of the cars were hired out. Such incentive schemes help to improve accountability because unless the managers perform their own welfare is affected. **(12 marks)**

(e) One of the reasons why StarCars was reorganised was to overcome some of the problems it was experiencing. For example, there were communication difficulties. Staff in many centres found it difficult to sort out wage queries with the head office at Oxford. Also, when a centre had a problem, such as a customer dispute, it was difficult to settle because no-one seemed to have any authority. This was because Ernie, who made all the key decisions, was often unavailable. After reorganisation communications should improve. This is because regional managers would be empowered to make decisions and resolve problems. Regional managers could be contacted immediately and would also be close at hand to sort out any difficulties that needed their attendance.

Another problem that StarCars had was maintaining the cars all over the country. The mechanic was overworked and not able to keep up with the workload due to the amount of travelling between centres. After reorganisation the maintenance of the cars was outsourced. This possibly meant that cars at the hire centre were maintained by local mechanics or garages. However, reorganisation meant that StarCars no longer had to worry about the responsibility of maintaining cars. Staff could focus on the provision of good quality customer service.

A further problem that StarCars had was a lack of leadership and motivation amongst staff at the centres. Because of the geographical distance between centres staff often felt isolated. Indeed, staff turnover at centres away from the South East had risen. After reorganisation staff should be better motivated. This is because they will enjoy direct leadership from the regional managers. They will get the opportunity to develop a proper working relationship with their manager and know who to go to when support or guidance is needed. The regional manager will visit each centre at least every day. Motivation might have been further improved if Ernie had recruited the new regional managers from existing staff. However, there is no information in the case to suggest that this has happened.

Finally, accountability is also likely to improve after reorganisation. Ernie was worried about accountability. Even though he trusted his staff he thought that there was a lack of incentive to perform well. The appointment of regional managers, whose salaries are linked to business performance, should help address this problem.

To conclude, there seems to be a number of strong reasons to suggest that the new organisational structure will help StarCars to overcome the problems it was experiencing. Communication in the business should improve, motivation and accountability should improve and the problem of the overworked mechanic will be eliminated. Arguably, the reorganisation will work better if some of the existing staff are given the opportunity to take up the positions of regional managers. **(18 marks)**

Question 1

(a) Productivity is being measured in the NHS by the labour productivity index. The index measures the value of output per trust employee. This is the worth of the service provided by each NHS trust employee. It is measured by multiplying each activity by its average cost, adding them together, and dividing this value by the total number of employees in the trust.

(b) Measuring employee productivity can benefit a business in many ways. In this case it could also be argued to benefit an organisation such as an NHS trust. It allows the organisation to evaluate how well employees are performing and perhaps the level of service provided to patients. This can be useful for comparisons. For example, a trust can see whether the productivity of employees has increased or decreased over time. It also allows trusts to benchmark themselves against other trusts. This comparison might indicate whether improvements to practices are required. Or it could help a trust to identify where training for staff might be needed.

(c) There are obvious benefits to NHS trusts in measuring employee productivity. It allows comparisons over time and between operations, which can help to identify problems or where a trust's employees are performing well. However, as the data indicate, such comparisons can be problematic. The index is distorted as certain important activities are excluded and subcontracted work is not included, much of which is done by NHS trusts. This might not be too great a problem if like for like comparisons are made. However, it could give a lower overall figure which needs to be interpreted carefully. Further, the amount of effort needed is different in different trusts. This could give a distorted figure. So it could be suggested that whilst NHS trusts will need some measure of employee productivity, the results must be treated with caution and evaluated in the light of the actual operations of each trust.

Question 2

(a) Royal Mail may measure absenteeism rates for a number of reasons. The absenteeism rate can be calculated by the number of staff absent as a proportion of the number of staff employed or alternatively as the number of days lost through staff absences as a proportion of the total time that should have been worked. Royal Mail will want to know the extent of absenteeism as there will be costs for the business. These may be the financial costs of sick pay, payments to temporary staff or overtime payments to existing staff. There will also be costs associated with disruption to work, possible delays in delivery of mail and the potential of lost mail if new staff are unaccustomed to new systems of work. Further, absenteeism can be demotivating to existing staff who may themselves then take time off. All of these factors are likely to result in a reduced quality of service provided by Royal Mail and so the measurement of absenteeism rates is vital if the business is to ensure the standard of its service.

(b) (i) Royal Mail may benefit from the scheme as it may help to reduce absenteeism rates. This may prevent some or all of the difficulties explained above, helping Royal Mail to provide a more efficient operation. Having 1,000 more people every day as a result of the scheme will help Royal Mail to provide more efficient services which will satisfy customers. The scheme will have costs associated with it. These have been estimated at £1.9m before discounts. However, Royal Mail may also feel that it is a relatively low cost method of motivating staff to attend work. The cost may be relatively less than a large pay increase to all employees, for example.

(ii) From the employees' point of view they will benefit from the rewards of the draw such as a Ford car or holiday vouchers. More than half of the 170,000 employees at Royal Mail and Parcelforce Worldwide qualified to be entered for the draw. Employees may be more motivated, feeling that they have a chance of winning the draw.

However, it is suggested that the scheme may be putting pressure on employees to turn up for work when they are genuinely ill. Workers may attempt to work in order to qualify for entry to the draw even if they are genuinely sick. This could not only affect their performance at work but also their health in the long run.

(c) The Communication Workers Union has argued that the fall in absenteeism was more a result of better pay and conditions than the incentive scheme. It could be argued that the scheme could be operating on a scientific management principle. Employees are rewarded for attending work. They are punished in the sense that non attendance means that they do not qualify for the draw and do not have a chance of winning the prize. Attendance is also closely monitored, which is a feature of this approach, holding that workers need to be controlled and checked to make sure they are doing their jobs. The union however is suggesting that better pay overall is a more motivating factor, and also that employees react better to improvements in their work conditions. This view might take into account that employees are motivated by other factors such as the possibility of flexible work conditions so they can achieve a better work/life balance. Therefore, it could be argued that improving pay and conditions over the long term is likely to be a more motivating factor and lead to falls in absenteeism. The scheme introduced by Royal Mail may work for a short period but if many workers do not see any benefit it is likely to have less effect on absenteeism rates the longer it continues.

Case study

(a) There is a number of reasons why supermarkets may want to reduce absenteeism and labour turnover. Absenteeism means that staff are missing from work, taking days off due to illness or accidents. The work of these employees may not be carried out if they are missing. Other workers may have to complete their work, reducing the amount of work they themselves are doing or adding to their work load. The other workers may not be as productive as the absent worker. Disruption can be caused to the operations of a business if staff are absent. For example, orders may not be placed which could affect other areas of operations. Temporary staff may need to be hired to fill in which can be expensive. The business would also have to pay sick pay to staff. There may be demotivating effects amongst staff if many people are absent and they may resent having to cover work. All of these effects can lead to a fall in productivity for a supermarket, with possible loss of sales or increased costs, which can reduce profit. It is estimated that it costs UK businesses £11 billion a year as 116 million working days are lost. High labour turnover can also be a problem for a supermarket. A high labour turnover measure means that staff are leaving a business more regularly. There will be costs associated with new staff. These will include recruitment costs such as advertisements and interview costs. New staff will need to be trained which will also be a cost. Other staff may need to take time off from work to train the new recruits, affecting their own work. It will take time for new staff to learn their roles and they might make mistakes, affecting productivity and potentially disrupting other staff. High turnover might also affect morale of staff and be demotivating. If employees are constantly leaving this can affect staff morale. Employees may wonder what these reasons are for the high staff turnover and question whether they should be looking for other jobs. **(8 marks)**

(b) Certain factors may affect absenteeism and labour turnover at supermarkets. Health and safety is one important factor. If employees work in a safe environment, they are likely to take fewer days off work through sickness and illness. Also, a safe work environment might motivate staff, as this is one feature of Maslow's hierarchy of needs that employees want to achieve. Or at least it could prevent dissatisfaction as work conditions are a hygiene factor in Herzberg's two factor theory. One important aspect of the health and safety of workers at supermarkets is stress. The Health and Safety Executive states that 13 million days are lost a year from stress related problems at work. This type of absence is on the increase. Stress in supermarkets may result from pressure to achieve targets for managers or to complete tasks before a supermarket opens, such as baking bread. Or it might result from the monotony of carrying out basic tasks continually, such as stacking shelves. Businesses must consider how to address both health and safety issues and stress. This might involve constant inspection to ensure that safety standards are maintained. But it might also involve communication with staff to make sure they are satisfied at work, such as staff reviews, or job redesign, rotation or enlargement to prevent a lack of motivation.

Another factor that might affect absenteeism and labour turnover is the nature of recruitment. For example, Asda is making an active effort to recruit more people over the age of 50. The business argues that this has resulted in a fall in labour turnover and absences from work and also an improvement in customer service levels. This may have been for a number of reasons. Older people may be more experienced. They may have worked before and be more aware of the requirements of the job. If they have either worked previously and been made redundant or returned to work they may be more committed to the job. They may also be concerned that if they leave this job at their age they may not be able to get another. Further, younger people may not see themselves as working in a supermarket all their lives and treat the job as just a stepping stone to other work. They may therefore be less motivated than older people. The flexible packages of work offered to staff has also helped. Offering older workers leave to be with the birth of grandchildren and a career break of two years is likely to be attractive to older employees and fit in with their need for a work-life balance.

(12 marks)

2 Tesco has various schemes which they have either introduced or are thinking of introducing to reduce absences. At Tesco, for example, two stores in the South operated a scheme where staff taking 1-3 days absent were not paid for those days. After three days they would be paid again and receive compensation for the first three days. This is possibly based on the idea that many absences are for a few days and that if staff are genuinely sick they would probably take off more than just one or two days. Removing pay entirely for taking one or two days off could be a real incentive to discourage absences of a few days. On the other hand, as stated it is possible that staff may simply extend their absences for longer periods knowing that they can receive compensation for the first three days. It may be that this scheme needs to be reconsidered to take this into account. Removing all pay could be very motivating to encourage staff to attend, but equally motivating to encourage them to be absent for a longer period.

An alternative scheme that Tesco is considering as an option is to offer staff a greater holiday allowance up front but reduce it every time a day is taken off sick. This gives employees the responsibility and the flexibility to organise their absences. If staff wish to take a day off they can do so although they will know that this will affect their holiday entitlement. The holiday entitlement will be increased to allow them to do this. This could be very motivating for staff as they will be able to manage their own absences. Certain motivation theories argue that giving employees greater responsibility over their working life can be very motivating. On the other hand some employees may not want this responsibility or may mismanage their absences and find that they have no holidays left when they need to take them, which may turn out to be demotivating.

Asda also has schemes designed to reduce absences and labour turnover. For example, it offers certain incentives for low absenteeism by employees. These include prizes such as an extra weeks' holiday, a weekend break or vouchers which can be exchanged for goods and services. The company also has an arrangement where employees who are parents can take leave or carers' leave for employees who may be responsible for others. Further, it has flexible working packages for over 50s which include grandparents' leave and career breaks. The business argues that the prizes for low absenteeism have been very effective because they force staff to consider whether they really need to be off as they may lose the opportunity of obtaining the rewards. Further, incentives offered to over 50s have greatly reduced both absenteeism and labour turnover. Older employees may feel they are more valued and less likely to leave the business or take time off. These incentives may have been effective because they take into account that employees are motivated by a variety of factors other than financial rewards. Although vouchers are to some extent money substitutes, many of the other incentives are non financial motivating factors which could meet the wide variety of needs of employees.

A further method which could affect absenteeism and labour turnover is the contracts offered to seasonal workers. They are entitled to the same benefits and job security as full time colleagues at Asda. However, the contracts would be over an annual period rather than a weekly number of hours. This would allow workers to be recruited at times of the year such as Christmas when extra staff are needed. Providing the same benefits as full time workers, but allowing the flexibility of working at different times of the year, would help to reduce absenteeism and could prevent labour turnover. Workers would only work at times when they were needed which may reduce absences and the relative improvement in conditions of work for flexible workers may encourage them to remain loyal to the business.

(20 marks)

Question 1

(a) A job description is a statement of the tasks to be carried out by the job holder and the responsibilities of the employee in the job. Examples from the data include the title of the job, broadcast journalist, that the job holder would work as part of the team and that the job holder would produce news and current affairs material for television and radio, which would involve research, writing scripts, bulletins and links, deciding what to include and what not to include, interviewing and reporting, assessing copy and sub-editing and managing resources, while following BBC guidelines and maintaining professional standards.

(b) Advertising internally for this post has certain advantages. The person would already be familiar with the BBC, know its procedures, may know the staff he or she will work with and could minimise disruption and reduce costs of application. On the other hand someone from outside the BBC may have fresh ideas and advertising externally would give a far wider range of candidates, perhaps with better abilities. The BBC might want to employ the best candidate it possibly can from as wide a range of candidates, so it might advertise externally.

Question 2

(a) Word of mouth has certain advantages over a local newspaper advert for Pete. It can be less expensive if someone is recommended. Pete will not have to pay for the advertisement. Also, he may not have to carry out time consuming and possibly disruptive interviews. If the person comes recommended then they may be skillful and suited to the job and he can base his decision on previous experience and advice rather than taking a chance on someone he does not know. On the other hand word of mouth advice may not always be reliable. Also, people react differently in different situations and when working with different people.

(b) Placing the advertisement for the cleaner in a local newspaper is likely to attract local applicants for the job. Local advertising is an appropriate form of advertising because cleaners are likely only to want to live close to their jobs. They do not want to travel a long distance and are unlikely to be prepared to move house for the job, especially as it is only two hours (5-7) five nights a week. Newspaper advertising is a relatively inexpensive way of reaching the ideal candidate.

Case study

(a) Using the Internet as part of the recruitment process would be an example of external recruitment. The Internet provides businesses with the opportunity of developing their websites that can be accessed by anyone interested in the company. By placing job adverts on their website a company has the potential of opening up vacancies to a much larger pool of potential employees than simply those existing employees within the business. In addition, using both general and specific job boards can help focus these opportunities more fully to an interested audience. Using the intranet, that is closed electronic networks specifically for employees of the business, would be an example of internal recruitment.

(6 marks)

(b) Even though businesses may use a variety of tried and tested recruitment methods, they may sometimes still lead to the recommendation of unsuitable candidates. This suggests that standard selection procedures are not 100 per cent accurate. This may be due to the capabilities of candidates in providing answers that the business may want to hear so that they can get the job but which may not fully reflect the totality of that individual. What network sites such as Facebook and MySpace can provide is certain biographical information about individuals such as qualifications which may or may not match the information on CVs. An indication of the type of activities individuals engage in and the sorts of information they may share about others or previous work may also say something about the nature of that individual and their suitability to the business. This might provide additional useful information to that gathered during an assessment.

(10 marks)

(c) The Internet can have certain advantages to a business when recruiting managers and professionals. It provides businesses with the opportunity of opening up vacancies to a much larger pool of potential managers and professionals. In addition, using both general and specific job boards can help focus these opportunities more fully to an interested audience. The Internet can also provide immediacy of information to potential applicants without having to wait for adverts to be drawn up through printed media.

However, what advertising jobs on the Internet can't provide is an initial screening of applicants for their suitability to the organisation. Often managers and professionals may be too busy to search for posts via the Internet and may rely on the services of recruitment agencies to highlight potential candidates. Recruitment agencies can therefore target potential applicants that might be on their books for particular jobs for which businesses were attempting to recruit. They will have a good knowledge of both the abilities of candidates and the needs of businesses. This may help to ensure that the most suitable candidate is appointed, avoiding costly and time consuming processes involved in re-advertising.

It might be suggested that in the case of managers and professionals, the skills of a recruitment agency could ensure that the most suitable candidate is appointed. However, there are factors that can influence the decision. If a business has its own website it may be relatively simple to advertise jobs. Small businesses may not have their own sites, but could make use of the employment sites that exist. Small businesses may be unable to afford the services of a recruitment agency.

(12 marks)

(d) Businesses may want to use network sites to gather additional information about candidates that might help them better judge whether they match the person specification for the vacancy. However, businesses may need to be very careful in undertaking such activities. They may be guilty of not processing personal data fairly under the Data Protection Act and could be in breach of guidelines in the Information Commissioner's Employment Practices Code. In addition, employers may discriminate against people using Facebook on the ground of age, since most users are aged between 18 and 24. One might also argue that the information gleaned from such network sites might be inappropriately used. Does a photograph showing a candidate drunk at the weekends imply that that person cannot do their job or that he or she might be an alcoholic? Further, businesses may need to think carefully about the message that web-vetting might be sending to prospective employees. Some may see it as intrusive although others may see it as a legitimate way of getting a feel for how a person behaves when not in a formal interview.

In conclusion, it could be argued that although such networks can help in the recruitment process, they should only really be a part of it. Given the possible problems some would suggest that they should only be a small part and only used in certain circumstances that the business feels are appropriate Any use of such networks would need to be carefully monitored to ensure a business remains within the law.

(12 marks)

Question 1

(a) The application form used by Frost Frame was the standard form used for general workshop employees. It did not go into any detail about a candidate's specific skills. It would be difficult for a company to match the candidate to a person specification if there was no opportunity for the candidate to actually document the skills he or she had.

Frost Frame could improve its application form by including a section which asks the candidate to outline experience in the given trade and what skills the candidate had acquired. This would make it easier for the business to identify whether the candidate had specific skills in working with stained glass, as well as other skills needed for the job.

(b) If the business decides not to interview the candidate this implies that the advert in the local press has been a waste of money. Frost Frame must make sure that all application forms and any accompanying materials will entice the maximum number of potential candidates to apply to the business. The small number of applicants might also be due to the fact that it was looking for a specifically experienced crafts person within a local geographical area, which may be difficult. It may need to place the advert in a specialist trade magazine.

The company will then have to decide whether to re-advertise, to advertise in a different way or to follow some other means of achieving its aims, such as training of existing staff.

Question 2

(a) It is important for interviewees to demonstrate a serious approach to the interview. Examples in the article where this was not demonstrated include inappropriate laughter, candidates' negative attitudes to tests, interviewees flirting with an interviewer and interviewees having a lengthy phone call on a mobile during the interview. In addition, there is an expectation that a candidate will demonstrate an honest and professional approach prior to the interview and show high levels of enthusiasm for the post. For example, one candidate in the article was recommended to second interview because of her honesty about previous illnesses. Another candidate was selected for interview because of his enthusiastic approach in his cover letter. One candidate also ensured that he was professional in his approach to other members of the firm. A calm, self-assured and appropriately confident approach will also be the type of work approach that most employers will look for in a candidate.

(b) Interviews can be useful for helping a business to select the most suitable candidate for the job in a number of ways. The interview provides a business with an opportunity of seeing how a candidate can relate to the core values of a business and, as importantly, to staff currently working in the business via the interview process. In addition the interview is an opportunity to probe candidates' applications in areas not fully covered by the application. So, for example, this allowed one of the candidates in the article to fully articulate why she had time off work that will have been apparent in the application form and reference. Most importantly, it provides an opportunity for a business to examine more fully the extent to which the candidate meets the criteria that a business are looking for in appointing a particular individual.

Question 3

(a) EasyJet does part of its selection via the Internet. For example, pilots are asked to fill in customised application forms online. Pilot workshops or assessments are also used as part of the selection process. These are likely to be sessions where the skills of pilots are tested or their ability to react to situations. Another feature of selection is the use of psychometric tests. These tests ask questions which are designed to find out the characteristics of pilots. They might indicate, for example, whether a pilot is calm or able to follow instructions.

(b) Online selection seems to be particularly useful early in the selection process. For example, some speculative applications or applicants, who clearly do not have certain basic levels of experience, are filtered out before being sent electronically to the appropriate person. Those that do not have the exact requirements may be added to an electronic database to build up a list of possible future recruits. This is a relatively quick and low cost method of selection. However, easyJet is less sure about online testing because of the problems of appropriate feedback. Further, it also holds other tests such as psychometric testing and workshops. Such tests might help decide on the specific skills and traits needed to be a successful pilot. So it could be argued that while online selection is useful for initial long listing, for example, other more specific tests need to take place for final selection.

Case study

(a) (i) CV stands for Curriculum Vitae. A curriculum vitae is a list of an applicant's personal details, experience and qualifications.

(ii) A face-to-face interview means that interviewer and applicant are able to see each other at the same place together in the interview situation. This allows the immediate exchange of information as well as actually viewing a candidate and how they respond to questions.

(4 marks)

(b) In undertaking a job analysis and then drawing out a job description and person specification it is likely that a skill required by sales people or call centre operatives is their ability to use the phone effectively. They must be able to communicate with a client, develop a rapport with the client and help respond effectively to client queries. They may also, possibly, have to deal with difficult issues or questions that the individual may not immediately have at hand. Interviews over the phone can help interviewers assess the extent to which candidates have these skills as they respond to questions and situations that the interviewer asks. The telephone interview might be able to accurately simulate the work environment of the candidate and as such could be a suitable assessment method.

(6 marks)

(c) Short listing is where a business selects a number of candidates from potential applicants to interview. Sometimes they are chosen from a longer list, which is then cut down. In some cases the interview may be carried out over the telephone. Short listing can be carried out using a variety of methods. Candidates' applications can be matched to the person specifications and/or job descriptions linked to the vacancy. This might be done electronically, online or manually. Scores or marks might then be allocated to particular levels of relevant experience that the candidates have, for example. Then, depending on the number that might be interviewed, a cut off point will be decided as to who does and who does not get interviewed. Those close to that cut off point are likely to be re-examined to check which side of the cut off point they should fall on.

(6 marks)

(d) (i) There are various advantages of telephone interviews to potential employees. Possible discrimination or bias may be removed. For example, the interviewer is unlikely to be aware of disability, age or ethnicity. Second, candidates may be able to organise interviews more easily without having to take time off work. Finally, interviewees don't need to think about what to wear at interview and this will not influence selection.

(ii) Businesses can also benefit from telephone interviews as they will reduce their costs. They don't have to find a location for the interview or pay travel expenses. In addition, they enable the business to judge the effectiveness of the communication skills of the candidate. Finally, the business may be able to interview more people because a telephone interview may be easier and quicker to organise and implement than face-to-face interviews.

(8 marks)

(e) There is a number of things that B&Q may need to take into account when interviewing by telephone. It will need to ensure that candidates have a quiet space at work or at home to enable an interview to take place. It will also need to train interviewers to make sure that they get the best out of candidates over the phone. For example, they should not ask too many close ended questions which would be less likely in face-to-face interview. Further, they should provide time for candidates to answer questions fully and also time for quiet moments to think about answers to questions. Evidence suggests that quiet spaces in phone conversations appear longer than in face-to-face situations.

(8 marks)

(f) Telephone interviews by themselves are unlikely to lead to successful appointments. There may be cost advantages and also chances to hear how applicants can communicate using telephone interviews. However, businesses more and more are asking applicants to undertake a battery of tests and selection exercises. A battery of tests will provide a fuller picture of what a candidate is like and what his or her potential is likely to be. In addition, telephone interviews often involve just one interviewer. There is evidence to suggest that panels of interviewers generally make better decisions about the full capabilities of the individual. This really can only be achieved by face-to-face interviewers. In a face-to-face interview candidates can be probed further by various interviewers about potential gaps in their applications. In conclusion, an effective selection process is likely to take into account a number of selection procedures. Even when costs are important, it could be argued that a business is unlikely to achieve a successful appointment using just telephone interviews.

(12 marks)

Question 1

(a) A full-time employee usually works 35 hours or more a week in the UK, although there is no specific number of hours that makes someone full-time. This will depend on what contracts for employment between the employer and the employee suggest is a full-time working week, month or year. A part-time employee is someone who works fewer hours than a full-time employee.

(b) Full-time employees may be taken on by businesses when work is guaranteed on a regular basis. Micah employs Carla on a full-time basis because she has to regularly, consistently and quickly respond to the professional clients of the business. This includes regular work on guitars for touring bands but also the ability to field a call from bands any day or time of the week and then provide immediate technical assistance if required. All of this work could not effectively be covered by someone part-time. There might be a lack of coverage at key times and days in the week to provide immediate technical assistance as well as the regular guitar maintenance work.

(c) Factors that might influence Micah's decision about whether to employ Ged as a temporary or permanent part-time worker include whether Micah believes increased orders are likely to be permanent features. If he believes this to be the case, he might decide to make Ged a permanent appointment. Being made permanent does bring obligations and in particular difficulties in making staff redundant if orders are not maintained. However, employing Ged on a temporary basis might make him less reliable as he may feel less committed to the business.

Question 2

(a) Rue du Paris clearly faces a number of problems, including the potential closure of two restaurants. It might be able to solve some of these by terminating the contracts of some of its staff in a number of ways. Some staff may have broken the conditions of their contract of employment. For example, they may have taken time off sick without being ill to work for other employers or left for half a day a week to work elsewhere whilst still being paid by Rue du Paris. Employees who break their contracts and are deemed to have misconduct in their employment may be liable for dismissal. This will reduce the overstaffing levels of the business and also cut wage costs. The business must ensure, however, that it complies with legislation, such as giving written or verbal warnings, before dismissing staff or they may be liable for reinstatement by an employment tribunal or fines. The business might also allow some of its older staff to take early retirement. They may be entitled to retirement benefits or even remuneration to encourage them to take early retirement. This will be a cost to the business, but could save money in the long run. Staff who are employed on fixed term contracts might simply not have these contracts renewed after the period of employment ends. This is a fairly low or nil cost option for the business. Rue du Paris might decide to make some of its part time workers redundant. To do this it must prove that their job no longer exists. It can not, for example, make a worker redundant and simply employ another worker at lower wages immediately to save costs. These options may help to save money for the business and could help to prevent the closure of two of the restaurants. But the business must be careful that it does not terminate the contracts of key staff or too many staff. Terminating the contracts of a key manager or some flexible workers may lead to

poor performance and closure anyway. So the choice of which staff to retain and which to sack is vital as well.

Case study

(a) The problems of employing permanent staff for a small business can be numerous. They can include the costs in advertising the position and time taken on interviews that may result in losing valuable time making sales or winning new business. There are training costs and time and effort spent to stay in line with employment legislations. There are also fixed costs associated with tax and National Insurance contributions.

(4 marks)

(b) Outsourcing means contracting, sub-contracting, or 'externalising' non-core activities to free up cash, personnel, time, and facilities for activities where the firm holds competitive advantage. Firms having strengths in other areas may contract out tasks such as data processing, legal work, manufacturing, marketing, payroll accounting, or other aspects of their businesses. This will allow them to concentrate on what they do best and thus reduce average unit cost. Examples in the article include virtual personal assistants. These are off-site staff who can work on small or large projects for a fixed fee.

(4 marks)

(c) Peopleperhour.com provides a platform for small businesses to advertise their personnel needs to a pool of freelance professionals who might be able to undertake support tasks. By providing an online market place, small businesses can compare the costs and specifications that different freelance professionals might provide to undertake particular tasks or projects. This may help them to reduce the cost of their recruitment. The Peopleperhour.com service is often much cheaper than standard recruitment agencies because these agencies often want to place people in permanent positions, as they would then get better commission. Small businesses may also find that identifying such professionals is difficult. Some employees, it is suggested, are hard to find, especially for a small firm looking for particular skills.

(8 marks)

(d) It could be argued that using the services provided by companies such as Peopleperhour.com have many potential advantages. They provide a relatively easy way of recruiting individuals to undertake particular aspects of work that a business needs completing, without many of the costs of employing staff directly, such as making National Insurance contributions or providing benefits. In addition, the freelance professionals are likely to be initially vetted by the outsourcing company thereby providing some guarantee of quality.

However, there may also be certain disadvantages with outsourcing services such as Peopleperhour.com. Businesses may want to develop their own recruitment processes. This means that they can find employees who fit in with the culture of the business. Keeping their own list of potential support staff may be expensive, especially if it needs updating, but good relations can be built up over time and businesses will know what each employee can do. In addition, freelance professionals can be expensive and businesses must take care that they get value for money for what they do. This may be easier if they carry out their own recruitment.

In conclusion, it could be argued that outsourcing can make financial sense as long as clear instructions are given about the needs of the business. Some companies may feel, however, that even outsourcing their temporary staff recruitment takes too much control away from the organisation. However, there appear to be major advantages for smaller businesses that have specific needs and limited resources.

(12 marks)

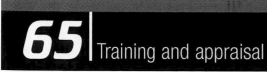

Question 1

(a) On-the-job training is training given in the workplace. It can include learning from other workers, being mentored by a more experienced employee and being given different jobs so that the trainee can develop a broad experience. One example of on-the-job training highlighted by the article is by the founder of the business, John Gill. It would appear that he learnt his trade by selling shoes on a market stall where he will have developed an understanding of how to sell shoes from other more experienced market traders around him. Another is the training given to Michelle and her deputy. They sat with a supervisor who discussed points about customer service afterwards.

(b) The article highlights a difficulty. There are often apprehensions amongst staff about training. This is often the case with younger staff, who may feel that they will have difficulties learning new skills. Another potential problem with training staff at Chockers is that the approach currently adopted is via the Modern Apprenticeship route. This would mean that any number of staff employed by the company might be either on or off site for aspects of training rather than working in the shops. This could create the potential of employee shortfalls at certain times for the business, perhaps leading to lower sales.

(c) Chockers would need to examine how cost-effective running its own training programme might be. At present the company is arguably too small to run its own complete programme efficiently and effectively as it would need specialist training staff, training materials and space to provide such comprehensive programmes. However, if the business was to continue to grown there may be enough economies of scale to warrant a training department in the business to operate bespoke in-house training programmes with appropriate accreditation for its employees.

Question 2

(a) (i) Modern Apprenticeships are schemes that aim to give young people an apprenticeship training which will equip them for a specific job in an industry. Businesses run Modern Apprenticeships and then receive a subsidy from government for each apprentice on the scheme. Typically Modern Apprenticeship training runs for three years.

(ii) In-house training is when a business develops its own training programmes that it delivers within the business. It may still call on outside help with these courses, however.

(b) The retail trade is highly competitive, perhaps nowhere more so than in the rivalry between supermarkets. This means that Asda will want to ensure that it can achieve as great a competitive advantage from every single input into the business as it can. The people that provide service to customers are very important and this is were there is a possibility of achieving a greater competitive edge. This competitive edge can be enhanced by training that focuses on making workers more productive through improving ways of working, familiarising them with new equipment and technology, developing new skills to improve flexibility, setting new standards of quality service, implementing health and safety policies, increasing job satisfaction and motivation and assisting in recruiting and retaining high quality staff.

(c) There is a number of arguments that Asda should provide its own training. If Asda provides the training, there is every chance that the training workers will receive will prepare them more fully for Asda's technology, procedures and working culture. In other words, it will be bespoke to the needs of Asda. In addition, because employees have been trained in Asda ways, there is less chance of employees using the qualification to transfer to other employment, so assisting with keeping labour turnover lower. However, employees may be less enthusiastic about gaining an accreditation that is Asda-specific and may not volunteer quite so readily to engage in training. They may be concerned that if they change jobs the training has less value. An external training provider might bring in new skills for employees that are not part of the scheme.

In conclusion, it could be argued that given the size of the organisation and the number of employees it has, Asda should provide its own training rather than making use of a training provider. Training its own staff may be costly, but so might using a training provider. Asda may also be better able to target where to spend the money provided by the Learning and Skills Council than an outside organisation.

Question 3

(a) The 'old method' of appraisal at Pettersford was for annual appraisals to take place. Once a year employees met with managers to discuss their performance over the previous twelve months. There was a number of problems with the old method of appraisal at Pettersford plc. First, the appraisal system was often a one way communication process. The line manager told the employee why they had done well or badly. Employees were not fully involved in the system and hence were unlikely to be committed to the process. In addition, the review was only every 12 months and it was difficult for employees to be able to recall what they had or had not achieved during that period, particularly as little time was given to this process.

(b) There were certain features of the new appraisal system which were designed to prevent the problems of the older system. As well as being appraised by a supervisor or manager, the new appraisal enabled peer group appraisal. Each employee could choose two employees who would undertake an appraisal on them. In addition, the appraisal system became quarterly as opposed to annually. Finally, managers/supervisors attempted to help implement employee 'personal commitments', discussed or agreed at appraisal interviews, into the work setting.

(c) (i) One advantage of the new system of appraisal is that employees had a stake in the system. They were listened to and the business attempted to help them implement their personal commitments agreed at the appraisal meetings. It was more of a two way dialogue. In addition, employees were provided with a more rounded appraisal of their achievement because it also involved peer viewpoints. Finally, appraisal was undertaken quarterly which would allow for more timely interventions based on current information. A disadvantage to the new system is that it may be quite time consuming for the employee to be involved in quarterly reviews. This may reduce the productivity of the business, which may offset the improved motivation.

(ii) One advantage to the business seems to be improved productivity. This was because employees who had been listened to rewarded the business with increased productivity. The personal commitment based on improved levels of information and more timely reviews provided a focus for the appraisal interview that seemed to result in improved performance. The disadvantages to the business may be in terms of administrative efficiency. The whole process is more time consuming and involved as it involves peer assessment. In addition, because peer assessors are chosen by the employee there may be an over emphasis on 'friendly raters' who may provide a more generous assessment.

Case study

(a) (i) Apprentices are often young employees or potential employees who receive training usually towards a skill or specific job in an industry. Today apprentices tend to be linked to Modern Apprenticeships. They receive apprenticeship training which equips them for a specific job in an industry and also they are employed by a business often get on-the-job training and experience working in the sector on a daily basis. In the cases study, social housing apprentices are given on-the-job training but also learn about the historical context of social housing.

(3 marks)

(ii) A graduate training programme is usually located in medium to large sized organisations. These programmes are typically designed to offer those with university degrees either professional training or managerial training. Businesses often feel that these employees are more suited to such posts.

(3 marks)

(b) On-the-job training is training given in the workplace by the employer. One example of on-the-job training is learning from a colleague. The article suggests that on-the-job training is given to apprentices in social housing. This could be working next to a worker dealing with a housing regeneration project, for example. They will experience the activities of the employee and the challenges faced by the job. They can see how the employee deals with these problems. Off-the-job training is training which takes place outside the business with an external training provider. The article suggests that the Chartered Institute of Housing provides a whole host of professional qualifications that will prepare employees to meet the challenges of the future.

(6 marks)

(c) The Modern Apprenticeship in social housing provides a detailed grounding of the historical context of social housing, its management and Housing Law. In addition, it provides the foundation for numerous professional qualifications in social housing that emanate from a Modern Apprenticeship. At present there are very few graduate training programmes for graduates interested in a career in social housing. So it could be argued that a young person looking to enter the industry stands a better chance taking a Modern Apprenticeship in social housing. On the other hand, for those few who can enter the industry through a graduate scheme, it could be suggested that their potential earnings will be higher and achievable far more quickly. They may also be able to achieve a higher position in an organisation.

(8 marks)

(d) The type of training that might be needed in the future should reflect developments in the sector. In the 1980s social housing was limited. It was mainly geared towards rent collection and bad neighbours. However, new job titles today include regeneration officers, tenant participation officers, urban designers, anti-social behaviour managers and financial inclusion officers. There is every suggestion that this will drive up the importance of multi-agency working that requires social housing employees to have people skills and an understanding of different professional perspectives.

This might mean that there is a greater uptake of Modern Apprenticeships in the industry by students. The contents of such course would need to change in order to take into account the changing needs of the housing sector. However, it might also be suggested that a greater number of graduate schemes will be set up. Traditionally graduates have not been attracted to the industry, but graduate schemes designed for specialists in areas such as urban planning might be needed.

(10 marks)

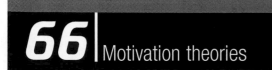

66 | Motivation theories

Question 1

(a) The case study suggests that management at Anmac has a laissez faire approach to the way work is organised. In addition, workers at Anmac work at their own pace, resulting in variable levels of output. These two features are exactly what Taylor found when he started to study work organisations - management that didn't understand the shopfloor and workers working at a rate set by themselves. Taylor's principles would suggest that management would need to undertake a study of the shopfloor to find out the best and quickest way of producing micro-electronic circuits and then train the workforce to complete their work in the most efficient way. Workers would then need to be paid piece rates to ensure that they met targets set by management.

If there is a shortfall of employees at Stafford then, using Taylor's principles of efficiency, Anmac should either move employees from a plant with sufficient capacity to an under resourced plant, if the work study suggests this to be most effective, or move employees from Chester to Stafford if the converse is true. Either way, one would expect increased productivity as a net result of the changes.

(b) The idea that the workers should either be moved or forced to do overtime to fit in with Tayloristic principles of efficiency does not take into account the social situations of the employees. Most of the workers are women with young families. This might make it difficult for them to do overtime if they have other responsibilities. In addition, most are married and their husbands already have jobs. It might be unrealistic or difficult to expect the whole family to move (including the husband leaving his current job) for the sake of one wage earner.

Question 2

(a) The table shows the results of different actions taken by Bryant and Gillie when introducing a piece rate system. Five different groups were involved. With groups A and C, management told the workers that a new system of payment was to be introduced next week. There was no discussion about the changes and none of the workers were asked for constructive opinions about whether they thought the changes were a good idea. This approach is Tayloristic. It assumes that workers only have financial needs and no personal and social needs. It follows the view that workers are there to work and managers to manage. As can be seen from the statistics on resignations and output, groups A and C had the highest percentage of resignations and the lowest positive percentage change in output. Group D had the idea of piece rates explained to them. In other words they were consulted about change. Management showed some appreciation of the fact that workers had an interest in their work and at least explained the need for change. This led to fewer resignations than in groups A and C and better output. Group E not only had the new system of piece rate explained, but also involved the workers in discussion about the changes. Here workers were even more involved in the process with some negotiation taking place. This led to better levels of output and no resignations. Group B was fully involved in the process of decision making about piece rates. They helped management devise a system that would be beneficial to both the company and the employees. In this situation output rose considerably higher than in any of the other groups and there were no resignations. Management had used the human relations approach fully in this situation and were best rewarded by the workers.

(b) From the results of this survey it is apparent that any changes that management feel they need to make in work practices should have workers fully involved in the decision making process. By doing this they are more likely to achieve greater work satisfaction and hence better productivity. Having said this, one has to be aware of changes in and outside the organisation which may affect the culture of the organisation. It might be that the market for children's clothing suddenly collapses, which may create uncertainty and insecurity about employment prospects. This may make the workers less amenable to being involved in decision making and could create potential for unrest if they have knowledge about future redundancy requirements.

Question 3

(a) Google could be said to motivate its staff in a number of ways. There is an interesting work environment, with open space and courtyards. There are activity areas, such as a beach volleyball court. Staff are helped to travel between areas via mini-scooters. They are given free drinks. There is also a wider variety of free lunches Staff are also encouraged to pursue their own activities by means of the 20 per cent scheme.

(b) It could be argued that staff at Google has elements of both hygiene factor and motivators that are addressed at Google. For example, they are treated well at work. They are given comfortable work conditions in which to operate. This in itself, according to Herzberg may not motivate staff, although it will prevent dissatisfaction. But importantly there are many examples of motivators. In particular staff are given opportunities for improvement and a sense of achievement. This can be seen in allowing staff to pursue personal projects.

(Note: this question could be answered with reference to other theories of motivation in this unit.)

Case study

(a) (i) Employees are motivated at work when they are encouraged to carry out tasks. It is possible for employers to motivate workers by various incentives. An employee with a lack of motivation means that the employee does not have the desire to contribute as fully as he or she could and so does not fulfil his or her potential at work.

(ii) Physiological needs are basic needs. On Maslow 's hierarchy of needs they are suggested to be needs such as eating food, drinking, resting and taking activity. They are said to be the most basic needs of employees at work, which need satisfying first before other, higher needs such as safety or gaining esteem from colleagues.

(3 marks)

(b) Lee Worsnip lacks motivation. He is not being encouraged to carry out tasks or fulfil his potential. This is likely to have implications for both Lee and the business.

(I) Lee's current lack of motivation has made him unhappy. This has resulted in him missing meetings, taking days off and refusing to take on low level work. He is also being offhand with other employees and seeing conspiracies where conspiracies may not exist. These actions could result in him facing disciplinary procedures if he breaks company regulations or conditions of service. He might also become ill with stress. His could lose earnings if he has to take days off sick. In the extreme he may have to give up or perhaps lose his job. His actions could result in problems obtaining another job, particularly if references have to be given, or he could have difficulty progressing in other areas of the business as a result of his attitude.

(ii) The problem to the business of a lack of motivation is that productivity is potentially affected through a lack of willingness of the employee to give their all to their work, as in Lee's case. Inflexibility may set in and clients of the business may be driven away by poor levels of customer service or responsiveness. In addition, the image of the company may be tarnished to future employees who may be put off applying to a company for jobs because of what they might have heard about the staff morale in the business. Further, other staff may be placed under stress and have additional work loads if they have to take over Lee's work. A lack of motivation can also lead to bad feeling in teams if they feel they are covering other people's work. All of these things are likely to affect the operation, productivly and profits of the business.

(10 marks)

(c) Lee is suffering from a lack of motivation at work. This could be indicated by his poor attitude to meetings, work time and other staff. If Lee's position is examined using Maslow's hierarchy of needs it may be possible to identify needs which are not being met.

It could be argued that his physiological needs are being met. There appears to be no indication that he has a problem with basic needs such as food, drink and rest. It might be suggested that there are no physical threats at work, although he may feel there are psychological threats, particularly if he feels that there are conspiracies. However, it might be argued that his real difficulties lie in meeting the belonging, esteem and self-actualisation needs, which he feels are not being met. For example, towards the end of the article he talks about constantly being checked on and therefore not being trusted. This would suggest that his belonging needs are not being met. In addition, his esteem needs were not being met. He felt that his views were not being listened to and that he had been passed over for promotion. Finally, he feels that his potential is not being utilised with him constantly being given routine work that he has shown he can undertake with ease. He wants to get on and be given the opportunity to self-actualise but the business has not recognised these needs.

(Note: it may be possible to answer this question using any of the other motivation theories in this unit.)

(12 marks)

(d) If Lee is to be re-motivated the business must consider exactly what incentives it can use that will be effective. Again using Maslow's hierarchy of needs, it may be possible to identify incentives which could satisfy needs at a variety of levels. Psychological needs may be satisfied by ensuring that he is involved in all meetings. This does depend to some extent on him attending. However, he could be notified of any decision by e-mail and asked to comment. Alternatively decisions which directly involve him could be made when he is present. The business would hope that greater motivation would mean that he would now be present at all meetings. This should also to some extent deal with some of his needs to affiliate with a group. Perhaps agreeing a rota for shared work during absence which everyone felt happy with could also deal with this aspect of his motivation and those of other group members. Lee also needs to believe that what he does counts and that he can be given additional responsibilities without having to be constantly checked on. It may be possible to give him tasks involving decision making with clear objectives, which particularly make use of any specialist skills he has developed through courses at night school for example. In terms of self-actualisation, he needs to be given the opportunity to achieve his ambition to progress within the business. He could be given career guidance and the opportunity of further study, for example as a release graduate student. This could give him a greater chance of promotion in future.

(Note: this question could also be answered with reference to other theories of motivation in this unit.)

(12 marks)

67 | Financial methods of motivation

Question 1

(a) Various payment systems are shown in the adverts. In the first advert payments are made per hour, for example the purchase ledger clerk in Wolverhampton is paid £7.00 per hour. This employee will earn a wage and the total amount paid each week will be the hourly rate times the number of hours worked. The finance director in the second advert is paid a salary of £60,000 a year. However, the successful candidate would also earn benefits on top of this. The last advert is for a salesperson. The employee would be paid a commission, almost certainly based on the amount sold. The employee could anticipate earning over £30,000 a year.

(b) Fringe benefits are payments over and above the wage or salary paid. In the second advert the finance director is being paid benefits over the £60,000 a year salary. Although not stated exactly, it is possible that the type of fringe benefits paid for this post could be a company pension, dental care or private health care. In the third advert there is a travel allowance for transport involved in visits for the salesperson. The employee can also take advantage of holiday incentives. These might be discounted flights or package holidays or even the use of company flats or other premises.

(c) Employees are to some extent motivated by money. They are often attracted to apply for a job based on the salary and wage, although other factors will also influence them, especially when they begin work. If a business offered a lower package of remuneration than the market rate it could find that either it received a very low number of applicants or that the quality of the applicants was poor. Well qualified people may be put off applying and look for better paid alternatives. Those who are desperate for a job and prepared to accept a relatively low wage might apply or people without the skills required could apply. In each case the business would either have to accept the quality of applicants given its wage structure or revise its package.

Question 2

(a) One advantage to Paul in paying overtime is that it will encourage staff to work longer and motivate them as they are earning higher rewards. One disadvantage is that overtime increases the wage costs of the business. These may not have been built into wage budgets for example.

(b) Financial rewards are monetary rewards to employees, or money in kind such as fringe benefits. In Nick Barnes' business financial rewards could be a problem. Employees sometimes become jealous if they feel that employees who do similar work get paid more. In this case Natalie, his longest serving employee, has been asked if she will take responsibility for an expanding area of work. Nick could argue that she is taking on extra work and so deserves to be rewarded. However, staff who previously did a similar job to Natalie may still feel aggrieved, especially if they feel that they are more qualified for the role of handling the printing of larger posters.

(c) Nick could motivate Natalie to take over the expanding area by offering share ownership. This can be a strong motivating factor for employees. They usually feel they have a vested interest in the performance of the business and will work hard to ensure its success.

However, in this case it could be argued that the benefits would outweigh the problems they may cause. Selling shares will dilute the ownership of Paul and Nick. They would still retain control, but they would have to consult with Natalie as a co-owner. But also, it is likely to have a very demotivating effect on other employees. They may also demand share ownership. It could, therefore, be argued that ensuring that the expansion goes well and trying to increase the rewards of all staff is a more effective way of motivating staff.

Question 3

(a)(i) Management incentives are usually linked to how well the company has performed. But they also can be used to help retain staff in a business by recognising the commitment made by managers to the business or to attract new managers to the business. In the article we have examples of WH Smith financial rewards through share option schemes to retain its management staff,
(ii) Performance related pay is a pay system designed to motivate staff, particularly white collar staff. The system directly links performance to pay. Managers are then rewarded financially for the performance of the company through things like bonuses or share option schemes. Examples include the chief executive at WH Smith who could generate £1.8 million on top of his salary.
(b) The main reason a business might use these incentive schemes is to drive up the performance of the business. This can be measured by its profitability, its market share, its value and numerous other measures. In order to achieve this a company has to recruit and retain the best staff to drive up company performance and then reward those staff for achieving that increased performance.
(c) It could be argued that a chain of five health and fitness centres in Yorkshire should introduce performance related pay for its managers. This would mean that managers may have their salaries increased if they met particular targets. Often these targets are agreed through appraisal and may include improved profitability, increased membership figures, improved evaluation data from clients of the centres, decreased costs and reduced staff mobility. However, the chain would need to consider the following. The bonus has to set at the right level to give managers an incentive to achieve their targets. Achieving the targets may have been more to do with staff within the centres rather than individual managers and hence created dissatisfaction with all employees.

Whether the business did this or not could depend on the reaction of managers to the system and whether it actually benefited the business. For example, managers may feel that the targets are unfair or that they are not set in the right areas. If this was the case then such as system could be demotivating and the service and profits of the business could suffer. If this was the case then the chain may decide against using it.

Case study

(a) (i) Employees are often rewarded in other ways than their basic earnings in order to motivate them. These are sometimes called 'perks'. Luxury rewards are perhaps examples of such rewards. They often have a high value and may be limited to one or two employees or businesses who may have shown the highest levels of performance in the business. For example, SolidWorks invited the top performing VAR to Hawaii.
(ii) Incentives are given to employees to motivate them. One form of incentive is money paid for performance. To incentivise on volume means that incentive schemes are based on the quantity of a product sold. So, for example, there may be a bonus for achieving particular sales targets.

(6 marks)

(b) There is a whole number of payment and incentive schemes documented in the article. Some rewards include elements that resemble fringe benefits. Fringe benefits are rewards which are used instead of or extra to actual money payments. These may include day trips, air miles, holidays to Hawaii, race days, or sailing around the Leeward Isles. Sometimes they may be linked to quality of performance. However, most incentive schemes are based on money and commissions paid to individuals relating to their performance in terms of sales.

Other incentives are team based and foster team building. They are rewards based on the performance of an entire group or team of workers rather than individuals. Some incentives are tied to particular business activity. For example, IBM offers VARs additional marketing funds to enable the business to make inroads into particular markets.

(6 marks)

(c) Fringe benefit types of incentives, such as day trips, may be useful to some VARs. They may provide recognition for individuals or businesses with status symbol rewards for work completed. In some cases they may enable VARs to avoid payment of taxes that they would incur if the incentives were paid in money. However, there are some problems with these approaches. The article makes clear that these approaches rarely act as incentives to perform better. Also they may become so established that VARs may expect them as part and parcel of normal rewards rather than as an incentive to increase performance. In addition, for some VARs it may just be difficult to take full advantage of the benefit, creating more administration than they are worth.

There is some evidence that monetary rewards are still valued by many VARs, particularly for salespeople. However some businesses are clear that payment incentive schemes can also act as potential barriers to particular types of work practice. Individualised incentives do not foster team work and hence there are some businesses that offer team incentives.

However, team incentives may also be problematic, particularly if there is a feeling within the team that certain individuals are not contributing equally to the team effort. In addition pressure on VARs to achieve particular targets that enable incentives to be paid may also distort the client relationship where the emphasis is on the short term and selling products rather than on developing a longer term relationship based on mutual understanding.

Other incentives mentioned in the article are clearly related to business practice. Hence IBM provides VARs with a marketing budget that will enable them to develop more effective client responses. This should help build longer term relationships that may result in longer term success.

(10 marks)

(d) It is clear that although the SME computer market is likely to be a potentially untapped market for computer manufacturers, the selling of computers to SMEs is potentially difficult to achieve. There is a number of potential reasons for this difficulty. Often SMEs don't have the resources to spend on computers that they may perceive to be irrelevant to their needs. Second, they may not have the computer skills to make best use of the computer and the commercial software available to them which may be better suited to bigger businesses. In this situation an incentive scheme to VARs that is based on selling 'boxes' may not achieve the desired result. Hence fringe benefits or money incentives to hit particular targets may not be useful incentive schemes in this case.

It is likely that VARs will need to be incentivised to listen to the needs of SMEs and develop a service of software and training that is accessible, affordable and points to real advantages that SMEs may get out of computers. Clearly this is the approach adopted by IBM. So it could be argued that team based schemes or even company wide schemes may be more effective. They may allow the sales representatives' manufacturer to tailor products to the needs of the small businesses rather than have individuals compete with each other to gain the largest sales on volume, which may not meet the needs of the small business, but may generate sales.

(12 marks)

68 | Non-financial methods of motivation

Question 1

(a) Job design is the process of organising tasks and activities required to perform a job. When designing the job being advertised the tasks and activities that were considered could have been that the overall task would be making up bespoke clothing. This would comprise activities such as sewing parts, adding buttons and pressing.

(b) Job enlargement involves giving an employee more work to do of a similar nature. It could be suggested that part of job enlargement could be carrying out tasks that were related to the main job. These might have included measuring, drafting patterns and altering patterns to fit customers.

(c) Job enrichment attempts to give employees greater responsibility. The business might decide to vertically extend the role of the tailor. This could include ordering fabrics. It might also involve helping to make decisions about the image of the business. For example, at the moment it makes bespoke clothing. But the team might want to move away from this in a small way in future to test the market. It might want to make a small unique ranges of off the peg clothing, for instance. Job enrichment gives employees a challenge and encourages them to use decision making skills.

Question 2

(a) In many respects St Lukes Communications adopts many non-financial methods of motivation. Staff are empowered. They are given authority and responsibility to work with others to achieved shared goals. Individuals work as part of teams and can also contribute to other teams if they feel they have something to offer. In addition, they take responsibility for quality. Further, through negotiations with others staff are more likely to be able achieve a better work-life balance by realising what responsibilities they have at work and when and how those responsibilities can be combined with responsibilities at home. Also, staff are encouraged to use their own initiative. They can contribute even incomplete ideas at meetings. They can also contribute to projects to which they are not specifically assigned.

(b) (i) This type of motivation benefits employees because they will feel more motivated to contribute to something if they have 'ownership' of it. This reduces stress. In addition, because staff have a direct input into decisions taken they will feel less frustrated by senior staff making decisions which they feel may be incorrect. Also, staff will feel as though they being both personally and professionally developed.

(ii) However, this approach is likely to also benefit employers. Productivity may be greater because of pooled talent. Staff who are not assigned to particular projects may bring knowledge to a decision which is 'outside the box' but helps the decision. Staff may attempt to take greater risks if they feel they are involved and supported that may provide the business with a competitive edge. It can also provide the business with flexibility and teams are also more likely to take responsibility for the quality of the product or service. Further, it helps reduce staff turnover, which can be very costly for a business. The industry norm is 25 per cent, but it is only 10 per cent at St Lukes, of which only one per cent goes to competitors. This suggests a high level of staff loyalty.

Case study

(a) (i) Empowerment is the management practice of sharing information, rewards and power with employees. Employees are given responsibility and authority. They are encouraged to take initiative and make decisions to solve problems and improve service and performance. Empowerment is based on the concept of giving employees skills, resources, authority, opportunity, motivation, as well holding them responsible and accountable for outcomes of their actions.

(3 marks)

(ii) Teamwork involves working collaboratively with a group of people, in order to achieve a goal. Teamwork can be a crucial part of a business, as it is often necessary for colleagues to work well together, trying their best in any circumstance. Teamwork means that people co-operate, using their individual skills and providing constructive feedback, despite any personal conflict between them.

(3 marks)

(b) There is a number of ways in which the organisation at Zinx might change to help motivate employees. Currently, it is a very traditional organisation that is hierarchical with a number of layers of management between the shopfloor and CEO. In addition, the functions in the hotel are clearly delineated so that employees only have responsibilities for the particular tasks allocated to them. By delayering the organisation and giving greater accountability and responsibility to staff there is every chance that employees will be far more engaged, enhancing the quality of the service they provide in the hotel. In addition, widening the activities that staff do may also create variety and at the same time enable staff to respond more quickly to the needs of clients. For example, restaurant waiting staff may take responsibility for running bars in the hotel if they are short staffed.

(6 marks)

(c) (i) Greater empowerment for employees will result in them feeling more trusted and more in control of their work. This can result in improved levels of self-confidence, improved pride in their work, reduced stress and enhanced levels of motivation.

(ii) Greater empowerment will also benefit employers. There are likely to be reduced levels of labour turnover, improved productivity with enhanced quality of service. This should help to improve sales and build the reputation of the hotel. Clients will get a better response from staff and their stay will be made more comfortable, providing improved levels of customer satisfaction. This is likely to encourage return visits and loyalty to the hotel, leading possibly to higher profits.

(8 marks)

(d) There is every indication in the case that empowerment would help the business. Employees will be more motivated. Employers may benefit from improved service, reduced staff turnover and customer satisfaction, possibly leading to greater sales and profits. But there is a note of caution with empowerment. Employers need to practice the art of 'trust but verify'. If employees are being given additional responsibilities and levels of accountability to improve service there is a need to test the levels of improved customer satisfaction through surveys and questionnaires. In addition, the business needs to ensure that empowered staff have direction so that the business goals of the hotel are still seen as vital.

In conclusion, it could be argued that empowerment should only be increased if employers can see real benefits for the hotel. If individuals pursue their own objectives and not those of the hotel, then greater empowerment may not necessarily benefit both employers and employees.

(12 marks)

69 Management

Question 1

(a) (i) According to Fayol's theory of management, she has fulfilled the following functions.

Forecasting and planning - for example anticipating a vacancy for an accounts executive and writing job advertisements in preparation for advertising the post.

Organising - organises applications for a training course for two workers in production.

Commanding - delegates task to 2 assistants and 1 secretary.

Co-ordinating - discussions with the head of marketing about personnel issues in the marketing department.

Controlling - checks progress of two job vacancies to see that applications are being received and the job will be filled.

(ii) According to Mintzberg's theory of management, she has fulfilled the following functions.

Interpersonal roles - figurehead role by passing out Basic Health Certificates.

Information roles - replying to emails to act as a channel of information.

Decision making roles - disciplining worker for persistent lateness working with trade union official.

Question 2

(a) Kaplin Price might be able to solve some of its business problems by utilising an MBO approach to business. First, the business would need to be clear about its objectives. At the moment the business appears to be unable to decide what its priorities should be - expand or rationalise. Once its business objectives have been set it then needs to organise work into manageable activities and jobs that will enable those activities to be achieved. If it wants to expand then it may need to develop infrastructures and recruit employees to undertake the additional activities. If it wants to rationalise it may need to merge departments, change job roles and make some redundancies. It will then need to motivate its staff. Expansion makes motivation easier in that staff can be rewarded through targeted bonus schemes to enhance their performance to meet enhanced business activity. Rationalisation may require that the business gives greater responsibilities and authority to staff so that they can be motivated by non-financial means. Whatever the nature of changed and developed job roles the business will need to outline the targets that staff will need to aid their development through appropriate training and promotion.

Question 3

(a) Managers face a number of dilemmas. It could be argued that one of the dilemmas at BP was the commando leaders' dilemma. Previously subsidiaries were given a high level of operational independence. But this perhaps contributed to lower level profits. Mr Hayward wanted to set stronger boundaries and standards for the business and have greater control. However, he would not want to restrict divisional heads so much that they were not free to make decisions and operate effectively.

(b) It could be argued that despite his desire to make the organisation more centralised, Mr Hayward has a Theory Y approach. He has argued that BP has failed to listen enough to what the bottom of the organisation is saying. He also uses the word collegiate. This suggests that he thinks that workers lower in the business have an important role to play and their views are important to the success of the business.

Case study

(a) Management by Objectives (MBO) can be a very effective method to help managers organise and control the operations of a business so that it can achieve its aims. It highlights the objectives clearly, so that everyone in the business knows what they are trying to achieve - their targets. It helps the coordination of operations, so that there is no conflict between the activities of employees. Workers, knowing what they have to achieve can be motivated, especially if incentives are given. However, despite these benefits there are problems. If it is poorly implemented or badly resourced MBO may not work. It can be confusing to employees. It assumes that employees understand the system and are motivated by incentives. Further, it can be inflexible and the business may not be allowed to change to meet changing conditions.

It could be argued that many of these problems were found in the implementation of MBO at the bank. The targets changed from month to month so employees had no clear idea about their real business objectives. Branch managers also did not really understand what the business was trying to achieve. Targets were often unattainable and so there was little chance that employees would earn their bonuses. In this case they were unlikely to be motivated. Further, some employees were given the bonus even if they didn't meet their targets as in the case of Patricia McGuire. Also, the performance appraisal process was very one way. There was no facility for feedback from staff.

So the business was not really gaining a clear picture about whether MBO was working or not. For all these reasons it could be argued that MBO was not successfully implemented at the bank.

(16 marks)

Question 1

(a) A number of different leadership styles may be identified. One is a bureaucratic, reactive or authoritarian style. It is suggested that many companies in the UK still use this style. Another style mentioned is an empowering style. This is perhaps a more democratic leadership style where employees' views are taken into consideration in decision making. A further style might be an entreprenurial style. This could be where a more laissez-faire approach is taken and employees are given power to make their own decisions within limits.

(b) Evidence suggests that there is a link between leadership styles and motivation. In a report by the Chartered Management Institute, an authoritarian or dictatorial style was said to lead to increased absenteeism, higher levels of sickness and lower productivity. In authoritarian companies only 44 per cent of managers said they got job satisfaction, compared to 71 per cent in other types of company. This suggests that authoritarian styles are demotivating for employees. A more democratic approach could increase motivation. It is suggested that the most successful companies have empowering leadership styles. This may also be the case with entrepreneurial styles. However, they can also be demotivating in some cases because of a lack of leadership. This style might only motivate employees if they are the type of people who enjoy the ability to organise themselves.

(c) There are some situations where an authoritarian leadership style might be appropriate. It is often argued that such as style might be necessary in organisations such as the army, where clear instructions need to be given and followed. A business facing pressure to deliver results with fewer resources may benefit for such as style. Decisions may need to be taken quickly and accurately by a single leader. Discussions or wide ranging decision making may lead to delays and a lack of guidance. People may not have the skills to make the decisions required. In a crisis, someone needs to take control and be clear about how the business will recover. On the other hand, this style may only be appropriate if the leader has a clear vision about how to improve the situation and the skills and ability to carry this out.

Question 2

(a) A number of factors may have influenced the decision to introduce a leadership scheme for the Fire and Rescue Service. One major factor was the need for leaders to develop the skills needed to cope with the demands of the job. It was argued that leaders needed to be more resilient. They also needed to be able to demonstrate respect and trust for colleagues and concern for service for customers. This implies that leadership would need a wider range of skills.

Another factor is the views of the organisation itself. The Fire and Rescue Service has a diversity strategy. It wants to ensure that its leaders fit in with the strategy. They need to have the ability to bring on board a diverse workforce. 'Transformational leaders' are argued to be more able to do this. In particular the strategy is designed to encourage more women into senior positions and more black and minority ethnic staff.

Case study

(a) It could be argued that Martin Guntac is a democratic leader. Such leaders take into account the views of employees when making decisions to varying degrees. They may ultimately make important decisions themselves, but they are more likely to consider what employees have to say before taking any decision than, say, a leader with an autocratic style.

Certain factors are likely to have influenced Martin's choice of leadership style. One is Martin' own opinions and personality. Martin sees himself as 'people person'. Given this view he is more likely to be able to appreciate the role that others might play in the business. He might be concerned about their motivation and also consider that they have a valuable role to play in the business. He allows people to make mistakes but he believes this is an important part of allowing employees to take responsibility.

Another factor is the tradition of the business. It has developed with regular weekly meetings with four site managers. These are the 'sort of' board of directors of the company. It has also developed a system of teamwork. An organisation based on teamwork is more likely to be one that is suited to a democratic leadership style.

A further factor might be the type of workforce at the business. Workers are encouraged to make their own decisions and are given training to allow them to develop skills that may help. In a survey over 90 per cent of staff felt motivated at work. This suggests that they feel that a leadership style that takes their views into account is important. Martin also relies heavily on the four site managers. They are very experienced and so the business might be suited to a more democratic leadership style. They are bale to handle day-to-day operation of the business.

The organisation of the business might also play a part. It is split over a number of dealerships. Allowing managers to make decisions and checking on targets may be more suitable than trying to make all decisions for parts of the organisation that are in different areas.

(12 marks)

(b) It might be argued that adopting a democratric style could have problems for Martin. He has to consider the views of others before making decisions. This might slow down the decision making process. Allowing workers to make decisions also leads to errors. This can be costly for the business. Training in decision making can also be expensive.

In some cases Martin's democratic style may not be appropriate. If the company faced a crisis then allowing dispersed decision making and many views could lead to problems in making key decisions. For example, Martin had to sack a site manager who was consistently underperforming. Some staff may not have the skills suited to delegated decision making.

On the other hand, Martin's style does seem to be appropriate for the business. 90 per cent of staff felt motivated at work. This may be because of his leadership style. A well motivated workforce will help the business to be productive and profitable. Listening to the views of experienced managers may also help the business. They run the business on a daily basis and this knowledge may prove vital in making the most important decisions.

In conclusion, although in the case of the underperforming manager, Martin may act in a more autocratic style, it does seem that his leadership style is suited to his organisation. Even when he took a difficult decision, he may still have consulted other managers for their views.

(16 marks)

71 | Individuals in organisations

Question 1

(a) Using information from the article, applied to Cattell's 16PF, it could be suggested that Ingvar Kamprad has some of the following personality traits. His care with money and the fact that he drives around in an eleven year old Volvo may suggest that he is quite highly sober, prudent and taciturn rather than happy-go-lucky. It could also be argued that he is intelligent, inventive, experimental and radical in his thinking. He was the first to think about flat packs and for customers to come to his store rather than deliver to the customer. He also appears to be self-sufficient, shrewd, hard to fool and tough minded. There is a suggestion that he is still in complete control of the business he founded. Also he did not immediately trust his sons and asked them to take responsibilities for different parts of the business to see who returned better results.

(b) IKEA entered a highly competitive market when it began. It could be argued that this needed an experimental and yet tough minded approach to business from an entrepreneur. There was a need for something new and different to break into the market. There was also a need to clearly understand market forces. His frugal approach to life is likely to be similar in the way he deals with staff. He would expect to get the maximum out of anything and not be wasteful with anything, particularly the business's resources. Such an approach can reduce costs and maximise efficiency. This can lead to greater profit.

Question 2

(a) It may be possible to analyse Padraig Cruikshank's personality using Eysenck's two dimensional matrix. The way in which Padraig started and operated his business and the types of decisions and actions he took might possibly classify him as extrovert-stable. Examples in the article may suggest that he is generally carefree, easygoing, responsive and talkative. In terms of carefree approach to life there is a suggestion that he views life as being more than work - he takes the view that people should 'live for the day'. He appears to be easy-going and responsive. For example, he wants friends as employees to be part of the business and be involved in the decision-making. And he attempts to consolidate this culture by setting up works councils that involve employees and managers talking together and making decisions. He also tries to be responsive to problems, particularly those highlighted in the Norwich area by talking with employees and finding creative and empathetic answers to problems of work overload by examining the possibilities of outsourcing, job sharing and/or flexible hours.

(b) Padraig's business faced certain difficulties. The rising demand for housing had placed a strain on the resources of the Norwich branch. Workers were being asked to work longer hours and claimed that they were breaking UK regulations. Padraig could at the time have simply stated that the extra work did not contravene legislation, if in fact he was correct. As long as extra time and flexibility was built into conditions of service, Padraig may have been justified in asking for extra time from workers.

However, such an approach is likely to have alienated staff. Padraig has tried to develop a culture in the business where staff are consulted over problems. His involved approach to business might enable employees to feel more fully engaged in decisions. Being open and responsive and including employees in decision-making is potentially empowering for employees. They may feel that their views are important in helping decide how best to cope with the increased demand. Some, as a result, may have been prepared to work longer hours. Others may give valuable information which could allow the business to decide whether other solutions such as outsourcing or job sharing would help. Padraig's personality and his approach to problems is likely to have minimised resistance to change and also to motivate employees, preventing disruption. It could also have allowed the business to make an effective decision to suit the challenges it faced.

Question 3

(a) There are certain problems for a business with employing knowledge workers. First, they may be intelligent, but this is only useful if they are working 'for' the business. Because they are potentially very skilled and make it their business to use existing knowledge, acquire new information, combine and process knowledge to create new solutions to problems and learn continuously from their experience, they often work to their own agenda. Second, for the reasons above, they can also be difficult to manage. This may lead to operational difficulties. For example, they may be unable to work in teams. Third, they know that their human capital is a transferable asset which they can take from one company to the next depending on who might be the highest bidder. So it is potentially difficult to make knowledge workers loyal to a business.

(b) The brightest people are likely to have the natural intelligence to analyse problems most effectively and think creatively about solutions to those problems. They are also likely to be quicker at seeing the issues and evaluating what needs to be done. All this makes for a better knowledge worker - someone who can acquire new information and combine and process different information to deal effectively with new problems that may arise. Also evidence from research suggests that a 10% increase in the workforce's education level leads to an 8.6% productivity gain. This can be compared with a 10% rise in plant and equipment values, which increased productivity by 3.4%. Having the brightest people should, according to these statistics, make those companies most productive.

(c) Knowledge in the form of processing and producing ideas, images, thought, concepts and symbols is often of more value to business than products themselves. If this knowledge resides in people, then it could be argued that knowledge workers are assets to an organisation, ie that knowledge workers have the capability of making a business more productive. If businesses do not view knowledge workers as assets they are likely to lose them to other businesses and hence a large part of the value of that business. Workers who leave the business take with them valuable knowledge. New workers may not have this knowledge. Costs may rise and productivity may fall if key employees leave.

The example of Maurice Saatchi in the article confirms the commercial value of knowledge workers. When key workers left, stakeholders became uncertain about the future performance of the business as important information on the running of the company left with the employees. Customers defected to other businesses. Shareholders sold their shares, causing prices to fall.

Case study

(a) Emma was keen to advance her career. She did this by developing her knowledge and skills through evening and weekend courses. She was intelligent and showed perseverance. After 4 years she had completed her Institute of Personnel Management qualifications - professional qualifications that most managers in personnel or human resource management strive to achieve. When Emma was promoted into personnel she was concerned to get practical experience of a variety of personnel specialisms - in employee legislation, industrial relations and recruitment. She was always keen to solve problems in new and exciting ways. All of these characteristics ensured that she achieved rapid promotion.

(4 marks)

(b) Emma is described as outgoing and popular with her peers. From the Eysenck test that she completed she is categorised as a stable-extrovert and innovator in problem solving. Her problem was to try and retain staff that had been recruited to the organisation and hence reduce labour turnover. Many employees had undergone extensive and expensive training and she felt it would be cheaper in the long run for the organisation to find creative answers to this problem. If she had been an adaptor she would have accepted the situation as given and tried to improve aspects of it, eg present recruitment strategies to see if these could be improved or present incentive payment systems to see if these could be altered. What she suggested was a far more radical idea; it meant capital investment in crèche facilities and an educational campaign aimed at men to try and persuade them to enter administration. Nothing like this had ever been suggested to senior management before.

(6 marks)

(c) Innovators sometimes generate a whole list of ideas to solve problems that may not always suit the business. Their solutions may be new and innovative, but they could be risky, initially costly and may require a reorganisation of other parts of the business. Emma's plans were rejected by management as being 'expensive in the short term and too far fetched'. Innovators can also be extrovert and irritable to many other employees who may be introvert and adaptors. This can cause unnecessary friction and poor staff relationships and, in the extreme, may force people to leave the business.

(8 marks)

(d) Emma's ideas were rejected by senior management in the business. There might be a number of reasons why this happened.

- Senior management were possibly adaptors and so found new and radical ideas threatening.
- The picture with the text shows all senior managers to be male. They may have felt a certain prejudice and resentment at being told by a woman, in an assertive manner, about creative ways of solving

problems that they might not have even recognised.

- It might be that finances were tight at the time and so in the short run no extra funds could have been made available for these ideas.
- Emma did not show any team approach in her work. It was her idea that was devised with little consultation and involvement from others. She did not communicate with others.
- She did not do any market research among the business's employees to see whether they would use the crèche facilities. She just thought they might.

(10 marks)

(e) Emma could have mentioned the problem, as she understood it, to senior management when she had noticed it. She might have sought approval for finding solutions to these possibilities and then set up a team to examine issues. First, this would have given her the opportunity of finding out about what senior management saw as priorities and secondly it might have made her final recommendations more acceptable. As the team generated ideas she might have mentioned them to senior management and acknowledged their responses to them. Again, this would have demonstrated a willingness to communicate with senior management and would have prepared them for the final report, of which they would have had previous knowledge.

(20 marks)

Question 1

(a) (i) One formal group that the first applicant might belong to is the management team at the business. The business may operate in the food and beverage industry and the management team would be likely to make decisions regarding production and marketing of its products, for example. The second applicant might belong to a formal group such as a group of park keepers at a zoo or other animal residency.

(ii) One informal group that the first applicant might belong to is a wine club made up from people at the business. Informal groups tend to be people with similar interests in a business. The second applicant might belong to a group of animal lovers or dog owners who meet with their pets.

(b) (i) There are likely to be certain benefits to a new employee of belonging to informal groups in a business. Workers may give practical advice and moral support about the job. They may also help a new worker who might initially be unsure about exactly what is required. The group will also be able to inform the new employee of the norms, values and regulations, both written and unwritten, of the departments and teams that he or she will be working with. This may help the worker to be both motivated and productive.

(ii) Businesses often see informal groups as an important part of the induction process. They help new employees to settle, which should ensure they work effectively as quickly as possible. This can save time and reduce costs. A business can also use informal groups to communicate its objectives to employees. An informal group may also act as a self-regulating means of discipline. If a group member develops a problem, such as consistent lateness, the informal group may subtly attempt to convince the employee of the repercussions of his or her actions. This will be especially true if group reward schemes are in operation.

Question 2

(a) There is a number of characteristics that appear to make the work of the group in the hotel effective. First, the group of employees operates as a team and this has been supported by the hotel management through obtaining Investors in People status. Second, each member of the team understands the others' contribution and they are flexible. When any one of them is absent the others in the team can cover for that person without reducing quality. Third, the team also demonstrates the ability to generate new ideas and solve problems. This was shown when a member of the team suggested that a reminder be sent in busy periods and this reduced unfilled rooms by 50%.

(b) There are still some problematic areas of group development that have yet to be ironed out. There is evidence, for the new wedding service that was introduced, that people in the group did not know precisely who should take responsibility. For example, there was a problem with the flowers and also with who should make decisions about when lunch should be served. This might indicate that roles have not been completely agreed. The communication in the group needs improving. Lastly, there is an issue about leadership that also needs to be addressed.

(c) There is perhaps a need to have a clearer understanding of the role of each person when new work is taken on board. There is also a need for greater leadership. There also needs to be improvements in communication between members of the group. Furthermore, the group needs to be fully motivated and able to carry on working effectively in the absence of its leaders. All of these issues could perhaps be solved by a clearer identification of roles in the business. This may be dealt with by a clearer job description and a clearer delegation of authority and responsibility. Another solution could be to carry out weekly or regular meetings to identify problems and

suggest solutions. This may be particularly important when key events are taking place.

Question 3

(a) IceCool was concerned with two major business problems - rising costs and a lack of corporate appeal to the youth market. It asked the production and marketing departments to put forward suggestions. Both departments were keen to impress because it could have meant greater resources being dedicated to them. Hence both the departments worked in isolation and on separate ideas. When their plans were unveiled to the management team they tried to criticise each other's approaches and highlighted the benefits of their own ideas. They were both hoping that they could win the argument and as a result have resources directed to them. This, therefore, caused the conflict between them.

(b) The benefit to the company of this conflict is that it has generated two possible solutions to the problems. The production department has highlighted poor productivity and the marketing team has developed a new product idea. If the two teams had not been competitive in their work they may have worked together and not generated both solutions. They may have been quite happy to put forward one idea. The company could use both ideas to help improve its performance. It is also likely that, in a desire to impress, the departments have been extremely well motivated and have put forward two good ideas.

(c) When the final decision is made, IceCool might ensure that the two departments work with each other by getting members of one department to work with members of the other department on a joint project. The heads of departments could initially work together or exchange roles. This can be further enhanced by communication and swapping of other department members. The business would also hope that, as well as these formal groups, informal groups would form which would help to motivate, support and pass ideas between employees.

Case study

(a) (i) There is a number of formal groups at Tyler Farndon. Formal groups are groups set up to carry out specific tasks. They have arranged meetings and rules determining their activities. Examples at Tyler Farndon might include the works council, the heads of department group, the union group and the shareholder group.

(ii) Informal groups are groups which are made up of employees in a business with similar tastes, but with few formal procedures which are not part of the formal business organisation. Examples at Tyler Farndon may include meetings between the head of finance and R&D who joined the business together and often attend conferences or an informal meeting between Nick and some managers to discuss possible redundancy.

(6 marks)

(b) Communication takes place through formal and informal groups in a number of ways. Certain formal groups have influenced communication. The works council, for example, which has 20 members, discusses various aspects of the business. These include production, changes in organisation and the future direction of the business. The heads of department group also allows communication to take place. For example, Sunita, the head of human resources, meets with other departmental heads to discuss human resource issues. The union group meetings will be organised to bring together union members to examine issues which are relevant to their needs and potential changes in business organisation. Shareholder groups will meet to discuss the benefits and drawbacks of potential developments.

Informal groups also enable communication. For example, the head of finance and R&D meet informally and tend to go to the same conferences where they discuss and communicate about industry trends. Various employee groups discuss and communicate about business developments and have heard via the grapevine about potential redundancies associated with the possible merger. Various manager groups have met, informally developing a strategy so that they all benefit from any future changes.

(10 marks)

(c) There are likely to be certain benefits of team operation and group decision making at the business. The clearest example of team working and group decision making is the works council. The council provides a forum for employees and managers from all parts of the business to work together as a team. This means that they can examine particular problems from a variety of perspectives. This may allow the group to generate more creative and realistic solutions.

Commitment and motivation between team members is likely to be enhanced by operating as part of the works council. Team members may feel that their views are being recognised and taken into account. They could feel that they are making a valid contribution to the business. In addition, being organised as a single status company with the same terms and conditions of employment for all is also likely to be motivating.

Groups can also provide accountability for the business. For example, the head of each department must argue for its budget each year at team meetings. They are likely to base this on the performance in previous years. The finance manager, for example, has stressed the need to remain within budget.

(10 marks)

(d) There is a variety of potential conflicts which can occur between groups in the business. One may be between employees and the business. Employees' groups are threatened by changes in status to their working. They are concerned about redundancies and changes to organisation and culture by mergers and the inclusion of new groups with different approaches to working and doing business.

Another may be between departmental managers. There is clearly a friendship between the heads of R&D and finance. This may result in R&D getting more resources than other departments, so causing resentment. Another conflict may be between the finance manager and other department managers. The finance manager seems to want financial restraint. Other managers may want to expand the budget in order to grow the business or develop their areas.

A further conflict may be shareholders and other groups, such as managers and employees. Shareholders may have different views about how they want the business to evolve. This may create conflict with the management of the business. So, for example, employees may feel that the business should continue to grow organically whereas stakeholders may want the merger to go ahead in order to maximise their share value or dividend payments.

(12 marks)

(e) In certain areas of the business there does appear to be effective group and team operations. For example, the works council appears to be the embodiment of the business's strategy of 'excellent products, ethically produced' and 'working together, working better'. Most workers appear to be willing to accept the decisions of the works council as they feel that their views are being represented. In addition, heads of departments meetings seemed to provide the possibilities of discussing business problems and sharing ideas about resource issues. Further, the single status approach to the business seems to motivate employees, who are not put in a position to resent exceptional bonuses given to management.

However, some of the informal groups appear to be creating some strains and difficulties for the business. The friendship between the R&D manager and the finance manager might create future resentment. The informal employee groups and grapevine are creating tensions within the workforce about possible ways the business might go. And informal management groups seem to be destabilising the business by developing strategies to look after their own interests.

It could be argued, therefore, that although the business has been relatively successful, it must make certain that all issues regarding uncertainty are discussed through formal channels set up to do this if it is to ensure that communication is effective and disruption does not take place.

(12 marks)

Question 1

(a) The Future Network plc has reorganised its UK business into three new operating divisions – games, computing and entertainment. Certain centralised services have been cut, particularly support services and each division now acts as a profit centre. In effect the company has decentralised by giving authority to the three divisions to develop their own strategy and make decisions within the overall framework of the business. This has meant that certain levels of management are likely to have disappeared and, in particular, long chains of command are likely to have been cut. In addition, each division is likely to need specialist functions working in finance, production, marketing etc to be working together. Hence there is every likelihood that the company will move from a bureaucratic, hierarchical organisational structure to one that is more matrix orientated.

(b) There are likely to be both benefits and possible disadvantages in the changes at The Future Network. A benefit of a more decentralised matrix structure is that employees and management are more accountable for the success or failure of the division as a profit centre. Hence they are more likely to have responsibility for decision making, which may lead to greater job satisfaction. In addition, because employees and managers in each division are likely to have a better working knowledge of their product and service, they are more likely to develop policy and practice that reflects the needs and demands of their customer base. Further, the divisions are likely to be more responsive to changes in the market and, because of delegated authority, more able to act quickly to respond to those changes. The article also suggests that the division may have led to reduced costs. These may have included fixed costs, such as centralised support, and other costs such as labour costs.

However, there are sometimes disadvantages of a decentralised compared to a more centralised structure. One disadvantage is that certain ordering and purchasing procedures might have been standardised and organised across the firm previously, which might have lowered costs because of economies of scale. In addition the managers of the divisions would need to ensure that they worked within the broad strategy of the business. Without this clarity of purpose and vision the divisions could work in isolation and create a skewed configuration of business operation that did not match the more strategic aspects of market development. There could, for example, be duplication of effort between the games, computing and entertainment, divisions particularly where the differences between the divisions at the boundaries of that provision are somewhat blurred, eg where there is the clear delineation between games, entertainment and computing for example with computer games. Finally, each division would need to ensure that its management team was clearly developed and trained to be able to undertake new responsibilities.

The previous organisational structure would have had numerous senior managers with significant management experience who may have helped lead the business through difficult times. The benefits of this experience may not be there with the new divisions.

Question 2

(a) There are both advantages and disadvantages to the Castle Gate Hotel of flexible working. One advantage is that resources can be tailored to demand at the hotel. For example, when the hotel is fully booked in July and August casual labour can be hired to provide extra help at the hotel. At other times of the year when the hotel is not fully occupied it will only retain the services of its full time employees. Further, it allows the management of human resources to be more flexible. Specialist services can be bought in

whenever they are required. Accounting staff, for example, are re-employed when accounts need to be produced. Other services can be subcontracted out to local firms, such as laundry services. The use of a flexible workforce in this way can benefit the business in a number of ways. The overall costs of hiring labour are likely to be lower as part time workers would lower overall wage costs. Subcontracting to other firms may also lower costs. It may also increase efficiency. For example, it is possible that laundry services offered by a local firm could be better than what the hotel itself could offer. Hiring fewer workers is also likely to reduce the use of resources and the need to make National Insurance contributions. Both of these would lead to reductions in costs.

However, one problem that the business may face is that casual staff may lack the commitment of full time permanent staff. They may also lack knowledge and experience in providing the services required by the hotel. This may lead to a fall in quality in the service provided by the hotel and customers may react against this, resulting in a reduction in bookings and harm to the reputation of the business. A further problem may be disruption to staff working as a result of having to employ casual or part time staff. For example, problems created by casual staff often have to be sorted out by permanent staff increasing their work load. The work load of Emma, Colin's daughter, also increased as a result of the constant need to hire casual staff. There could also have been costs associated with this such as any recruitment agency fees. Further, the strain placed on permanent staff as a result of extra work led to high absenteeism and also a resentment on their part. These are both likely to have affected the efficiency of the business. Finally, subcontracting does not always guarantee that costs will be reduced. For example, Emma felt that subcontracting the marketing operation to a local business was expensive and may not have been value for money as the marketing may not have achieved the desired effect that the hotel required.

Case study

(a) Businesses, such as Lloyds TSB, may benefit in a number of ways from teleworkers. Teleworkers can help to reduce the cost of the business. For example, a business may employ 100 workers, each requiring a workstation and a computer and an office would need to be large enough to take all staff. If half of these workers operated from home, the office size could be reduced, cutting rent, for example. So could the office equipment. This suggested in the evidence firm Internet service provider Eclipse Internet. Major savings of £14,778 can be made on workstations in London and £6,422 elsewhere. Also, staff would not have to travel to work. So they would not be affected by rail strikes or other inconveniences. Again, evidence from Eclipse Internet suggests that 20 per cent of workers spend over an hour a day commuting. Further, teleworkers give flexibility. They could be asked to work in the evening, increasing the operating time of the bank. Self employed teleworkers may also be hired in busy periods.

There are also benefits for teleworkers themselves. They might argue that they would be better motivated as they are allowed to determine their own work conditions. If they were self employed, this might help them to operate more efficiently and earn more. They might also benefit from a better work life balance. For example, they could be in a better position to look after children, they could work when they want, and not travelling, will reduce time spent 'getting to work' and stress. They may even be free to undertake leisure activities in the day and work at nights or weekends if they wished.

(8 marks)

(b) Certain types of worker may be suited to telework. Some of these are suggested by the information in the tables. For example, certain occupations tend to operate as teleworkers more than others. These occupations include managers and senior officials, and professional and technical occupations. Examples might be the manager of the overseas marketing function of a large plc, with operations in many countries, technical staff responsible for setting up businesses with entire bespoke computer systems or writers of computer software. The majority of these workers tend to be male.

Teleworker homeworkers are also found in administrative occupations, but tend to be female. Also, most teleworkers who work in their own home or work from home as a base tend to be self-employed and full time from the information in Table 2. Males are often full time employees and females part time.

A number of reasons may be put forward to explain these trends. The nature of certain job demands makes telework effective in some cases. Businesses often want employees in some occupations to be flexible, to be able to respond quickly to changing situations and to meet people immediately when required. So, for example, it may be far more effective for a manager controlling a large operation with branches abroad to work from home as a base, travel to branches when required, and communicate via IT with head office and other employees. Also the skills of some employees lend themselves better to teleworking. Employees in technical occupations, such as the computer industry, are familiar with IT and can easily operate from home without the need to 'attend' work every day. Employees' own needs also affect their suitability for telework. Increasingly women are making up a larger proportion of the workforce. They are also returning to work. Part time telework jobs in administrative work or technical work makes it easier for them to work from home and look after children. However, this is also the case for males looking after children. Also, as lone parent families become more common, parents are looking for ways to work from home in order to achieve a better work life balance. Further, the nature of telework makes it attractive to the self employed. They can work from home, operate their own conditions of work and hours of work, be flexible over work time and offer their services to many businesses. They are also flexible, which may be attractive to businesses hiring their services.

(12 marks)

(c) There are many potential benefits to taking on teleworkers for Footballfangs.com, both for the business itself and its teleworkers, as explained in (b). These include potential cost savings, improved flexibility and the ability to react to change, improved motivation and a better work life balance. Employing teleworkers rather than premises based employees might therefore be a cost efficient way for the business to expand. Further, the type of operation the business conducts, selling outfits for dogs over a website, lends itself to teleworkers rather than using a large office where workers are employed. The teleworkers can work from home, for example, either updating the website or contacting potential customers via telephone or email.

But there are also potential problems with teleworking. Such methods of work require technology to operate efficiently and not break down. Workers with websites in their own home may feel isolated from their work colleagues and lack self motivation, which could affect the efficiency of the business. The business may also find it difficult to monitor how long and how efficiently teleworkers work. Teleworking can also have communication problems and the disparity of the staff mean that it may be difficult to establish the corporate culture the business wants. Further it could be argued that the potential benefits of teamwork and sharing knowledge are not gained when individual employees are working in isolation.

Overall, however, it may be argued that these problems tend to exist when businesses grow large. Small operations may be able to get over technical and communication problems and as long as regular communication takes place, the required culture can be established. Span of control problems also tend to be reduced in smaller organisations. And the nature of the operation lends itself very well to teleworking. The business may also need to hire premises as the operation currently takes place in their home. So it could be argued that employing teleworkers rather than full time or part time employees based on the premises is a low cost and less risky expansion strategy.

(20 marks)

Question 1

(a) (i) Number of new staff required = number of posts ×
% turnover = 6,258 × 38% = 2,378.
(ii) Number of new staff required = number of posts ×
% turnover = 4,780 × 52% = 2,486.
(iii) Number of new staff required = number of posts ×
% turnover = 3,524 × 125% = 4,405.
(b) If labour turnover fell by 20% then labour turnover would be
38% - 20% = 18%.
The number of new staff required is number of posts ×
% turnover = 6,258 × 18% = 1 126. So staff required would be
1,126.
(c) Posts filled by students aged 16-25 are likely to have a higher
staff turnover than young women aged 21-30 at Pickerell's for a
number of reasons. First students will probably only be looking for
part time jobs or temporary jobs in their college or university
holidays. Or they might be only looking for a little extra income for a
period of time. Also, students at the business were often from EU
countries who would work for a while before moving to other jobs
with longer hours or perhaps returning home. On the other hand,
young women aged 21-30 were likely to remain with the business as
they saw the chance of developing a career and perhaps moving into
management.

Question 2

(a) External recruitment involves hiring employees from outside the
organisation who do not work for the business at the moment. They
may be employees who work for other businesses or people who do
not have a job at present. There is a number of examples of this type
of employment suggested in the article. Seasonal workers employed
at Christmas or other periods, for example, could be unemployed
people who are willing to take temporary jobs to earn extra income.
They might also be students looking for part time or temporary
work over the Christmas period. They might even be workers in part
time or full time employment looking for extra income. In all these
cases the employees before the Christmas period may not have
previously worked for the business. In this case the business is
planning to bring in extra workers from outside the organisation to
cope with surges in seasonal demand.

Another example of planning to increase the supply of labour
using external recruitment is the recruitment of over 50s employees.
Many businesses including Asda are recruiting older staff, recognising
that they bring knowledge and skills to a job which younger people
may not have. Some businesses are targeting older workers when
vacancies occur as customers may value their experience. These may
be workers who have retired from other businesses and are looking
to be re-employed.

A further example of planning external supply is the recruitment
of workers for new call centres such as the BT call centres in Delhi.
BT would not have previously had an operation in this area of the
world. So it would have to recruit new employees who are unlikely
to have worked for the business. It is unlikely that many workers in
UK centres who are already working for BT would move to centres
in India.
(b) The factors that might influence the recruitment of workers
from outside the organisation in these situations are numerous. One
factor that might affect the recruitment of staff in seasonal periods
is the level of unemployment. Asda requires extra staff at peak
periods. Its existing employees are unlikely to be able to cover all
the jobs required at that time. If there is a large pool of
unemployed labour then a business might easily be able to attract
workers from outside. On the other hand if employment rates are
relatively high the business might find it more difficult to attract

workers.

Demographic trends may influence recruitment of older workers
at Asda. It is argued that the UK has an ageing population. If there are
more people in the age group 50-70 who are retiring, then this will
give a larger pool of potential employees for the business. Their
attitudes to work will also be important. If many wish to continue to
work, perhaps because of low levels of pensions, then again the pool
of labour should be greater from which to recruit.

The degree of flexibility might also be important. For example, if
workers are increasingly prepared to work in more than one job, or
work at different times, this gives a larger number of potential
workers, particularly at times of high seasonal demand.

Cost is likely to have been a major factor influencing recruitment
at BT call centres. For BT, the costs of opening call centres is 30%
lower in India, for example, than in the UK. In addition there is a high
level of skilled workers, many of them graduates, to choose from. The
skills available are also likely to be important. It could be argued that
recruiting from so many graduates in india gives a higher skills level to
the labour force at BT call centres.

The benefits offered by businesses in relation to those of
competitors are also likely to be an influence. Asda for example
provides the same benefits and job security for its flexible part time
staff as it does for its full time staff. In addition it has a flexible working
package for its target group of over 50s. It has introduced a week's
leave for new grandparents and up to two years career break. These
factors could encourage greater employment of older workers. It
might even encourage part time workers to work full time or staff to
move from one business to another.

Case study

(a) Certain factors may have affected the ability of the business to
promote employees to higher posts. One factor could be the training
and qualifications of staff. The business encouraged staff lower down
the hierarchy to obtain extra law qualifications or take the Institute of
Law examination. This would allow them to be promoted to higher
positions. Second, the ability of staff to be flexible. More flexible staff
may be of more use to the organisation. For example, a secretary
working in two legal areas may remove the need to have two
specialist secretaries for the business. Third, the policy of the business
towards promotion. If the business is strongly committed to
promoting internally and rewarding its staff for service then this will
increase the promotion chances of employees. Fourth, the number of
higher level posts available. The larger the number of higher level
posts, the more chance of internal promotion, although there is also
perhaps more chance of external promotion. Fifth, the age of the
workforce. A business may prefer to employ younger workers in
higher posts as they are likely perhaps to give longer service in those
posts. Finally, the motivation of staff. Well motivated staff are more
likely to be promoted than those with high absences and poor
motivation. **(6 marks)**
(b) There is a number of ways in which Stewart and Mathers could
have forecast the increased need for employees. First, it could use
past information in the form of time series or backdata. The table
shows figures for sales revenues, total employees working in the
company and number of employees leaving over a six year period.
This shows an increasing percentage of employees joining the
company on a year in year out basis. In addition the figures, with
some straightforward calculations, can provide a labour turnover
index. This index over the same period shows only slight increases,
suggesting a marginal increase in percentage wastage rate. In
addition, there is also a need to take into account workers'
productivity. Since 2004 there appears to have been a 27% increase
in productivity per worker, perhaps due to potential economies of
scale. In addition, by using business and management knowledge
about the sector Stewart and Mathers detected a growth potential
in particular aspects of the legal market for cases taken out in
relation to personal injury. All these factors taken together can
provide data on which to forecast the increased need for employees
after the year 2004.

(10 marks)

(c) (i) A labour turnover index shows the number of employees leaving as a percentage of those that could have left. It is calculated by:

$$\frac{\text{Number of staff leaving per period}}{\text{Average number of staff in post}} \times 100$$

In 2004 the labour turnover index was:

$$3 \div 70 \times 100 = 4.3\%$$

In 2004 the labour turnover index was:

$$6 \div 100 \times 100 = 6.0\%$$

There has been an increase in 1.7 per cent in the labour turnover index over that period. **(4 marks)**

(ii) Increasing levels of labour turnover can lead to a number of effects on the business. First, it will increase the number of times that businesses need to advertise new posts. There will also have to be interviews and perhaps training every time an employee leaves. Second, it will take time for many new employees to settle into a new post. Productivity may suffer as a result. There may be lost business if the company cannot fill these posts. Internal appointees may settle in more quickly, although they themselves will leave a vacancy elsewhere in the organisation. Third, the business may need to reorganise if turnover is high, especially if important members of the business leave on a regular basis. Furthermore, all of the above are likely to lead to increasing costs for the business. Also, higher labour turnover may be demotivating for existing employees. The business may attempt to improve staff morale and retain staff by increasing the levels of motivation through better working conditions, more interesting and responsible jobs and better pay.

(10 marks)

(d) (i) For jobs at the base of the hierarchy both local and national factors external to the organisation will have an impact. The company is based in Skelmersdale with population and demographic trends that might suggest that it has a ready pool of potential entrants to the business, with a relatively easy and available public transport system. In addition there is a number of colleges in the area that provide specialist courses for relatively low entrant employees. In addition, government training and subsidies on the New Deal also provide the organisation with the possibilities of recruiting low entrant employees at reduced costs.

(ii) It would appear more difficult to recruit for managerial jobs external to the business. The article suggests that managerial posts need to be advertised in national newspapers and that the company may need to provide subsidies to potential employees to attract them to the area immediately. This suggests that the local labour market has a deficit of this type of employee. The business is also likely to have to fill higher level posts more quickly because of the potentially damaging effect on the organisation of the loss of key workers.

(12 marks)

Question 1

(a) (i) The type of approach taken by many traditional publishing companies tends to be a hard approach to human resources. This approach often requires an authoritarian leadership style. There are certain features of each of these which can be found in a traditional publishing organisation. A hard approach sees human resources as being like any other resource in the business, such as materials or machines. A business will manage its human resources by predicting what type and how many workers it will require in future, assessing its current employees and then deciding where to fill any gaps or how to reduce employees if necessary. This is often referred to as workforce planning. There is little attempt to integrate human resources into the strategy of the business or see the development of staff and their motivation as integral to its success. At many publishing companies, for example, and at *Metro* previously, people are given a low priority. They were often not seen as being important.

Further, this approach often requires an authoritarian leadership style. The leaders tend to be task-orientated. They focus on getting things done and completing tasks. They organise subordinates to achieve this and make sure they are given clear instructions about how to complete tasks. At *Metro*, previously, it is suggested that the style was very autocratic. Such a leadership style usually means that most if not all decisions are taken by the leader. This would fit in with a task-orientated approach and authoritarian leadership. It is also suggested that publishing businesses often need to meet deadlines and so they have little time to spend on 'people issues'. An authoritarian leadership style which was task-orientated could be suited to a business that needed to meet deadlines.

(ii) Originally *Metro* was 'a classic start-up'. It was autocratic and people were not the most important aspect of the business. However, in 2003 it wanted to change its approach. It could be argued that the new approach would take into account many aspects of the soft side of human resource management. This sees human resources as vital to the success of the business. It is also usually accompanied by a democratic leadership style, where employees' views are valued, their needs taken into consideration and they make a contribution to decisions and take initiative.

This approach appears to have had certain benefits for *Metro*. Workers tend to feel more valued by the business. As a result they may be more motivated. This can help improve the efficiency and productivity of the business. For example, workers in the past may have refused to work late when there was a deadline to meet if it involved them working past their leaving time. Now they often stay late because they want to. Staff are also likely to be motivated by appraisal meetings where their needs are discussed. Commercial staff at the top of grades are given special projects to retain their interest and motivation. The greater motivation may also be reflected in the fall in attrition rates, the rates at which people leave the business. If workers are more motivated they are likely to remain with the organisation, rather than leave for other work. This can help the business to retain staff with key knowledge and also reduces the costs of finding replacements.

Further, this approach may allow the goals of the business to be more easily achieved. There is evidence that staff understand the goals of the business under the new system. There was a 25 per cent rise in staff who understood Metro's goals between 2003 and 2004. One of the key goals, 72 per cent argue, is to develop people. This suggests that the business is increasingly considering that human resources are important in its success.

There is also evidence that the stress on training of employees can benefit Metro. The business calculates that there has been a 1 per cent improvement in skills for every £1 spent. Training can improve the efficiency and productivity of employees and the business itself, helping to increase profitability. For example, the induction process helps employees to understand the audience that the business is targeting. This is important if the product is to meet customers' needs and sell well. Training can also help employees to make progress through the company. Taking courses, for example, can provide better skills which may allow employees to become managers in future.

Even if trained employees leave to go to other jobs, taking a soft side approach to human resources can also be of benefit. Trained employees often take the good name of Metro elsewhere. The good reputation of the business might spread to customers, possible improving sales. But other employees looking for jobs may also consider working for the business. This could help Metro to attract well qualified and suitable applicants for jobs.

(b) It could be argued that there are many potential benefits for a new small publishing company in taking *Metro*'s approach to human resources management. Employees could be more motivated, leading to a more efficient workforce and increased productivity. They may want to remain with the business, reducing the costs associated with high labour turnover. They may be prepared to take on extra work or work later as they feel they are valued. They may be more skillful or have greater knowledge of the market, which can help the business to better target its customers. They may make better managers in future. Even if they leave, spreading the good name of the business can help future recruitment and possibly sales. Employees will also understand the goals of the business, perhaps helping it to achieve its aims and objectives.

However, taking such an approach is not without problems. There are inevitably likely to be increased costs. One simple example might be the extra costs of employing a human resources specialist, such as Laura Ashworth at *Metro*. This could be just one extra salary for a small business, although the costs may be difficult to meet. However, there are other associated costs which are likely to be far higher. These could include the costs of training, the costs of regular appraisal meetings and the cost of induction. There are also likely to be time costs. If employees are being trained or attending meetings they may not be working and production may be lost. Other workers may have to take over from them, resulting in lost production from other workers and disruption. The business may also have to reorganise greatly to take into account the new approach and incorporate the needs of employees into its operations.

In conclusion, it might be argued that, given the potential benefits of a soft HRM approach and a democratic leadership style, small publishing businesses starting up should follow *Metro*'s approach. There are costs, but if £1 spending on training results in a 1 per cent increase in skills, this may be considered a cost worth accepting. However, it is interesting that Metro actually started like all other publishing businesses, with a more autocratic style and taking a hard HRM approach. Only when it grew to be successful did it change its approach. Therefore it could be argued that small publishing companies need to start out being task-orientated, especially given the importance of deadlines and the relatively high costs of a people centred approach. As they grow they might then be in a position to follow *Metro*'s approach to human resources.

Question 2

(a) One of the reasons why remuneration at Gerham-Nevis may need to change is for retention purposes. If employees leave a business this can be costly and create problems. Paying the 'going rate' for a job or the rate which employees feel is appropriate could ensure that a business retains staff and could help to reduce staff turnover. At the motor repair company one of the problems stems from the fact that there appears to be pay differentials between its wages and those of local competitors. The dissatisfaction of one employee at this situation led to him leaving to take a job at a higher rate elsewhere. The vacancy caused difficulties for the business as it was unable to fill the post with a suitably qualified worker. In the end it was forced to employ a trainee and productivity fell as the trainee needed time to learn the trade.

Another reason why remuneration may need to change is to accommodate the move of the business into a new operating area. It has made a strategic decision to move into the market for respraying vehicles. This would require a change in the operations of the business.

But the requirements of employees would also need to change. For example, they are likely to need to develop skills which could involve training. They are also likely to have to work extra hours or perhaps change the times at which they work. This would require greater job flexibility from employees. In order to ensure that this change in operations takes place successfully a change in remuneration is likely to be needed so that employees would be able to carry out the new tasks and be motivated to fit in with new work arrangements.

A further change in operations would also require a possible change in remuneration. The owners of the business want to introduce a computerised accounting system for all invoices and to produce thecompany accounts. It is suggested that one of the current admin staff could take over this role. However, currently, admin staff are paid at a lower rate than mechanics. Further, it is likely that training for the new accounting system would be required and, again, the member of staff may have to work extra hours compared to their existing time at work. Remuneration would lead to change to provide an incentive for an administrative member of staff to take on this role.

Another potential reason why the business may need to change its remuneration system is the lack of progression through the business. Currently, if posts become available higher in the business they are often simply filled by an experienced worker when they become vacant. But there is no system to ensure that the worker has the skills, training or other requirements necessary for the job. A vacancy left further down is simply filled by employing another mechanic to take the place of the worker who has filled the higher position. A change in the remuneration system may be needed to prevent this haphazard method of dealing with vacancies and ensure that the appropriate staff are employed.

(b) To deal with the issues associated with the employee who left to join another business and the resulting vacancy problems the business may consider changes to its remuneration. First it could ensure that employees in its garages are paid the market rate for the job. This may be the wage that is currently being offered by local businesses, although there may be a need to take into account the national rate. This would depend on whether employees would consider moving to another area of the country to work as a mechanic. The business may also consider offering a slightly higher wage rate than local competitors if this could be afforded. Although matching or bettering the wage rates of rivals is a cost, there are also potentially damaging costs associated with losing staff. If key staff leave, cannot be replaced, or are replaced with less productive workers then output could fall which can be damaging in the long run, as appears to have been the case at Gerham-Nevis. Therefore, matching or bettering local wage rates is likely to be a cost worth paying to retain key staff.

To deal with the changes in operations the business may consider various changes to its remuneration system. Some of the mechanics are concerned that they do not have the necessary skills to carry out the respraying operations and are worried about the extra hours they will have to work. One solution is simply to offer them higher wages to take on a more skilled task and to offer them overtime for the extra hours that they have to work. This may be satisfactory for some employees. However, as many motivation theories have shown workers are not necessary motivated only by financial means. The two workers with young children have to travel long distances to work and may not necessarily find increased overtime an incentive to work extra hours or to take on board extra responsibility. In this case the business may need to consider non financial methods of motivation. For example, it might consider that job design is an important motivating factor. Allowing workers to vary their hours of work to suit their own personal needs could be more motivating than being paid overtime. More flexible working may allow them to achieve a better work/life balance. Further, the business could also introduce a job rotation system so that mechanics are working on different aspects of both car repairs and respraying at different times. This would allow them greater variety in their working life which could be motivating. So the business may consider adding a combination of both financial and non financial incentives to its remuneration system

to ensure an efficient change to the new service being offered.

Encouraging a member of the administration staff to take on the role of invoicing and accounting using the computer system is also likely to involve a change of remuneration. Currently administration staff are paid a lower rate than mechanics. So once again an increase in the wage rate for taking on this extra role may be required. However, as in the case of the mechanics with young children there may be a need to introduce non financial incentives. This could involve flexible work arrangements. But the business may also consider delegating a certain amount of responsibility. Empowering the member of staff to allow decisions to be made about the operations of the invoicing and accounting system may not only motivate the employee but help the business to operate more efficiently.

The rather haphazard method of appointing managers also needs to be addressed. The business could introduce a system of progression whereby employees are encouraged to train in management skills so if posts become available in future staff within the business have the ability to take on these roles. Financial rewards could be provided to encourage staff to train and higher grade posts could be established with higher rates of pay or other fringe benefits. Managerial staff may also be offered other incentives such as profit sharing. This would motivate employees as they would feel they were being rewarded for developing their skills and also have the potential to progress in the company and earn higher rewards in future.

Question 3

(a) B&Q has attempted to develop a human resource approach that is sensitive to the Chinese market. It decided not to saturate new businesses in China with ex-pats. Instead it intended to develop home grown talent and meet local requirements. A benefit with this approach is that it is likely to gain a competitive advantage over rivals. The business may be able to respond and adapt more quickly to the needs of the Chinese market. Further, Chinese HR professionals may be more likely to understand employee needs, customs and cultures in their own country. This could prevent problems when setting up new stores. Most importantly, perhaps, they may also understand how to tap into appropriate supplies of labour in their own country.

(b) A problem that B&Q may have faced in managing human resources in China was the difficulties of importing a foreign cultural concept and then adapting it to Chinese requirements. So, for example, the business struggled initially to attract appropriate personnel for their HR function. This was because the culture in China was for HR to have a policing and administrative role. This meant finding the right sort of employees was a problem. Further, performance appraisal may have also been difficult to administer given cultural differences. The application procedure, for example, did not operate in the way that B&Q envisaged given cultural differences in approaches.

Case study

(a) The soft side of human resource management includes motivation, organisational culture, support for employers and employees and industrial relations. Soft side human resource management in the article includes employees initially having a view about the organisational culture of working at Claridges. They felt a mistrust of management. Further, the core values developed for the business included soft side factors, such as commitment, passion, team spirit, interpersonal relations, responsibility of actions.

The hard side of human resource management includes analysing current needs of employees, predicting future demand of employees, predicting future supply of employees and predicting labour turnover. The article mentions issues of labour turnover, particularly the reduction from 73% to 27% in 2002. Future supply of employees is also highlighted through the internal recruitment policy the business instituted.

(6 marks)

(b) A number of factors may have influenced the business to change its approach to human resources management. One might have been the results of the staff survey. Only 47% of staff bothered to respond to a survey on the extent of problems at the hotel. Of those who did, only 67% felt they were proud to work for the hotel. This suggests that the business could have had a poorly motivated staff lacking the enthusiasm for working at the business. It argued that 'if you don't get it right for employees, you won't get it right for customers'. Staff may not have been happy working for the business, with staff turnover running at 73%.

Another factor may have been competition from other businesses. It was suggested that Claridges was 'battling to maintain its place in the market'. Other hotels were also offering a luxury service to compete with Claridges. And more competition was coming from cheaper hotels offering fewer services perhaps but reduced prices. As a result occupancy rates were down. Further, there had been complaints from customers.

In addition, demand for hotels, especially from the American market, had been affected by the events of 9/11. Many hotels in the UK, not just Claridges, had experienced a fall in trade. Foreign tourists were less willing to travel and this had cut the number of potential customers in the market. **(10 marks)**

(c) The changes in the management of human resources appear to have affected the business in numerous ways. There have clearly been certain benefits. First, pride at working for the hotel has risen to 99% and every member of staff responded to the survey as opposed to only 47% last time. This suggests that staff motivation has improved as a result of the changes. Second, people who visit the hotel say that they recognise the same faces. This implies that labour turnover has reduced. And various changes in culture, particularly in relation to staff enjoying their work, have altered the somewhat 'straight-laced' approach that traditionally dominated the service ethos. Staff are also likely to be better trained and encouraged to be promoted within the business. These changes are all likely to improve service and reduce costs. This could improve the profitability of the business.

However, there are likely to be some costs involved in the changes. First might be the reorganisation required. Working in teams may be new for some staff and managers. This would take time to get used

to and there may have been some 'teething problems'. There would also have been some costs, such as the prizes given as incentives. There will also be costs of training. However, the business would hope that these costs would be more than offset by the increases in trade due to improved service, which should result in increased profit. **(10 marks)**

(d) There is a number of methods which can be used to measure the effectiveness of human resource management. These include labour turnover, absenteeism, labour productivity, industrial relations, relations with stakeholders, profitability and health and safety. These can sometimes be condensed into the 4Cs model developed by the Harvard Business School - commitment, competence, congruence and cost effectiveness. It might be possible to examine some of the changes that have occurred using this model.

Commitment is part of the seven core values. It includes loyalty and motivation and is measured by labour turnover and absenteeism. The article suggests that the same people seem to be staying longer in their jobs. Customers see the same faces. Employees look to the future in the business rather than elsewhere. Competence is linked to employes skills and training, assessed through appraisal and skills inventories. There is evidence that this has improved with 450 employees now encouraged to look to the future through internal recruitment and promotion. In addition skills are being enhanced through staff being encouraged to move across departments to develop their skills. Congruence is whether employees and managers share the same values, assessed by absence of grievances and conflict. New core values have been developed and now 99% seem satisfied with working at the company. This suggests a lack of grievance or conflict. Cost effectiveness is linked to employees' efficiency, assessed by cost, output and profit figures. The business would hope, as suggested in (d), that any costs would be offset by improvements in trade, although there are no figures to support this in the article. Using these criteria it may be possible to conclude that in many cases human resources management has been successful at Claridges. **(14 marks)**

Question 1

(a) (i) Internal communication is communication within the business - internal emails from colleagues.
External communication is communication with people outside the business - site visit to discuss aspects of business with clients.
(ii) Message - request for information about the day's work.
Sender - other colleagues.
Receiver - Leila.
Feedback - discussion of problems and advice.
(iii) Channels of communication are the routes taken by messages - reports for clients based on the site visit.
(iv) A medium of communication is the method used to communicate - memos, briefings.
(v) Formal communication is communication through channels set up and approved by the business - internal meetings.
Informal communication is through non-formal channels - chat between Leila and Elle.
(vi) Vertical communication is by people at different levels of the hierarchy - discussion between Leila and her secretary.
Lateral communication is by people at the same level in the hierarchy - discussions with others at internal meeting or at coffee breaks in the morning.

Question 2

(a) One barrier to communication was the language barrier. Although Juan spoke English his Spanish accent was difficult to understand for his employee. He also used Spanish words which his employee, Jason, did not understand. A second problem was that an intermediary did not communicate the information. Jason informed his colleague, Emily, about the reasons for his absence. A third barrier was perhaps the perceptions of each person. Juan may have felt that the lateness of Jason and his non-attendance were signs of a lack of motivation and interest in the job. But in fact they were a result of genuine problems and concerns in his private life which unfortunately spilled over into work.
(b) One solution to the language difficulties might be simply for Juan to speak slower and not use Spanish words. Or alternatively Jason perhaps could ask questions if he does not understand exactly what Juan is telling him. If there was another member of staff who spoke Spanish and English they could translate. If Juan had some complex instructions then he could perhaps write them down and leave Jason to read them before asking about anything he didn't understand. It could be argued that if Emily had told Juan about Jason's situation then there would not have been a communication problem. But Jason should perhaps have taken responsibility to tell Juan himself. If this was not possible then he could have left a message, texted Juan via mobile phone or emailed him from home. Perhaps also Juan needs to set up some system to let him know if staff are going to be late or absent. The difference in attitudes and perceptions might be solved by a face to face meeting. Both Juan and Jason need to explain their view of the problem to each other. They will then be in a better position to appreciate the situation each person is faced with.

Case study

(a) Certain communication problems appear to exist at Jenning's Brewery Distribution Depot. There are problems with vertical communication at the business. Poor vertical communication is apparent between the office and the delivery workers. This has resulted in poor relations between the two.

There are also problems with lateral communication. Poor lateral communication is apparent between the four clerical assistants who took the orders and the four load planners. The two groups appeared to work in isolation.

Further, there are problems with communication between the business and external sources. Poor communication is apparent between the public houses, the customers of the business, and those in the business itself. **(4 marks)**

(b) Certain reasons may explain the communication difficulties between the office and the delivery workers. There appears to be no coherent policy on the handing out of orders to delivery workers. The supervisor is so keen to get work out on time that delivery is ad-hoc. Delivery workers do not get a chance to set up an established rota or relationships with public houses. Delivery workers also seem more motivated by their own interests rather than the most efficient way of working. The inability to contact the delivery workers if stock is left behind is a major problem. It would involve another journey which adds to costs or taking deliveries later which may cause difficulties for the customer.

Some reasons may also be put forward for the poor communication between the clerical assistants and the load planners. The sectioning off of areas makes each group isolated. Furthermore, a lack of a written record means that incorrect orders cannot be checked against the orders placed on computer by the load planners at a later date if there are computer problems.

One reason why the business may have communication problems with its customers is that the publicans feel that no one at the brewery wants to help them when, for example, they have a rush order or when they are trying to find out why a delivery has not been made. The barriers to communication appear to be caused by negative perceptions and attitudes.

The office staff appear not to give weight to the needs of publicans and, therefore, are not viewing the messages as important. Perhaps also, an impersonal telephone call is not the best way of dealing with consumer problems. A face-to-face discussion with a representative and some written evidence of their complaint may make the publicans more satisfied.

(8 marks)

(c) The changes could be explained to the workforce using team meetings/briefings. Face-to-face communication in this situation has a number of advantages:
- it encourages co-operation to take up the new ideas;
- it allows information to spread quickly among the staff;
- communication is two way so that points can be elaborated where needed (in addition, views can be exchanged and any constructive criticism listened to);
- involvement in the process may help to motivate employees.

Once the meetings have taken place, some written outline of the proposals with time for comment and further consultation may help. The changes could be explained to the publicans in a number of ways. They could be sent a formal letter. This could be backed up by the company newspaper publishing an article on the new approaches to customer service. In addition, the drivers could communicate the new systems informally on their delivery rounds. The brewery could also organise an official presentation for its publicans, where it might again explain the changes and show it is willing to listen and improve customer relations.

(10 marks)

(d) Possible solutions to the problem of poor communication between the office and delivery workers might be to ensure all delivery workers have a mobile phone or pager and to give delivery workers some form of incentive related to their performance. A simple communication device such as a mobile phone may be a relatively cheap way to prevent delivery problems. Incentives based on performance will tend to motivate workers better than the threat of sacking. This would only lead to increased costs of replacing the staff and costs involved in them being trained.

Possible solutions to the problem of poor communication between the assistants and the load planners might be to reorganise the office area and to merge and then retrain the two groups of staff in each other's skills. This may help to avoid isolation and lateral communication problems. It may also be possible to set up a more rigourous system of checking and reporting. So, for example, weekly meetings could take place between the two groups and information passed between them. Also information could be sent by e-mail telling each group what the other is doing. An alternative may be to appoint a customer services officer. This employee could be based at the office and visit the publicans regularly to hear their views. One way to prevent problems of orders being kept is to ensure that there is rigorous 'backing up' of all orders at the end of each day. This will prevent the need for a written copy.

Possible solutions to the poor communication between the business and its customers might be to train workers in customer care, to issue computers or faxes to publicans and to give delivery workers a regular route. This will help them to build up a rapport with the publicans and deal with their needs. For example, they may be able to communicate problems that publicans are having.

(e) Two possible solutions to communication problems between the office and delivery drivers were suggested. The use of mobile phones should be a way in which drivers could be informed of changes to plans or to pass on information if, for example, deliveries were left behind. Of course, the business would need to make sure that drivers did not answer the phone when driving. This could mean that they already arrived before they got the message, so it would not always be effective. There is also the cost of setting up phones for 65 drivers. Further, there could be abuse of the system with private calls being made. It could be argued that the offer of financial incentives for reaching targets is more effective. This would place the onus on the drivers to contact the depot. If they made the incorrect delivery, they would know that they would not receive their reward. Incentives can

be costly, but if they lead to greater efficiency and more trade they can be effective.

Backing up of orders at the end of the day is a fairly standard practice which should be carried out by all computer operators. The reorganisation of the office might be better than keeping the system the same and instituting numerous rigourous checks. There is no guarantee that new systems will be any more effective than old ones. The changes suggested should make employees multi-skilled. They could then be more productive and motivated. It could also help to develop a stronger corporate culture and feeling of team work between the two groups as they share tasks.

It could be argued that appointing a customer relations officer is a relatively cheap way of solving the communication problem with publicans. They can build up a relationship with the publicans and have the skills to communicate problems and solutions. It is debatable whether this is a better solution than training delivery workers and office staff in customer care and also allowing other technical methods of communication such as by email. On the one hand, it is cheaper for the business. And the level of care may be better as it could vary from one employee to another. On the other hand, having the immediate contact with a delivery employees may be preferred by publicans. Perhaps the business should try to find a more cost effective solution first and see how that works. If it fails it can then use the alternative.

(10 marks)

Question 1

(a) (i) In 1992, Eurotunnel, in an attempt to harmonise conditions and representation for both UK and foreign employees of Eurotunnel, set up a company council. At this time there was no union recognition. The council was only involved in consultation over business and employee issues. So the council was only asked for its opinions, it did not have any real influence over the decisions of the businesses. The Employment Relations Act, 1999, influenced many businesses to recognise trade unions, some for the first time. Employees were given the right under certain circumstances to vote and force employers to accept union recognition. So in 2000 Eurotunnel made its own decision to recognise the T & G for negotiations over the pay and conditions of non-managerial employees. A single union agreement was reached, which meant that only the T & G and no other union would be recognised in negotiations for pay and conditions by the business. This left the business with two types of employee/employer bodies - the council, representing all employees, and the T & G representing non-managerial employees for negotiations over pay and conditions.

(ii) A number of reasons may be put forward for the recognition of the T & G and for a single union agreement being negotiated. First, as stated earlier, the Employment Relations Act, 1999, influenced many businesses to recognise trade unions. Employees were allowed under certain circumstances to vote for recognition of unions by employers. In some cases employers, perhaps knowing that recognition was likely to take place anyway, agreed to recognise unions. Second, agreeing to recognise a union meant that to some extent the business could be involved in how this would take place in the business. Further, in the case of Eurotunnel, a single union agreement was reached. This may have saved costs for the employer. Negotiating with just one union over pay could reduce negotiation time and other expenses. It may also ensure that further industrial action or disagreements did not take place, especially if most employees belonged to the T & G. Lastly, the industrial climate at the time may have been an influence. Many businesses were recognising unions or agreeing to union/employer partnerships. They were increasingly taking the human resources view that workers were stakeholders in the business. Taking a stakeholder approach means that the views of many stakeholders are taken into consideration when making decisions. Involving employees, through unions, may have been one way to help this take place.

(b) It could be argued that employee representation has improved at the business. First, union recognition was given. The business agreed to negotiate with the T & G over pay and conditions. The T & G is a large and powerful general union, which might have helped to improve the conditions of workers, especially when compared to the situation of non-collective bargaining and simple consultation which existed before 2000. It could also be argued that having two bodies representing employees, the T & G and the council, meant that there were now more avenues for the views of employees to be heard in the business. Further, some of the figures on changes after 2000 seem to suggest that employees felt that their chances of representation at Eurotunnel had improved. The number of union members at Eurotunnel more than doubled after recognition, for example. So they were more likely to contribute to decisions through union representation. More than half of employees felt that there was a greater active union presence after recognition.

However, there is also evidence to suggest that representation may not have improved after recognition. The results of the survey show that although employees felt that there was a greater presence, the effectiveness of the union was debatable. Less than 30% of employees felt unions had been effective in representing their views, and only 1 in 10 felt that their pay and benefits had improved. Many employees wanted the council to be retained as well as having union representation. But they also suggested that both the council and the union had been ineffective in representing views.

It could therefore be argued that, in principle, the representation of employees increased as a result of changes in 2000, as employees had two bodies to further their interests. In practice there may also have been greater consultation over decision making. However, employees may also argue that the effectiveness of representation has been restricted, as illustrated by few real improvements in pay or conditions.

Question 2

(a) The major factor influencing employee representation at Newquest is likely to be the support of unions for employees. Every worker in a vote for union recognition voted in favour of recognition. A second factor was legislation. The employment Relations Acts set in place a process to allow union recognition. Although there were sufficient members to achieve recognition, the company still asked for a vote, which was unanimously in favour. A factor in future could be the view of employers about the role of unions. Amicus stated that it would be working hard in future to promote a mutually beneficial relationship for the business and employees.

(b) In many respects employee representation can benefit the company. First, representation can lead to the workers of the company achieving higher rewards or better working conditions. Second, if workers feel their views are being represented to employers and employers are paying attention to them, they may feel more valued. This in turn is likely to lead to greater motivation for employees which may result in greater output, lower staff turnover and lower absenteeism. Representation is also likely to increase the ability of workers to contribute ideas to the business and a greater exchange of information. Employers are likely to understand worker needs more keenly which may help when thinking about human resource changes. Finally, representation can help develop a common culture that allows the business to achieve its objectives.

However the business will also need to understand some of the potential drawbacks of employee representation. This includes the possibility of the decision making process being slowed down by constantly taking into account employees' views. In addition it can be expensive and time consuming with constant meetings with employee representatives. Strong representation can also lead to conflict as employee and employer objectives may differ.

Case study

(a) The objectives of a trade union are the goals that it is trying to achieve. Among the goals of a trade union are to protect and improve the work conditions of employees and protect them against job losses. At Ryanair, for example, the Irish Airline Pilots Unions (IALPA) attempted to protect the interests of pilots. It argued successfully in the Labour Court in Ireland that pilots should be given a copy of their terms and conditions of work. This would enable pilots to see exactly what was expected of them by employers and what they had agreed to when taking the job. It might enable pilots, for example, to refuse to carry out certain tasks that were not stipulated in their contract of employment. Further, the union attempted to raise the issue of victimisation against pilots. This centred around training for new aircraft, where pilots who were union members would have to pay a charge, or face possible redundancy. The union could have argued in court that this represented victimisation in the workplace.

A further objective of trade unions is to raise the earnings of workers. It is claimed that the business was attempting to recruit in Eastern Europe and employing workers at a firm called Crewlink, who were then hired to Ryanair. These workers received two-thirds the pay of other aircraft workers. Ryanair countered by saying that its staff earn higher wages than comparable businesses which have a high level of union presence in countries such as Scandinavia. But against this it was suggested that the business contracts out work to lower paid workers such as ground staff, boosting the average pay of all its workers. This might suggest that Ryanair has a policy of employing workers on lower wages. An objective of a union dealing with the business might therefore be to ensure that all workers are being paid a wage comparable with workers in the industry in the UK.

(b) There are arguments that the objectives of trade unions are to protect their members' interests. Unions are organisations which are formed by workers to promote their interests. They also exist to allow employees to combat the negotiating power of employers in discussions about conditions and pay. It is suggested that individual employees can be in a weaker bargaining position when negotiating with employers than if they join together and are represented by a specialist who has negotiating skills. Also, joining together gives them the power to disrupt business and put greater pressure on employers to gain increased pay and better work conditions.

Further, members that join unions pay a contribution from their wages. These funds allow unions to operate and without them unions would have to find funding from other places. In this sense employees are paying to be represented and their views should be taken into account. Employees also elect union members in the same way that voters vote for members of Parliament to represent their views. Members are likely to feel that elected officials should take into account their needs as this is the role they have been elected to carry out.

On the other hand, it could also be argued that the interest of passengers should also be taken into account. Paying customers of any airline such as Ryanair provide income for the business. If customers do not fly with the airline then the business will find that earnings and perhaps profits may be reduced. If, for example, a union negotiated for high wages, this could force up wage costs and reduce profits. Higher costs or reduced profits may lead to the business increasing its prices, resulting in a loss of passengers and possible redundancies. This is suggested by Ryanair's Chief Executive when he argues that Siptu, the union representing baggage handlers, was happy to have £200 airfares and a monopoly on flights in and out of Ireland. He suggests that this position of strength was only arrived at by controlling wage costs.

In conclusion, it could be argued that the main priority of trade unions is to look at and try to improve members' interests. However, although it might appear that the interests of passengers are secondary, they can be very important. If, in raising wages, unions increase the costs of Ryanair, passengers may use other airlines if Ryanair is forced to raise prices to cover costs. If this happens then employees may lose their jobs in future.

(12 marks)

(c) There are many stakeholders of a business such as Ryanair. The stakeholders of a business are individuals or groups that are affected by the operations of the business. They usually include the owners of the business and its employees, including managers as well as workers. But they can also include other businesses which are suppliers and customers of the business who buy its products. They can also include government and the local communities in which the business operates. These groups are likely to be affected in different ways by the anti-union stance of Ryanair.

Existing employees may feel that they suffer as a result of the anti-union stance. Unions protect employees' interests. It is suggested that at Ryanair employees have low wages so the business can control costs. Employees may feel that belonging to a union may help them to gain higher wages, especially those that felt there were no pay increases and little chance of promotion. A greater union presence may also help to ensure that conditions are protected, as in the case

of the pilots who may have faced victimisation. On the other hand some workers may feel that an anti-union stance could benefit them. The business argues that its low cost approach has led to a strong position for the business, which may help protect jobs. Employees from other countries can also benefit as they can gain training in English and become employed, when they may have not been able to get a job.

The owners of the business are likely to feel that an anti-union stance is of benefit. Low costs as a result of individual bargaining are likely to allow the business to pursue the low price policy that has become successful. Low costs may also allow greater profits. So the business may be able to retain profit for future investment or pay higher dividends to its owners. Perhaps one way in which owners may feel that the business could benefit from greater union involvement is that it may force the business to comply with legislation. Even individualised bargaining can lead to claims against the business in court and the business may be able to work with unions to ensure that it complies with EU law.

As suggested earlier, the anti-union stance may allow the business to set low prices for passengers. Driving down costs, including wages, is a key strategy for the business in competing with other airlines. The low costs and low prices of Ryanair would not only lead to low fares for Ryanair passengers, but may also force competitors to lower prices. Perhaps one effect of the anti-union stance that could affect passengers adversely is if the business does not comply with legislation. For example, unions may force the business to train workers more efficiently and meet safety requirements and maintain standards. This is likely to be very important in the aircraft industry. If the business is not pushed by unions to comply with legislation it may take a chance to 'cut corners' in important areas. This could adversely affect passengers if, for example, workers are not trained to an adequate standard. In the same way, suppliers may both benefit and perhaps suffer. They may gain from dealing with a business that is not constrained by 'red tape' and bureaucracy. On the other hand in an attempt to ensure costs are reduced this could lead to a lack of rigour in ordering for example.

Government is also a stakeholder of any business. Employing workers at relatively low wages may mean that the business contributes less in National Insurance contributions. Workers will also pay less tax as they are earning less. On the other hand, greater union involvement might lead to more cases being raised in courts, unless unions can work with employers to ensure that legislation is being complied with.

In conclusion, it could be argued that in the short run taking an anti-union stance might benefit employers and passengers if this results in lower costs and prices, but may not be in the interests of employees and perhaps government. In the long run the effect will depend on a variety of factors. If taking a non-union stance allows the business to employ more workers and stay in business then some employees and government may benefit. The extent to which an anti-union stance will affect the choice of the business to comply with legislation will also determine the extent to which all stakeholders benefit. If the business sees non-compliance as a way of bypassing legislation then many stakeholders could suffer. Employees may face problems with conditions, suppliers may face operating difficulties and the business may also face problems if it is taken to court and fined.

(20 marks)

Question 1

(a) Collective bargaining is a situation where employees join together in negotiations with employers over issues such as basic pay, holidays and overtime. The views of similar minded employees are then represented by bodies such as trade unions in negotiations with employers. Collective agreements are reached on behalf of the employees concerned, which apply equally to all employees represented. In the case of the Asda depot, they were likely to have been represented by unions such as GMB. The two depots seemed to have different conditions, which might imply that some workers belonged to the GMB union, which had negotiated different conditions to other unions.

Asda put forward a package of changes to conditions. Part of this was seen as a move towards individual bargaining. A move to individual bargaining would have meant a moving away from collective agreements. Asda would then have negotiated with individual employees over their conditions, rather than with a union which agreed conditions for many workers. Different individuals may have negotiated different conditions as a result.

(b)(i) From Asda's point of view, there may have been advantages and problems with a move towards individual bargaining. Asda may have wanted this system as it allowed the business flexibility. It could negotiate different conditions to suit its needs. Negotiating with individuals may also have given it more power to control conditions. Wal-Mart, the US owner of Asda, is fiercely anti-union, perhaps for these reasons. On the other hand individual bargaining can be time consuming and expensive for employers. It is also a more complex system which may lead to increased costs.

(ii) Employees at Asda may have been concerned by a move to individual bargaining. They may have felt that they would not be supported by a strong union in negotiations and their conditions may become eroded. On the other hand, some employees may benefit. Those individuals who are valued by the business may find an improvement in their conditions, compared to a collective agreement.

Question 2

(a) Binding arbitration is a solution to an industrial dispute where both sides agree to appoint an arbiter, an individual or organisation, to rule on the dispute. The arbiter will listen to both sides and then make a judgement. In the case of binding arbitration, the ruling by the arbiter is legally binding, which means it must be accepted by law. This type of dispute resolution may have been unpopular with members of the T&G at Morrisons as it forces them legally to accept the ruling, which may go against them. Members had to accept the pay offer which went to arbitration even though 87 per cent rejected the offer.

(b) In this case binding arbitration suggested that the original pay offer should stand. So binding arbitration acted against the interests of union members. However, this does not necessarily have to be the case. The arbiter might have decided that the pay offer was too low. After considering the views of both sides in the dispute, the decision may have been to raise the pay offer. If this were the case, then union members might have benefited from arbitration.

Question 3

(a) Certain services which are offered to companies by ACAS can be identified from the article. First, ACAS can offer conciliation services to both employers and employees. LRS had experienced this aspect of the work of ACAS at industrial tribunal cases. The role of ACAS could be to offer suggestions to solve disputes before they reach the tribunal stage. ACAS also provides advice to businesses. For example, it helped Merseyrail to bid for funds from the Department

for Trade and Industry. Further, ACAS develops codes of practice for employers and employees to follow. For example, as a result of the industrial relations cases, LRS approached ACAS to develop preventative action. This led to agreed procedures for staff to follow in certain circumstances. ACAS also becomes involved in industrial relations. It helped to set up a committee of enquiry at Merseyrail and then led a joint working group.

(b) Involving ACAS in industrial relations can have a number of benefits for a business. It may help to improve industrial relations with employees. Employees may feel that solutions to disputes or codes of practice suggested by an outside body may be less biased towards the needs of management. Recommendations for improvements may also lead to improve efficiency. Sometimes an outside organisation, especially one with the experience of ACAS, can make suggestions for improvements in working practices which may lead to improvements in productivity of employees and employers. An example of this might be the greater training initiatives at Merseyrail which may lead to a more productive workforce. Further, recommendations which lead to preventative action could stop harmful disputes taking place and save costs for a business. Other costs may also be saved or reduced, including the costs of claims made by employees against a business. Conciliation by ACAS may also reduce costs for both sides in any dispute before it reaches tribunal stage. In the case of LRS the involvement of ACAS helped to legitimise new systems. Again, the involvement of an impartial outside organisation may help employees to accept changes, which could prevent disruption for a business. Lastly, ACAS can help to gain funds for a business. In the case of Merseyrail, funds were gained through a Department of Trade and Industry grant. This could help pay for changes taking place, more employment or investment.

Case study

(a) Industrial democracy is where employees' views are represented in business. Part of this involves allowing employees to elect representatives who will then be involved in decision making even at the highest level, such as deciding business strategy.

Many aspects of industrial democracy and participation can be seen in the operations of Suma. The business was set up in 1970 as a workers cooperative. A worker cooperative is a business organisation which is owned by employees in the business. At Suma the 100 employees own the health food and whole food wholesaler and run the business in a democratic way. As owners of the business they are likely to have a major input into its overall running and decision making.

A general meeting of members takes place 6 times a year. This is where business strategies and policies are decided. All members attend this general meeting and can make proposals which will affect all workers if they are passed at the meeting. This way employees have a major influence on the plans of the business and how it operates. Further, the general meeting elects 6 members to the management committee which meets every week. The management committee implements the business plan. This includes appointing company officers and issuing action points when the operations of the business differ from the plan. The 6 elected members are therefore directly involved in the weekly control of the direction of the company. Workers also report aspects such as finance, quality and productivity in the management committee.

Worker involvement can also be seen in the responsibility that Suma expects of its workers. Instead of coordinators operating as overseers, workers support each other so that tasks are completed on time. In this way workers are often taking decisions that management may make in a traditional hierarchy. It is suggested that the business can only be effective if all employees have the skills and responsibility to make these decisions. Further, workers are expected to make urgent decisions to ensure the business operates efficiently. For example, if orders are waiting workers can vary their hours to ensure they are completed on time. Workers are also expected to take on a far wider range of jobs and responsibility than at other businesses. This often involves warehouse or office workers doing manual work and vice versa. Employees who may be given limited responsibility as drivers for example, in other businesses, may be making important decisions at Suma.

(8 marks)

(b) There are certain advantages of introducing industrial democracy and participation at Suma. One advantage is that all workers share in the responsibility for the performance of the company. If the company does well they are likely to be rewarded equally well given that they all earn the same wage and are given the same allowances. If the company does badly then they are all likely to suffer equally. Being responsible for the performance of the company is likely to be very motivating for all workers. They are therefore more likely to be productive to help the company survive in a competitive market. Further, workers are unlikely to resent their colleagues which may be the case in businesses with differential pay structures as they are all in the same position.

Allowing employees' views to be taken into account in decision making may also be beneficial to the business. They can take initiatives when they are necessary to make sure orders are carried out on time and customers' needs are fulfilled. They can take these decisions exactly when they are needed rather than having to request permission as may be the case in a more traditional organisation. Further, working as a team and supporting each other may not only be motivating but may also ensure tasks are carried out effectively as skills are being combined in particular operations.

As all members are owners of the business and have an input in general meetings and the management committee it is possible that they can bring a wide variety of skills and knowledge to the decision making process. Having an input from a variety of angles and perspectives may produce innovative ideas and may allow the business to deal more effectively with problems. However, the input of large numbers of ideas into the decision making process also highlights one of the potential problems of the use of industrial democracy at Suma. Too many ideas and too many influences on the decision making process can lead to muddled and confused decisions being made. Unless someone is in charge and can guide the process this may delay decisions or lead to incorrect decisions being made. Alternatively, in an attempt to appease many decision makers the final decision may not be the best for the business.

There may be other problems with industrial democracy and participation at the business. For example, allowing employees to carry out different jobs could be counter productive. For example, allowing a driver to work in an office without the necessary skills could lead to incorrect decisions being made. Similarly, encouraging an office worker to carry out production tasks without the specialist skills needed may lead to faulty products or reductions in quality. Even if employees are multi skilled they may not be the best people to carry out the jobs and efficiency may suffer.

In conclusion, it could be argued that the advantages of industrial democracy and participation at Suma outweigh the disadvantages. Operating as a workers cooperative is motivating for employees. They also have the incentive as co-owners to take responsibility for decisions and make them in the best interests of the company. In traditional organisations individuals may make decisions in their own interests which are not to the advantage of the business itself. This is less likely at Suma. Although there could be problems with multiple decision makers, this can be avoided if there is clear agreement on the procedures and methods by which decisions are made.

(12 marks)

79 | Industrial disputes

Question 1

(a) Certain methods of industrial action may be identified in the businesses in the articles. At Argos employees were brought in to meet managers' and it was suggested that action might be taken against them if they joined a union. The actual action was not stated in the article. Another form of employer action being used was bringing in outside workers to cover for Argos workers, so that shops could stay open. At the Trellebourg chemical company workers took strike action. This may be an example of employees' industrial action. At Culina Logistics employers' industrial action threatened to change the work standards and conditions of employees. This included a reduction of break time and a loss of bonuses.

(b) In the social security dispute the employers may have justified their actions on the basis of the potential disruption to others of the strike action. The Secretary of State argued that bringing in workers to ensure that social security benefits were provided was necessary to ensure that benefits were paid to those most vulnerable in society. Without bringing in outside workers benefits would not have been paid and people would have been left without money. In the chemical company dispute workers took strike action in response to management action which introduced tags to be worn at break time by staff. Workers may have felt that management was attempting to put pressure on workers over time keeping, which possibly may be used in future for disciplinary reasons and possible dismissal. They may have also felt employers were trying to change their work conditions. At Culina Logistics employers' industrial action was designed to influence staff to vote against union recognition. The employers suggested that union recognition may result in a deterioration in rewards, perhaps as a result of higher costs to the business.

Question 2

(a) Strike action may be taken to further the position of employees in an industrial dispute. Firefighters at Glasgow airport may perhaps have hoped to resist changes to the way fire safety was organised proposed by the British Airports Authority (BAA). Previously the 59 firefighters were responsible for fire safety on the runways, airport land and at the terminal. BAA proposed that safety at the airport building would be transferred to Strathclyde Fire Service. This would allow staffing levels at the terminal to be cut to a two person fire service team which was not given equipment to fight fires.

(b) If the intention was to stop the changes taking place completely then it could be argued that the objectives of the Glasgow firefighters were not achieved. A month after the dispute the proposed arraignments were confirmed. In this sense the action had failed to achieve its objectives. On the other hand, if the intention was to prevent the changes taking place in the form that the BAA wanted because the firefighters disagreed then it did achieve this to some extent. Eight specialist officers were recruited to improve fire safety at the terminal, six staff more than was originally proposed. Further, if the objective was to be compensated for accepting the changes, then this was also achieved as a one-off payment of £1 500 was made.

Question 3

(a) Contingency plans are often prepared by businesses to avoid problems which may occur as a result of unforeseen events in future, which do not take place in the usual trading environment. Such unforeseen action may be industrial action by unions and employees to further their case in a dispute, for example, the 24 hour strike staged by employees at Sainsbury's distribution centre. In this case the business would want to try to minimise the impact of the strike, which would remove the work of labour for 24 hours at the distribution centre. It might be able to do this by ensuring that shops had enough stock to cope with deliveries not taking place for 24 hours. It could take extra products each week or month to hold in case of emergencies to prevent shelves running out and not being replenished. However, holding too much stock is costly, which can be a financial burden for a business. And this solution does not perhaps solve the problem of deliveries for fresh produce or newspapers which may have to be made daily.

An alternative to this is to make sure that there are plans to deliver daily goods in other ways. One method might be to deliver straight from producers, importers or suppliers. This could add extra costs if, for example, a delivery business has to be employed to deliver the goods. Another solution might be to employ workers to deliver the products from the warehouse. This would mean employing extra staff which is also costly. Staff may also need to cross picket lines, which could prove disruptive. So perhaps storing extra products in case of short term emergencies may be a solution which leads to less conflict. Newspapers, however, might have to be sourced from the publisher in some way. On the other hand, if the strike was longer, the business may have to turn to other solutions.

(b) A number of factors may affect the strengths and weaknesses of both sides in this dispute. A major factor is the potential impact on the revenue and profits of the business. If the strike causes problems which lead to falls in revenue and increases in costs, and therefore a loss of profit for the business, then this could add strength to the union's position. However, if as suggested the business has contingency plans which it has already budgeted for, then the potential impact on profits may be small. Another factor which is likely to affect the relative positions of the two sides is the reaction of customers. For example, if customers feel that essential products are not being delivered, this could harm the reputation of the business. The impact may go beyond the 24 hours of the strike and sales in future could fall. A further factor could be the relative impact on employees. A short term strike is unlikely to lead to a large loss of earnings. But if unions feel that further strikes are necessary to strengthen the position of employees, the loss of earnings may be greater. Also, the unions must ensure that too much damage does not result. A large loss of spending will result in reduced revenue for the business. As a result it may have to make employees redundant. Lastly, the relative bargaining positions of the business and unions will have an impact. The business appears to suggest that the overall package was one of the best in the area and that pay offers had been above inflation in the last three years. Inflation at the time was relatively low and the employers may argue that this gave employees an increase in their real living standards. On the employees' side, the pay offer was below the regional average of £8 promised by the company and was below comparative depots. Also, employees had recently agreed to changes in work practices, which they may feel deserved rewarding.

It could be argued that a single one day strike would not significantly affect the outcome, especially as the business appears to have contingency plans to deal with supplies. However, if employees were willing to accept the costs of more sudden stoppages or if longer strikes took place, the business may find it harder to deal with the possible effect on consumers, which may lead to them switching retailers. This could then weaken the employers' position.

Case study

(a) (i) Employees' industrial action is the methods used by employees to further their interests in a dispute. The industrial action by employees in the first case was the Express Newpaper journalists 'guerrilla' tactics where a planned one-day strike was cancelled at the last minute, costing management large sums of money for cover staff they had lined up backed up by a 24 hour stoppage for the following week. The industrial action in the second case study was a two day strike backed up by picket lines.

(ii) Employers' industrial action is the methods used by employers to further their interests in a dispute. The industrial action by employers in the first case included Express newspapers lining up casual workers, the Press association and shuttle buses to lessen the impact of the strike and the DPW. In the second case employers had put into place contingency plans to minimise the disruption. **(6 marks)**

(b) Certain reasons for the industrial actions by employees may be suggested. In both cases there is a suggestion that the work of staff who are union members is undervalued and lacks recognition. The PCS claimed that levels of pay were 'appalling'. It argued that low wages were 'endemic' in the public sector. It might have been comparing the wages of employees in the public sector to those of employees doing similar jobs in the private sector, for example. The PCS might also have been aggrieved about 'unacceptable performance appraisal systems'. It may feel that the appraisal methods used by the DWP to evaluate staff performance are too stringent and restrictive. It may also feel that they are being used to restrict the earnings of employees, to keep costs down, or for disciplinary reasons. A further reason may have been the proposed job cuts of 80,000 in the civil service. This may have been a cost cutting exercise by employers. However, it might also have been employers' industrial action designed to improve its bargaining position in wage negotiations.

(10 marks)

(c) The benefits of industrial action are that they can clear the air. The action can bring grievances out in the open and once these are settled this could improve the atmosphere of the business. So issues of pay for the journalists and pay and jobs for the civil service will be examined in more detail. In addition, new rules are likely to be developed in response to the action to which both employers and employees will agree. This might be how pay settlements are negotiated in the future. Finally, management may change their goals and the way they are achieved in response to the industrial action. For example, the DWP may decide against a 80,000 jobs cut.

The problems of industrial action for employers is that it can lead to lost production for the Express and 5,000 driving tests that are likely to be cancelled because of picket lines in the second case. Express Newspapers will have machinery not being used and plant costs that are still incurred even if no production is taking place. In addition, the industrial action can lead to poor relationships between employers and employees with this being evident in the Express Newspapers case study. For employees in both cases, industrial action will lead to loss of pay and if the action were to continue in the future the possibilities of job cuts as the newspaper lost market share. If the action didn't work then employees' position is likely to be weakened in the future which may result in employees leaving the union.

(10 marks)

(d) Various factors are likely to affect the relative strengths and weaknesses of the dispute. One factor could be the extent to which a business can minimise the disruption of the dispute. In the case of the Express Newspapers dispute, management had lined up casual staff to cover the strike. Another factor could be the costs of the dispute to employers and employees. In the case of a strike both lose. But if one side is affected more than another this could affect the result of a dispute. The NUJ, for example, suggested that Express

Newspapers had spent a lot of money to cover the dispute. Another factor could be the length of time the dispute continued. If employees lost a great deal of income through a lengthy dispute, they may be in a weaker position, although this may also be the case for employers. A further factor may be support for the strike. If all workers support the strike then the union may be in a strong position. If some are against it, their position may be weakened. A further factor could be public support or how the public is affected. For example, they are likely to be greatly affected by the cancellation of 5,000 driving tests. It would then depend on which part in the dispute that the public felt was responsible. In the case of Express Newspapers, failing to bring out a paper may result in the public changing to another, losing revenue for the business, which may then make workers unemployed.

(12 marks)

(e) There is some evidence to suggest that employers will have problems if strikes took place at Express Newspapers. The cancellation of newspapers can be a very important influence in a newspaper dispute. Employers will be very concerned that customers will change to buying a competitor if the paper does not come out. The strike was timed to come at a time that could have the most impact, just when the Champions League was taking place. Employers also had to spend large amounts to cover for the strike. However, it might also be suggested that the position of employees in the Express Newspapers dispute has been weakened over time. It seems that any disruption could be covered by casual workers. Employers had laid on transport to bring in such workers. This cost the business, but failure to bring out the paper may have cost even more. Strikes were cancelled. The union stated that this was a disruption tactic, but may also have feared that the strike would actually have had little impact given the actions of the employers. The fact that workers were now passing a resolution calling for a genuine partnership may suggest that employees and their representatives were looking for a settlement to the dispute.

In the case of public sector dispute the result of the action could depend on how the public consider the action of employers and employees. In the public sector the employer is the government. Pay settlements would be taken from taxpayer's contributions, provided from people's incomes. Public anger at public sector disputes can be a factor influencing their outcome. If the public felt that members of the PCS did indeed receive appalling levels of pay they may have support for the dispute. Further, government may argue that increased pay could result in unemployment. But, again, if this led to the disruption of vital services such as the New Deal or immigration, then the government may be forced to retain employees, fearing a public backlash.

(12 marks)

Question 1

(a) Production occurs when a business takes inputs, carries out processes and produces an output or product. Inputs are the raw materials and components. Processes are the methods used to convert raw materials and components into products. Such processes usually need tools, equipment and machinery. Outputs are the products or services produced when inputs are converted. For example, the manufacturer of wheels might be using aluminium or a metal alloy. Different processes will be used to cut and shape the metal wheel. The output will be the finished wheel. This is production. Production also includes the provision of services. For example, the dentist in the photograph is providing an oral hygiene and maintenance service. He uses inputs such as filling materials as well as his own labour skills to provide the service, which is the output.

(b) The first photograph shows some of the resources needed to extract oil from the earth. Oil extraction is a primary production activity. The second photograph shows a potter making a pot. This is an example of manufacturing in the secondary sector. Finally, Pret A Manger is providing services, such as the provision of food and drinks. Its operations are part of the tertiary sector.

Question 2

(a) Examples of inputs used in this case might be water, malt, hops, yeast and possibly sugar.

(b) For production to be effective, it needs to be planned. There is a number of planning activities which brewers might undertake. The business must plan how much to produce in order to satisfy its current demand. Producing the right quantity in this case is very important. If brewers produce too much, it may be left with unsold stock which may be wasted. This is because beer is perishable with a limited life. On the other hand if it does not produce enough, it may not be able to satisfy demand. This could be a problem because it takes several days to produce more to satisfy an order. Another planning activity is ensuring that the business has enough resources to meet demand. Brewers may hold some resources, such as hops, in stock. Others may have to be ordered. If the business runs out of key resources this may halt production. Brewers will also have to plan its product range and decide what quantities of each brew should be produced and marketed. It may also plan to produce new brews. Many breweries produce brews for special occasions like Christmas and St. Valentines Day.

Case study

(a) Production takes place when resources, such as raw materials or components, are changed into 'products'. Land, labour, capital and enterprise - the factors of production - are used in the production process. Secondary production involves manufacturing, processing and construction. In this case Ben and Jerry's process milk, cream, sugar and other ingredients into ice cream. This is clearly an example of secondary production.

(4 marks)

(b) All businesses need to plan production. A large company like Ben and Jerry's is likely to employ production planners to ensure that production runs smoothly. A production planner may have to ensure that the ice cream factory is going to produce enough to meet orders. A production planner may do this by setting daily or weekly production targets. Planners will also have to ensure that there are enough resources such as milk, cream and sugar to meet production targets. If there is a break in supply the ice cream plant may be idle for a while which would be expensive. A production planner may be responsible for loading. This involves deciding how resources in the

factory can be best used - which staff should be employed in which tasks for example. A production planner might also be responsible for dealing with problems in the ice cream factory. For example, a production planner might be involved in contingency planning to deal with unexpected problems such as machinery breakdown or mass staff absence due to illness.

(6 marks)

(c) (i) Inputs are the raw materials and components used by a business when producing goods or services. In this case the raw materials used by Ben and Jerry's are milk, cream, liquid cane sugar, stabilizers, flavourings, marshmallow, fudge, peanut butter or caramel and fruits, nuts and sweets. These are all used to make the wide range of ice creams and other products marketed by Ben and Jerry's.

(ii) Processes are the methods or activities used by a business to convert raw materials into final products. Ben and Jerry's use many processes in their ice cream factory. Examples of processes include mixing, pasteurisation, homogenisation, cooling, chunk feeding, variegation, packaging and many others. Some of these processes are self explanatory. However, others may need explaining. For example, pasteurisation involves heating the ice cream mix to 180 degrees to kill off any harmful bacteria. Homogenising involves breaking down the fat globules in the mix to make them smaller. This makes the ice-cream smoother. It will whip better and won't melt as easily. Chunk feeding is a process which means adding any fruits, nuts, sweets or biscuit bits to the semi-frozen mixture. Variegation is the process that adds the swirls to Ben and Jerry's ice cream. The frozen mix passes through a variegator where swirls of marshmallow, fudge, peanut butter or caramel, for example, are injected into the ice cream.

(iii) Outputs are the products or services produced by a business. In this case Ben and Jerry's makes ice cream products. Their main product is a pint carton of ice cream. They come in a wide range of flavours such as vanilla, chocolate, peanut butter, marshmallow, peppermint and banana. Ben and Jerry's also make yoghurts and other ice cream products.

(12 marks)

(d) All business activity adds value to the raw materials used up in production. This means that the value of output a business produces is much greater than the value of the inputs used up in production. The value of the output is measured by the price paid by the customer. The value of the inputs is the cost of raw materials bought from suppliers. Value is added by a business because the products they make are more marketable than the materials they use. In this case Ben and Jerry's adds value by transforming basic ingredients like milk, cream, sugar and flavourings into luxury ice cream. These raw materials have little value on their own. However, people are prepared to pay more money for the luxury ice creams produced by Ben and Jerry's. Such products have a much higher value. There is not enough information in this case to calculate the value added by Ben and Jerry's.

(8 marks)

(e) Ben and Jerry's will have to make a number of production decisions during the course of its operations. Deciding what to produce, where to produce, which production methods to use, what scale to operate at and how quality can be ensured are some examples. One important production decision which Ben and Jerry's might have given some serious thought to before production began was the location of their ice cream factory in Waterbury, Vermont. The location decision is a key decision because it can affect the future plight of the business. Generally a business will be located where costs are minimised. In this case Ben and Jerry's ice cream factory may have been located in Waterbury because it needs a constant supply of milk and cream. The Waterbury factory is located near to the St Albans Co-operative Creamery. Hundreds of local farmers supply this creamery with milk. The location of the factory in Waterbury will mean that the cost of transporting very large quantities of milk and cream will be minimised.

Another key decision that Ben and Jerry's would have considered is the production method. Ben and Jerry's produce very large quantities of their ice cream cartons. They are mass produced and sold in a wide range of markets. This means that certain production methods may not be appropriate. Production takes place on a large scale at Waterbury. Ice cream is produced continuously on a production line using lots of specialist machinery. On the production line a large number of processes are carried out such as mixing, pasteurising, homogenising, flavouring, and so on. Other methods of production, such as making it by hand in a small dairy, would not be appropriate for Ben and Jerry's.

(10 marks)

81 | Types of production

Question 1

(a) Job production involves the production of a single product at a time. It is used when orders for products are small, such as 'one-offs'. Production is organised so that one 'job' is completed at a time. There is a wide variety of goods and services which are produced or provided using this method of production. In this case, Alex Stone is providing a financial service to his clients. He uses job production because every single job he undertakes is unique. Every client is different and every set of accounts produced by Alex will be different. The accounts will contain different financial information because his clients run different businesses. Alex is likely to work on one client's accounts, complete them, and then move on to the next client.

(b) It is argued that job production will help to motivate people at work. The tasks Alex and his trainee carry out may require a variety of skills, knowledge and expertise. For example, they will be dealing with different clients and different businesses when producing accounts. Their work may be more demanding and interesting. They will also see the end result of their efforts and be able to take pride in their work. This should help raise the level of job satisfaction.

Question 2

(a) Batch production involves performing several processes on a number of identical units all at the same time. The group or collection of identical units is called a batch and can vary in size. After a particular process has been performed on the entire batch, the batch is transferred to another work station where another process is performed. In the clothes industry the processes might involve making patterns, cutting, sewing, attaching buttons and zips, finishing and packaging.

(b) Batch production is common in the clothes industry because manufacturers produce a variety of different clothes and uniform designs in different sizes and colours, for example, In the same factory. For example, Uniform+ might make some outfits for hotel staff, overalls for industrial workers and sportswear all in the same day. The same processes are likely to be used, the same staff and the same machinery. Only the designs and materials are likely to be changed. Demand is not likely to be high enough to continually produce one variety of outfit all day, every day.

(c) One of the problems with batch production is that different machinery and tools might be needed when switching from one batch to another. To overcome this problem the manufacturers of machinery have tried to develop more flexibility and diversity in their machinery. In this case, Uniform+ has invested in flexible machinery to help overcome this problem in batch production. Flexible machinery can cope with a wide variety of designs and materials that Uniform+ need to offer their customers. Uniform+ also employ multi-skilled staff. This means they are adaptable and can use the variety of skills needed when switching production from one design to another.

Case study

(a) The production of breakfast cereals requires a number of processes. These include compounding and mixing, extrusion, cooking, drying and coating. **(4 marks)**

(b) Businesses are making increasing use of new approaches to production. In this case Nacional has combined two production methods. It uses both batch production and flow production to manufacture breakfast cereals. By using extrusion, production has been made more efficient by combining several processing steps into a single, continuous flow. PV Baker has supplied and installed a complete process plant for Nacional, which incorporates the entire production process from compounding and mixing of the recipe 'dough' through extrusion and cooking to drying and coating of the final extruded product shapes. This is flow production. However, at the same time the plant can switch from the production of one breakfast cereal to another. The new facility can make a variety of different products, including corn-balls, coco-balls, choco curls, golden squares, stars and rings, as well as co-extruded filled pillow shapes. A key design feature of the facility is the ability to rapidly changeover between products in response to market demand, including those where different raw materials and syrup are involved. This suggests that batch production is also used. **(10 marks)**

(c) The current state of technology is likely to affect all production decisions. As technology advances, new materials and machinery become available. Changes in technology often result in firms adopting new methods of production. In this case, Nacional has carried out a major refit and expansion plan that involved a massive investment of around 11.2 million euros. Nacional has purchased new technology which enables it to produce breakfast cereals in a continuous flow. However, the new machinery is flexible because it be used to produce different types of cereals - different shapes and flavours, for example. New technology has played a very important role in the production of breakfast cereals at Nacional. **(6 marks)**

(d) Nacional will enjoy a number of significant benefits following its 11.2 million euro refit. It should be able to meet the growing demand for breakfast cereals more easily. This is because the flow production techniques adopted by Nacional are capable of much larger volumes. Flow production will also reduce unit costs as Nacional is more able to exploit economies of scale. This will help to improve the profitability of the business. A very important benefit to Nacional is the increased flexibility. The new production line is capable of producing different products including corn-balls, coco-balls, choco curls, golden squares, stars and rings, as well as co-extruded filled pillow shapes. This means that customers can be offered a much wider range of choice.

The new production line might enable Nacional to organise production more easily. For example, once the line is set up to produce a particular product, production should run smoothly without any problems. The increased automation should also make it easier for staff. Generally, the Euro 11.2 million investment should result in better efficiency, lower costs, more flexibility in production, and therefore, greater profits.

However, when using flow production it is important to remember that there may be some drawbacks. The set up costs are very high. An enormous investment in plant and equipment is needed, 11.2 million euros in this case. Nacional must therefore be confident that demand for the product is sufficient over a period of time to make the investment pay. Also worker motivation may be a problem. Most of the manual operations required on the production line will be repetitive and boring. Factories with production lines tend to be very noisy. Each worker will only be involved in a very small part of the job cycle. As a result of these problems worker morale may be low and labour turnover and absenteeism high. Finally, breakdowns can prove costly. The whole production system is interdependent. If one part of the supply or production line fails the whole system may break down.

To conclude, there is no evidence in the case to suggest that Nacional has experienced any of these problems. Overall the company looks set to benefit from the investment quite significantly. **(20 marks)**

82 Capacity utilisation

Question 1

(a) Operations management is the organisation and control of the process by which inputs, such as labour, materials and machinery, are transformed into final products. Production managers, such as the one just appointed at Oliver Handy, are therefore responsible for making key production decisions. These might include what production methods are to be used, what combinations of resources such as labour, machinery and materials are needed, how to best utilise the firm's capacity, what stock levels are required to support production, how to ensure that work is completed on time and how best to ensure quality.

(b) (i)

	2004	2005	2006	2007 £
Total output	12,000	13,500	14,000	17,000
Total cost	252,000	297,000	305,200	297,500
Unit cost	21	22	21.80	17.50

(ii) The calculations made in (i) show that unit cost falls quite significantly after the appointment of the new production manager. Unit costs fall from £21.80 in 2006 to £17.50 in 2007.

(c) One approach which operational managers are likely to use is to set operational targets. Setting targets can help managers monitor the performance of the production function. Production managers may set targets for unit costs. These costs can be measured at the end of a production run and compared with the targets. If actual unit costs are higher than the targets the production manager is likely to search for reasons why so that appropriate action can be taken. Generally, businesses are always looking for ways to reduce unit costs. In this case the new production manager emphasises the use of production targets and unit costs. It is possible that targets were set for unit costs. The impact on unit cost following the arrival of the new manager suggests that such targets may have been used.

Question 2

(a) (i) Capacity utilisation compares actual output with capital output (the potential output of the capital of a business). Capacity utilisation measures actual output as a percentage of the maximum potential output of the capital of the business. For example, if a business could be in operation for 100 hours a week but only operated for 95 hours its capacity utilisation would be 95 per cent. In this case it would be operating at near to full capacity. This would benefit the business as it would be productively efficient, operating at its lowest average cost of production. If it operated for only 20 hours a week its capacity utilisation would only be 20 per cent, which would make the business productively inefficient.

(ii) Rationalisation is a situation where a business reduces the

July		August			
Week 3	Week 4	Week 1	Week 2	Week 3	Week 4
78%	52%	68%	75%	75%	78%

number of resources it puts into the production process. Businesses often rationalise by reducing the number of workers in the business or selling off capital equipment. Rationalisation usually takes place because a business has excess capacity. This is a situation where there are too many resources in the business to produce the actual level of output that it wants to produce.

(b) Capacity utilisation can be found using the formula: current output ÷ maximum potential output x 100%. Maximum potential number of hours worked is 60, shown in week 2 of July.

(c) Capacity utilisation could be increased in a number of ways. A business might consider sub-contracting further to increase its current output levels. In the second week of July the business actually worked to 100 per cent capacity. This is unusual and as the calculations above show, in most weeks in July and August the business is working at around three quarters of its capacity. When it has attempted to work at full capacity at other times machines break down and workers take time off, perhaps due to stress. Sub-contracting work to other businesses is one way in which the current output can be improved. There may be some advantages to the business in sub-contracting. The other businesses may be operating more efficiently, for example they may have newer machines. This could mean that production costs are lower. Another advantage is that, as production orders are met, the business may maintain the goodwill of its customers. It may have had to turn away orders due to lower levels of capacity utilisation and lost customers as a result. Another method of increasing capacity is to increase sales. Greater sales generate increases in output. This means that spare capacity is then used. However the business has found that when it tries to work to full capacity it often experiences problems. One way around this might be to try to reorganise sales patterns. At the moment the business faces seasonal patterns of orders. For example, sales are down in late July and early August due to other firm's workers taking holidays. Perhaps the business could offer discounts to customers to send orders in early or move production to different times of the year. This would increase sales at times when orders are low.

(d) One method often used by businesses to improve capacity utilisation is to rationalise. Rationalisation involves reducing the number of resources to produce a given quantity of output. This lowers costs and so increases profits. Sometimes businesses have spare capacity, too much capacity for their current level of output. This might be the case at Zaman & Nazran. Working at 100% capacity is unusual and in a typical week it is working at 75% capacity. If Zaman & Nazran is unable to make use of the spare capacity then it might be better to reduce its plant size, by selling it off and moving to smaller premises. Or it could lease some of its existing plant that it is not using. It might also consider reducing its workforce or using sub-contractors as the business does at times already.

However, reducing resources by 50% and therefore, presumably, reducing capacity by half, could pose problems for the company. It may mean that it would lose out on profitable orders unless it can sub-contract work. It is currently sub-contracting to rivals and it would not want this to continue for a long period. Moreover, further increases in sales could solve spare capacity problems. The business expects that sales will rise by another 50 per cent in the next five years. To solve the problem of the strain on machinery it is committed to an investment programme. This should all mean that in future the business is able to work to nearer full capacity and that rationalisation would not be an advisable strategy.

Case study

(a) Capacity utilisation is about the use made of resources in a business. It compares actual output with the output that could be produced if the business was operating at full capacity. In this case, Gibson's could produce a maximum of 18,000 buggies a year, however, in every year since 2003 it has produced less than this.

(3 marks)

(b) (i)

	2003	2004	2005	2006	£ 2007
Output p.a	14,000	12,000	11,000	10,500	10,900
Total capacity p.a	18,000	18,000	18,000	18,000	18,000
Capacity utilisation	78%	67%	61%	58%	61%

(5 marks)

(ii) In 2003 the capacity utilisation of Gibson's was 78%. This means that the factory was operating at about three quarter capacity. However, over the next four years this fell to 61%, which is only just over half capacity. This means that the factory is underutilised. The underutilisation has resulted from a fall in sales caused by competition from overseas, particularly China. **(5 marks)**

(c) Capacity at Gibson's is being underutilised. This means that resources are being wasted. A business can lower its unit costs if it can increase its capacity utilisation. This is because some of its costs are fixed. Higher levels of capacity utilisation, and higher levels of output, will make a business more efficient. However, Gibson's will need some spare capacity. This is because demand for golf buggies is likely to be seasonal. Golf is more popular in the summer than in the winter. Therefore, during the summer the factory might be operating closer to full capacity than in the winter. Despite this, it is very likely that Gibson's would want to improve their capacity utilisation.

(6 marks)

(d) Like many other business, Gibsons has to cope with seasonal demand. They have to organise their operations to deal with 'peak' demand in the high season and very low demand out of season. To cope with seasonal demand production operations have to be flexible. There is a number of measures a business like Gibson's could take to cope with seasonal fluctuations in demand.

Gibson's could ask staff to work overtime during the busy periods. Overtime is often popular with workers because overtime rates are usually higher than basic wage rates. They may be time and half or double time. However, not all workers will want overtime because they have other commitments. Gibson's could employ temporary or part time staff during the spring and summer months. Temporary staff can be 'hired and fired' according to demand levels. They will be employed on very short-term contracts. However, temporary staff will have to be trained and may not be as reliable as permanent staff. Part-time staff are generally more flexible than full-time staff. They can

often adapt to changes in the hours they work. Gibsons might also decide to lease more machinery and equipment. For example, vehicles, tools and machinery can be leased during busy periods and returned when orders fall. Gibson's might also use flexible suppliers. When orders increase Gibson's might need to call on suppliers to make emergency deliveries. Suppliers that cannot offer flexibility and reliability might be avoided. Finally, a common way of dealing with seasonal demand is to keep production fairly constant and accumulate stocks during the quiet times. Stocks will then be drawn on when orders start to flood in. However, stock holding costs need to be taken into account when using this approach. **(10 marks)**

(e) Gibson's is likely to be very keen to improve capacity utilisation. One option is to cut capacity. It might do this by rationalising. This involves reducing excess capacity by getting rid of resources that the business can do without. Gibson's might decide to cut staff by making people redundant, employing more part-time and temporary staff and offering early retirement. They may sell off unused fixed assets such as machinery, vehicles, office space, warehouses and factory space. They may lease out some of their spare capacity to another business or mothball some resources. This means that fixed assets, such as machinery, are left unused, but maintained, so that they can be brought back into use if necessary. It might be cost effective to move to smaller premises where costs are lower.

An attractive option would be to increase sales and use up the capacity. However, Gibson's have tried this by investing in a new marketing campaign. Unfortunately the impact was not significant. Capacity utilisation can vary considerably within a business. Where capital equipment at Gibson's has low utilisation rates, it might be more efficient for the business to subcontract or outsource the work. This means hiring or contracting another business to do work which was previously done in-house. For instance, Gibson's might run a small fleet of delivery vans which on average are on the road for 4 hours per day. It is likely that it would be cheaper for the business to sell the vans and employ a company to make the deliveries. An alternative outsourcing strategy is to take on outsourcing contracts for other businesses. For example, Gibson's could accept contracts from rival buggy producers to improve its capacity utilisation. Outsourcing then becomes a strategy for increasing demand for the business.

Gibson's has already tried to increase demand without much success. Therefore it probably has to look at cutting capacity. Depending on its circumstances - which equipment is being underutilised, whether production is labour or capital intensive and whether activities can be effectively outsourced - Gibson's will have to choose between rationalisation or subcontracting. They may have to use a combination of both. **(20 marks)**

Question 1

(a) (i) Raw materials are the unprocessed materials that are used to make other goods. The middle photograph shows sand which is used in glass manufacture.

(ii) Work-in-progress is the unfinished goods that are currently being manufactured, but are not yet ready for sale. The bottom photograph shows glass bottles on the production line.

(ii) Finished stock is stock that is completed. The top photograph shows bottles of wine which are ready to be sold to customers.

(b) Many businesses hold stocks of finished goods. The main reason for this is so that a business can cope with fluctuations in demand. Businesses do not usually get a constant flow of orders. If there is a sudden rise in demand, a firm can meet urgent orders by supplying customers from stock holdings. This avoids the need to step up production rates quickly.

Question 2

(a) (i) Maximum stock level is 350 sheets.

(ii) Buffer stock level or minimum stock level is 100 sheets.

(iii) Re-order level is 200 sheets.

(b) (i) There was an unexpected large rush in week 3 of March. Here the business had to reduce its stock below its buffer stock level due to unforeseen circumstances.

(ii) In many weeks (1,2 January, 3,4 February, 1,2 March) stock falls by 125 a week. However in some weeks it falls by less, which is likely to reflect disappointing sales. These are week 3 of January (about 63), 4 of January (around 62), 1 of February (about 63) and 2 of February (about 62). In week 4 of March sales are 100, which is still down.

(c) If the business experiences cash flow problems it may not have enough liquid assets to meet its day-to-day expenses. One way around a cash flow problem is to reduce stock holdings. Money tied up in holding stocks is a cost for the business. It could be used for other spending. So, faced with a cash flow problem, the business may decide to reduce the maximum level of stock it holds, freeing up cash which is needed for other expenditure.

Case study

(a) (i) Regular monthly stock takes are made by Regal Jewels. This involves recording the amount and value of stocks which the business is holding. In this case, a stock take would be made at each of the nine outlets. The total stock of the business would be found by adding together the value of stocks held at each store. This task is usually done manually. **(3 marks)**

(ii) A stock take is required for security reasons - to check that the items actually in stock match the stock records kept by the business. This would be particularly important for Regal Jewels. Pieces of jewelry are small and can be highly valuable. They may be a target for thieves. Regular stock checks will be vital to ensure that stock does not go 'missing'. The stock take is also necessary to help determine the value of total purchases during the year for a firm's accounts. **(6 marks)**

(b) The costs of holding stocks can be very high. In this case one of the main costs will be the opportunity cost of holding stocks. Capital tied up in stocks earns no reward. Regal Jewels has £3,560,000 tied up in stocks. This money could be put to other uses that might have earned the business a bigger return - such as opening more stores. Storage can also prove costly. In this case stock has to be stored securely because it is valuable and vulnerable. It will be necessary to keep stock in specialised, secure display cabinets during the day. When the stores are closed stock might be transferred to high security safes. The handling costs and specialised storage facilities may be significant. There may also be very high insurance costs for stock. **(6 marks)**

(c) (i) Lead time = about 1 week.

(ii) Re-order quantity = 2,000 bags.

(iii) Re-order level = 1,500 bags.

(iv) Minimum stock holding = 1,000 bags. **(8 marks)**

(d) Information in the Figure shows why Regal Jewels found a new supplier for the bags. Between January and June the supplier seemed reliable - delivering 2,000 bags every month. However, at the beginning of July the supplier only delivered 1,000 bags. Assuming that the usual 2,000 were ordered, this is likely to leave Regal Jewels short. However, another delivery was made three weeks into July, another 2,000 bags. After this no delivery was made again until the middle of September, presumably from a new supplier. It seems that after the delivery of 2,000 bags in July, Regal Jewels ran out. At the end of August stocks of bags were zero. Indeed, for two weeks the business did not have any bags. This must have been very irritating for Regal Jewels. Not being able to pack customer purchases into their high quality, customised bags, may affect their image. Consequently, it appears that a new supplier was found. Two weeks into September a delivery of 3,000 bags was received. **(6 marks)**

(e) Increasingly, small businesses are turning to computerised stock control systems. At the moment the owner of Regal Jewels is having trouble keeping up to date with the stocks held in each shop. A manual, paper-based stock system is currently being used which is proving to be inefficient as the business grows. The owner is thinking of setting up an online stock control system. Computerised stock control systems have many advantages. Online systems can hold details of a firm's entire stock on computer databases. All additions to, and issues from stocks, are recorded and up to date stock levels can be found instantly for each of Regal's nine shops. Some systems are programmed to automatically order stock when the re-order level is reached.

A new online system has been developed which allows small businesses, such as Regal Jewels, to login and manage their stock levels. It is perfect for a business with more than one location. It is possible to monitor stock movements and react to information delivered to a computer from anywhere in the world. The system has a number of benefits such as cost effectiveness, no new hardware is needed, it is available from multiple locations, its easy to use, has free support, is easy to train staff and a 30 day free trial is available.

If Regal Jewels is having problems monitoring stock levels the new online system is likely to be of benefit. Stock is the most valuable asset of this business. Stock management is crucial to the effective performance of this business. Therefore, providing the cost of the online system is not prohibitive, Regal Jewels would be advised to invest in the new technology. **(10 marks)**

Question 1

(a) (i) Quality may be described as those features of a product or service that allow it to satisfy customers. In this case, airlines regard safety, reliability, comfort and maintenance costs as crucial when buying aircraft from Airbus.

(ii) Few would disagree that the most important quality feature identified in (i) is safety. Safety is of the utmost importance to airlines when buying aircraft. If any aspect of an aircraft's safety is compromised the effect could be catastrophic. If failure to meet safety standards results in passengers being harmed, or worse, the airline might have difficulties recovering from an incident.

(b) Airbus' approach to maintaining quality standards is very thorough. To achieve the very highest standards in an aircraft's performance the question of quality is addressed by Airbus at every stage from design to final assembly and beyond. Repeated checks are made. Tests are applied and Airbus ensures every supplier of parts meets the strictest standards on quality. Defective work, parts and materials are rejected.

Delivering aircraft on time, on cost and on quality - getting it right first time - is the goal Airbus continually strives for. Airbus has a network of key employees who identify problems at various stages of design, production and assembly and recommend action to eradicate them, pre-empting possibly costly delays at a later point. These employees also ensure continuous improvement in standards and efficiency by pinpointing ways in which people could work better or where tools and materials could be improved.

Question 2

(a) (i) Quality assurance is a method of ensuring quality that takes into account customers' views in the production process. Quality assurance attempts to guarantee that quality has been maintained at all stages in the production process. The aim is to stop problems before they occur rather than finding them after they occur.

(ii) Many businesses work to quality assurance codes of practice. These show that a production process has been carried out to a certain standard and to the required specification. Once a business has been assessed and has achieved a certain standard, it is regularly checked by the awarding organisation to make sure standards are maintained. In this case, Compsoft has been granted ISO 9001 certification, the internationally recognised standard for the quality management of businesses.

(b) The BSI is the body responsible for awarding the ISO 9001 certificate. They visit businesses to ensure that business processes meet the required standards for certification. Some of the basic requirements include a set of procedures that cover all key processes in the business, monitoring development processes to ensure they are producing quality products, keeping records, checking outgoing applications for defects, with appropriate corrective action where necessary, regularly reviewing individual processes and the quality system itself for effectiveness and ensuring continual improvement. Regular monitoring by the BSI ensures that these standards are upheld and that Compsoft remains worthy of its title as an accredited ISO 9001 provider.

(c) Compsoft should enjoy a number of benefits as a result of ISO 9001 certification. The award can help a business to examine and improve systems, methods and procedures to lower costs, motivate staff and encourage them to get things right first time. It can define key roles, responsibilities and authorities and help Compsoft to assure that orders are consistently delivered on time. It can also highlight product or design problems and develop improvements, record and investigate all quality failure and customer complaints and make sure that they do not reoccur. The ISO 9001 award gives a clear signal to customers that Compsoft are taking measures to improve quality. Finally, it can help the business produce a documented system for recording and satisfying the training needs of new and existing staff regarding quality.

Case study

(a) A TQM readiness assessment is the first stage in the process when implementing TQM in an organisation. It involves carrying out an investigation to determine areas in the business where TQM will be particularly important. In this case, over a five day period all of the senior management team and several hourly employees were interviewed. This highlighted several areas for targeted customer service improvement and cost reduction. **(4 marks)**

(b) GNY Building Materials was faced with two problems - escalating costs and ailing customer service. After an important board meeting it was decided to create a new business culture, a culture which valued quality, customer service and continuous improvement. GNY employed a consultant and when it began work it was apparent that the company did not have a history of participative management and reacted slowly to opportunities. Initial interviews confirmed that management was viewed sceptically. Poor internal communication fed fear and resentment on the part of employees. It was hoped that TQM could address all of theses issues and improve the performance of the business. **(6 marks)**

(c) Training is important when introducing TQM because it may be a completely new concept to many of the people in the business who are expected to adopt it. One of the key steps when introducing TQM at GNY was training. A quality steering committee was organised to train the management team. Training was further developed in the six TQM training sessions. By incorporating their culture, credibility was improved. In addition, training improved the application of TQM ideas and broke down barriers to change. Four groups of twenty employees were then trained. The consultant trained in-house trainers to continue the training of employees.

Also, the business faced increasingly aggressive competition. A major objective for implementing TQM was to eliminate the waste in delivery and improve the reliability of delivery. The chairman made it plain that the savings from improvements would fund the culture he needed. **(8 marks)**

(d) A number of costs would have been incurred by GNY Building Materials when implementing TQM. GNY employed a consultant to introduce TQM. Business consultants are notoriously expensive and their fees would be significant. Another huge cost would be the cost of training. GNY employs 350 workers and all of them would have to be trained in TQM. The successful introduction of TQM requires thorough training and it is not a cost which can be 'squeezed'. There is likely to be a great deal of bureaucracy and documents and regular audits are needed. This will all add to costs. It may be necessary to monitor the new quality system which could incur a cost - the salary of a supervisor, for example. Finally, if the whole quality system fails, there may be costs in setting it up again. Time may be needed to 'rethink' or adjust the system. Retraining might also be necessary. Although quality control systems are costly, it is argued that their benefits outweigh the costs. **(10 marks)**

(e) Generally, TQM will help a business focus clearly on the needs of customers and relationships between suppliers and customers. It will achieve quality in all aspects of business, not just product or service quality. It will help the business critically analyse all processes to remove waste and inefficiencies, find improvements and develop measures of performance and develop a team approach to problem solving. It will also help to develop effective procedures for communication and acknowledgement of work and continually review the processes to develop a strategy of constant improvement.

GNY Building Materials felt the benefits of TQM quite quickly. Three months after the introduction of TQM the business generated cost reduction initiatives worth £600,000 and implemented over £300,000 of cost savings. This major victory by hourly and first line management demonstrated the effectiveness of TQM. GNY Building Materials realised a 25:1 payback on their investment in Total Quality

Management. This is highly significant. In addition, their premier service reputation was restored and they became the preferred supplier to many contractors. According to the chairman, the company has become much more flexible and responsive. Improvements to the profitability of the company confirmed this. The actual quality of the product should be improved, so customers are more likely to purchase the product. Business costs may be cut if faults in products are identified before the product reaches the market. The costs of failure once the product has reached the market are likely to be much higher than those during manufacture. The main benefits in this case are clearly financial and hopefully long lasting.   **(16 marks)**

85 | Customer service

Question 1

(a) Customer service is about meeting the needs of customers. According to Turban et al, 2002 'Customer service is a series of activities designed to enhance the level of customer satisfaction - that is, the feeling that a product or service has met the customer expectation'. In this case Asda offers its customers a number of services to enhance the level of customer satisfaction. For example, Asda provide 'Greeters' in the stores. These are customer care specialists who are trained to help customers with all their enquiries. Greeters go out of their way to give customers a genuine welcome as they walk into the store and provide a range of help from selecting the right shopping trolley to suit customers' shopping needs, helping wheelchair users and directing customers to the right aisle. Another example is the exchange policy offered by Asda. When customers purchase an electrical item they can ask for their receipt to be placed into a free Guarantee Wallet. This means that their purchase is guaranteed for a full year. However, customers will need to keep their own receipt to cover the warranty.

(b) One way of meeting customer expectations is to train staff in customer service. Training in customer service will help staff to do their job more effectively. Without proper training the quality of customer service is likely to be poorer. Training will also motivate staff. Without training they may become frustrated because they cannot do their job. Training is also likely to make staff more flexible. For example, staff from one Asda department might cover for an absent colleague in another if they have been widely trained. Training is often necessary to bring staff up to date with new technology or new legislation in customer services. Asda specially train all of their Greeters. They are customer care specialists which will help Asda to meet customer expectations.

Question 2

(a) TSO gathers quantitative data to measure its performance in the provision of customer services. It sets performance targets and then compares actual performance with these targets. Examples of the targets set in 2006 were to answer 80% of their telephone calls in 10 seconds, 90% in 20 seconds and 95% in 30 seconds. TSO also aimed to achieve an abandon call rate of no more than 2% of call volumes answered and process standard written post order requests within an average of 2 working days of receipt. It also aimed to deliver a service that achieves a benchmarked satisfaction score of 83.1% and achieve a fair outcome for customers when things go wrong and achieve less than 1.4% of complaints received against overall despatches.

(b) The quality of customer service provided by TSO seems good. The company appears to have met the vast majority of its targets in most months. For example, the 80 per cent target for answering telephones calls within 10 seconds was met in every single month in 2006. In fact the actual performance was 90 per cent or over in every single month. The percentage of calls abandoned was also generally better than the target. TSO aimed to abandon less than 2 per cent of its calls. It managed this in every month except December when it was 2.2 per cent. However, the average time it took to answer calls was less impressive. Its target was 6 seconds. This was exceeded in several months and in one month, September, the average time was 10 seconds.

(c) Businesses like TSO will particularly benefit if they can produce quantitative data when monitoring customer service performance. Quantitative data is much easier and quicker to analyse. It is easier to make quick comparisons between different time periods using numeric performance indicators. Businesses that use quantitative data are likely to set performance targets. At the end of the year actual performance can be compared with the targets. This was the approach used by TSO. They set a number of performance targets and then compared actual performance with the targets. For

example, TSO's target for the number of complaints as a percentage of orders dispatched was 1.2%. TSO missed this target in four of the twelve months. For example, it was 1.4 per cent in October. Quantitative data like this is simple to understand and helps to clarify performance in customer service.

Case study

(a) ScottishPower provides a significant amount of its customer service online. One of its main services is providing answers to customer questions. About 95 per cent of these questions are answered automatically. Recently, there have been a growing number of queries on energy efficiency. ScottishPower customers can also enter meter readings online, view and pay bills, change services, update personal details and notify the company when changing address. This should help to enhance customer satisfaction.
(6 marks)

(b) Much of the information in this case is about the customer service provided online by ScottishPower. The provision of customer service online is a relatively new innovation. Ten years ago it is likely that most of ScottishPower's customer service was provided over the telephone - perhaps from a call centre. Now it is possible to enter meter readings, view and pay bills and ask questions online. It was not possible to do this years ago. Online customer services are increasingly popular. Nicola Morrison, online manager at ScottishPower, says, 'We are committed to making it easy for our customers to benefit from the flexibility and cost savings of managing their accounts online'. **(6 marks)**

(c) Transversal is the UK's leading provider of multi-channel eService solutions for customer-facing websites and contact centres. The company has provided ScottishPower with a new system. The software system ensures customers receive rapid responses to their online account queries. According to Nicola Morrison, 'Working with Transversal has not only helped underpin our online growth, but has given us an unparalleled insight into our customers' requirements through the ability to analyse the questions they are asking'. By investigating the type and number of questions asked on its site. ScottishPower has been able to ensure that the right information is immediately available to its customers - without needing to invest in costly market research. For example, after seeing a growing number of queries on energy efficiency, this information was made more visible on the new site. Consequently the software also helps ScottishPower to monitor the quality of customer service.
(10 marks)

(d) The provision of high quality customer service is very important to ScottishPower. The company has over 5 million customers and is aiming to be the industry's number one for customer service. Its aim to be number one shows that it takes customer service seriously. ScottishPower will also use the quality of customer service to help differentiate its product from those of competitors. This is because there are few opportunities to differentiate a product such as electricity. It is a homogenous product. If ScottishPower provides high levels of customer service it may be able to keep ahead of its competitors and win more customers.

Competition in the supply of electricity has intensified in recent years. A number of new providers have entered the market following deregulation. This means there is more pressure on ScottishPower to provide good customer service. If it provides a poor service customers are more likely to switch suppliers. Finally, ScottishPower may be able to charge higher prices if it provides high levels of customer service. **(10 marks)**

(e) Generally, there are significant benefits from providing high levels of customer service. It has been argued that customer service is the critical factor in determining whether a customer buys and is retained. This will be particularly important to ScottishPower. It has over 5 million customers and will be extremely keen to retain them. Retaining current customers helps future growth, by sustaining healthier sales volumes and margins, for example. High levels of customer retention through effective customer service also improves staff morale and motivation. No-one enjoys working for a business where customers are not valued and customer service systems are either ineffective or non-existent. When customers are happy staff are likely to be happier too. As a result they will be more productive. Improved staff morale and motivation resulting from reducing customer dissatisfaction also benefits staff retention and turnover, recruitment quality and costs, stress, grievance, discipline and counselling pressures.

Reduced customer dissatisfaction will obviously reduce legal action from customers or fair trading laws. Retaining customers also enables the business to focus more on proactive opportunities such as growth, innovation and development, rather than reactive tasks such as fire-fighting, crisis management and failure analysis. Having a culture of delighting and retaining customers improves the image of a business. A company's reputation in the media, and increasingly on the web in blogs and forums, for example, can be improved. The converse also applies. For example, one disgruntled customer and a reasonable network of web friends may cause a significant public relations headache. A large company such as ScottishPower would probably attract quite a measure of adverse publicity if its customer service was poor.

Finally, the most important benefit to ScottishPower of providing high levels of customer service is that customers will be retained. When a company has 5 million customers, it will not want to lose them. **(18 marks)**

86 | Purchasing

Question 1

(a) McPhersons Ltd, the butcher chain, currently undertakes all purchasing on a central basis. It is considering the decentralisation of the purchasing function to its shops, so that each shop will carry out its own purchasing. Following decentralisation certain costs would rise and others would fall. Each shop manager would be given an increase in salary of £2,000. Thus total costs would rise by £40,000 (£2,000 × 20). In addition, the discounts lost from bulk buying would be £60,000.

However, certain costs would fall. Cold storage, distribution and handling costs are expected to fall by £50,000 and administration costs are expected to fall by £5,000. Overall, total costs will rise by £5,000 (£60,000 - £55,000). Thus on purely financial grounds decentralisation appears not to be viable.

(b) There is a variety of non-physical advantages and disadvantages which McPhersons might experience if the business decentralised purchasing. If shop managers buy in meat for individual shops it is argued in the case that quality might improve. Managers may buy their meat locally, enjoy a better relationship with suppliers and have more control of quality. Local managers will also be in touch with the needs of local customers. These needs can be reflected in the buying patterns of managers. It might also be argued that managers might be better motivated. They will have a little more responsibility if they have to buy in the stock for their own shop. This extra responsibility might be an indication of the value which senior managers or owners place on them.

One of the non-financial disadvantages of decentralised buying is that the range of stock or meat sold in each shop might differ too much. If this happens, different standards may be set in each shop. McPhersons might find this unacceptable. The owners and managers might also lose too much control as a result of decentralised purchasing. They will be allowing key decisions to be made by subordinates. They might as a result be unable to control the purchasing strategy of the business.

Question 2

(a) Vi-Spring has just adopted JIT manufacturing. Businesses that use just-in-time (JIT) manufacturing techniques depend very heavily on their suppliers. JIT manufacturers need supplies delivered at regular intervals at specific times. In this case Vi-Spring gets deliveries the day after they have been ordered. JIT manufacturers do not hold stocks of materials and components, so a break in supply will leave them vulnerable. If one of Vi-Spring's suppliers fails to deliver, or delivers the wrong order, the company may have to close down production for a time. This could be very expensive. For JIT manufacturers suppliers need to be 100 per cent reliable. Their role is critical.

(b) JIT manufacturing does require businesses to have good relations with their suppliers. It appears that Vi-Spring has developed good relations. Vi-Spring was around 200 suppliers but 30 of them are key to operations. The company prefers to build close and reliable relationships with its suppliers, regarding them as key business partners. If a problem develops, rather than dropping a supplier Vi-Spring will work with it to overcome the issue concerned. This suggests that Vi-Spring values its suppliers highly and treats them well.

Case study

(a) (i) IXO uses a vendor rating system to choose effective suppliers. This involves measuring a supplier's performance according to a set of important criteria. In this case IXO uses five criteria when evaluating supplier performance. These are price, quality, reliability, flexibility and payment terms. The best supplier is the one with the highest rating. This is found by adding all the scores together. **(4 marks)**

(ii) In this case, IXO attaches more importance to price than any other single performance criteria. This is evident because it gives a score out of

20 for price. All other criteria get a score out of 10. This shows that price is more important to IXO. This is probably to be expected since IXO Instruments Ltd is always looking for new suppliers to help keep costs down. The people who own the company set demanding financial targets, which often means that managers have to continually cut costs.

(6 marks)

(b) The total ratings for each vendor in this case are shown in the table below. There is not a great deal of variation in the ratings but there is one clear winner. Reynolds Ltd appears to be the best performing supplier. It has a score of 47. This is 4 better than the next best which is AGT and Williams & Co with ratings of 43. This means that IXO Instruments Ltd will ask Reynolds Ltd to supply the FFD 339 component. **(8 marks)**

Supplier	Price	Quality	Reliability	Flexibility	Payment terms	Total
Reynolds Ltd	18	8	7	8	6	47
AGT	12	8	9	9	5	43
Adco	14	6	7	5	8	40
Veelle	8	9	9	9	9	44
Williams & Co	20	8	6	4	5	43

(c) Suppliers are an important business stakeholder and will benefit from the success of a business. However, they can also contribute to the success of a business. Having good suppliers, and effective relations with them, will help to improve the operational performance of a business. In this case, IXO's relationship with suppliers may not be very good. The main reason for this is because they are on the constant look out for new, cheaper suppliers. The operations manager is under pressure to meet demanding financial targets which means that cheaper suppliers must be found. This will not help to develop good relations between IXO and suppliers. Suppliers will feel that they could be 'dropped' at any moment by IXO, leaving them with less revenue and unused capacity. This view is supported by the new operations manager. She was particularly concerned about the treatment of suppliers. She felt that IXO could not develop effective relations with suppliers if they continually looked for cheaper ones. **(8 marks)**

(d) One of the changes which the new operations manager wants to make is to use eSourcing. This is a relatively new approach to supplier management. It involves the use of Internet technologies and electronic communications in the whole purchasing process. It is a systematic approach that can handle all stages in the purchasing process, including identifying appropriate suppliers, tendering, negotiation and award and contract management. The various eSource tools available enable buyers and suppliers to connect and contract quickly and efficiently in order to improve the company's competitiveness.

IXO Instruments Ltd may be able to benefit from this new approach. eSourcing significantly reduces the length of time spent on the whole purchasing process. It also reduces the need for paper-based systems and labour-intensive processes. In general, eSourcing helps to improve operational efficiency and can benefit both buyers and suppliers. IXO might benefit from eSourcing because it is quicker - it enables a faster sourcing process and faster results. The whole process could be 70 per cent faster. eSourcing eliminates the need for multiple face-to-face meetings, reduces travel time and eliminates geographical barriers. It also provides more transparent, uniform and predictable pricing, it improves the enforcement of corporate purchasing policies and gives better process transparency.

IXO's suppliers will benefit from eSourcing as well. It is a more efficient and objective sourcing process and provides a more level playing field. It is easier to respond - negotiations and travel are eliminated. Costs are lower such as selling and customer acquisition. It is also more convenient for buyers, leading to more transactions. Providing benefits to suppliers should help IXO to develop better relations with suppliers. Consequently, the introduction of eSourcing could benefit IXO considerably.

(14 marks)

87 | Using technology in operations

Question 1

(a) Automation occurs when machinery replaces labour. In this case Barclays Bank has automated one of its systems. For instance, cheques which were previously processed by hand will now be handled by computers. Automation will help Barclays to save money because less people and less space will be required. The bank will also shut its Barclays House operation in Poole and seek out smaller premises in the town or nearby Bournemouth. The new premises will be 100,000 sq ft compared with the 300,000 sq ft currently provided by Barclays House.

(b) Unfortunately, one of the main problems when introducing new technology is that people are made redundant. Automation in particular means that machines will replace people. In this case Barclays is planning to cut 1,100 jobs in its processing centre in Poole, Dorset, over the next three years. The redundancies are the result of automation in a number of its systems. Unite, the newly formed union which incorporates finance branch Amicus, expressed concern about the 'large reduction of jobs in Poole'. Union official Steve Pantak said: 'Unite does however have robust agreements in place and the bank's plans are spread over the next three years, so we will be working with the bank to ensure the maximum number of redeployments and voluntary redundancies'. This will help to reduce the pain of redundancies.

Question 2

(a) Coilcolor has used computers in a number of its operations. The original stock control and sales processing system was implemented in 1992. Since then Coilcolor's business model has undergone substantial changes and the original system with its ageing technology no longer serviced the demands of this highly competitive industry. Consequently the company had to invest in an upgrade. A company called Computerisation developed two highly sophisticated, bespoke systems for Coilcolor - a Sales Order Processing System and Stock Control System. The new systems efficiently manage Coilcolor's complex product portfolio. This consists of many product variables including stock code, material, colour etc. The new systems were created to work alongside Sage MMS, a computerised accounts system.

(b) Generally, the introduction of computers in a business will improve efficiency. In this case computerisation has reduced administration time and costs by avoiding the need for multiple data entry. Coilcolor have also achieved a sustainable competitive advantage through their quick turnaround times within the intensive manufacturing process. Improved administration has enhanced that advantage which was made possible by the implementation of Computerisation's systems. From a customer service aspect their new systems provide the company with the ability to monitor stock efficiently, satisfying customer demand with low minimum order quantities.

Case study

(a) Robots are increasingly used on assembly and production lines. They have some form of arm, which moves to instructions given by a computer. Repetitive tasks, such as installing components, can be carried out many times with great accuracy. In this case robots are used in production cells for a variety of tasks such as operating lathes. However, Minco is considering adding more robots, to load the initial paint station for example. They may also be used to unload rollers off a conveyor after the coating has cured. Brian Duff, Minco's manufacturing engineer says, 'robots are also ideally suited for Minco's packaging process'. **(6 marks)**

(b) Automation involves replacing workers with machinery. New technology means that more and more jobs in the workplace can be done by machines. In this case robots have been employed to carry out tasks that were previously done by people. Robots keep labour costs down allowing Minco to compete internationally, according to Brian Duff. Once the robots have been programmed they just run. The introduction of robots means that people are not required to load lathes for 10 to 12 hours a shift. Brian Duff says, 'Before the robots were installed, this process required an additional finish turning lathe. We had an operator manually feeding two lathes to work the ends and then feeding a third lathe to do the finish turn work. The finish turning machine was actually capable of twice the production than was possible by hand.' Thus the introduction of robots is a form of automation. **(6 marks)**

(c) Robots tend to do tedious repetitive work. Consequently, as robots are introduced at Minco Manufacturing, the workers are released from tedious jobs which are boring and demotivating. In one area the introduction of robots in a cell means that operators are free to do other tasks. In this case the operator can do inspections and move parts in and out of the cell. Minco is also thinking about using robots to load the initial paint station. This is very labour-intensive, because every roller made gets painted. Rollers weigh up to eight pounds so it is exhausting work. Brian Duff said that workers get fatigued in this area and production begins to drop. The introduction of robots in this area will therefore make it easier for workers. **(6 marks)**

(d) As a result of adopting 16 new Stäubli robots in its production cells Minco Manufacturing has improved product quality and reduced costs. Robots keep labour costs down allowing Minco to compete internationally. 'By using robots and reducing labour costs, we can compete with companies that make parts in China, for example.' said Brian Duff. 'We are able to keep the work in the United States and still be competitive with the cheaper labour rates in Asian countries.'

The robots are known for high-speed performance, and this speed also generated savings. Before the robots were installed, a certain process required an additional finish turning lathe. Operators were employed to feed lathes in the process. The finish turning machine was actually capable of twice the production than was possible by hand,' Duff explained, 'With three robotic cells currently running, we've saved three lathes that we can transfer into making another cell'. They've also saved about 50 per cent more floor space. 'It allows us to design extremely compact work cells'.

Robots have also improved the quality of products and consistency in production. The quantity of fuser rollers produced and the level of quality needed, demanded repeatability as well as speed. 'Repeatability is key to the robot's performance in this application because of how we are locating the part into the draw tube. If we don't place the part against the stop very accurately then we would have too much fluctuation and we could not control the quality of the roller,' Duff said. 'We need to meet a length accuracy of less than .005 of an inch, but we're not seeing even that much variation. We're seeing .002 or less.'

Generally, robots are more accurate, can do repetitive work without complaint, save labour and improve quality and consistency in production. This will help to improve the financial performance of Minco Manufacturing. **(10 marks)**

(e) The increased use of robots at Minco Manufacturing has clear benefits. However, the introduction of new technology can be problematic. One of the main drawbacks is the cost of new technology. Development, installation and maintenance can often prove costly. Also, businesses may have to retrain staff. There is evidence in this case to suggest that the nature of workers' tasks change significantly after the introduction of robots. Another problem may be labour relations. Workers may feel threatened by robots. If robots replace workers there may be significant redundancies and industrial unrest. There is no mention of redundancies in this case but job losses may have been likely. New technology creates jobs which require new, technical skills, but replace manual jobs. These new jobs cannot be done by the existing workforce unless they can be retrained. Often, this is not possible. In this case operators have been asked to inspect work after the introduction of robots. Some operators may not have the skills to do this. Automated production lines are interdependent. If one part of the line breaks down the whole process may stop. There may also be teething problems. Breakdowns often occur when technology is first installed. Minco may have encountered such problems when installing robots.

The management of technological change is considered very difficult. One reason is due to the rapid pace of the change. When new technology becomes available business managers have to decide whether or not to purchase it, or wait for the next important breakthrough. Deciding when to invest in new technology is very difficult. In this case Minco is thinking of buying more robots to do other jobs, in the paint shop, for example. The management of the human resources leading up to the change, and during the change, requires great skill. People are often unhappy about change in their lives. Finally, there may be problems with computer software. Minco may have to constantly buy the latest software to be compatible with clients or suppliers who use more modern versions. Modern machines may not run older software. New software may not be able to convert older programs. Although none of these problems are highlighted in the case, it does not mean that some of them have not been encountered. **(12 marks)**

Question 1

(a) Whichever definition of size is used QinetiQ is a large company. For example, a large firm is one that employs more than 249 staff. QinetiQ employs around 13,000. According to the EU a business is considered large if its turnover exceeds 50 million euros (about £37.9 million). QinetiQ's turnover in 2007 was £1,149.5 million. According to the information in the figure QinetiQ has been a large company according to this measure for the last five years. Finally, according to the EU a firm is considered large if the amount of capital employed exceeds 43 million Euros (about £32.6 million). QinetiQ's capital employed is £477.4 million.

(b) (i) Market capitalisation = share price × no. of shares

Market capitalisation (Low share price) = 161p × 660,000,000 = £1,062.6 million

Market capitalisation (High share price) = 218p × 660,000,000 = £1,438.8 million.

(ii) In 2007 the value of QinetiQ according to market capitalisation varied between two levels. When the share price was at its lowest it was valued at £1,062.6 million. However, when the share price was at its highest the value of QinetiQ was £1,438.8 million. According to this method of measurement the company grew by around 40 per cent in less than a year. Although this might be possible, it is very unlikely that a company as large as QinetiQ could grow quite so quickly. For example, it took five years for the company's turnover to grow 50% from £774.4 million to £1,149.5 million. This case highlights one of the problems with using market capitalisation to measure the size of a business. Share prices can fluctuate wildly which means that, technically, the size of the business is also changing in the same way. However, this would not happen. Share prices are influenced by a range of factors such as interest rates, the state of the economy and activity in the financial markets. Consequently share prices may not reflect accurately the size of a business at a particular point in time.

Question 2

(a) According to the EU, a firm is considered to be medium-sized if it has a turnover between 10 million and 50 million euros or has between 50 and 249 employees. In this case Ot2k employs 79 staff and has a turnover of £20.1 million (about 27 million Euros) in 2006. Therefore, according to both criteria, Ot2k is a medium-sized firm.

(b) According to the Sunday Times Fast Track 100, Ot2k was the second fastest growing private limited company in 2007. Sales have grown 206% a year from £700,000 in 2003 to £20.1m in 2006. This means that sales trebled every year (on average) for three consecutive years. This represents a very fast pace of growth for a business.

(c) Some businesses prefer to operate on a small scale, however, many others prefer to grow and become much bigger. Ot2k has grown very quickly and there are some strong motives for growth. For example, in some industries firms will not survive if they remain small. Staying small might mean that costs are too high because the firm is too small to exploit economies of scale. In addition, small firms, even if they are profitable, may face a takeover bid from a larger firm. In this case one of the main motives for growth may have been economies of scale. As firms grow in size they will begin to enjoy the benefits of economies of scale. This means that unit production costs will fall and efficiency and profits will improve. Growth will also help to increase future profitability and increase market share. In this case, demand for the services provided by Ot2k has been fuelled by hurricanes in the Gulf of Mexico, the high price of oil, and a shortage

of diving vessels. This has helped the company to grow quickly.

Case study

(a) Figure 3 shows the share of employment in small businesses by industrial sector. The financial sector is the industry with the smallest number of small businesses. Less than 20 per cent of the firms in finance employ less than 49 people. This is perhaps not surprising because the financial sector is dominated by some very large banks such as HSBC, NatWest and Royal Bank of Scotland. Other sectors which have a below average number of firms employing less than 49 staff, include retailing, manufacturing and transport.

(2 marks)

(b) Rodney Wooliscroft's fishing tackle business is a small enterprise. Its turnover is just £190,000 pa. Also, the only people employed in the business is Rodney and his son. Tianna Nyles's financial advice business is also a small enterprise. It employs a total of 19 people and has a turnover of £3.4 million. This is below the 10 million euros which would make it a medium sized firm.

(4 marks)

(c) Barriers to entry are obstacles that prevent or discourage a business from entering a particular market. In the case of the two businesses described above, there are no real barriers to entry. The supply of fishing tackle is a simple retail business which requires few resources. Such an enterprise would not require a great deal of capital for example. Premises could be rented, fixtures and fittings would be modest and the value of stock would be fairly low per item. It might even be possible to buy stock on sale or return from manufacturers. There is little to stop new businesses entering this market.

Tianna Nyles provides financial advice to people. This sort of service is usually provided by financial experts. Such people may be educated to graduate level and have experience in the financial sector at a fairly high level. The supply of people with these skills may be fairly limited. This provides a barrier to entry into this industry. However, there is nothing to stop anyone supplying financial advice and operating a financial services business. This means that the barrier may not be so high therefore competition in this industry is likely to exist. However, it could be argued that it is a little more difficult to establish a business providing financial advice than one selling fishing tackle. However, in either case the barriers are not insurmountable.

(8 marks)

(d) Both of the firms described above are likely to remain small. However, the reasons may be different. In the case of the fishing tackle business, it appears that the owner Rodney Wooliscroft, has no desire to grow. The business is run by him and his son. It states in the case that Rodney likes to spend time fishing and he does not appear to want the extra responsibility and hard work that comes with growing a business. The business diod grow when Rodney asked his son to set up an online shopping service for fishing tackle. However, this was to cope with growing competition from new online businesses. Now that Rodney's own online business is established, he seems satisfied with the current situation. This is in common with many business owners who will not grow their business because they are happy with the current level of profit.

Tianna Nyles's business may remain small for different reasons. Her business is already bigger than Rodney's. She employs 19 staff and has a turnover of £3.4 million. It might be argued that she does want to grow her business. However, there may be a limit to how far she can grow. At the moment her business serves Harrogate. This is a fairly small town and the demand for financial advice may be limited in this particular catchment area. If Tianna wants to grow her business this might mean opening branches in other towns in Yorkshire or further afield. However, operating in other towns may not suit her business style. She would find it difficult to supply the personal service, widely recognised in Harrogate, in other areas. It is difficult to supply a personal service when a business becomes larger. For this reason Tianna may decide not to grow any further. People in other towns may prefer to buy financial advice from a local firm. This would make it difficult for Tianna to spread.

(10 marks)

(e) Despite the advantages of large scale production many firms survive operating on a small scale. There are a number of reasons for this. As in the case of Rodney Wooliscroft's fishing tackle business, some business owners are happy to remain small. They may not want to take on the extra responsibility of growing and becoming large. Some owners avoid growth because they want to remain below the VAT threshold. Another reason why firms choose to remain small is because they are often flexible and efficient. They can be innovative and respond quickly to market changes. For example, Rodney Wooliscroft was quick to set up his online business when competitors entered the market. In some very large firms decision-making is very slow. In some cases small firms can survive because their costs are lower than their larger rivals. For example, a micro brewery will not have to buy a fleet of delivery lorries. In some markets, as in the cases above, there are no barriers to entry which means it is cheap to set up a business. In these circumstances there is little to stop a new firm taking a small share of the market. Some businesses enjoy a degree of monopoly power. This is because they supply a service in a local area where it is not worth a competitor challenging the market. It might be argued that Rodney Wooliscroft and Tianna Nyles enjoy some monopoly power for this reason.

In recent decades there has been a growth in the number of small firms operating in the UK. In the 1980s and early 1990s unemployment was high and many people may have set up small businesses because they couldn't find a job. They may have used redundancy payments to help fund business start-ups. Government schemes have also encouraged people to set up small businesses in recent times. For example, some start-up schemes provided funding for small business to help them get going. Organisations such as Business Links provide advice on running a business and obtaining finance. European initiatives have included loans from the European Investment Fund and finance for training from the European Social Fund. There have also been changes in the structure of the economy. The growth in the tertiary sector has contributed to the growth in the number of small firms. The provision of many services is often best undertaken by small enterprises.

(16 marks)

Question 1

(a) Premier Foods may be able to exploit a number of economies of scale following the acquisition of Campbells. For example, there may be significant marketing economies. On the distribution side, Premier Foods will be able to distribute the Campbells brands at little extra cost. This is because Premier Foods will already have an established distribution operation. Also the extra administrative costs of selling the additional brands will not rise in proportion to the size of the sale. Premier Foods may also enjoy purchasing economies. For example, it will need to buy much larger quantities of raw materials to make the soups and other products. As the size of their orders increase, cost per unit purchased should fall as the company enjoys the advantages of bulk buying.

(b) In addition to the marketing and purchasing economies of scale outlined above, there may be other economies which Premier Foods can exploit. For example, technical economies may arise because some of the plant, machinery and equipment owned by Premier Foods may be better utilised. It is possible that the new brands will be produced in factories that the company already owns. Production facilities at Campbells may eventually be closed down. Premier might also exploit managerial economies. As businesses grow they can afford to employ specialist managers. For example, in this case a manager might be appointed to manage each individual brand. Brand managers are specialists and efficiency might improve. Premier might also exploit financial economies. Larger firms have advantages when they try to raise finance. They will have a wider variety of sources from which to choose. For example, large firms will often find it easier to persuade institutions to lend them money since they will have large assets to offer as security. Finally, large firms borrowing very large amounts of money can often gain better interest rates.

The extent to which Premier Foods is able to exploit further economies probably depends on how effectively it can integrate the activities of Campbell Soups. Businesses often struggle to absorb new businesses and the costs of doing so are often higher than expected. For example, Premier may find it difficult to exploit managerial economies. During the integration process managers working for Campbells may be released in favour of those already employed by Premier. This could result in a loss of knowledge and therefore the opportunities for managerial economies may be diminished.

Question 2

(a) Diseconomies of scale are when the average costs of a business begin to rise as output increases. At some point the opportunities to gain economies of scale from increased size will become exhausted. After this point increased output only leads to rises in costs. Diseconomies can occur as a result of poor co-ordination of activities, problems with communication or a lack of motivation as a result of large size. At IBM, for example, there were communication problems and poor co-ordination of activities. Part of the business argued that the future lay with small personal computers. Another part was successful, making software. However, the business persisted in making large mainframes, so different activities in the business lacked a co-ordination of strategy. This was largely a result of poor communication. Those at the top did not listen. The business only solved these problems by operating a co-ordinated strategy. It also reduced size and operated as small segmented operations. This dealt with another major reason for diseconomies of scale at large businesses, a lack of motivation. Employees became more motivated as a result of the changes as they were empowered to look for solutions and be innovative.

Case study

(a) The term scale in business means size. When managers and owners talk about increasing the scale of operations they mean that the business should be bigger. Large scale businesses use more resources and produce more output. They also have higher turnover, enjoy lower unit costs and generally make larger profits. In this case Timmings has increased the scale of its operations several times. Timmings began as a small engineering company in 1978. It repaired agricultural implements for farmers. The business was successful and eventually began making its own agricultural implements. The company grew and by 1996 it had a work force of 240. Between 1978 and 1996 it increased its scale of operations three times. In 1996 Timmings moved to a spacious new factory on an industrial estate in Birmingham. The move was the result of receiving a large contract to make and supply potato harvesting equipment. The company expanded again by taking on more and more staff. Timmings may now be regarded as a large scale operator. **(4 marks)**

(b) The size of a business has a major impact on average costs of production. Typically, there is a range of output over which average costs fall as output rises. Over this range, larger businesses have a competitive advantage over smaller businesses. They enjoy economies of scale. Over the years Timmings has increased the scale of operations several times. It has expanded and moved into bigger premises. After each move it is likely that Timmings improved its productive efficiency. This is because Timmings would have enjoyed lower average costs due to economies of scale. By increasing the scale of operations, Timmings moves closer to the optimum scale of plant. Each time it does this average costs fall. It is not clear from the information given whether Timmings has reached the optimum scale of plant when it moves to the Birmingham factory. It may be possible for the company to increase productive efficiency further in an even larger plant. **(6 marks)**

(c) One reason why Timmings may have switched to capital intensive production methods is because of the difficulties it was having trying to recruit skilled engineers. Information in the case suggests that in 2001, after the company had moved to Birmingham, it experienced difficulties recruiting high quality engineers. If the company had not switched to capital intensive production Timmings may have found it more difficult to grow. The switch also coincided with the new ownership of the company. The US parent company may have had a new vision for Timmings. It may have felt that capital intensive production methods were more suitable. **(6 marks)**

(d) Timmings plc has grown consistently over the years. It has changed location to bigger premises a number of times. During this time it has probably been able to exploit technical economies of scale. Technical economies arise because larger plants are often more efficient. The capital costs and the running costs of plants do not rise in proportion to their size. One technical economy that Timmings may have exploited is that of indivisibility. Many firms need a particular item of equipment or machinery, but fail to make full use of it. Timmings may have needed a laser cutting machine that cost £100,000. The fixed cost will be the same whether it is used for 4 hours a day or 8 hours a day. As Timmings expands, more use will be made of it and so the average cost of the machine will fall.

Firms often employ a variety of machines which have different capacities. A slow machine may increase production time. As the firm expands and produces more output, it can employ more of the slower machines in order to match the capacity of the faster machines. This is called the law of multiples. It involves firms finding a balanced team of machines so that when they operate together they are all running at full capacity. Timmings may have enjoyed this benefit. As the scale of operations expands the firm may switch to mass production techniques. Flow production, which involves breaking down the production process into a very large number of small operations, allows greater use of highly specialised machinery. This results in large improvements in efficiency as labour is replaced by capital. Timmings may have experienced this when it invested £180 million in CNC machinery and robots. **(8 marks)**

(e) When Timmings was bought by the US engineering company in 2001, it switched to capital intensive production strategies. It invested £180 million buying CNC machines and robots. Two categories of robot were purchased by Timmings - processing operations robots which perform a specific task such as spot welding or spray painting and assembly line robots used to perform a single task in the assembly line process such as fitting a component. The benefits of this investment could be numerous. For example, capital intensive production is generally more cost effective if large quantities are produced. Certainly Timmings plans to produce more and more output. The advantage of machinery is that it is often more precise and consistent, it can operate 24/7 if necessary and machinery is a lot easier to manage than people. The robots purchased by Timmings perform monotonous or repetitive and often dangerous work involving heavy machinery, industrial pollutants, poisonous chemicals or other hazardous materials. Also, with a more capital intensive operation there is less reliance on people. This is an advantage because people are more difficult to manage than machines. They have feelings and react. People can be unreliable - they may go sick or leave suddenly. People cannot work without breaks and holidays and finally people sometimes need to be motivated to improve performance.

Unfortunately there are some drawbacks when employing a greater proportion of capital. Capital is very expensive initially. £180 million was invested in new machinery. It will take a lot of output to get this back. Also, there could be huge delays and costs if machinery breaks down. Large portions of production could grind to a halt if there is a breakdown with a crucial machine. Machinery can also be inflexible - much machinery is highly specialised and only suitable for producing standardised products. Machinery also poses a threat to the workforce and could reduce morale. In this case around 30 staff were laid off as a result of the switch to capital intensive production.

In this case, the benefits of switching to capital intensive production probably outweigh the costs. Timmings is an established firm with good products, a sound customer base and a good reputation. There is no mention in the case of disruption when the machinery was purchased and no mention of poor morale. Only 30 staff were laid off and these may have been voluntary redundancies. Arguably, Timmings needed to change. They had difficulties recruiting staff and the new owner probably had a new vision. **(16 marks)**

90 | Mergers and takeovers

Question 1

(a) Horizontal integration occurs when two businesses operating in exactly the same market join together. In this case, Blizzard and Activision are both gaming companies. US-based Activision makes console games such as the Tony Hawk series and Guitar Hero. Blizzard is the biggest player in online gaming and World of Warcraft is the global market leader of what are known as massively multi-player online role-playing games.

(b) There are numerous reasons why businesses merge. In this case the two firms are hoping that their different strengths will combine to form a business which is powerful on every gaming platform and in every territory. Blizzard is strong in Asia, where its Starcraft series has proved hugely popular. Starcraft, a strategy game first released in 1998, is played by millions of South Koreans in gaming cyber-cafes, and by professional gamers on television. Activision has developed a presence on all three new generation game consoles - Microsoft's Xbox 360, Sony's PlayStation 3 and the Nintendo Wii - with franchises such as Spider-Man and X-Men. The two firms may have joined together for defensive reasons. Operating independently they may have become the victims of a hostile takeover. By joining together they have more resources and can resist such approaches. They may also develop and dominate the market. Finally, one of the main motives for integration is to exploit the synergies that might exist following the merger. This means that joining two businesses forms an organisation that is more powerful and efficient than the two companies operating on their own. Synergy occurs when the 'the whole is greater than the sum of the parts'. For example, when 2 + 2 = 5. Synergies may arise from economies of scale, the potential for asset stripping, the reduction of risk through diversification or the potential for gains by management.

Question 2

(a) A demerger is where a company sells off a significant part of its existing operations. GUS has a history of demerging. For many years GUS was one of the best performing stocks on the London Stock Exchange. However, in 2000, the company embarked on a new strategy aimed at delivering long-term shareholder value by focusing on a small number of businesses with above-average growth potential. Other parts of GUS were to be disposed of over time and the proceeds reinvested. By 2003, GUS had been successfully repositioned around three major businesses - Experian, Home Retail Group (formerly Argos Retail Group) and Burberry. In December 2005, GUS completed the demerger of Burberry and, in March 2006, announced the separation of its two remaining businesses, Experian and Home Retail Group.

(b) One of the main motives for integration is to exploit the synergies that might exist following a merger or takeover. This means that joining two businesses forms an organisation that is more powerful and efficient than the two companies operating on their own. Synergy occurs when the 'the whole is greater than the sum of the parts'. For example, when 2 + 2 = 5. Synergies may arise from economies of scale, the potential for asset stripping, the reduction of risk through diversification or the potential for gains by management. In this case, GUS recognised that there were no compelling synergies between their current businesses and that their eventual separation was likely to create the most value for shareholders. GUS believed that Experian and Home Retail Group would achieve their greatest potential and value by becoming independent businesses. In this case GUS believed that the sum of the parts was greater than the whole and that there was no scope for economies of scale or asset stripping, for example.

(c) GUS believed that Experian and Home Retail Group would achieve their greatest potential and value by becoming independent businesses. They felt that a number of benefits would be achieved. The main benefit would be to shareholders, the demerger was expected to enhance shareholder value. There would also be the creation of two separately listed companies offering discrete investment propositions, each with clear market valuations, transparent capital structure and efficient balance sheet. Experian and Home Retail Group would also enjoy greater flexibility to manage their own resources and pursue strategies appropriate to their markets. There would be sharpened management focus, helping the two businesses maximise their performance and make full use of their available resources. Finally, it was hoped that management rewards would be more directly linked with the business and stock market performances, helping to attract, retain and motivate the best people.

Question 3

(a) A management buy-out is where the ownership of a business is transferred to the current management team. The team is likely to buy shares from the existing owners. Funds for the buy-out might be provided by members of the management team itself or financial institutions, such as banks or venture capitalists. In this case, Warrington Internet search engine marketing company, Latitude Group, has undergone a management buyout worth more than £50m. The buy-out was led by chief executive Dylan Thwaites, winner of the Ernst & Young Technology and Communications Entrepreneur of the Year award in 2006. The management team also includes finance officer Julie Moran, operations officer Richard Gregory, and technology officer Rob Shaw.

(b) Venture capitalists are specialists who are prepared to take the risk of investing directly in a business. The capital they provide is sometimes called risk capital. In this case, Private equity investor Vitruvian Partners invested what is believed to be as much as £55m. The money will be used to re-capitalise the business and fund a rapid growth programme. Vitruvian Partners is a recently formed London-based private equity firm dedicated to investing in middle-market buyouts, growth buyouts and growth capital across a range of industries in Northern Europe. Investors like Vitruvian Partners aim to make a profit on their investment and often 'cash-in' their investment after a few years.

(c) Latitude is the UK's largest independent search engine marketing specialist offering both paid and natural search, with household-name clients including Tesco Finance, House of Fraser, Kwik-Fit Insurance, Crystal Lakes & Ski, Alliance & Leicester, William Hill and Bank of Ireland. Latitude has seen turnover rise from £500,000 in 2002 to more than £30m in 2006, while headcount has risen from eight in 2002 to more than 100 in 2007. After the management buy-out, Dylan Thwaites, said: 'This is a fantastic development for Latitude and its clients. This will help us fund future expansion through acquisition and internal growth. 'We will be looking at new geographic markets and diversification into other digital marketing products including further development of social media and display advertising. All with a view to providing our clients with an even better and more complete service'. It is often argued that the efficiency of a business will improve after a buy-out. This is because there is an increased incentive for managers to perform well. Following a buy-out the management team will benefit financially from any profit made by the company, so there is an incentive to keep costs down and motivate the workforce, for example. Latitude may benefit from this.

Case study

(a) James Barnes is the current chief executive of Dobbies and led the management buy-out of the company in 1994 before taking it public three years later. The sale will net a windfall of £10 million for James Barnes. Mr Barnes owns 6.7 per cent of the company. His father and sister own another 2 per cent.

(4 marks)

(b) (i) Tesco acquired Dobbies in June 2007 for £15 a share. At the end of April 2007, Dobbies' share price was £11.53. Clearly, Tesco's bid for the company increased the share price. It is quite normal for the share price of a company to rise following a takeover bid. The amount paid for a business listed on the stock market when taken over is nearly always greater than the current share price. The price of Dobbies' shares rose because of increasing demand for their shares. When Tesco decided to take over the company they will have started to buy their shares. Also, news of any takeover usually results in a rush to buy the shares. This adds to the demand and forces the price up further.

(6 marks)

(ii) Although Tesco eventually bought Dobbies, other parties were also interested in buying the company. According to information in the case, venture capitalists Apax Partners were interested and so was Sir Tom Hunter, the Scottish entrepreneur, who owns Wye-vale Garden Centres and Blooms of Bressingham. Initially, their interest forced the share price up to £17 a share as speculators joined in the frenzy to buy Dobbies' shares. In the end though these two other potential buyers withdrew their interest and the share price fell back to what Tesco finally paid for the company. However, if they had pursued their interest there may have been a bidding war and Dobbies' share price would have risen further.

(6 marks)

(c) One of the motives for buying another company is to lower costs. Cost can be lowered by exploiting economies of scale. In this case Tesco might enjoy some buying economies if they buy larger quantities of stock which both Dobbies and Tesco currently use. However, the opportunities to bulk buy might be limited because Tesco does not currently cater well for this market. The stock overlap might be small. Administrative economies are likely to be exploited. Tesco is likely to absorb some of Dobbies' administrative activities by merging their accounts function for example. There may also be opportunities to save on distribution costs. Tesco has a very large

distribution operation and it is likely that Dobbies' stores could be served by the same system. This would save money. Finally, the scope for exploiting economies of scale might be limited in this case because although Dobbies is a large retailer operating 21 stores, their product lines are very different from those of Tesco's. Also, most of Dobbies' stores are in Scotland where Tesco is arguably less dominant. The main motive for acquiring Dobbies was not to reduce costs. It was to diversify.

(10 marks)

(d) As explained in (c), Tesco may enjoy some cost savings as a result of buying Dobbies. However, the main benefits from the acquisition are those associated with diversification. Tesco said that the acquisition would give it access to a market to which it was not catering at present and it reflected a strategy of developing the company's non-food operations. Andrew Higginson, the Tesco finance director, said that the supermarket saw potential to expand the range of environmentally-friendly products in Dobbies, adding that it offered a 'big emerging market' in consumer spending. 'I think garden centres can go after that green pound and they are already in an attractive and growing market,' he said. Tesco is keen to capitalise on the current boom in gardening and related 'green' products, including composting kits and water butts. Tesco wants to extend the firm's range of environmentally friendly products to offer wind turbines, home insulation and services such as carbon footprint calculators. It would also seek to expand the chain, particularly in the south of England, to offer 'greater choice and keener pricing'. It is clear from these statements that Tesco is looking to enter a new market. Tesco's growth opportunities in its current market might be dwindling. It obviously sees a great deal of potential in this new and growing market. Tapping into this completely new market will also reduce risk for Tesco.

(14 marks)

91 | Innovation, research and development

Question 1

(a) Wolfson spent $29.3 million on R & D in 2006. Research is the inquiry and discovery of new ideas in order to solve a problem or create an opportunity. In this case much of Wolfson's research is channelled into the search for ideas for new products. Development involves changing ideas into products, materials, systems or processes. Quite often a business will identify a number of possible ideas which have scope for development. The first stage is to select the idea which shows the most promise. The time spent on development can often be very lengthy. Innovation in business is the commercial exploitation of an invention. It involves committing resources and bringing a new idea to the market. In this case evidence of innovation is the stream of products that Wolfson has bought to the market including the audio in products such as MP3 players, personal media players and mobile phones

(b) Expenditure in R & D is very important to Wolfson. This is shown by the large proportion of revenue which is channelled into R & D. In 2006, Wolfson invested about 14 per cent ($29.3m ÷ $204m x 100) of its revenue in R & D. Also, in 2005 the profit made by Wolfson was $29 million. This means that the amount of money allocated to R & D in 2006 was the same as profit made in 2005. This shows how committed Wolfson is to R & D and innovation. Wolfson also employs some of the most experienced and innovative designers and engineers in the industry.

(c) Generally, if a business invests in R & D it may gain a competitive edge over its rivals and increase future profitability. However, some specific purposes of innovation can be identified. In this case the main purpose of Wolfson's R & D is to develop new products. One of the main reasons why businesses invest in R & D is to extend its product range or replace products that have come to the end of their life cycle. Wolfson is a global leader in the supply of high performance mixed-signal chips for the digital consumer market. Its products can be found at the heart of consumer electronic applications in the home, in the office and on the move. Many of the world's leading electronics manufacturers are customers, with its chips providing the audio in products such as MP3 players, personal media players, mobile phones, digital cameras, games consoles, flat screen TVs and hi-fi systems. The company has developed a broad range of products and continues to invest heavily in research and development to expand its product portfolio.

Question 2

(a) Rolls Royce is a big spender on R & D. It is the UK's 7th biggest spender in all. The amount of money allocated to R & D by different businesses varies greatly and may depend on a number of factors. For example, certain industries, such as pharmaceuticals, chemicals, motor cars, computers and defence, tend to have high levels of spending on R & D. This is due to the nature of the industry. In this case Rolls Royce is in the aerospace sector. Together with pharmaceuticals, aerospace accounts for 45 per cent of all R & D expenditure in the UK. Larger public limited companies tend to be more committed to R & D. They are better able to meet the cost and bear the risk involved than smaller businesses. Rolls Royce is a very large company. Finally, some businesses are committed to high levels of R & D spending because it is part of their corporate objectives and culture. This is certainly the case in the aerospace industry.

(b) There is a great deal of evidence in this case to suggest that Rolls Royce is committed to reducing environmental damage through its R & D. During 2006 Rolls Royce launched a new £95 million technology demonstrator programme, the Environmentally Friendly Engine (EFE). This will deliver improvements in turbine efficiency and combustion emissions. Also, Rolls-Royce is a lead partner in the development of the European 'Clean Sky' Joint Technology Initiative.

Alongside its industrial partners, it hopes to gain European Commission approval to launch this seven-year programme in mid 2007. In combining this programme with the EFE programme, Rolls Royce will continue with its progress towards achieving the Advisory Council for Aeronautics Research in Europe (ACARE) goals for environmental improvements by 2020.

(c) A patent aims to protect the inventor of a new product or manufacturing process. In 2006, Rolls Royce filed a record 330 patent applications. A patent allows a business to design, produce and sell a new invention and attempts to prevent competitors from copying it. New inventions are protected for fifteen years. The developer must make details of the invention available to the Patent Office and pay annual fees which become more expensive after the first four years. This is to encourage production of the new idea. Some of the benefits to businesses of patents are a higher level of sales, reduced competition and legal protection that encourages continued research.

Case study

(a) (i) The global market for video games is huge. The market is currently worth $37.5 billion. However, the potential for future growth is also significant. By 2011, the worldwide gaming market will be worth $48.9 billion at an annual growth rate of 9.1% during the five-year period. **(4 marks)**

(ii) Nintendo, which has outsold Sony and Microsoft in the videogame console market, recently became the leader in game revenue, toppling Sony. Worldwide revenue from Nintendo DS and Wii gaming software amounted to $1.2 billion in the quarter, up more than 31% from $943.6 million Nintendo enjoyed in the second quarter. In comparison, Sony generated $1 billion in gaming software revenue for its PlayStation 3, PlayStation 2 and PSP players, while Microsoft posted revenue of $317.8 million for Xbox and Xbox 360. Nintendo is also expected to maintain its lead, as it ships about 200 additional titles by the end of the year, bringing the number of games to more than 350, many from outside publishers. Nintendo has achieved mass-market appeal through easy to use games, and the Wii's motion-sensing control that allows players to get more physically involved in games, which could involve swinging a virtual tennis racket or golf club. **(4 marks)**

(iii) Sales of PlayStation 3 software have been suffering due to the console's high price and a lack of compelling titles. One of Sony's third party publishers, EA, is losing revenue due to meagre PlayStation 3 sales and the company is rooting for price cuts and improvements to the console in order to encourage software sales. Sony cut the price of the PlayStation 3, but because the company was slow to drop prices and produce compelling games, third-party publishers are flocking to other platforms. **(4 marks)**

(b) Generally, if a business invests in R & D it may gain a competitive edge over its rivals and increase future profitability. However, some specific purposes of innovation can be identified. In this case, one of the main purposes of R & D is to generate new video games. One of the main reasons why businesses invest in R & D is to extend their product range or replace products that have come to the end of their life cycle. In the video games market products have quite a short life cycle. They need to be updated fairly regularly. There is also intense competition. The three market leaders, Nintendo, Sony and Microsoft, are all under pressure to continually innovate and bring new games to the market. This is the nature of the industry. **(8 marks)**

(c) Allocating resources to R & D is extremely risky. Expenditure on R & D does not guarantee new products. Quite often money spent on R & D is wasted. For example, in the video games market there is intense competition. A company like Sony may bring out a new game only to find that a rival has launched an even better game. This could mean that sales of the new Sony game are so low that the R & D expenditure is not recovered. Indeed, Sony is having trouble with its PlayStation 3 game. Sales are said to be meagre.

Setting a budget for R & D expenditure is also fraught with uncertainty. R & D departments often spend more than they are allocated. In 2007, Sony cut its R & D expenditure on games by nearly 10 per cent to 97.9 billion yen. The cost of a particular research project may be difficult to estimate accurately. This is because researchers will not know when a breakthrough is going to occur. Some research has been ongoing for many years. Also, during an R & D project there may be unforeseen spending. For example, a business might have to unexpectedly recruit staff with specialist knowledge and experience to further the programme. And, because some R & D programmes run for many years, their costs tend to rise with inflation. This all adds to the uncertainty. **(8 marks)**

(d) Many companies use computer aided design (CAD) to help develop new products. CAD is an interactive computer system which is capable of generating, storing and using geometric and computer graphics. It helps design engineers to solve design problems. CAD is used in many industries today. Companies such as Sony, Nintendo and Microsoft may enjoy a number of benefits if they use CAD.

CAD has meant huge cuts in lead time, ie the length of time between the initial design and actual production. Long lead times result in lower profits as firms lose out to competitors in the race to launch new products. A wide range of designs can be shown on the computer screen. Two and three dimensional engineering drawings, wire-framed models, electronic circuit board designs and architectural drawings are examples. CAD systems handle repetitive work, allowing the designer more time to concentrate on 'creating' the design. The need for specialists is also reduced, which helps keep down costs. Modifications and changes are easily made. The size or shape of a design can be changed in seconds, for example. Problems are often more quickly identified. This sometimes prevents the need for expensive reworking later on. Also, the final design, once manufactured, is more likely to be right. Since the speedy introduction of new products is so important in the video games industry, all of three of the leaders are likely to use CAD. **(8 marks)**

(e) Innovation and creativity are hugely important in the video games industry. Video games appear to have quite short product life cycles. People get bored with them and are eager for new, stimulating and more exciting games. The amount of money spent by companies like Sony, Nintendo and Microsoft on R & D and innovation is huge. For example, in 2007 Sony spent a massive 97.9 billion yen. Nintendo and Microsoft will have spent similar amounts. Competition is also very fierce in the industry. There is enormous pressure to grab a bigger slice of the lucrative and growing market. Nintendo has recently become the market leader. This will annoy Sony and it will want to fight back. To do this it must develop more and better new games. Nintendo is currently enjoying the success of its new Wii games. It has recently developed a flagship title for the Wii, called Wii Fit. The game encourages players to engage in full-body exercises using Wii Balance Boards, performing activities including yoga, push-ups, aerobics, and stretching. Sony's R & D team will be under pressure to match and exceed this development.

However, innovation and creativity are not the only factors which affect the financial performance of firms in the video games industry. Other aspects of the business have to be right. For example, once new games have been developed they have to be manufactured and the quality of manufacture must match customer expectations. Games must be reliable and easy to use. Technical products such as video games need high standards of manufacture. Customers would be very easily irritated if there were technical faults when they started playing. The marketing of the games will also be vital for success. For example, companies must get their launch right. They will have to invest on an effective advertising campaign and make sure the games are available in outlets where customers can buy them. The pricing must also be right. In this case there is some evidence to suggest that Sony has got its pricing wrong. Sales of PlayStation 3 software, have been suffering due to the console's high price. The problems have affected third-party game publishers, such as leading game maker Electronic Arts. EA is losing revenue due to meagre PlayStation 3 sales and the company is rooting for price cuts.

To conclude, there is a range of factors that can affect the financial performance of a business in any industry. These might include the quality of products, the strength and quality of leadership, the effectiveness of marketing, the skills of the workforce, the quality of financial control and the vision of the directors. However, in the fiercely competitive video games industry it is likely that the most important key to success is the ability to generate a constant stream of innovative new games. **(14 marks)**

Question 1

(a) Product ideas come from a number of sources. These include ideas from competitors, ideas from staff, ideas from R & D and ideas from other products. In this case the idea came from a consumer - Deborah Brady. Deborah, a keen equestrian, identified the need for carrying basic equipment whilst horse riding in a more convenient and comfortable way. The idea was developed during a horse orienteering competition where various equipment including map, phone and pens were used on a regular basis but were difficult to access from a coat or rucksack whilst 'on the move'.

(b) One of the steps involved in the design process is to investigate alternative solutions. Deborah undertook this step over a four year period. She developed a range of prototypes in collaboration with local fashion designers and manufacturers and with the support of Design Wales and the Wales Innovation Network (WIN) refined the initial concept into a functional activity vest. The vest is a multifunctional piece of outdoor apparel incorporating an integral, detachable map case for improved accessibility, together with specifically shaped ergonomic pockets for carrying essential safety equipment and field kit such as compass, space blanket, mobile phone, hand warmer, medical card, whistle, etc. The vest also incorporates high visibility edging to improve safety whilst on the road. Deborah also found that although the product was initially designed for use during equestrian orienteering events, many other sporting activities could also benefit from a product of this nature. These included walking, rambling, cycling, mountain biking, climbing, orienteering, fell running and rescue units.

(c) Ergonomics is the study of people in their environment and the adaptation of machines and conditions to improve efficiency. This means that the design should be efficient and take into account user convenience and safety. In this case, people enjoying outdoor activities, such as those described above, will often need to remove objects from pockets. Due to the nature of their activities such a task may be difficult and potentially dangerous - when riding a bike or a horse for example. However, with an ergonomic design such a task will be easier. The i-Quip Explorer has ergonomically designed pockets. This allows users to remove objects from pockets more conveniently and safely.

Question 2

(a) When developing a product a number of design features have to be considered by the designers. These might include safety, maintenance, environment, aesthetics and legal. In this case there were arguably two or three key design features. The Home and Garden Tidy solves the two most common problems for gardeners when tidying their gardens - keeping a refuse bag open and upright and keeping tools in one place. Consequently, the product was designed to improve the efficiency of gardening and make gardening more convenient. It is a very simple labour saving device. It may be the product does make gardening a little easier. For example, it has 8 handy size pockets to keep all garden tools in one place, it can be easily wheeled around the garden, the pocketed support easily removes from frame to facilitate removal of heavy bags or for cleaning, it is at a convenient working height for standing or kneeling and at the end of the day it folds away for easy storage. Convenience and efficiency are often important design features.

Another important design feature in this case is reliability and durability. Consumers do not want to buy products that wear out quickly or fail to perform under certain conditions. In this case the B-tidy range has been manufactured to the highest of standards. Materials used are strong, robust and will withstand the rigors of climate changes. It has a robust steel frame with a tough tear resistant

waterproof polyethylene pocketed support. It will support up to 15 kgs and supports and keeps open any standard size refuse bag. If the product was flimsy and prone to breakage it would fail in the market.

Finally, another important design feature is commercial viability. Businesses must be able to produce and sell a product at a profit. Before launching the Home and Garden Tidy Barbara and Peter had to be sure that it would make a profit for them. Their original product was exhibited at the Geneva Inventors and New Products Exhibition in April 2006, at which they were awarded a Bronze Medal in their category. This has resulted in considerable public, media and trade interest in the product, both in the U.K. and in Europe. Also, the product had extensive trials with consumers during its development and comprehensive market research indicated very positive potential consumer interest. Consequently Peter and Barbara were able to launch their product with confidence. Their research carried out before the launch suggested that the product would be commercially viable.

Case study

(a) Chrysler has a strong history of building concept cars. According to Virgil Exner, Chrysler's first vice president of styling, concept cars are 'idea cars'. These one-of-a-kind concept vehicles provide opportunities to explore new design ideas. Customer reaction to future products can be more effectively gauged as senior management gets comfortable with new design trends. Concept cars may influence new products, as the Portofino influenced the first LH sedans. The Viper and the PT Cruiser concepts were so well received they became production cars. Concept cars also offer engineers a platform to explore advanced technologies on functioning vehicles. The building of these advanced vehicles helped propel Chrysler to the position of styling leadership it enjoys today.

(4 marks)

(b) Many designers have to consider ergonomics when designing products such as cars. Ergonomics is the study of people in their environment and the adaptation of machines and conditions to improve efficiency and comfort. In this case, ergonomics is an issue when comes to the design of the car interior. Ergonomically, the customer's interaction with the vehicle must be natural and allow for quick response. Controls must be placed within easy reach, instruments clearly visible and placement of components logical. This is important to Chrysler because drivers expect high standards of comfort when buying a car today. A car designed to high ergonomic standards may give a car manufacturer a competitive edge in the market. However, interior designers face the difficult challenge of blending aesthetic, functional and ergonomic features, often within tight constraints.

(6 marks)

(c) (i) When designing any product a number of features have to be considered by the design team. With some products the environment is an important design issue. Some consumers are more likely to buy products if they are environmentally friendly. In this case, many drivers would prefer to buy cars that are environmentally friendly. Cars are blamed for contributing to global warming. Consequently car designers have had to come up with designs with reduced emissions. Also, as global oil stocks are dwindling, many drivers want cars that are fuel efficient. Consequently, designers have to develop engines that are more economical. Clearly, environmental issues are very important to Chrysler when designing cars.

(ii) Some consumers are very particular indeed about the appearance of products. For many drivers the shape, style and colour of a car are very important. Chrysler has a strong history of building beautiful and exciting concept vehicles and their world-class designers develop fresh, bold, trend-setting exterior designs. In the market, car producers can increase their market share if they can design better looking cars than their rivals. Consequently, again, this is an important design feature for Chrysler.

(iii) Designers must ensure that their design solutions are safe. Safety is particularly important in the design of machinery. Cars are potential 'killers'. Over 3,000 people a year are killed in car accidents in the

UK. Car designers have to consider a wide range of safety issues. For example, in particular, brakes have to be thoroughly reliable and effective. The structure of the car has to be designed so that it can absorb impact, doors must be designed so that young children cannot open them whilst the car is in motion and lights must be designed so that they do not fail when driving at speed. In recent years designers have added special safety features to cars such as seat belts, airbags and a range of warning systems. There are many more safety issues that car designers have to take into account. Arguably, safety is the most important design feature for car manufacturers.

(12 marks)

(d) Chrysler uses computer aided design (CAD) in its design process. CAD is an interactive computer system which is capable of generating, storing and using geometric and computer graphics. It helps design engineers to solve design problems. At Chrysler CAD software is used to develop the designer's interior and exterior themes. Data generated by the CAD software links the designer's concept to all other supporting activities in the corporation such as, manufacturing, marketing, finance and purchasing. The CAD operator receives input from various sources: oral direction or sketches from the designer, engineering sections, or scan data from clay models. The design often evolves between a physical clay model and the CAD data. As more realism is required for full size evaluation, three-dimensional elements such as mirrors, tyres and wheels are developed and added to the CAD data. The final concept data is then sent to engineering for final production surfacing and release.

CAD can benefit Chrysler in a number of ways. It will reduce lead times significantly allowing Chrysler to bring their new cars to the market more quickly. Long lead times result in lower profits as firms lose out to competitors in the race to launch new products. A wide range of designs can be shown on the computer screen. Two and three dimensional engineering drawings, wire-framed models, electronic circuit board designs and architectural drawings are examples. CAD systems handle repetitive work, allowing the designer more time to concentrate on 'creating' the design. The need for specialists is also reduced, which helps keep down costs. Finally, modifications and changes are easily made. The size or shape of a design can be changed in seconds, for example.

(8 marks)

(e) The aim of value engineering is to reduce costs and avoid unnecessary costs before production begins. This technique, which is very important in the design process, is used by most manufacturers in Japan. It aims to eliminate any costs during the design stages which do not add value to, or improve the performance of, products and services. Value analysis is a similar process, but is concerned with cost reduction after a product has been introduced. With raw material costs rising, the need to succeed in world-wide markets and low wage economies applying hostile price competition, value engineering and value analysis are essential tools in the fight to remain competitive.

Value engineering helps businesses to design products at the lowest cost. It is usually carried out by cross-departmental teams. Team members might include designers, operations managers, purchasing specialists and cost accountants. The process involves carefully checking components of a product to find ways to reduce their costs. The team will analyse the function and cost of each element and investigate ways to reduce the number of separate components, using cheaper materials and simplifying processes.

The success of value engineering will often depend on how departments work together. Value engineering cannot be undertaken by an individual. Costs can only be reduced if departments take into account each other's needs. In this case there is plenty of evidence to suggest that Chrylser uses a cross-departmental approach to design. For example, data generated by the CAD software links the designer's concept to all other supporting activities in the corporation such as, manufacturing, marketing, finance and purchasing.

The advantages of value engineering include lower costs, resulting in lower prices for consumers, more straightforward methods of manufacture, fewer components in products, resulting in lower maintenance and repair costs, improved co-operation and communication across departments and possible 'spin-offs' for other products. Because of these advantages it is very likely that Chrysler uses value engineering and value analysis.

(10 marks)

Question 1

(a) (i) Qualitative location factors are those to which a monetary value cannot be attached. In this case examples might be the distance from his home, whether the unit satisfies health and safety legislation or how pleasant the immediate environment is.

(ii) Quantitative location factors are those that can be measured in monetary terms. Examples might include rent or leasing charges, business rates, conversion or refurbishment costs or the cost of obtaining planning permission.

(b) Arguably, the most important location factor is the cost of rent. This is likely to be a significant business cost. Clevon is probably going to look for the cheapest possible location. When setting up a business it is important to keep costs as low as possible because cash is always short in the early development stages.

Question 2

(a) A footloose business is one that is not tied to a particular location. It means that the business could locate anywhere without being disadvantaged. In this case, Mobile Fun is located in Birmingham. However, it does not matter where this business is located. It is an online business and has customers all over the country plus some overseas. Its goods are small and lightweight and are delivered using the postal system. The location of Mobile Fun was probably not a big issue when the company was formed.

(b) (i) A variable cost is one which fluctuates with the level of output produced by a business. When more output is produced and sold, variable costs will increase. Transport is a variable location cost because when a firm is busy and sells more goods, there have to be more deliveries. If a firm is located close to its customers and suppliers, transport costs will tend to be lower.

(ii) Some businesses have to consider the cost of transport when choosing a suitable location, particularly if materials and components or finished goods are bulky or heavy. However, in this case, transport costs are not really an issue for Mobile Fun. The goods being delivered are very small and lightweight. More importantly though, Mobile Fun charges its customers for delivery. Goods are delivered using the postal system and the different charges are listed clearly in the case. For example, if customers choose the Royal Mail First Class option, they are charged £2.50 for their order. Consequently, transport costs will make little or no difference to the location of Mobile Fun.

Question 3

(a) Enterprise zones are small geographical areas, perhaps just a few hundred acres of land, located in urban areas. They are designed to encourage private sector businesses to create jobs in these areas and develop derelict land. Enterprise zone status lasts for ten years. Local governments use a range of incentives to attract businesses to these areas. The East Durham Enterprise Zone is located in the heart of the North East and is home to some of the region's major industrial estates. Parts of East Durham, around the Peterlee and Seaham areas, have been designated an Enterprise Zone. Companies locating in these Enterprise Zones can benefit from freedom from business rates for 10 years, 100% tax allowances on the costs of industrial / commercial buildings, a streamlined planning process and possible rent free periods from developers. Other possible inducements include Regional Selective Assistance, SME Enterprise Grants and Property Development Grants.

(b) Prima Windows is located in the East Durham Enterprise Zone. The company moved into a 15,000 square foot factory in Seaham Grange in 2002. A total investment of £0.75m has bought the business a new factory, offices and state of the art CNC machinery

for its UPVC profile manufacturing business. The company will increase staff from 25 to 40 and double sales within two years. One of the reasons why the company was attracted to this location may have been the facilities available at the site. Director, Paul Hewitt, said Seaham Grange is a quality estate and the Enterprise Zone benefits made this a massive investment for the company. Another reason for locating at Seaham Grange is likely to have been the numerous financial inducements offered. For example, Prima Windows probably qualified for Regional Selective Assistance. This is available to most manufacturing and some service type businesses provided they are expanding their business, creating jobs and spending over £0.5m on equipment, plant and machinery and associated building costs. Prima Windows might also have qualified for a Property Development Grant. These are offered to manufacturing businesses and those providing a service to business on at least a regional scale which are building new premises. Grants are given towards the cost of various areas of site preparation in the form of £10 per square metre of floor space constructed to a maximum grant value of £25,000.

Finally, there may have been many other benefits from location in Seaham Grange. It may have good transport links which will aid distribution and supply of materials and components. There may be a ready supply of labour and plenty of land if the business needs to expand again in the future.

Case study

(a) In this case location is an important issue. The location of a campsite is likely to affect the performance of the business. A good location with attractive views, good facilities and proximity to shops, pubs, restaurants and other amenities, is likely to generate more revenue. More people are likely to choose a campsite with a good location when looking for somewhere to camp. They may also return once they have seen how good the location is.

(4 marks)

(b) Gordon will almost certainly require planning permission for his campsite. One reason is because he plans to convert some buildings into a toilet block and wash room. Construction work that is likely to change the outside appearance of a building usually requires planning permission. Permission might also be needed to operate a camp site on some land that was previously used for something else. In this case the land was probably used for agricultural purposes, for example cattle grazing.

(4 marks)

(c) Search costs are the expenses incurred when looking for a suitable location for a business. Finding a suitable location may take time and cost money. In this case Gordon will have incurred some travelling expenses. He will have paid for return transport to Skye from Doncaster. He will also have had to meet some accommodation costs during his four week stay, hotel expenses for example. Gordon will have spent time travelling around the island looking at potential locations. He may have paid to use public transport or hired a car. Gordon may also have incurred some legal costs, employing a solicitor to carry out legal searches for example. Finally, Gordon may have needed to use a camera to photograph sites, a laptop computer to store information and a mobile phone to arrange meetings with land owners and estate agents, for example.

(6 marks)

(d) When setting up a business some 'one-off' costs will be incurred in relation to location. These are fixed costs because they do not vary with output. In this case the 'one-off' costs will be the expenses incurred when converting the derelict buildings into a toilet block and wash room. These will include building costs, painting and decorating, arranging for water and electricity supplies to be connected, fitting and meeting hygiene standards. The search costs outlined in (c) are also 'one-off' location costs. There are also some 'other one-off costs' for the two locations. These might have included planning permission to operate as a camp site and the conversion of the derelict buildings. Once these costs have been met they will never be incurred again. Some location costs are 'ongoing'. This means they will be incurred over the life of the business. In this case, since the sites are not going to be purchased outright, rent will have to be paid to the land owners. These costs will not vary according to the number of campers using the site, they will be the same each month. Indeed, rent will have to be paid during the winter months when the camp site is likely to be closed. Business rates, tax paid by businesses to the local authorities for certain public services, also fall into this category.

(10 marks)

(e) After a meeting with his accountant Gordon decided to locate his camp site at Portree. There is a number of reasons why he probably chose this site. The 'one-off' fixed costs are significantly lower. The 'one-off ' costs for the Dunvegan site are £15,500, this compares with just £9,000 for the Portree location - quite a difference! One of the reasons why these costs may be lower is because the building on the Portree site already has a water supply. Another important issue is the capacity of the two sites. Portree can accommodate more tents and caravans than the Dunvegan site. This means that the Portree site has the potential to generate more revenue for Gordon's business. There may also be some qualitative reasons. Portree is the main town on the Island of Skye. It has more amenities than Dunvegan such as pubs, restaurants and shops. Many campers might prefer this.

However, there is a case for choosing the Dunvegan site. The 'ongoing' fixed costs are lower for the Dunvegan site. In a year the total rent for Portree is £14,400 (£1,200 × 12), for Dunvegan it is only £12,000 (£1,000 × 12). This is a difference of £2,200 in a single year. In the long term, the money saved on the lower 'one-off' fixed costs at Portree would be offset by much higher ongoing fixed costs. The business rates are also lower at Dunvegan (by £200 pa). This adds further weight to the argument. There is also the problem of midges at Portree. Evidence in the case suggests that the Portree site suffers more from midge infestation. Midges are a very serious problem for campers, they can make life very miserable when camping. Therefore, the Dunvegan site might be a better option.

It could therefore be argued that Gordon has made the right choice. The financial benefits from choosing the Portree site are significant. When setting up a business cash is usually limited so choosing the Portree location, with the lower 'oneoff' fixed costs, will help to keep the overall setting-up costs down. Also, the extra capacity of the Portree site, nine more tents and five more caravans, means that more revenue can be generated. This will more than help to offset the higher rent paid. It might also prove easier to convert the Portree croft into a toilet block and wash room because it is already connected to a water supply. Finally, although it is suggested that midges are possibly worse in Portree, midges are a problem all over the Scottish Highlands. In which case the Portree site may not be significantly worse than the Dunvegan site.

(16 marks)

Question 1

(a) (i) Location A. Payback period is 3 years (£4.5m = £1.0m + £1.5m + £2.0m).

Location B. Payback period is 2 years and 7 months (£6.0m = £2.0m + £2.5m + [£1.5m ÷ £2.5m] × 12).

(ii) Location A.
Net cash flow = £16m.
Average net cash flow over 7 years is £16m ÷ 7 = £2.29m.
Initial outlay = £4.5m.
Average rate of return = £2.29m ÷ £4.5m × 100% = 50.8%.

Location B.
Net cash flow = £15.5m.
Average net cash flow over 7 years is £15.5m ÷ 7 = £2.21m.
Initial outlay = £6.0m.
Average rate of return = £2.21m ÷ £6.0m × 100% = 36.8%.

(ii)

Location A			Location B		
Initial cost	£4.5m			£6m	
Net present values	£1.0m x 0.83	= £0.83m	£2.0m x 0.83	= £1.66m	
	£1.5m x 0.69	= £1.04m	£2.5m x 0.69	= £1.73m	
	£2.0m x 0.58	= £1.16m	£2.5m x 0.58	= £1.45m	
	£2.5m x 0.48	= £1.20m	£2.5m x 0.48	= £1.20m	
	£3.0m x 0.40	= £1.20m	£2.0m x 0.40	= £0.80m	
	£3.0m x 0.33	= £0.99m	£2.0m x 0.33	= £0.66m	
	£3.0m x 0.28	= £0.84m	£2.0m x 0.28	= £0.56m	
Total cash flow		= £7.26m		= £8.06m	
Net cash flow	£7.26m - £4.5m	= £2.76m	£8.06m - £6m	= £2.06m	

(b) Using the payback method of appraisal, location B would be chosen as this has the shortest payback period. However, the other two measures, average rate of return and discounted cash flows, give higher values for location A. Location A also has the lowest initial costs and yields higher revenue over the seven years, although it does lead to greater disruption in the initial stages, shown perhaps in the lower revenues earned. It could be argued overall that location A would be chosen when the overall effects of all methods are taken into account.

Question 2

(a) In this case the main reason for relocation is clear. Burberry is moving production of polo shirts from South Wales to China because costs are lower. According to information in the case the cost of manufacturing polo shirts at the Treorchy site is £11 each. The production cost in China is about £4 per shirt. This is a huge saving and should help Burberry to increase long term profit.

(b) One of the main drawbacks of moving production from South Wales to China is that 300 hundred people will lose their jobs. This may cause hardship for these people and their families. It will also cost Burberry because they have to make redundancy payments to those laid off. The closure of the Burberry factory in Treorchy has also attracted a great deal of negative publicity. One of the reasons was due to the size of the original redundancy offer made to the 300 workers. It was a meagre £1000 each; not even enough to buy this

year's hottest Burberry accessory, the Beaton handbag, priced at a lucrative £1,095. It was also reported that the company could lose its royal warrants as the row intensified over the closure. Chris Bryant, Labour MP for Rhondda, allegedly wrote to the Lord Chancellor to demand that MPs have a say in which firms get the warrant. This is currently determined by the Queen and the Prince of Wales. Bryant also called for a Constitutional Affairs Select Committee investigation into the same issue. This could damage the image of Burberry - perhaps turning some customers against them.

(c) Burberry operates from multiple sites. This means it has production facilities in more than one location. One advantage of this is that Burberry can exploit what local towns and other regions have to offer. For example, by moving to China it is able to take advantage of lower labour costs. Some of its other factories in other locations may enjoy other benefits such as proximity to a pool of skilled labour.

Case study

(a) The original location for Debenhams was in London. The business, then called 'Debenham & Freebody', was based at number 33 Wigmore Street, London. The modern Debenhams group grew from the acquisition of department stores such as Marshall & Snelgrove in Oxford, Harvey Nichols in Knightsbridge and Browns of Chester. Most stores retained their former identities until a unified corporate image was rolled out across the stores. Debenhams was listed on the London Stock Exchange in 1928 and continued to expand. In 1985 the company was acquired by the Burton group. At this point the company owned 65 stores. Since then the company has changed ownership several times and now operates as a plc. It has 140 stores in the UK and Ireland with 36 franchises in 16 other different countries. Expansion has taken Debenhams from one location in Wigmore Street, London to more than 140 locations worldwide. **(6 marks)**

(b) (i) If businesses make good decisions about location they may find that they have found the optimal location. The optimal location is the best possible site for the business. It is the site where costs are minimised and benefits maximised. In the case of Debenhams, the optimal location for one of their stores would be in a high profile shopping area. For example, their store in Oxford Street, London, is probably in an optimal location. Oxford Street is arguably one of the most famous shopping destinations in the world. The location would have direct proximity to a huge army of shoppers. There are good transport links into the area and it is a well known shopping location. However, the costs would have to be taken into account. If the operating costs such as rent, rates and wages were too high, the costs might outweigh the benefits and such a site would not be the optimal one. However, since Debenhams has operated a store there for many years it has to be assumed they are happy with the location. **(6 marks)**

(ii) The location of large stores, like those operated by Debenhams, is crucial for their success. An optimal location will generate a number of benefits for Debenhams. One advantage is good access to markets. Customers will find optimal store locations convenient. They will be able to get there easily, using effective public transport links perhaps, and the shopping environment will be to their liking - close to other facilities like, cafes, restaurants, pubs and other shops. If Debenhams can locate their store in places like this they will enjoy much higher 'customer traffic'.

Another benefit of an optimal site is that costs will be lower. Lower costs such as rent, business rates, maintenance and servicing costs will help to increase profit. Some of the new purpose built shopping complexes like the Trafford Centre, near Manchester, provide competitively priced sites for stores like Debenhams. An optimal location would also provide easy access for staff. This is important because travelling to work is becoming increasingly difficult and stressful. Most of the stores run by Debenhams are well served by public transport because they are in central locations. An optimal location will also provide staff with a good working environment. This will help to improve the quality of life and improve the morale of all those who work there.

Finally, an optimal location will give Debenhams a competitive edge over its rivals. If Debenhams occupies the prime site it may be at the expense of a competitor. Consequently it will have the advantage over that competitor. **(10 marks)**

(c) Debenhams now operates over 140 of its own stores in sites all over the UK and Ireland. It also has 36 franchises in 16 different countries. One of the main disadvantages of multi-site operations is that it may be more difficult to exploit economies of scale. For example, it may be difficult to exploit managerial economies because each store will require its own managers. Also, there may be some duplication of resources. It is possible that some of the resources purchased for each store are not fully employed. This underutilisation of resources will be a waste of money. Operating on over 140 different sites may mean that it becomes difficult for senior managers to keep a tight control on every single site. This might result in some sites underperforming because there is an inadequate level of control, supervision and accountability. This could lead to diseconomies of scale if a business has too many different sites.

Communication is likely to be more difficult. For example, because of geographical distances between Debenhams' different stores, senior managers are less able to have face-to-face meetings with workers much lower down the hierarchical structure. There may also be language problems with some of the 36 international sites. It may also be difficult to foster a positive and successful organisational culture when operating over 140 different stores. What could happen is that some stores develop their own unique culture. This might be a problem when bringing together stores for meetings and cross-store ventures, for example. Finally, it may be more difficult to standardise systems, procedures and other activities if there are lots of different stores. This could be confusing for customers and also employees if they have to move around different stores. However, it is fair to say that in retailing this is less likely to happen because great efforts are made to emphasise standardisation. **(12 marks)**

(d) Debenhams operates 36 international franchises across 16 different countries. One of the main advantages of this is that the business is able to expand into new markets and generate more revenue and profit. Debenhams already has very good coverage of the UK and Irish markets with their 140 stores. Setting up outlets overseas provides the company with new opportunities. Also, Debenhams could not serve international customers from its UK stores. Another advantage to Debenhams of having international exposure is that it will help to build the strength of the brand. In the future, if Debenhams can become a global brand its sales are likely to rise significantly.

Debenhams will benefit from cheaper labour in many overseas locations. The cost of labour in Asia, where Debenhams has located some of its franchises, is much lower than in the UK. This will help to increase the profitability of these franchises and attract more franchisees. Sometimes foreign governments are keen for businesses to locate operations in their countries to provide employment. It is possible that Debenhams may have received some financial incentives to locate their stores in certain countries. This will also help to reduce costs.

Unfortunately, locating operations overseas does come with problems. Some countries are politically unstable and consequently attract very little inward investment. Equally, some countries are currently boycotted by western companies because of the nature of their political regimes. To locate in these countries, which may have a poor record on human rights, could attract consumer boycotts or shareholder disapproval. Debenhams has stores in some 'difficult' areas. For example, it has a number of stores in Indonesia and the Middle East where political problems are notorious.

Language can be an important factor in location decisions. One reason why the UK is favoured as a location by US companies is because the UK and the US share a common language. However, most of Debenhams overseas stores are in non-English speaking countries. This might cause communication problems. It may also be necessary to alter packaging and other information provided for customers which can add to costs.

Debenhams may also be affected by fluctuations in exchange rates. When payments are received from franchisees overseas it may be necessary to convert currencies into sterling. If the pound is strong, money flowing in from abroad will be worth less. This will affect Debenhams' profits.

For Debenhams the advantages of locating stores abroad surely outweighs the disadvantages. The benefits of higher sales, increased global exposure and lower costs are far more significant than the threat of political instability, language barriers and fluctuating exchange rates. The threat of political instability will always remain but language barriers can be overcome with effective training and communication systems. And over a long period of time fluctuations in exchange rates may even themselves out. The fact that Debenhams has 36 international stores supports this view. **(16 marks)**

95 | Lean production

Question 1

(a) Cell production is an alternative manufacturing approach to flow production and involves dividing the workplace into 'cells'. Each cell occupies an area on the factory floor and focuses on the production of a 'product family'. A 'product family' is a group of products which requires a sequence of similar operations. Inside a cell, machines are grouped together and a team of workers sees the production of a good from start to finish. In this case New Balance Athletic Shoes Ltd employed a consultant to run a series of team workshops with process workers to introduce the basic principles of lean manufacturing. These teams were then challenged to analyse their current process, which led to the development of a new cellular layout requiring 35 per cent less space and only four operatives instead of five. The total work content was balanced between the four operatives to create product flow around the cell. Once the cell footprint had been agreed, an 'ideal' factory layout was developed to convert freed up space into additional cells.

(b) One of the advantages of cell production is that it encourages team working. Team working involves dividing the workforce into fairly small groups. Each team will focus on a particular area of production and team members will have the same common aims. In this case the factory was divided into cells containing four operatives to create product flow around the cell. The four workers in each cell represent a team with a common aim. They would be responsible for the production of a family of products from start to finish. Both the business and the employees might benefit from teamwork. Workers should develop relationships with colleagues and a 'team spirit' which may improve motivation and productivity. Flexibility might improve. For example, team members might be more willing to cover for an absent colleague. Teams might plan their own work schedules, share out tasks, choose their methods of work and solve their own problems. This should lead to quicker decision making and the generation of more ideas.

(c) Generally, there is a number of advantages of cellular manufacturing. These include the release of floor space because cells use less space than a linear production line, improved product flexibility, shorter lead times, a reduction in the movement and handling of resources, less work-in-progress and a safer working environment and more efficient maintenance. In this case New Balance Athletic Shoes Ltd was able to increase output from 10 to 14 pairs of shoes per person per hour, reduce staffing from five to four in each cell, reduce space taken up by manufacturing cells by 35 per cent, create new cells, cut manufacturing costs by £1.5 million and avoid the £1.5 million cost of building an additional factory.

Question 2

(a) One of the benefits of introducing lean production at Jenx Ltd was that stock levels fell. This would help create more space, cut storage costs and reduce the opportunity cost of holding stock. The technique used to achieve this benefit may have been JIT manufacturing. JIT involves holding very low levels of stock and organising a new delivery regime with suppliers. Suppliers are required to make more frequent deliveries of stock and arrive with components and materials just when they are needed. Stocks are then taken directly to the point where they will be used in production. They are not stored. JIT also involves cutting stocks of finished goods. This is achieved by only producing goods that have been ordered.

(b) An important part of Jenx's improvement programme was the introduction of 5S. 5S is a Japanese approach to housekeeping in the factory. It is a method of organising, cleaning, developing and sustaining a productive work environment. What does 5S stand for? **Sort**. This is about getting rid of the clutter in the factory. Only items

such as necessary work tools should be in the factory environment. All other items, such as excess inventory, should be removed. Set in order. The work area should be organised so that it is easy to find what is needed. **Shine**. This is to do with keeping the work area clean. Make it 'shine'. **Standardise**. Once the most effective cleaning and sorting methods have been established, they should be used as standards for the whole factory. **Sustain**. Mechanisms should be implemented to ensure that the standards achieved are recognised by everyone and used in the future. This approach has helped businesses to improve efficiency because the work environment is less cluttered and more organised.

(c) The improvement programme implemented by Jenx Ltd was based around 5S. This technique, along with other lean methods, helped to bring about a number of efficiency gains. To begin with there was a noticeable change in employee commitment and contribution to business improvement. Productivity increased by 15 per cent as a result of introducing manufacturing cells. The distance travelled to manufacture products has reduced by 93 per cent from 80 metres to 5 metres, lead times have been cut by 60 per cent and stock levels and WIP have been cut. Jenx has also invested in a new extraction system and sawing equipment, improved work flow and increased space utilisation by 20 per cent.

Case study

(a) (i) FTL Company Ltd implemented kaizen principles to reduce costs and improve output. FTL had been successful in winning new contracts which required an increase in production of 50 per cent to support the continued company growth. The company also had an underlying need to reduce waste and improve productivity to respond to competitive pressures and offset recent energy cost increases. FTL therefore decided to bring all of their production in house - a vital step for the company if they were to continue to grow and remain competitive, fighting off competition from India, Turkey and China. It was felt that the introduction of kaizen principles could help FTL deal more effectively with these issues.

(4 marks)

(ii) Kaizen means continuous improvement. It is perhaps the most important concept in Japanese management. In Japan every aspect of life, including social life, working life and home life, is constantly improved. The introduction of kaizen must involve everyone in the business. Kaizen is said to be an 'umbrella concept'. This means that a wide range of different production techniques and working practices must be carried out for it to be effective. Some examples include TQM, quality control circles, JIT, zero defects, 5S and SMED. By introducing some of these methods improvements should be ongoing. This approach argues that a day should not pass without some kind of improvement being made somewhere in the business.

(6 marks)

(b) Manufacturers like FTL Company Ltd offer a wider variety of products. This has resulted in companies having to reduce the size of batches they produce. Consequently, it is important to reduce changeover or set-up time when switching from one batch to another. FTL Ltd have recognised that their change over and set up times are too long and therefore adopted SMED. This is an approach to reduce output and quality losses due to changeovers. It was developed in Japan by Shigeo Shingo and has allowed companies to reduce changeover times from hours to minutes. He developed a method to analyse the changeover process, enabling workers to find out for themselves why the changeover took so long, and how this time called be reduced. There are four key steps in SMED. Suppress useless operations and convert IS operations (those which must be done while the machine is stopped) into ES operations (those which can be done when the machine is running). Simplify fittings and tightenings. Work together. Suppress adjustments and trials. SMED has often resulted in workers approaching changeovers with a 'pit-stop mentality'. At FTL Ltd SMED training was given leading to a full analysis of the process using video footage. Opportunities for improvement were identified, which resulted in a reduction from 27 mins/shift to 9.5 mins/shift in set up for turning and grinding.

(8 marks)

(c) Training has played a huge role in the introduction of kaizen and lean principles at FTL. To begin the programme of work, a presentation was delivered to the entire workforce explaining, in simple terms, the need for change. The principles of 'lean' were introduced along with the need for 'total employee involvement'. A kaizen project team was formed comprising operators from the multi spindle auto production area, engineers and supervisors. The team was invited to discuss the current method of manufacturing for turned parts and identify any areas of concern. In Japan kaizen is part of their culture and training in continuous improvement is probably not needed. However, in the UK kaizen is a new concept. It needs to be explained to people - its purpose, benefits and how it works. Kaizen cannot work if people do not understand it.

Training was also important when a quality plan was developed and introduced. This was to ensure that defects were checked for as they happened moving forward. The operators were fully trained to carry out the checks independently, giving them greater control of their working environment. The kaizen team was also trained to monitor the machines' ongoing performance and react to any output loss causes. Their training also covered how to deliver these results via a Power Point Presentation to management on a monthly basis.

(8 marks)

(d) There is some evidence in the case to support the view that FTL Company Ltd is committed to quality. To begin with the management team at FTL operate with continuous improvement in mind, and have always encouraged employee involvement in the development of new processes. The company has so far achieved ISO9001:2000 quality standard and is currently working towards BS EN ISO14001. Obtaining certification for BSI quality awards demonstrates a commitment to quality.

FTL Ltd also developed and introduced a quality plan as part of their improvement programme. This was designed to reduce defects. The idea was to ensure that defects were checked for as they

happened moving forward. The operators were fully trained to carry out the checks independently, giving them greater control of their working environment.

Quality is likely to be very important for FTL Ltd. This is because it faces growing competition from countries like China, India and Turkey. The company also plans to bring 100 per cent of its production in house. This was regarded as a vital step for the company if they were to continue to grow and remain competitive.

(8 marks)

(e) Evidence in the case suggests that FTL Ltd has benefited considerably from the introduction of lean principles. As a result of a 10 day manufacturing efficiency project, FTL has achieved the following. It has created an extra 30 new jobs to help boost production by the 50 per cent needed to match demand. It has also achieved a 65 per cent reduction in set-up times using SMED analysis, increased added value by £72,000, improved labour productivity by 60 per cent and reduced the amount of rework by 75 per cent.

Customer demand is now being satisfied by 100 per cent in house production. This means that the company has complete control over quality. It does not have to rely on sub-contractors. There has been no loss of customers to the low cost labour economies of China, Turkey and India despite increasing competition. A quality plan has been introduced which checks for defects as they happen. This should help to improve quality further and may lead to the business achieving zero defects. A self-managed kaizen team has been established to monitor and improve production. This should ensure that improvements are continuous and will show the entire workforce that the changes made are permanent. Finally, staff morale has improved as the multifunctional team has driven improvement - all ideas have been listened to and actions deployed as a team. This will help to motivate workers and make it easier to recruit high quality staff in the future.

(16 marks)

Question 1

(a) Most of the waste generated is the result of some form of business activity. For example, the amount of waste attributable to commerce and industry is 12 per cent and 13 per cent respectively, in total a quarter of all waste. However, some of the other sectors that contribute waste are also the result of business activity. These include construction and demolition, 32 per cent, and mining and quarrying, 29 percent - the two largest contributors. The only waste in the chart that it is not the direct result of business activity is household waste and sewerage (and possibly dredging). However, it could be argued that much household waste is the result of business activity. This is because much of the waste discarded by households is produced by businesses, mainly packaging and unwanted goods that have worn out, are broken or are no longer needed. Consequently, private and public sector business activity is responsible for nearly all the waste generated in our society.

(b) (i) Waste management is about how businesses deals with waste material. Why is waste a problem for a business and the environment? For a business, unnecessary waste is expensive. It will raise costs and reduce profit. A firm may try to raise its prices to pay for these extra costs, which might deter customers. Also, businesses have to comply with the law when disposing of waste. This is particularly important for businesses that produce hazardous waste. Therefore, effective waste management can help businesses to reduce waste, reduce costs, operate within the law and improve their corporate image.

(ii) Waste management is also important for the environment. If not treated properly waste can harm people or the environment. For example, hazardous waste such as radioactive material may kill people if not disposed of carefully. Other types of waste such as chemical waste may damage plant and wildlife. Also, some resources that are wasted may be non-renewable, such as oil. Consequently, if waste is reduced and disposed of sensitively, this will mean that such resources will last longer and the environment will be protected.

Question 2

(a) Viridor Waste Management is one of the UK's leading waste management companies. At the moment it operates 25 regional landfill sites, numerous regional recycling facilities and 189 waste processing sites UK-wide. Viridor provides a full range of waste management services such as recycling, composting, clinical and confidential waste services, hazardous waste treatment and safe and efficient landfill disposal. Companies like Viridor have flourished in recent years for a number of reasons. One is because of tougher UK and EU laws relating to the treatment and disposal of waste. Companies have to comply with such laws which means they have to dispose of waste properly. To help them do this they employ companies like Viridor. Businesses are also conscious that reducing waste can lower their costs. For example, if they use less energy and can make better use of recycled materials their profits may be higher. Finally, people are more aware of their environment today and are critical of businesses that are environmentally unfriendly. As a result they may stop buying their products. Companies like Viridor can provide businesses with a range of services which will helps them to manage their waste more effectively.

(b) (i) One of the services offered by Viridor is the disposal of hazardous waste. This sort of waste can damage health. Clinical waste, for example, is materials from hospitals and vets, which may be contaminated with blood. It must be disposed of by being burned. Other examples of hazardous wastes include toxic (poisonous) materials such as lead, rat poison and cyanide; materials which cause health risks if inhaled, swallowed or absorbed by the skin, such as asbestos; corrosive materials, such as acid, which can burn the skin,

eyes and lungs and flammable wastes, such as gas cylinders which may ignite.

(ii) Around 90 per cent of all solid waste in Britain is landfilled. This is a fairly safe way of disposing of waste which involves burying it in the ground. This is not without problems. In the past gas has escaped leading to explosions. Today landfill sites contain 'liners', such as clay or polythene to prevent escape. Pipes and pumps are used to release them. When a landfill site is full, a top is constructed, which is covered in clay and layers of soil so rain water can drain off. It is then planted with crops or plants.

(iii) A good way of disposing of organic waste is composting. This involves collecting organic waste such as potato peelings, kitchen scraps, grass cuttings and other garden waste and allowing it to decompose. It can then be returned to the soil, where it will act as a natural fertiliser. Composting tends to be carried out in people's gardens rather than as a business activity because compost can vary in standard and there is a problem finding markets for it.

Case study

(a) Perth Leisure Pool is likely to use a range of resources such as water, gas, electricity and chemicals.   **(4 marks)**

(b) Perth and Kinross Leisure (PKL) appears to understand the importance of waste management. Waste management describes how businesses deal with waste material. In this case for example, PKL has adopted a waste minimisation approach to waste management. It has introduced a number of measures to reduce waste. For example, Perth Leisure Pool has changed its lighting arrays to reduce the consumption of electricity. Also, the 10 x 400 watt lamps in the training pool have been replaced by 10 x 250 watt lamps. Bells Sports Centre has undertaken an audit carried out by the Carbon Trust. As a result a mechanical and electrical consultant was hired. This led to taps in the centre being replaced by spring loaded push caps. This will help to reduce water consumption.

(4 marks)

(c) The waste minimisation approach used by PKL is probably the best way to manage waste. The reason is quite simple. If the amount of waste generated by an organisation is reduced or eliminated, the cost of dealing with it will also fall. As a result the financial performance of the organisation will improve. In this case PKL has made significant costs savings as a result of its waste minimisation strategy. For example, in an effort to save water one centre has been piloting a waterless urinal system. The initial signs are that it has worked very well. The cost per month of the system is only £20. The centre will save £350 per cistern each year. It is hoped that all centres will adopt this system very soon. Other methods of waste management tend to focus on the disposal of waste after it has been generated. This will obviously cost money - there will be no financial benefits.

(6 marks)

(d) One of the measures taken by PKL to reduce waste was to carry out 'audit tours'. Centre managers have organised audit tours in sports halls, swimming pools and other leisure buildings belonging to PKL. The purpose of these audit tours is to identify where energy savings can be made. For example, the tours will identify locations and areas where lights can be switched off or heating levels can be reduced. This is a simple idea but will help to save money. It is often publicised that if households turn down their central heating by one of two degrees, the savings would be significant. The same doctrine is being adopted by PKL. The cost of energy is rising so quickly now that saving it has become even more important. The figure supports this view. Both gas and electricity prices have increased from around 30 to 55 in just one year - nearly 100 per cent.

(6 marks)

(e) PKL will enjoy a number of benefits from its waste minimisation policy. The introduction of colour coded recycling containers at Perth Leisure Pool should cut down on the number of general waste collections which will reduce the amount of waste sent to landfill and save money in the long term. All PKL centres have plug in time clocks to ensure that non-essential equipment is switched off overnight. This has helped to save £100 per machine per year. One centre has been piloting a waterless urinal system. The initial signs are that it has worked very well. The cost per month of the system is only £20. The centre will save £350 per cistern each year. Perth Leisure Pool has changed its lighting arrays to reduce the consumption of electricity. Also the 10 × 400 watt lamps in the training pool have been replaced by 10 × 250 watt lamps. This saves approximately £400 per year. In the leisure pool hall a heat recovery unit has been added to the dehumidifier. This has reduced gas consumption and saved around £600 per year. Bells Sports Centre has undertaken an audit carried out by the Carbon Trust. As a result a mechanical and electrical consultant was hired. This led to taps in the centre being replaced by spring loaded push caps. This will help to reduce water consumption.

(8 marks)

(f) The measures taken by PKL to minimise waste have generated modest financial savings since the amount of money saved is only £100s. However, over a long period of time the savings will be significant and will help to improve the financial performance of the organisation. It might be argued that a large multinational commercial bank might not be interested in such an approach because the savings are not large enough. However, a large bank is likely to have branches all over the world - perhaps many hundred in total. Such an organisation is also likely to have office blocks, call centres and other properties around the world. The scope for energy savings could be enormous. In many cases it is likely that energy is being used frivolously. For example, it is common to see office blocks artificially lit for 24 hours a day. This is extremely wasteful. If a commercial bank carried out audit tours, similar to those used by PKL, in all of its buildings, the potential energy savings could be huge. Also, if a large commercial bank was to install waterless urinal systems, like those used by PKL, in all of its buildings, since it has so many buildings, the savings could be very large. Generally, because a multinational bank is such a large organisation with huge energy bills, the amount of money it could save might well increase its profit significantly. Given the recent rise in energy bills, the savings could be even more attractive.

(12 marks)

Question 1

(a) In recent years many firms have attempted to improve their efficiency by downsizing. This term, coined by US management theorist Stephen Roach, has been used to describe the process of reducing capacity, ie laying off workers and closing unprofitable divisions. In this case, Airbus has opted to shrink its operations using measures involving 10,000 staff cuts, the closure or sale of three plants in France and Germany and plans for widespread outsourcing - some of which is likely to go to lower cost countries such as China. Unfortunately 1,600 jobs will be lost in the UK. Most of these will fall on Filton, near Bristol, which manufactures parts for wings, fuel systems and landing gear on Airbus aircraft such as the workhorse A320 jet. Airbus said it would deal with most of the excess jobs through natural wastage. Three other sites - Saint-Nazaire-Ville in France plus Varel and Laupheim in Germany will either be sold or closed.

(b) Downsizing is a strategy used by businesses to improve efficiency. In this case, Airbus has appointed a new chief executive, Louis Gallois, to put the company back onto an even keel following new aircraft delays and the impact of a falling dollar. Mr Gallois, who has a reputation for bold and decisive moves following the successful restructuring of the SNCF national railway business, said the financial gains to be obtained at Airbus were a necessity. 'We have no choice ... we have to reduce our costs.' Laying off 10,000 staff and closing down sites will obviously save Airbus a great deal of money.

(c) In an effort to reduce costs Airbus has plans for widespread outsourcing - some of which is likely to go to lower cost countries such as China. Outsourcing involves finding a contractor to supply components or to carry out processes that a business may have undertaken. Airbus may contract out the manufacture of components that were once made at Filton in Bristol or at other sites which are due to be closed down in Saint-Nazaire-Ville in France or Varel and Laupheim in Germany. Airbus will outsource such production because it will improve efficiency. Quite often sub-contractors are specialists and can undertake certain types of production more cost effectively.

Question 2

(a) According to David Smith from Unilever, 'Knowledge management is strategy and processes to enable the creation and flow of relevant knowledge throughout the business to create organisational, customer, and consumer value'. The aim of knowledge management is to unlock the information held by individual members of the workforce and share it throughout the company. If this can be done, efficiency should improve. In this case Lowe Partners Wordlwide, a large advertising agency, created a portal called 'Lowe Go'. The portal provides a virtual 'desktop' for Lowe users and supplies fast access to the information, people and business tools needed to add substantial business value.

(b) Before the creation of Lowe Go it was common for knowledge to be kept in personal folders or in users' mail files resulting in a loss of knowledge when employees left the agency. The new portal has allowed users to upload case studies and important documents to be used as reference when pitching and on other campaigns. Before Lowe Go there was no easy way to share information and promote creative excellence across the group. Now Lowe share company news, industry news and promote creative excellence throughout the group. This increase in knowledge in turn provides increased accuracy in the business decision making process, and enables any one office to call on the resources and expertise of other people within the Lowe Network.

(c) One of the key benefits to Lowe of its new portal is the ability to bring people in different parts of the business (account management,

planners, creative, finance etc) into one workplace to generate ideas and review new creative work. This helps account directors to gain an insight into how the new advertising campaign is perceived and provides valuable information to a wider audience that was not possible before. For example, posting up the latest Nokia advert (from the DAM), then asking selected users for their feedback results in a more accurate business decision before the advert is previewed to the client. The results/feedback is kept and can be used for future campaigns (knowledge management).

Case study

Note: in the first impression of the 4th edition there was a misprint. This has been corrected in reprints. The second paragraph should start 'In 2008 Gregsons attempted to diversify into furniture by mail order.'

(a) Many traditional organisational charts are hierarchical, with many layers of management. Delayering involves removing some of these layers. This gives the organisation a flatter structure. At Gregsons three management and supervisory layers were 'stripped out'. The purpose of this was to cut costs, improve communications, empower staff and speed up the decision-making process. It was also felt that delayering was necessary to help introduce flexible working practices such as flexible working hours and multi-tasking. It was expected that delayering would cut the wage bill by several million pounds per year once voluntary redundancy and early retirement payments had been met. Quite big wage cuts may be achievable by Gregsons because delayering involves laying off highly paid managerial staff. Delayering should improve communications because the organisational structure will be flatter at Gregsons. This means that messages and information should flow through the organisation more quickly. Staff will be empowered because they will be required to take on some of the responsibilities of the managers who have been laid off. They will also have to make decisions and solve problems. However, this should improve their motivation because their jobs will be more interesting and challenging and they may feel more highly valued.

(6 marks)

(b) Reengineering involves fundamental changes to business processes in order to achieve huge improvements in efficiency. In this case Gregsons reengineered the entire ordering process at its mail order depot in Staffordshire. Before reengineering was undertaken, orders were received by post or over the telephone and dealt with manually. A new system was introduced which could cope simultaneously with telephone orders and online orders and process them automatically. A voice recognition system is now used for telephone orders. Mail orders are still accepted but order forms were redesigned to be read by computer. About £21m was invested in IT to run the new system. The complex IT system also allows customers to track their order status on the Internet. Staffing was cut from 120 to 32. This case highlights some of the typical features of reengineering. For example, jobs in the organisation are likely to change. Repetitious work is usually replaced by multidimensional work. At Gregsons many of the staff were retrained to work in a new customer services function. The purpose of this function was to deal swiftly and sympathetically with customer complaints and try to sell more products by developing relationships with customers once an order had been dispatched successfully. Workers are likely to be empowered and make decisions and solve problems for themselves. At Gregsons delayering took place which resulted in a more empowered workforce. A flatter organisational hierarchy is also a feature of reengineering. Another feature of reengineering is that employees must believe they are working for customers and not their bosses. At Gregsons a new customer services function was created. Staff were trained to focus on customers and deal with their needs swiftly and effectively.

(8 marks)

(c) Tom Peters identified eight key characteristics of good performing companies after some comprehensive research involving interviews with managers and the analysis of financial information. One of these was that the organisation charts in leading companies tended to be flatter. As a result of its delayering process, where three layers of management were stripped out, Gregsons now has a flatter organisational structure. Tom Peters found that top companies recognised the qualities and potential of their workforce. Given the opportunity, workers would act creatively and solve their own problems. As a result of the delayering process and the introduction of flexible working practices, workers at Gregsons were empowered. Since managers were laid off the remaining staff were granted the opportunity to take on managerial functions such as decision making and problem solving. Staff were trained in more tasks and encouraged to solve problems. Successful businesses stressed values such as good customer service and dependability. At Gregsons a new customer services function was created. The purpose of this function was to deal swiftly and sympathetically with customer complaints and try to sell more products by developing relationships with customers once an order had been dispatched successfully. This shows that Gregsons is beginning to focus seriously on customer needs. Finally, Tom Peters found that diversification could weaken a company and that expanding through the development of strengths would be more profitable. Gregsons discovered this to its cost. In 2004, the company attempted to diversify into furniture by mail order. However, this was unsuccessful and Gregsons withdrew from the operation after two years at a cost of £5.6m. It was in 2006 that the directors decided to embark on a new strategy. They decided to continue with their core activities but improve efficiency across the whole organisation and increase sales by going online.

(10 marks)

(d) Gregsons introduced flexible working practices as one of its strategic initiatives. For example, staff would be able to choose 80% of their hours of work in return for being on call at certain times. One problem that Gregsons often experienced was a surge in demand immediately after a TV advert. This often meant that staff were overworked for a period and mistakes were made with order picking and dispatch. Vehicle drivers were also included in this arrangement. Staff would also be trained in more tasks and encouraged to solve their own problems. One of the main benefits of this measure was that Gregsons could deal with surges in demand without incurring any high overtime costs. Because of the new flexible practices, staff can be called in at short notice. In addition to the cost savings enjoyed employing this practice, customers get a better service. This is because there were fewer mistakes at busy times as there were more staff to deal with the surge in demand after TV adverts. Staff were also trained in different tasks. This will provide extra flexibility when moving staff around the organisation, to cover for absent colleagues, for example. Worker motivation is likely to have been improved at Gregsons for a number of reasons. They received training, they were empowered, they were given the chance to choose 80% of their working hours and they were given more interesting work to do. All of these are likely to improve worker motivation and productivity.

However, there may be some disadvantages of the new flexible

practices. The training needed could have been very expensive. The short term costs could have plunged Gregsons into the red. There may also have been some resistance to the introduction of new flexible practices. Some workers may have been very happy with the 'old' ways of working. For example, some staff may have objected to being on call some of the time. Another problem may have been overloading staff with extra responsibilities. When staff are empowered they are expected to make decisions and solve problems. It is possible that some staff feel that they are not capable of taking on these extra, more complex tasks. They may lack confidence in their own abilities or may actually have serious difficulties carrying out such tasks.

(12 marks)

(e) Between 2005 and 2008 Gregsons saw its sales revenue rise from £231m to £275m, an increase of around 20%. It is likely that the increase is partly due to the strategic changes made by the company in 2005. Sales revenue may have increased as a result of the new customer services department. Staff were trained to develop relationships with customers and try to sell them some more goods once an order had been dispatched. If staff did this effectively there would be an increase in sales. Sales might also increase if customers were now getting a better service with fewer mistakes. For example, customers can track the status of their purchases on the Internet. Satisfied customers are likely to return and buy more goods from a tried and trusted supplier. Finally, Gregsons' sales will also benefit from the new online ordering facility. An increasing number of people are buying goods online as they become accustomed to new trends in shopping. One of the main advantages of offering goods online is that people can buy goods 24 hours a day 7 days a week. It is also convenient for people who are not able to or who choose not to visit shopping centres and other types of retail outlet.

It is also possible that the increase in sales was caused by other factors. For example, the advertising budget may have been increased so that Gregsons' adverts appeared on television more. A competitor may have left the market which would mean that Gregsons would benefit from more customers. Economic factors might have been influential. For example, interest rates may have fallen, making it cheaper to buy goods with credit cards. Many of Gregsons' customers probably pay using credit cards.

Many of the strategic initiatives introduced by Gregsons were designed to improve efficiency. This is more likely to have an impact on costs rather than sales. For example, the wage bill came down from £34m to £28m between 2005 and 2008. This would not affect sales but it would help to increase profit. Other measures such as delayering, empowerment, flexible working practices and reengineering are designed to improve efficiency rather than raise sales. However, it is likely that shorter lead times, fewer order picking errors, fewer customer complaints and the new customer services department have also helped to increase sales.

(14 marks)

Question 1

(a) 12 + 20 + 15 minutes = 47 minutes.

(b) Yes - the minimum time would now be 12 + 16 + 15 minutes
= 43 minutes.

Question 2

(a)

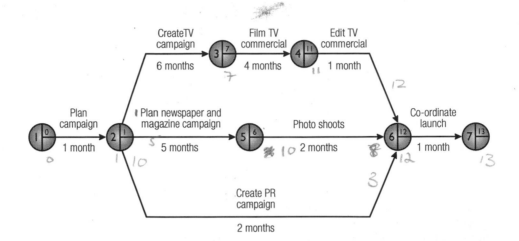

(b) 13 months

(c) (i)

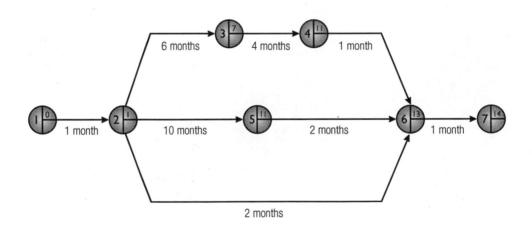

(ii) The overall time taken will increase to 14 months.

Question 3

(a), (b) and (c)   A B C D H K L

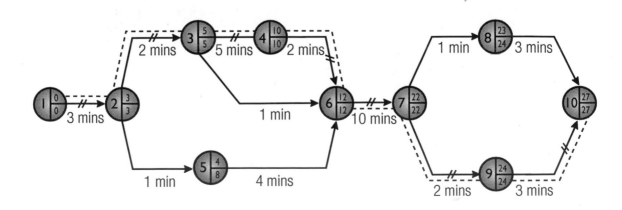

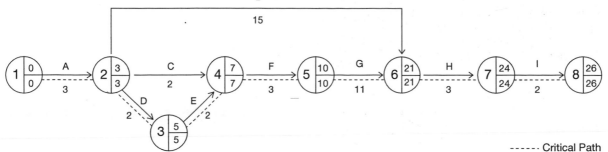

------ Critical Path

Case study

(a) Critical path analysis (CPA) is a quantitative technique that allows a business to calculate the amount of time it will take to complete a complex project made up of many different tasks. The technique is used to find the minimum amount of time that the entire project, such as the construction of a building, will take to complete. CPA can also be used to identify those tasks, needed to complete the project, which can be delayed if necessary without delaying the whole project. CPA also helps a business to use its resources more effectively. This is because resources can be switched away from a task that can be delayed. **(4 marks)**

(b) (i) See Figure at the top of the page.
(ii) See Figure at the top of the page.

(12 marks)

(c) See Figure at the top of the page.

(4 marks)

(d) According to the diagram above the construction time will be completed in 26 days. All nine tasks will be completed before the stocks accumulated by the business run out. Newport Holdings can store a maximum of 30 days of stocks. Therefore the company has four days spare, assuming the project is completed on time.

(4 marks)

(e) If task B is delayed by 4 days it will take 19 days instead of 15 days. This will change the EST at node 6 to 22, at node 7 to 25 and at node 8 to 27. So, the minimum completion time has increased to 27 days. However, this is not a problem because the construction can still be completed within the 30 days. However, the critical path is changed. Task B is now critical and cannot be delayed. Tasks C, D, E, F and G are no longer critical. The critical path is now A, B, H and I. This is shown on the Figure at the bottom of the page. **(6 marks)**

(f) One of the advantages of using CPA is that it provides a visual image of a complex project. The network diagram shows the order of each task and provides a range of useful quantitative information. When decision makers are confronted with a picture of a problem it may be easier to solve. CPA might be used by Newport Holdings to reduce the time lost between tasks, ensuring that projects run smoothly. CPA will encourage the company to plan ahead. This is because CPA requires staff to identify all the tasks required in a particular operation and how long each task will take. The construction of the network diagram forces decision makers to consider all aspects of a project. CPA should help Newport Holdings to improve efficiency. For example, during the construction of the new assembly line the level of working capital can be minimised by ordering and receiving resources 'just-in-time'. By identifying critical and non-critical tasks, resources such as labour and machinery can be used more effectively. Finally, Newport Holdings may improve its cash flow using CPA. This is achieved by not ordering supplies too early and only making purchases when they are required.

However, there some disadvantages of CPA. The construction of the network diagram alone will not guarantee the smooth running of a complex project. The co-operation and commitment of the entire workforce is needed to ensure that each task in the construction is completed on time according to schedule. It is important to consult staff and not assume that they can complete tasks in certain times. CPA is only a useful tool if the information used to construct the network diagrams is accurate. For example, if the task durations are wrong then the minimum completion time that is calculated will also be wrong. The critical path will also be inaccurate and misleading.

To conclude, provided Newport Holdings is aware of the drawbacks of CPA and takes measures to avoid the pitfalls, it should be a useful tool for the business. **(10 marks)**

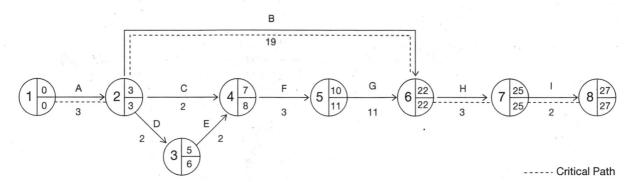

------ Critical Path

99 | Operations management techniques

Question 1

(a) In any simulation process the first step is to collect information about how the system operates at the moment. The information regarding the tipping of corn at the warehouse has been collected. The table shows arrival intervals of successive lorries and tipping times. This information will form the basis of the model used to simulate the arrival of lorries at the warehouse. The next step is to allocate random numbers to the time between arrivals and the time spent tipping. The table below contains this information.

Time between arrivals	Cumulative frequency	Random numbers	Tipping time	Cumulative frequency	Random numbers
3	5	01-05	10	12	01-12
4	15	06-15	11	32	13-32
7	60	16-60	12	62	33-62
10	90	61-90	13	90	63-90
13	100	91-100	14	100	91-100

The simulation can now begin to show the arrival time and tipping time of 10 lorries arriving from 9.00 am onwards. One tipping facility is used in this first simulation. The random numbers are used in the order shown in the students' book. The first three lorries arriving are described below.

Random number 20 - lorry 1 arrives after 7 minutes
Random number 84 - lorry 1 takes 13 minutes to tip

Random number 27 - lorry 2 arrives 7 minutes after lorry 1
Random number 38 - lorry 2 takes 12 minutes to tip

Random number 66 - lorry 3 arrives 10 minutes after lorry 2
Random number 19 - lorry 3 takes 11 minutes to tip

The results of the entire simulation are shown in the table below. The random numbers are excluded.

						Minutes	
Lorry	Simulated times Arrival	Tip	Arrived at	Tipped at	Leaves at	Lorry wait	Tip wait
1	7	13	9.07	9.07	9.20	0	7
2	7	12	9.14	9.20	9.32	6	0
3	10	11	9.24	9.32	9.43	8	0
4	7	10	9.31	9.43	9.53	12	0
5	7	11	9.38	9.53	10.04	15	0
6	7	11	9.45	10.04	10.15	19	0
7	10	12	9.55	10.15	10.27	20	0
8	10	13	10.05	10.27	10.40	22	0
9	13	10	10.18	10.40	10.50	22	0
10	7	10	10.25	10.50	11.00	25	0

With the use of just one tipping facility lorries are kept waiting for an increasing amount of time. For example, the second lorry is kept waiting for 6 minutes compared with the tenth lorry which is kept waiting for 25 minutes. After the first lorry has arrived the tipping facility is kept fully employed throughout the time.

(b) Using the same procedure as in (a), but with two tipping facilities, the results of the simulation are shown in the table below.

								Minutes	
Lorry	Simulated times Arrival	Tip	Arrived at	Tip No.	Tipped at	Leaves at	Lorry wait	Tipping wait Tip 1	Tip 2
1	7	13	9.07	1	9.07	9.2	0	7	
2	7	12	9.14	2	9.14	9.26	0		14
3	10	11	9.24	1	9.24	9.35	0	4	
4	7	10	9.31	2	9.31	9.41	0		5
5	7	11	9.38	1	9.38	9.49	0	3	
6	7	11	9.45	2	9.45	9.56	0		4
7	10	12	9.55	1	9.55	10.07	0	6	
8	10	13	10.05	2	10.05	10.18	0		9
9	13	10	10.18	1	10.18	10.28	0	11	
10	7	10	10.25	2	10.25	10.35	0		7

(c) As the information in the table above shows, the operation of two tipping facilities eliminates all lorry waiting time. Lorries arrive with their loads and can tip immediately. With one tipping facility, lorry waiting time had risen to 25 minutes in just two hours. By the end of the day this waiting time will have increased, probably to intolerable levels. When operating two tipping facilities it was the tips that were kept waiting. However, the wait was never more than 14 minutes on the basis of this simulation. Whether or not the investment in a second tipping facility would be beneficial depends on the priorities of the business. If it was important not to keep the lorries waiting, then a second tip might be worthwhile. However, if it was important to keep the tips fully employed, then the operation of one tip might be preferred. More information on the costs and benefits of investing in a second tip would be needed to draw a final conclusion.

(d) The main disadvantage of using a simulation in this case is that if the original data is not accurate, the results shown in (a) and (b) will be unreliable. Indeed, the business could draw some incorrect conclusions from the simulation and make some bad decisions based on these conclusions. For example, on the basis of the results in (a) the business may decide to operate a second tipping facility. However, if the tipping times were overstated in the original data, the second tipping facility may not be needed and therefore resources would be wasted. Simulations rely very heavily on the quality of data supplied.

Question 2

(a) The time constraints for the three brewing processes can be represented by the following three equations.
(Malting) $4BB + 6SA \leq 240$
(Mashing) $8BB + 4SA \leq 240$
(Fermenting) $2BB + 3SA \leq 150$

(b)

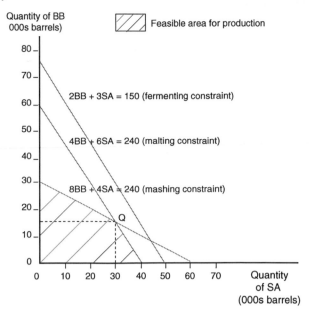

Quantity of BB
000s barrels)

☐ Feasible area for production

2BB + 3SA = 150 (fermenting constraint)

4BB + 6SA = 240 (malting constraint)

8BB + 4SA = 240 (mashing constraint)

Q

Quantity of SA (000s barrels)

(c) On the graph, the point which shows the resource allocation which maximises profit is point Q on the edge of the feasible area. At this point 15,000 barrels of best bitter and 30,000 barrels of strong ale can be produced.

(d) The total profit would be:

$(15,000 \times £34) + (30,000 \times £30) = £1,260,000$.

Question 3

(a) The matrix representing the transportation model in this question is:

	R1	R2	R3	Supply
W1	1	3	6	20
W2	4	10	3	40
Demand	14	20	26	60

(b) One feasible solution to this transportation model could be:

	R1	R2	R3	Supply
W1	14 [1]	6 [3]	[6]	20
W2	[4]	14 [10]	26 [3]	40
Demand	14	20	26	60

The cost of this solution is:
$(14 \times £100) + (6 \times £300) + (14 \times £1,000) + (26 \times £300) = £25,000$.

	R1	R2	R3	Supply
W1	[1]	20 [3]	[6]	20
W2	14 [4]	[10]	26 [3]	40
Demand	14	20	26	60

Another feasible solution can be given by:
The cost of this solution is:
$(14 \times £400) + (20 \times £300) + (26 \times £300) = £19,400$.
This solution results in a lower transportation cost than the previous one. Any other change would result in an increase in transportation costs over this figure. By trial and error, this is the lowest cost solution. To prove this point, another feasible solution might be:

	R1	R2	R3	Supply
W1	5 [1]	15 [3]	[6]	20
W2	9 [4]	5 [10]	26 [3]	40
Demand	14	20	26	60

The cost of this solution is given by:
$(5 \times £100) + (9 \times £400) + (15 \times £300) + (5 \times £1000) + (26 \times £300) = £21,400$ This is more than £19,400 (the lowest cost solution).

Case study

(a) The three equations representing the constraints are given by:

Turning $1.5MK + 4.5MG < 90$
Milling $4MK + 2MG < 80$
Inspection $2MK + 2MG < 50$

(3 marks)

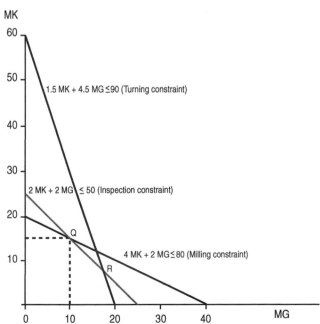

MK

1.5 MK + 4.5 MG ≤90 (Turning constraint)

2 MK + 2 MG ≤ 50 (Inspection constraint)

Q

4 MK + 2 MG≤80 (Milling constraint)

R

MG

(b)

The points on the graph can be calculated as follows.

Turning constraint	MK	$90 \div 1.5 = 60$
	MG	$90 \div 4.5 = 20$
Inspection constraint	MK	$50 \div 2 = 25$
	MG	$50 \div 2 = 25$
Milling constraint	MK	$80 \div 4 = 20$
	MG	$80 \div 2 = 40$

(6 marks)

(c) (i) On the graph positions which maximise profit are those that that on the edge of the feasible region. On the graph there are two points which lie on the edge of the feasible region, Q and R. However, point Q is the point which maximises profit.
(Note that the calculation for this answer is in (d). Q is the answer to this question rather than R because profit at Q is $(15 \times £100) + (10 \times £80) = £2,300$, whereas profit at R is only $(7.5 \times £100) + (17.5 \times £80) = £2,150$.)

(2 marks)

(ii) To maximise profit Westmoore should therefore produce 15 MKs and 10 MGs.

(1 mark)

(d) The weekly profit made from producing the two components at the profit maximising point is given by:

Maximum profit $= (15 \times £100) + (10 \times £80) = £2,300$ **(4 marks)**

(e) The economic order quantity (Q) for the steel is given by:

$$Q = \sqrt{\frac{2CA}{HP}}$$

$$Q = \sqrt{\frac{2 \times £100 \times 500}{0.2 \times £200}}$$

$$Q = \sqrt{\frac{£100,000}{£40}}$$

$$Q = \sqrt{2,500}$$

$$Q = 50 \text{ tonnes}$$

(6 marks)

(f) The current ordering policy for Westmoore Metal Products is not cost effective. According to information in the case the company currently orders 80 tonnes each time it places an order. However, according to (e), where the economic order quantity is calculated, the most cost effective order size is 50 tonnes. Therefore, in order to minimise stock holding and ordering costs the company should lower its order quantity to 50 tonnes.

(12 marks)

100 | Aims and vision

Question 1

(a) The aims of a business are what the business intends to achieve in the long term, its purpose. Tomkins may have had a number of aims, suggested in its Annual Report and Accounts. These may have included the creation of shareholders' value and growth in sales revenue and profit.

(b) In terms of sales revenue, Tomkins increased its sales revenue from £2,70 million in 2003 to £3,125 million in 2006. Although there was a fall between 2003 and 2004 overall it might be said to have achieved its aim in this area. Profit rose from £193 million in 2003 to £245 million in 2006. Again it could be argued that the business achieved its aim, although between 2005 to 2006 profit fell. If this continued in 2007 this conclusion may be revised slightly.

In terms of shareholder value there is perhaps some conflicting evidence. The dividend paid per share went up each year. Shareholders will have benefited from this. However, the ordinary share price rose between 2003 and 2005 before falling back below its 2003 price in 2006. Further, comparing the shareholder return to the average of all engineering companies, Tomkins performed better than average before 2006, but then not as well. On this basis it could be argued that the aim to create shareholder value was achieved before 2006 but not as well in 2006.

Question 2

(a) A vision statement is a statement about the purpose and values of a business. It outlines, ideally, what the business would like these to be. The vision statements in the data include aspects of these features. For example, General Motors states that it will earn customers' enthusiasm through integrity, an aspect of its values. McDonald's wants to make people smile through the quality of its products and service. Each business also has a purpose. General Motors wants to be the world leader in transportation products and related services and Ford in automotive products and services. McDonald's wants to be the world's best quick service restaurant. Simmons group wants to be the 'first choice' provider of high quality construction, development and consultancy services.

(b) Some vision statements may not reflect reality. They may be vague and optimistic. They may not describe accurately the world in which businesses operate. It might be suggested that certain parts of the vision statements in the data are very optimistic. For example, it might be extremely optimistic of McDonald's to think that every customer in every restaurant will smile after eating a meal. Similarly it might be optimistic to think that every business customer buying construction, development and consultancy services will use Simmons Group. Other aspects might be more achievable. For example, it might be suggested that Ford, GM and McDonald's could be the market leaders in their industries.

However, it could be argued that the reflection of reality is not important for a business. What is important is that the vision statement illustrates the purpose of the business. This will show where it intends to go in future and what it is striving to achieve to all its stakeholders. If the statement is motivating and shows a clear direction then the business has a greater chance of being successful.

Case study

(a) It could be argued that Michael Ashley and City shareholders could have different aims for the company. Michael Ashley is a successful entrepreneur. He has built up Sports Direct International plc to become a company worth £2,2 billion when floated on the stock exchange. Business people often take a long-term view of growth. As he says 'I am building a long-term business'. They may take decisions that may be costly in the short term and may take years before they bear fruit. Initially these decisions may not create large profits. Michael is planning for the next 25 years. He is not concerned about the short-term share price. He has a clear vision to buy brands. These strategies are risky and could affect short-term profits and share prices. But he sees the business as being eventually worth £4 billion as a result.

City shareholders are likely to want the company to be profitable and successful. Successful companies that make profits can pay good dividends. Successful companies have higher share prices. This means that shareholders can sell their shares and make a profit if they want. But share prices halved within months of them buying shares at flotation. Shareholders need financial information about the performance of the business in order to assess their shareholding. This was not available.

In conclusion, it could be argued that although they both have similar aims for the business, to make profits and be successful, City shareholders want this in the short term. They also do not want it at the expense of lower share prices. Michael Ashley takes a longer-term view and is unconcerned about short-term changes, preferring to look a the long-term value of the business.

(40 marks)

(b) A vision statement is a statement about the purpose and values of a business. It outlines, ideally, what the business would like these to be. Vision statements may not always reflect reality. They may be vague and optimistic. They may not describe accurately the world in which businesses operate.

Certain features of the business would not perhaps be included in a vision statement for Sport Direct international. For example, it would be unlikely to include detailed information about the operation of the business. It would not include details of where it sources its stock. It would not include details of its share price nor perhaps exactly what it expected the share price to be in future. It would not state exactly what markets the business operates and what it would move into in future.

However, all of these aspects might be taken into account to some extent. The wording would reflect the purpose of the business and its values. These might be optimistic, but would reflect what the business believed it could be in future. A vision statement might include that the business wants to be the first choice, market leader or leading provider of products that satisfy customers in the low cost sporting goods and clothing market. It might include that it intends to achieve this by expansion into new and exciting markets, so it might state that it wants to be the leading European supplier. It could also stress that the business has safe, long-term growth prospects. It might stress its values of quality brands at low prices, providing value for money for customers.

All of these issues would need to be included in a short, one or two line statement. This should be enough to include the main purpose and values of the business. But it must also be short enough to be motivating and easily remembered by stakeholders.

(40 marks)

Question 1

(a) The objectives of a business are the goals or outcomes that allow a business to achieve its aims. Departments within a business may have particular objectives. The marketing department of the national brewery in the case may have the objectives of retaining the overall value of sales of beer over the next two years, maintaining its market share over the next two years, arresting the decline in sales of mass market brands from previous years and continuing the rise in sales of specialist brands from previous years.

Achieving these marketing objectives can help the business to achieve its corporate objectives of increasing profits by 3 per cent. Arresting the fall in sales and maintaining this for the next two years should lead to higher profits than previous years as sales revenues will be higher. Increasing sales of specialist beers will also lead to higher revenues. Maintaining market share might also help. If the market is static then maintaining market share might not in itself increase sales. But the business may be able to raise prices without losing sales and increase profits. In an expanding market even maintaining market share might result in higher sales.

Question 2

(a) A mission statement is a statement written by the business stating its purpose and values. It states the aims of the business and provides a vision. Plastering Contractors (Stanmore) Ltd has written a mission statement which contains these elements.

(b) The statement of Plastering Contractors (Stanmore) Ltd contains a number of the elements of a mission statement. It states its aim and purpose, to provide an able highly trained team of workers to the construction industry. It also states its values, to provide a just and harmonious working environment, with security, job satisfaction and excellent remuneration.

(c) In terms of profit and sales it could be argued that the company might be willing to profit satisfice rather than maximise profits. It states that it wants a just and equal working environment with excellent remuneration. This could suggest that it is prepared to pay higher costs and perhaps accept a satisfactory level of profit in order to achieve these aims.

Case study

(a) A functional objective of the transformation programme was to deliver cost savings of £600 million per year. The failure of the programme would have had a major effect on the ability of the business to achieve its corporate objectives. Well planned strategies allow businesses to achieve their corporate objectives. There is a link between function and corporate objectives. The best run companies make sure they are linked. Achieving functional objectives allows a business to achieve its corporate objectives. For example, if the cost savings were designed to achieve a growth of profits, then failure to make these savings may mean that the business was not able to achieve its corporate objectives.

However, there is evidence to suggest that the failure of the transformation programme may not be the only factor that could affect the ability of the business to achieve its corporate objectives. It could be suggested that the business is also failing to achieve its marketing objectives. It has lost market share to Tesco. Further, customers do not appear to value the price differences that exist between Sainsbury's and its competitors. If this is the case then it may have marketing problems with its branding or its pricing strategies.

In conclusion, it might be argued that the failure to achieve the cost savings will have affected the ability of the business to achieve its corporate objectives. But there is also evidence to suggest that the possible failure in achieving other functional objectives is likely to play a major part, given the link between functional and corporate objectives.

(15 marks)

(b) The mission statement of Sainsbury's sets out certain objectives that it intends to achieve. It intends to be the consumer's first choice for food. It intends to deliver products of outstanding quality and provide a great service at competitive costs. It intends to achieve all of these by working faster and simpler and working together with its stakeholders.

It could be suggested that in the early 2000s the business struggled to achieve some of these objectives. One of the objectives stated was to provide goods at competitive costs. The business transformation programme was designed to save £600 million a year. In 2004 it was stated that this had failed and £260 million was written off. If it was planned to pass any savings on to customers as it gained economies of scale, then it could be argued that this objective was not achieved. Further, it is also stated that stores had stockouts - empty shelves. A further problem was that there was an increase in wastage at warehouses. Customers were lost and people spending at the store were spending less. Again it might be argued that the business was not providing a great service, not supplying products of quality. It could also be suggested that the objective of working faster was not achieved. In fact stores were not getting deliveries on time, so the failed system may actually have been working more slowly. Further, the business faced competition from Tesco, in particular. In 2008 it had twice the market share of Sainsbury. So whether it achieved its objective of being customers' first choice for food is also debatable.

On the other hand, it might be argued that despite its problems the business was still able to achieve some of its objectives. Just because there was wastage does not mean that the quality of its products were not good. The new system may have been simpler to operate. There are often teething problems with new systems and changes made have improved the system. Further, Sainsbury's is not the cheapest supermarket. It may still be the first choice for those customers prepared to pay a higher price for better quality products.

In conclusion, there appears to be a large amount of evidence in the article to suggest that, although Sainsbury's was still likely to have been a profitable business in the early 2000s, it may not have been as successful as it intended in achieving its objectives.

(40 marks)

Question 1

(a) (i) Selling off the Littlewoods high street chain was an example of corporate strategy as it changed the size of the business and also the markets in which it operates. Selling off this part of the operation would have reduced the size of the organisation. It was sold for £409 million. Its stores had disappeared completely by 2006. It also meant that it no longer sold to high street shoppers.
(ii) Creating Littlewoods Shop Direct Group expanded the size of the business. It also moved into another market, sales to customers via the Internet.
(b) It could be argued that the corporate strategy of Littlewoods has ultimately proved to be successful for a number of reasons. First, it was able to sell off its retail stores. Although they had a target market, it may have been deemed unsuitable for the new strategy and image of the business, to move up-market. Second, the business has changed its catalogues so that they fit in with the new image. They are selling pergolas to ABC1s rather than D and E social categories. ABC1s are likely to have higher incomes. They have attracted customer using well known names. Further, they have established a successful online store, which many see as the future of retailing. Today it is the fourth largest Internet retailer and intends to double sales over three years.

Question 2

(a) The strategic direction of a business is the path that the business plans to follow to achieve its goals. Burberry intended to open another ten stores in the US, taking its total to 50. One of the goals stated in its strategic review in 2006-07 was to accelerate growth from its chain of retail shops. Opening ten new stores might allow it to achieve this goal. Another goal was to invest in under-penetrated areas. The US was deemed to be an under-penetrated area by Burberry, as peers had 70 or 100 stores, compared to Burberry's 50. Opening ten new stores might have helped it to achieve this goal as well.
(b) It is likely that expanding in the US might help Burberry to achieve its strategic objectives of raising sales and profits, for a number of reasons. There appears to be untapped potential in the US. Successful similar style competitors have 70-100 stores. Burberry will only have 50 even after it opens another ten. The market also favours luxury goods, exactly the type of products that Burberry produces. Further, the Burberry brand is particularly highly rated in the US, perhaps even more than in the UK according to some

observers. This should mean that customers will be attracted to the brand. Lastly, sales through retail outlets have for the first time exceeded the value of other merchandise. This suggest a growing demand for products sold through Burberry's retail shops.

Case study

(a) Corporate strategy is the plans and policies that a business develops to allow it to achieve the objectives of the whole business. It involves not only the range of activities a business carries out but also the size of the business organisation.

One part of the corporate strategy is to operate in and target a particular market. It is located in Northern Ireland and is able to put Made in Britain on its shirts. It is selling high quality shirts and this is an important part of its market. It is targeting customers abroad, 45 per cent of sales are overseas. In the UK it has moved its target market away from supplying the City to supplying professionals and fashion shirts for special occasions. Another part of this strategy is to sell through a network of independent shops.

Another part of the business strategy is to be organised in a particular way. It is organised into parts. Each part specialises in a particular area. Some products are sub-contracted, such as the shirts supplied to Thomas Pink. Others make products such as the shirts sold under the Thread & Bone label. The latest venture is to buy Coles, an Internet-based mail order business.

(40 marks)

(b) It could be argued that a number of factors have contributed to the success of Glenaden's strategy. First it has made use of its ability to use the Made in Britain label. It might, for example, have chosen to relocate production to a low cost country. But it made a virtue of its high cost label, marketing itself as a high quality product. This proved to be successful for its purchases in the US and Japan, who want a product that is made in Britain rather then a low cost country.

Further, it has effectively targeted its customers. It sells through independent retailers rather then high street shops. It also changed it strategy to take into account changing tastes and perhaps to gain a wider market. Rather then limiting its sales just to City of London employees, it targeted a wider market for professionals who wanted a work shirt or a shirt for a special occasion.

Its business organisation has also helped the company to achieve a successful strategy. It is sub-divided so that parts of the business produce for particular markets. This may help it to specialise in the needs of these markets. It is also taking advantage of future trends rather than remaining static. It has identified the growing trend of online purchasing and has bought a company with an online presence. This is likely to be important in future, especially as professionals recognise the need to save time through online purchasing.

(40 marks)

Question 1

(a) (i) Internal audit:
- production facilities and capacity - moving to a new plant which expanded production;
- efficiency - four weeks' work time was lost during the move;
- human resources - difficulties recruiting skilled production workers;
- stock management - orders were sent out late;
- finance - cash flow problems as a result of late orders;
- profits - spending on R& D would affect profits and last year profits fell from £3.5m to £0.1m.

(ii) External audit:
- exchange rates - strength of pound meant that exports were expensive;
- competition - rivals were bringing out innovative products;
- markets - operating in home market and markets abroad;
- prices - competitors were charging lower prices abroad;
- technology - new technological developments in machinery meant that new ideas had to be incorporated into products;
- customers - changing customer needs required constant improvements in products.

(iii) The factors that might be included in a PESTLE analysis are:
Political - the tax on exported products;
Economic - the movement into mild recession of the economy
Social - whether people would go out for meals more often which would increase demand for food equipment and the latest developments;
Technological - new technological developments in machinery meant that new ideas had to be incorporated into products;
Environmental - the need to develop more environmentally friendly equipment, perhaps which could be recycled.

(b) Short term problems were likely to have been:
- a mild recession, which would perhaps last for a few years and then the economy would recover;
- the strength of the pound, which might recover at a later date as currencies tend to fluctuate for short periods.

(c) It might be suggested that the business faces a number of real problems. The first could be the problems associated with the move to the new site. The business appears to have suffered in a number of ways. First, it lost four weeks' production time. There was also the problem of recruiting sufficient skilled labour. If it was unable to find this labour then it may have to retrain staff, which could be costly. Or it may not be able to find the right staff. Orders were sent out late, with the marketing department reporting that this had affected repeat orders. It also affected cash flow. These are serious problems for the business. Operating at less than full capacity can increase costs. Losing sales and damaging the business's reputation can reduce revenue. Both will hit profit.

Another major problem is the investment decision that the board needs to make. If it does not invest in R&D it may not be able to keep up with the new developments of its rivals. They are introducing new and innovative products to the market. The business knows that investing in R&D now will be costly. But failure to do so may be even more costly in future. Ensuring that long term profits are maintained may depend on investing now even though this would require funding at extra cost and may affect cash flow adversely.

Question 2

(a) SWOT analysis is an investigation of the Strengths, Weaknesses, Opportunities and Threats to a business.
(b) Phipps has a number of strengths. These include that it is a global operator with plants across the world, that it is a specialist manufacturer with particular skills which are likely to be in demand and that it has experienced substantial growth which has built up its

profits and reputation. Its weaknesses are its relatively high costs, the fact that the current MD left leaving a gap which could take months to fill and poor management decisions taken over allowing stock to build up in the USA.

The opportunities, the chances that exist as a result of factors external to the business, include the growth of the Far East market, the possibility that some rival companies will go out of business in the US or Far East and the launch of a new pigment. The threats, the problems that exist as a result of factors external to the business, include the level of competition from low cost Far East manufacturers, the predicted downturn in the markets in the US and Japan and that the MD has moved to a rival company.

It could be argued that based on this SWOT analysis there is likely to be a number of challenges for Phipps in the near future. It has to decide how to fill the gap in its management structure, decide on a suitable pricing strategy for its new product and use strategies to cope with the downturn in its markets. In the longer term, if it is able to launch its new product and sort out difficulties such as overstocking, it would hope that its reputation and quality will allow it to weather the recession in some markets and continue to be profitable. If it makes the wrong choices, however, it could face difficulties.

Case study

(a) SWOT analysis is a technique used by businesses to examine the internal strengths and weaknesses of the businesses and the external opportunities and threats it faces. SWOT analysis can be used to evaluate the position of Premier Foods in 2008.

The main internal strength of the business could be said to be its size and reputation. It has grown rapidly by acquiring companies with well-known products. It will have a large customer base that is loyal to these products. Only as recently in 2006 it was valued it £2.8 billion on the stock market. Its size would also allow it to achieve large economies of scale. This should reduce production and other costs in many areas.

However, it could be argued that since 2006 and in 2008 it has certain weaknesses. One is it debt problem. It has net debts of over £2 billion, largely as a result of raising funds for its acquisitions. It is was suggested that it was unlikely to pay a dividend, which might antagonise shareholders.

Its opportunities in future lie in a number of areas. It could try to make greater use of its economies of scale. It has great buying power which might enable the business to make use of marketing and purchasing economies. The company estimates that eventually its operating costs would be £113 million lower than if Premier Foods and RHM, the company it bought in 2006, were operating separately. But there are clear threats to the business. Warburtons, a leading competitor to its bread products, has seen its market share grow from 15 to 23 per cent in five years. If this continues, the business may lose greater sales in this area. Higher wheat prices have also been a problem. They have forced up the production costs of a loaf of bread by 7.5 pence and the business was faced with the dilemma of raising prices to cover this or accepting lower profits.

In conclusion, it could be argued that although Premier Foods is still a major business with many internal strengths, it also has certain weaknesses. In 2008 it also faced major external threats in the form of higher costs and competition. It would perhaps hope that using certain strategies and the main strengths of the business that it could overcome these difficulties.

(40 marks)

(b) Premier Foods might make use of certain strategies to improve the position in which it found itself in 2008. As it states in its Annual Report, it should make use of its large buying power to gain purchasing economies of scale and reduce its costs. It might also make use of marketing economies, so that promotion can be across many of its brands. It might also consider rationalising to some extent. This would reduce costs further. It might decide to consider its recent acquisitions and sell off any of its unprofitable operations. This might cut turnover, but could cut costs further. There is a suggestion that the business might sell some of its non-core assets, such as a French company.

Another strategy might be to raise new equity. The business faced a debt problem, largely as a result of borrowing to fund acquisitions. However, it must be careful how it raises further funds. Borrowing more form financial institutions may increase interest payments. Selling shares is a possibility, as is not paying a dividend for a period. But not paying a dividend will not be attractive to new shareholders so its could not continue doing this for a period of time.

It could attempt to use marketing strategies. It could offset the price of higher material costs by raising price. It risks that sales would fall as a result. But it would need to take into account the elasticity of demand for its product and also the competition. Other bread manufacturers would also face rising costs. If they raised their price, Premier may be able to do the same. It might also consider its other brands. The company has many strong bands, with customers who are loyal. It may be able to raise prices to some extent without affecting sales, although again, it would need to consider the price changes of the competition.

In conclusion, it could be suggested that a combination of strategies might help the business. Some might be short term operational strategies, such as raising price. Others may be longer term strategies, such as gaining economies of scale or investment. All of these strategies carry risk to some extent.

(40 marks)

104 Decision making

Question 1

(a) Strategic decisions concern the general direction and overall policy of a business. They are far reaching and can radically influence the performance of the organisation. In this case Tata has paid a great deal of money for a two iconic motor car brands. To fund the acquisitions the company has had to raise around $3 billion. Winning the Jaguar and Land Rover brands is likely to open a radical new chapter in the company's history.

Although Tata's trucks dominate the highways of India and the company has made passenger cars since 1991, acquiring the Land Rover and Jaguar marques would represent a foray into uncharted luxury territory. Tata has no experience in this field of business. The decision to buy the brands may have far reaching consequences. The performance of the company could be adversely affected if the new ventures prove unworkable. On the other hand, if the acquisitions are successful, Tata may benefit considerably.

(b) Tactical decisions tend to be medium term decisions which are less far reaching than strategic decisions. They are tactical because they are calculated and their outcome more easily predictable. In this case the decision involves the possibility of choosing a new parts supplier for Land Rover. The outcome of such a decision can be predicted fairly accurately. For example, Tata can make accurate judgments about the cost of such a switch. They would expect costs to be lower and possibly the quality to be improved, for example.

Question 2

(a) Decision making is often constrained in some way. Some constraints are internal which means that restrictions come from within the organisation. The most troublesome constraints are likely to be those which are external - restrictions which come from outside the organisation. In this case Sir James Dyson has encountered an external constraint. He was planning to build a new design and engineering school in Bath. However, the project is now under threat ahead of a planning vote by local councillors and faces an uphill battle for approval. Council officers earlier this month recommended rejection of the scheme on the grounds that it would damage the historic character of the proposed site, a former craneworks. The Environment Agency is also arguing that the centre would pose an increased flood risk to the city. It is the latest setback for the project, conceived four years ago on a site initially suggested by the council. It is now possible that the decision to build the school in Bath may have to be cancelled.

(b) When choosing a site for the £56 million school, a number of locations were considered. For example, Dyson's team rejected other possible sites in Bristol and Swindon. Before deciding on the Bath location a range of data would have been gathered and analysed. This is part of the decision making process. For example, the cost of acquiring the land would have been an important factor. The price of land can vary considerably and could have a huge impact on the overall cost of building the school. The project team would also have compared other costs for each site such as business rates, construction costs and other operating costs. Proximity to users may also have been a factor when making the final decision. The project team eventually chose Bath because of its close links to the local university.

Case study

(a) Carparts has to choose a growth strategy for the future. The company has reached the stage in its development where further growth cannot be generated by acquisitions in the UK. It has identified two growth strategies for the future, either setting up an online sales business or buying a French car parts distributor. Thus, the objective of the decision is to select a future growth strategy for the company.

(4 marks)

(b) Operational decisions are lower level decisions and are sometimes called administrative decisions. They are short term and carry little, if any risk, at all. Such decisions can be taken quickly and require much less evaluation than tactical and strategic decisions. In this case, on the morning of the final board meeting, the chairperson has delegated some tasks to his Personal Assistant (PA). These tasks require some operational decision making. For example, the PA has to decide which restaurant to book for the chairperson and some important shareholders. The PA also has to decide which four distribution centres the chairperson should visit the next day. These are both operational decisions. They are very short term and can be made by a junior member of staff.

(6 marks)

(c) (i) Internal constraints are the restrictions on decision making that are imposed by the organisation itself. The organisation has some degree of control over internal constraints. In this case, the decision might be restricted by the attitudes of some of the directors. This is because some are said to be averse to risk. Consequently they are drawn towards a particular course of action in the decision. It could be argued that the risk averse directors are not sufficiently open-minded and consequently their judgment is impaired. If this is the case then the decision is being constrained because one of the options is being overlooked to some extent. Another internal constraint is finance. The cost of the online service is £2.2m whereas the purchase of AutoPlus will cost £4.5m. The business must decide to what extent it has internal funds, such as retained profit, to meet these costs.

(ii) External constraints in decision making are those which the firm cannot control. In this case the main external constraint is the possible emergence of a competitor when trying to buy AutoPlus. AutoPlus is a French, medium-sized distributor of motor car parts which Carparts is considering to buy. However, if another firm was also interested in acquiring AutoPlus a bidding war could start. This could force up the price of AutoPlus and impact on Carparts' decision. There is nothing that Carparts could do to control this external constraint.

(12 marks)

(d) In this case the board is faced with quite a difficult strategic decision. The company wants to continue growing but needs to change its growth strategy. The scope for further acquisitions in the market is very limited. The growth in turnover has flattened out in the last five years. One of the main difficulties faced here is that the new growth strategies are unfamiliar to the company. The company has no experience in computer sales and a lot of money would have to be spent on staff training and computer equipment. Money would also have to be invested in expanding the delivery service since all online purchases would have to be delivered. Further, the company has no previous experience developing a business overseas. The French market for car parts might have different characteristics to the UK market. There is also the language barrier and possible problems due to exchange rate fluctuations. Selling car parts in northern France could be a high risk strategy. The general problem here is one of uncertainty. The company is moving into unknown territory. Another difficulty faced by the decision makers is the attitude held by some of the directors. The directors who appear to favour the online selling option have often been criticised for being too risk averse. This means they will be drawn to the course of action that carries the least risk. This cautious approach could force the firm into making an inappropriate decision. Another difficulty in this case is that the board is split regarding the decision. The chairperson has a casting vote but is not prepared to use it on such an important decision. Therefore, the company is being caught on an indecisive footing.

One solution may be to postpone the decision and gather some more information. However, during this time, the opportunity to buy AutoPlus might be missed and another company might develop a first class online retail facility for car parts.

(16 marks)

(e) The quality of decision making could improve if a business has a range of useful information to analyse. In this case, the directors might benefit from more information on the performance of AutoPlus. If they were a quoted company it might be possible to get copies of their annual reports to analyse their recent financial performance. If AutoPlus was happy to sell out it might provide some internal financial information such as budgets and cash flow forecasts. It might also be useful to have some information on the French market for car parts. For example, it states in the case that Carparts does not have any experience in overseas development. It would therefore benefit from some market research data. This might be provided by a specialist in the area. With regard to the other growth option, the directors might benefit from more information about the online selling of car parts. For example, there may be other online retailers selling car parts which could provide information. The business could set up a working party to gather a comprehensive set of information on online selling. This would take time but might help the board reach a more informed decision. It might also be useful to find out whether existing customers would use an online selling facility. This could be done quite easily, using a telephone or Internet survey perhaps. Finally, some economic data might be helpful to see whether the economic environment is suitable for the types of growth strategies that Carparts is considering. Forecasts for interest rates, inflation rates and growth rates for example might be useful.

In conclusion, it could be argued that the decision making process could have certain problems. Carparts has some information that will help it to make a decision. But perhaps it does not have enough information about customers. In particular given its lack of overseas experience it would need to research this market carefully. Perhaps, therefore, more market research is needed before making a decision.

(40 marks)

105 | Decision trees

Question 1

(a)
Probability of failure
3-4pm = 0.5 (1 − 0.5)
4-5pm = 0.5 (1 − 0.5)
5-6pm = 0.3 (1 − 0.7)
6-7pm = 0.4 (1 − 0.6)
7-8pm = 0.4 (1 − 0.6)

Expected values
3-4pm EV = 0.5 × £1,300 + 0.5 × -£200 = £650 - £100 = £550
4-5pm EV = 0.5 × £1,700 + 0.5 × -£400 = £850 − £200 = £650
5-6pm EV = 0.7 × £400 + 0.3 × - £1,200 = £280 - £360 = - £80
6-7pm EV = 0.6 × £1,000 + 0.4 × - £800 = £600 - £320 = £280
7-8pm EV = 0.6 × £1,100 + 0.4 × - £400 = £660 - £160 = £500

(b) On financial grounds the 'happy hour' should be arranged for 4-5pm. This is the hour that has the highest expected value.

(10 marks)

Question 2

(a) In the diagram points B and C represent chance nodes. These chance nodes show that there are different possible outcomes when a particular course of action is chosen. For example, at node B there are three possible outcomes. These are a good crop of potatoes, an average crop or a poor crop. At point C there is only a chance of a good crop or a poor crop.

(4 marks)

(b) The expected values of each course of action are given by:
Potatoes Expected value = (0.3 x £50,000) + (0.3 x £30,000) + (0.4 x £10,000)

$$= £15,000 + £9,000 + £4,000$$
$$= £28,000$$

Swedes Expected value = (0.5 x £40,000) + (0.5 x £10,000)
$$= £20,000 + £5,000$$
$$= £25,000$$

When using decision trees to make decisions a business should choose the course of action with the highest expected value. In this case Colin should plant potatoes because the expected value is £28,000, £3,000 higher than for swedes.

(6 marks)

Question 3

(a) The expected values of each research programme is:

VAC 1 EV = 0.3 x £20m + 0.7 x £2m - £2m = £6m + £1.4m
-£2m = £5.4m

VAC 2 EV = 0.4 x £17m + 0.6 x £4m - £2.6m = £6.8m + £2.4m
- £2.6m = £6.6m

VAC 3 EV = 0.5 x £9m + 0.5 x £6m - £1.4m = £4.5m + £3m
- £1.4m = £6.1m

The research programme with the highest expected value is VAC 2. Therefore, on financial grounds, Trumed should adopt this one.

(10 marks)

Case study

(a) Decision trees have a number of features. Points where decisions have to be made are represented by squares and are called decision nodes or decision points. At these points a decision maker has to choose between different courses of action. For example, at point B in the diagram, Opal Media have to decide whether to use thorough development or rapid development when launching a new magazine. Points where there are different possible outcomes after making a decision are represented by circles and are called chance nodes. At these nodes it can be shown that a particular course of action can result in a number of outcomes. For example at node D there is a chance of success, moderate success or failure if Opal Media decide to launch a new magazine and use thorough development.

(6 marks)

(b) The expected values of each option are:

Withdraw and thoroughly develop 2012
EV = 0.5 × £3.5m + 0.3 × £1.8m + 0.2 × £0.9m - £0.4m
EV = £1.75m + £0.54m + £0.18m - £0.4m
EV = £2.07m

Withdraw and rapidly develop 2012
EV = 0.6 × £2.8m + 0.2 × £1.2m + 0.2 × £0.5m - £0.1m
EV = £1.68m + £0.24m + £0.1m - £0.1m
EV £1.92m

Retain and advertise
EV = 0.4 × £3.9 + 0.6 × £0.7m - £0.5m
EV = £1.56m + £0.42m - £0.5m
EV = £1.48m

Extension strategy (relaunch)
EV = 0.5 × £3.0m + 0.5 × £0.6m - £0.3m
EV = £1.5m + £0.3m - £0.3m
EV = £1.5m

Extension strategy (new markets)
EV = 0.3 × £8.0m + 0.7 × £0.8m - £0.6m
EV = £2.4m + £0.56m - £0.6m
EV = £2.36m

According to these calculations, on financial grounds, Opal Media should launch *Squash Monthly* in new markets in Canada and the USA. This option has the highest expected value.

(14 marks)

(c) Answer (b) above suggests that on financial grounds, Opal Media should launch *Squash Monthly* in Canada and the USA. This option has the highest expected value of £2.36m. This is higher than the other alternative strategies.
Withdraw and thoroughly develop 2012
EV = £2.07m
Withdraw and rapidly develop 2012
EV £1.92m
Retain and advertise
EV = £1.48m
Extension strategy (relaunch)
EV = £1.5m
Extension strategy (new markets)
EV = £2.36m

With the adjusted revenues for the second extension strategy, the expected value of entering the Canadian and US markets is now:

EV = 0.3 × £6.5m + 0.7 × £0.6m - £0.6m
EV = £1.95m + £0.42m - £0.6m
EV = £1.77m

The change in revenue means that this option is now not the best. The best option is now to withdraw *Squash Monthly* and launch

2012, following thorough development. This has an expected value of EV = £2.07m compared with only £1.77m.

(16 marks)

(d) Using decision trees to make important decisions will benefit Opal Media. Constructing a tree diagram will help the marketing department to visualise the different courses of action very clearly. Decision trees place numerical values on decisions and outcomes. This tends to improve results. Most people agree that the use of quantitative decision making techniques improves the quality of decision making. One significant advantage to Opal Media of using decision trees is that it forces decision makers to take into account risk. This is important because many decisions in business have an element of risk. Certainly in this case every course of action is subject to risk because the outcomes are not certain.

However, despite these advantages, the use of decision trees has a number of drawbacks. Decisions are not always concerned with quantities and probabilities. They often involve people and are influenced by legal constraints or people's opinions for example. These factors cannot be represented quantitatively very easily, if at all. Decision trees ignore qualitative data such as the effect of Canadian and USA legislation if trying to launch the magazine in those countries. Another problem is time lag. By the time numerical data is gathered, collated and processed it may be out of date. Making decisions based on out-of-date information could result in Opal Media choosing the wrong course of action. Some might argue that the whole process is too time consuming and expensive on business resources. However, if computerised decision making models can be used to analyse decision trees this would save time. One serious problem with decision trees is that decision makers might manipulate the data to encourage a particular course of action. For example, a manager might be biased when estimating probabilities for certain outcomes. In this case for example, the success of the overseas launch of *Squash Monthly* might have been given an exaggerated probability value by a manager for personal reasons. This will obviously distort the final result and influence the decision. A problem also exists with the general accuracy of the numerical data. Because the financial values and the probabilities have to be estimated the data is naturally imperfect and could lead to inaccurate decision making. Finally, decision trees fail to take into account the dynamic nature of business. In this case for example, the exchange rate forecasts could be subject to external forces and turn out very differently. This would affect the final decision.

To conclude, Opal Media would have to consider these drawbacks before relying on decision trees when making their final decision. If the numerical data can be gathered and processed quickly, if it is accurate and impartial and if qualitative factors are not too important, then Opal Media may consider that the benefits of decision trees outweigh the drawbacks.

(40 marks)

Case study

(a) A fishbone diagram is a decision making tool used by businesses. It is also known as a cause and effect diagram as it examines the possible causes of problems, both general causes and more refined causes. This allows a business to see clearly the factors which are contributing to problems. A business may then be in a better position to deal with these problems.

The figure below illustrates the issues at Decolt. Its problem is the performance of the offices it has set up in Europe, in Paris and Berlin. Both have missed targets set for profit. This is likely to be because sales are relatively too low and costs are relatively too high, as shown in Table 1. These are general causes. Certain refined causes are contributing to the poor sales performance. Some of these, such as relatively high prices and possible poor design are applicable to both offices. But some, such as the failure to close a sale or the extent of competition, are specific to the French office. The inability to have a co-ordinated sales policy, so that sales appear in one team rather than another is also a problem.

(b) Force field analysis is a decision making tool designed to examine the force of change. In the model driving forces promote change and restraining forces prevent change. If the driving forces are equal to the restraining forces then there will be no change. To promote the change that a business requires, the driving forces must be greater than the restraining forces.

This type of analysis can be used to examine the situation that Decolt faces in both the French and German markets. Both sales managers agree that the failure to achieve profit targets are the result of the products being unattractive to customers at the current price when compared to designs by French or German competitors. The solution is to reduce the price by 20-30 per cent in order to make them more attractive.

In this case the driving force is the cut in price. This is designed to attract European buyers in two countries to buy the British style products. However, the restraining forces are the tastes of buyers in France and Germany. If the reduction in price is a stronger attraction to customers than the apparent dislike of British styles or perhaps like for European style, then the business may be able to achieve the change it wants, and increase sales and profit. The extent to which it can achieve change will depend on the relative effects of the fall in price and strength of desire for European styles. If they can cancel each other out then there would be no change. In the worst possible situation the tastes of French and German buyers could be so strong that any cut in price has no effect and sale and profits continue to fall.

The two managers suggest that a cut in price will increase profits. This seems to imply that the cut in price, the driving force will more than offset the restraining force of tastes for European designs. This present situation is shown in the diagram below. If the price cut has more effect than the tastes for European designs then the situation will change in the way that the business wants, with higher profits resulting.

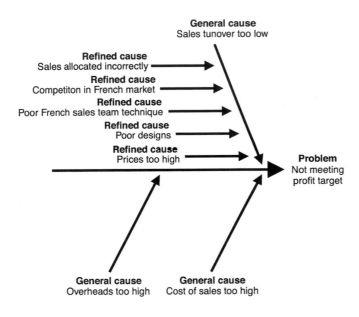

(40 marks)

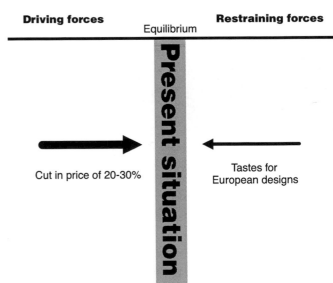

(40 marks)

Question 1

(a) Just-in-time manufacturing is where operations take place exactly when they are required. So, for example, supplies are only delivered just before they are needed in the production process. Although very effective in reducing time and costs, this method of production can lead to problems. For example, in 1997 a supplier of parts to Toyota was destroyed by fire. This was the only supplier of brake parts, which delivered supplies just before they were needed. When its production stopped as a result of the fire Toyota was left with no supplier of parts and production ready to begin almost immediately. It did not have the parts available and had no time to find an alternative supplier. It was forced to close production until it could find replacement parts. If Toyota had not operated this system then parts would have been ordered earlier or from multiple suppliers and the problem could have been averted.

(b) Holding large stocks of components and materials might have prevented the problems experienced by Toyota. If the supplier had failed to deliver the products due to fire destroying its production process then Toyota would simply have used its stocks of components or materials until the supplier could resume production. This would have avoided the closure of the Toyota plants and its resulting losses. It would also have prevented the closure of other Toyota suppliers who were unable to supply Toyota's assembly lines which were not operating.

On the other hand holding large amounts of supplies is a costly exercise. Just-in-time manufacturing has proven to be very effective for some businesses in reducing costs and ensuring efficient operation. It could be argued that a fire at a suppliers with a closure of all supply is a fairly unusual experience which is unlikely to occur often. Holding large amounts of components for something with a low probability of occurrence may be an extreme strategy. However, it has now diversified its component base to ensure that it never has to close a plant again. Ensuring a more efficient system of just-in-time manufacturing, with alternative suppliers, may therefore be a more effective solution to problems experienced by Toyota than increasing its stockholding.

Question 2

(a) Reid Architecture may have needed a contingency plan to deal with being a terrorist target for certain reasons. The plan would have been needed to ensure the safety of staff at the business. This could have included plans for evacuation of the building and being a safe distance away in case of any explosion. Planning would also be necessary to be sure of the continuation of the operation of the business. This might have included plans to continue trading in the case of damage to property or equipment. Further, contingency plans would have been required to ensure the costs associated with any disruption were minimised. For example, this may include the cost of recompilation of data or delays in the activities in the business or disruption to its operations.

(b) Reid Architecture drew up certain measures in its contingency plans. These would have been essential to an architectural practice. One of the measures involved what key workers were to do if they could not get into the building. This may have included working in other locations or accessing important information. This would have been essential for an architectural designer as delays in the design process could delay the building project, possibly resulting in penalties for the construction company. There were also plans to ensure information on the computers was saved and could be retrieved. An architectural practice would draw up many plans in its daily operations which would be amended to meet the needs of customers. It would be essential for employees to have the latest plans and information about the projects to ensure deadlines were met and mistakes were not made in the designs. Another measure was to ensure communication was maintained. Internal communication would have been necessary between employees who may be responsible for many aspects of projects. It would also have been vital to communicate not only with clients to inform them of the progress of planning but also with government agencies responsible for approving plans.

Case study

(a) A crisis is usually an unforeseen event that threatens a business in some way. The crisis that faced Maya Lim was the result of a leak and an explosion destroying her shop. There is a number of functional aspects of the crisis that faced Maya.

From a finance point of view, some aspects of the crisis affected the monetary situation at the business. For example, Maya's business had made a small net profit of £4,672 after expenses. The business had been struggling and to fund her working capital she had nearly reached her agreed overdraft limit of £8,000. On the day of the explosion she was still overdrawn by this amount. Had she continued trading she would have hoped to earn the funds to pay back this amount. But unable to trade as a result of the leak and explosion, she would be unable to regain revenue to pay back the money. Further, she had £10,450 in outstanding trade credit. This would have been given by her suppliers, who would expect to be repaid after a number of days. Maya would have received this stock before the accident, but it was destroyed or damaged in the explosion or by the leak so it was unsaleable. So she had no means to earn the money to pay suppliers back. Any insurance payout would take months to come. By this time she would be likely be liable for payments of stock and other payments to creditors such as interest on the overdraft. Financial records were also damaged. Businesses have to keep past records to present to HM Revenue and Customs or Companies House about their trading. This may make Maya's annual accounts more difficult to complete next year. She may also be contravening legislation by not keeping past records.

From a marketing point of view, some aspects of the crisis will have affected her image and publicity. For example, the business was unlikely to begin trading immediately. In the time it would take to reopen it may have lost its customers to rivals. Customers may find alternative places to purchase their products. Any customer loyalty that the business had built up may disappear in the time before it reopens. Further, customers may be concerned about safety in the shopping centre. Having already faced an explosion, customers could be worried about a repeat. It may deter customers from visiting the centre and even if the premises reopened there may be fewer potential customers. Records were destroyed. This may have been useful market research information that Maya may have used in future for say mailings about promotions or to give her ideas about future new products to stock and the nature of her target market.

From a production point of view, some aspects of the crisis affected output. Most if not all of the stock was destroyed or damaged so that it was not possible to be sold again. This would mean that the business would need completely to reorder stock before it could begin trading. Faced with the difficulties over payment for outstanding stock, suppliers may be unwilling to provide Maya with more products or extend her trade credit. Most of the records were also destroyed. This may make any stock ordering more difficult as there would be information that could help to monitor ordering patterns and how often stock sold amongst the destroyed records.

From a human resources point of view some aspects of the crisis may have affected employees at the business. If she employed any other staff there would not be work for a period whilst the premises were unusable. But if staff were permanent full time staff she may have had to continue paying their wages or fear that they may find work elsewhere. If they were temporary or non-essential staff they may have had to be made redundant. When Maya found that she no longer wanted to continue with the business she may have had to make redundancy payments to some staff. She may also have felt obliged to help some staff to find jobs, as she herself had done.

(40 marks)

(b) Businesses always need contingency plans in case of a crisis. It is impossible to predict exactly what will happen in business. That is why businesses insure against fire and other insurable risks. They can also insure against interruptions to work in progress as a result of fire damage or other risks. This will help the business to cope with any period of disruption until it is able to resume its operations. Businesses are increasingly putting contingency plans in place to deal with problems that are non-insurable. It is impossible to insure against loss of profit such as a fall in demand for example. So businesses may hold back money in case of trading difficulties or have alternative strategies that they can use in case conditions change.

In Maya's case it could be argued that she did have contingency plans. She had insured against fire and flood and would eventually receive the money. But she did not take out cover for disruption to work in progress and so had no cover for loss of earnings. So when her business trading was interrupted by the damage to premises she had no means of supporting her interest and other payments. This forced her to go out to work and find another job.

It could also be argued that given the financial position of the business, it was likely that any major problem would have forced the business to close. Even without the fire, a period of slow trading may have brought working capital problems to the fore. Many smaller businesses fail even though profitable because they can't meet their day to day expenses. Maya was very close to her overdraft limit. She had large amounts of trade credit, much of which was already overdue. She was unlikely to get any more finance if she needed it as a result.

However, perhaps the most important factor influencing the effectiveness of her contingency plans was the sheer scale of the effect on her business. Some of the other problems she may have experienced could have been overcome. But planning for such a major disruption to all her activities for a long period was unlikely to have been in any contingency plan. As such it could be argued that no amount of contingency planning would have saved her business given its position at the time of the crisis.

(40 marks)

Question 1

(a) (i) Surface manifestations are aspects of the business that can easily be seen by stakeholders. At Lands' End they include the following. The name itself with its incorrect spelling which first appeared on a letter head is a symbol intended to show the integrity of the business. It has been deliberately left to illustrate that the company is prepared to own up to its mistakes. It is printed on the first page of every catalogue and can be seen every time the company name is used. Stories, such as how this came about and the fact that the company could not afford to change it at the time, can also be used. For example, the story of the customer on her wedding day asking a Lands' End employee to wake her up the following morning could be used to show other employees how the business cares for its customers. Lands' End also has norms to explain the ways in which employees should behave. These are set out on the Lands' End website under the principles of doing business. The website makes use of other manifestations such as slogans and mottoes. These include phrases such as 'we do everything we can to make our products better' and 'we price our products fairly and honestly'.

(ii) The organisational values of a business are the consciously thought out values and policies that are expected by the business of its employees. They often come from leaders and are intended to guide the organisation. At Lands' End, for example, the president Mindy Meads suggests that some of the values of the business include quality of the fabrics used in the product and the workmanship as well as being customer driven and working together to give customers what they want.

(b) If these surface manifestations and organisational values permeated the whole of Lands' End then employees at the business might have certain beliefs, such as ensuring that quality is maintained at all times, that attempts are made to make improvements to products, that every effort should be made to meet the needs of customers and that the business should be honest in all its dealings.

Employees would be expected to behave in ways which were consistent with these beliefs. For example, there would need to be constant checking and appraisal of production to make sure quality standards were maintained. There would need to be constant testing to ensure that products met with the standards that were claimed in the brochures, for example, that stain resistant trousers were exactly that. There would also be attempts to improve quality where possible such as the introduction of new fibres or other materials that may improve the quality of the products being sold. Employees would also have to operate in a fair and honest way, ensuring that if mistakes were made they were admitted and a solution was quickly and effectively found. Employees at the business would constantly seek ways to ensure that customers' needs were being met. They would attempt to anticipate customers' needs but also to react when needs were not being met, as in the example of the 800,000 replacements that were sent out for defective products.

Question 2

(a) Although BP puts safety above profit a BP enquiry suggested that the organisational culture at the business may have contributed to an explosion at the refinery. It suggested that there were problems with the company's global management culture. There was a lack of responsibility, procedures were ignored and a lack of respect for audit findings. There was also a lack of corporate memory and incompetent workers left in post by managers.

(b) Certain changes might be made to the management organisational culture that might help prevent such problems in future. There appears to be a culture gap between the current culture and the culture needed to prevent accidents. The views of

managers towards audit reports and safety procedures need to change. Management must communicate effectively to staff that it is vital that procedures are followed and accept the importance of findings that might suggest that problems exist. Further, there needs to be a more effective system of monitoring. This might prevent the loss of knowledge about safety procedures when employees leave. It will also help to prevent incompetent workers working in jobs that could create accidents. They can either be retrained or replaced.

(c) Certain obstacles might exist that could prevent such change. One might be the views of managers and workers. Managers may have developed attitudes over long periods. They may find it hard to change their views. Employees may also find it difficult to change. The size of the business may also be a problem. BP is a multi-national organisation. Communicating and implementing the new culture with all employees may be difficult. Even if the new culture is established, the physical environment in which BP workers operate may lead to difficulties. Drilling for oil is a difficult and costly process and constantly carrying out safety checks may be a problem.

Question 3

(a) It could be argued that successful corporate cultures have certain features. Some of these exist at Royal Dutch/Shell, the oil group, and Pentland. First, a successful culture often has shared values, beliefs and norms. These must be shared over time and carried by senior people. At Royal Dutch/Shell there is a belief that young recruits are attracted by the values and beliefs of the organisation. Its culture therefore stresses honesty, integrity and respect for people. At Pentland, the immediate supervisor is massively influential on productivity. They are likely to have a strong influence on communicating the corporate culture of the business. Second, the culture must be 'packaged' and embodied in everyday operations. For example, the Royal Dutch/Shell group has developed a set of principles which place honesty, integrity and respect for people at the core of its corporate culture. Third, the culture must be communicated and understood by employees. The Royal Dutch/Shell group surveys employees to find out how they feel about the company. At Pentland there are management surveys of management behaviour.

(b) There are certain benefits to these businesses of the cultures they have.
- The businesses are more likely to retain staff because they feel good about the company they work for.
- Empowered staffed are likely to be more motivated and hence add to the competitive advantage of the business.
- Employees are more likely to identify with the business and its aims and objectives. This might make change easier to manage.
- Each employee might appreciate the position of other employees who have the same values.

Case study

(a) Brian Strode needs to change the organisational culture at Radigan's in a number of ways. Currently, the business is experiencing a major culture gap, the difference between the organisational culture of employees and managers and that which Brian would hope to set in place to achieve a more harmonious and efficiently operating business.

Brian would need to introduce an entirely new set of basic assumptions at the business. These would be the culture of employees at Radigan's and would influence how they would behave. The new culture would need to stress that employees should see themselves as part of one organisation rather than separate groups operating in their own interests. It should also stress the need to be customer centred and ensure that quality should be maintained at all times. Employees also need to feel valued and encouraged, aiming for improvement through training and possible promotion. This could be achieved by setting in place training schemes and also encouraging workers under the age of twenty five to aim for management posts, perhaps, taking appropriate qualifications, supported by the business. Further, staff need to be prepared to change their views so that they can react to changing requirements of the business from the market in which they operate.

Brian would also need to set in place organisational values. Currently, the business has no mission statement. Brian could express his views about the organisational culture of Radigan's in the mission statement. For example, he could include phrases such as 'one business, one goal' or 'working together for a better future' to reflect that employees should be seen as one operation rather than a series of disparate groups. The mission statement as well as including words which would reflect the basic assumptions would also include policies designed to develop the organisational culture that Brian wants. These could include increased team working, training for all the workforce and the need to take responsibility in order to ensure that customers' needs are being met. There is a need to examine whether the payment system motivates employees sufficiently. This may need to be changed so that employees do not run out of the door at 5.30pm, especially if urgent orders are required. Brian would also need to consider policies which would help ensure improved industrial relations. For example, the business might consider a works' council, where employees and employers are represented. It might also consider involving trade unions in any negotiations on changes in the business in order to take into account their views.

There are many elements of surface manifestations that could be introduced to encourage the organisational culture that Brian wants. For example, the business may consider calling all employees by the same title in an attempt to prevent a 'them and us' attitude at work. It may also introduce its own posters to replace the 'I'm the boss' and 'Over worked and under paid' posters. The business also needs to consider addressing the practice of working to the clock. For example, it may think about introducing activities after work or social arrangements to replace worktime which carry on after 5.30. This may give employees a feeling that they do not need to leave exactly at 5.30 every evening. Staff may also be encouraged to take training days and group building courses regularly to break down the informal groups that have developed. Changes in the physical nature of the workplace could also help to prevent the isolation and cramped feeling that staff feel. For example, changing the layout of the offices into a more open plan area may encourage greater interaction. Reorganising equipment on the work floor, perhaps as cell production, with team work, could encourage greater interaction in the manufacturing process. Brian may also consider introducing a weekly newsletter or some form of email communication. This could include stories about the contribution of either workers or managers to the overall success of the business. It would help to show how all employees are making a valuable contribution.

All of these changes may help to introduce an organisational culture that is more conducive to improving the operation of the business. Whether they will be successful will depend on a number of factors. For example, it may not always be possible to change work practices to introduce teamwork. Further, informal groups always develop in a business and it can sometimes be difficult to break these down especially if workers are artificially forced to work as part of another group. There would also need to be changes in outside factors such as the attitude of trade unions to negotiations at the business. If union representatives continued to be resistant to the needs of Radigan's then it may be difficult to break down the feelings of dissatisfaction of employees.

So in conclusion it could be argued that although in principle the changes made to improve the organisation culture at Radigan's have great potential, they are not guaranteed to be successful, especially if factors beyond the control of the business play an important role.

(40 marks)

(b) It could be argued that having a strong organisational culture shared by all staff could solve many of the problems of the business. Having a strong culture would provide an identity for the business. At the moment there is no mission statement or view for where the business is intending to be in the future. A strong culture might help all employees to identify where the business intends to be and their role in the company. A strong culture also helps employees identify with each other. One of the major problems faced by the business is the them and us attitude. Managers see shop floor workers as lazy. Workers see managers as pen pushers. A strong culture which all employees shared could allow each employee to better appreciate the role and contribution of others. Staff might start to identify and even develop friendships with people in other areas of the business. Further, a strong culture helps motivate staff. At Radigan's staff have signs which imply that they do not see hard work as important. They also do not want to take responsibility. A shared culture could motivate staff to appreciate that if they work hard and the business benefits, they may benefit as well. Also, perhaps, a strong culture can help a business to become aware of what is going on around them. This might be internally. But it might also be externally. Currently there is little appreciation of the competitive pressures faced by the business. Lastly, a shared culture could help maintain control of the organisation. Brian had to change the culture so that it was more responsive to customers' needs and to reduce costs. Having a shared culture may make these tasks more achievable.

On the other hand a shared culture is not necessarily a guarantee that a business will be successful. For example, what if the business agreed that the culture they would share would be a task culture? This is where power is given to those who can accomplish tasks. It is suited to teamwork. But given the intense competition and problems facing the business, Brian may need to establish more of a role or a power culture. The type of culture established must suit the needs of the business and its situation. Further, simply sharing a culture does not guarantee success. It may be that making organisation and operational changes, or changes to marketing policies may be just as effective in competing with other business as establishing a strong culture. Also, it may be that the different groups in the business are necessary to give different perspectives. Having a management and workforce with exactly the same views may not allow ideas to develop which can sometimes result from conflict. For example, if there are disagreements on approaches to competition, this could result in healthy debate and alternative solutions may be found.

In conclusion, it could be argued that establishing a strong culture could help to make Radigan's more successful. However, such a culture would need to suit the organisation of the business. It is also no guarantee of success and other factors may be equally as important.

(40 marks)

109 | Implementing and managing change

Question 1

(a) Various factors appear to have influenced change at the business. One is rising costs of production. Developments in the manufacturing process have resulted in increased amounts of waste metal. This has meant increased charges at landfill sites used to dispose of the materials. Legislation requires that businesses pay charges for the disposal of materials to protect the environment. Another factor has been comparison with other businesses, particularly in the USA where the directors visited to benchmark their activities. They found that, given the right production processes, experience, knowledge and perhaps equipment, it may be possible to move into the production using recycled materials. Further, there were changing consumer tastes, particularly in relation to the demand for more environmentally friendly products. Businesses were also prepared to pay a higher price for recycled metal knowing customers may be prepared to pay more when recycled materials were used in products.

(b) There is a number of implications that are likely to result from the changes made by the business to its operations. First, it is likely that the overall corporate strategy and culture of the business may change as a result of using recycled materials. This could affect the aims and objectives of the business. Second, there is likely to have to be a major investment in new machinery which conforms to new standards. This could be a major cost given the changing nature of production methods. Employees will also need to be trained in using this new machinery, again increasing the costs of the business. It could also be suggested that the business will now be looking for new markets. It may target business customers who are specially looking for recycled metal. New marketing strategies will need to be developed in order that new customers for the recycled products can be found. There may need to be changes in human resource planning with the recruitment of new staff and the retraining of current staff in the use of new equipment. In addition, the business will need to be aware of how competitors are dealing with the notion of recycled waste metal so that it can compete on price and quality. This will require market research.

Question 2

(a) The approach adopted to manage change at Remploy was a negotiated total package. This is where a total package for change is put together and negotiated between employers and employees. Remploy decided that its corporate strategy was to increase staff from 12,000 to 25,000 and triple output over five years. In addition, it wanted to develop a change programme that examined all the weakest links in the production process. It conducted detailed consultations with every person in the business to see how processes could be improved. This meant that ideas could be shared to the benefit of both staff and employers.

(b) (i) The benefits to employees are that working practices could be improved and they would have more say in how these practices emerged and developed. For example, staff suggested that a huge overhanging machine be moved so that they could see each other and help communicate when a constraint in the flow of work had built up.

(ii) One benefit to the business is that productivity may improve in the short term by incorporating employees' ideas in the work process, for example the coloured tape to improve accuracy and speed of the machinists. There has also been a long term change in culture – one that meant employees were less likely to fear change in the future.

Case study

(a) When Lowke's, a former leading company in the food processing sector, bought Feraday's it had certain decisions to make. A new combined company would require changes and they would need to be managed an implemented carefully. Lowke's chose to adopt a longer, consultative model of change. It could have simply bought Feraday's, kept those parts it wanted and quickly sold off and discarded the rest. But it chose the alternative strategy of implementing change.

There were likely to have been costs in using this strategy. A major cost would have been the resources that it continued to employ from the former Feraday's business. Workers at Feraday's feared their days were numbered. Despite the overlap of skills and job roles, there was not initial move the make staff redundant. This would have led to a large wage bill, especially as the new company was to take shape over two years. Many staff could have been employed for that period. There may also have been costs involved in involving many people in the process of managing change. Workers at Feraday's, for example, may have been obstructive of new measures, fearing job losses. This may have delayed or prevented the new business from establishing efficient methods of working. Some were not interested in the process, simply concerned with their own situation. There would also have been other financial costs. These could have included the costs involved in finding new jobs for workers or in paying higher redundancy packages as a result of longer service.

On the other hand there were also potential benefits of a longer, more consultative process. Lowke's would have retained the knowledge of certain key staff in Feraday's. This knowledge management is vital for business. Staff who leave may play key roles in a business and their opinions, views and skills are lost when they leave, never to be replaced adequately. This knowledge may have been vital if the new company was indeed keen to push forward and expand. Further, taking into account other views may have helped identify the most efficient methods of change. Retaining the skills of the two businesses meant that effective comparisons could be made. The best practice of each business could then be used. A consultative process also helped to boost morale. Many businesses find that when takeovers occur, staff lose motivation and performance suffers. In this case workers at Feraday's saw that there was no favouritism. This helped develop a climate of trust and perhaps more interest and faith in the changing systems. Lastly, the longer process meant that the business could take time to consider its options and not rush into things. It also meant that the needs of customers could be considered.

In conclusion, it could be argued that whether the costs of the process outweighed the benefits or vice versa would depend on whether the business is able to achieve its objectives. It was attempting to raise sales within the two year change process and by 25 per cent over five years. If it did achieve this then it might decide that the longer, perhaps more costly process was worthwhile.

(40 marks)

(b) A private limited company is a business that is owned by its shareholders. Private limited companies tend to be either family run businesses or businesses that are co-owned by people with the same or a similar approach who may or may not know each other. They are often medium sized operations, although some are very large. Public limited companies, however, often have many owners. The owners are still the shareholders, but shares are traded on stock exchanges. They can be bought and sold by anyone wishing to invest in the business. Shares in private limited companies are usually only traded between the owners or with new owners with consent of other shareholders.

Lowke's is a private limited company. Limited companies have a board of directors and a managing director. Sometimes directors are also shareholders. They often have a similar vision. When Lowke's bought Feraday's the intent was to re-establish the company as a major food manufacturer. It saw this a long-term strategy. They were prepared to accept lower profits in the short term in order to achieve the longer-term objective. The board of directors, some of whom might have been shareholders, had the same vision. Senior managers also seem to feel the same.

In a public limited company, however, with larger numbers of shareholders who are owners, this strategy may have been more difficult to implement. Shareholders buy shares for two reasons perhaps. They want to be paid a dividend. A business may only pay a dividend if it is making relatively good profits. Also, shareholders hope that the price of their shares will rise, so they can sell them for more than they paid. Share prices rise when companies are performing well and making profits. It could be argued that shareholders may have disagreed with the change strategy used by Lowke's. They may not have been prepared to sacrifice short term profit for longer-term growth. Further, in large companies a divorce of ownership by shareholders and control by managers also may occur. Shareholders want one thing and managers another. This may have resulted from the strategy used by Lowke's.

In conclusion, if Lowke's were a public limited company, this does not mean that the management model adopted by the company could not be implemented. However, it could be argued that it would be more difficult given that shareholders may be less prepared to sacrifice short term profits for longer-term growth.

(40 marks)

Question 1

(a) Economic growth is the change in the productive potential of the economy, usually measured as changes in national income. In periods of growth, more is produced. People have more income and more to spend. Living standards increase. Birmingham suffered in the past as its manufacturing industry declined. But growth has seen increased demand for business services in the area and these business are now demanding office space.

(b) It is suggested that in 2008 and 2009 the UK economy could be going into recession. If this was the case then demand for office space at Colmore Plaza may fall. Whether rents may need to fall to attract tenants may depend on the extent of the recession. If spending fell and businesses suffered then there may be offices that can not be rented. The only alternative may be for the owners to lower rents. However, it may also depend on supply. If some businesses want this type of office and there is no other similar offices then rents may not have to fall, or may only need to fall slightly.

Question 2

(a)

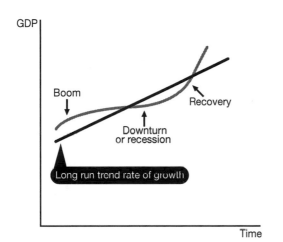

A slowdown or downturn in the economy is where the rate of growth of the economy begins to fall. This is usually shown as a slowdown in the growth of GDP as in the figure above. As a result people start to spend less, there may be some unemployment, wage increases start to slow and further cuts in spending take place.

(b) Faced with a slowdown of US and European markets JCB could look to expand in other markets. It is suggested that there might be growth opportunities in countries such as India, Russia South America and the Middle East. India, in particular, appears to be an area into which JCB has been successful in recent years. However, JCB might need to take into consideration certain factors in these countries.

There may be legislation which could affect the business. There might be high costs such as the setting up of factors. Demand for building might only be short lived, so setting up factories may leave unused capacity. If it was sure that there was a long-term market in these countries then expanding abroad might be a successful strategy. It would also be appropriate for the business to maintain its presence in the US and the UK. The UK appears to be holding up fairly well. In recessions some business cease operations. JCB would be well placed when these economies begin to grow again.

Case study

(a) Hip Housebuilding may consider a number of strategies faced with a possible UK recession. One strategy may be to reduce its prices or offer deals like its rivals. It had 300 unsold properties. Reducing their prices may help to sell the properties. This may reduce the profit on these houses.

Another strategy may be to take advantage of the situation of other companies. For example, the company has experienced an increase in job applications. It may be able to employ well qualified staff waiting for an upturn in the market. It may be able to take advantage of a fall in land prices. Buying land now may be a lot cheaper than in future. It could then have available land waiting to expand building when the economy picks up in future. It might also consider some of the projects that other businesses have not taken up, selecting those that are most profitable.

Whether it can take advantage of these opportunities depends on certain factors. Whether it should reduce the prices of its unsold houses may depend on the effects on costs and profits. If it was costing the business to have unsold properties, this may be a strategy worth pursuing. Whether it can take advantage of other strategies may depend on just how much the business has been affected. It may only be able to take advantage of falls in land prices if it has the funds available to buy land or to take on labour. It would also need to be convinced that profitable opportunities existed on these plots.

(40 marks)

(b) On the one hand a recession will be a problem for businesses. Some businesses are affected more than others. It could be suggested that the house building market is particularly affected. Falls in income result in cutbacks in luxury purchases or major expenditure such as moving house perhaps. Hup Housebuilding has unsold properties. Other businesses were cutting back on new projects. Confidence was low and sales were suffering.

But there are also opportunities. Other house building companies were not taking advantage of opportunities for potentially profitable projects. Land prices were falling. Labour was available.

Whether the downturn is more of an opportunity than a threat may depend on the financial position of Hup Housebuilding compared to its rivals. If it is able to take advantage of the opportunities that present themselves then it may be in a good position to grow when a recovery takes place. If some businesses are forced out of the market then there may be more changes for Hup Housebuilding during any recovery. However, if, like its rivals, it is facing difficulties then the problems may outweigh the benefits.

(40 marks)

Question 1

(a) Overhead costs of a business are the indirect costs. These are the costs which cannot be linked directly to production. For example, if a business produces more it will have to buy more materials or ingredients, so direct costs increase. But if a business increases output the interest paid on a loan or overdraft, for example, does not change. So interest payments are not linked directly to production.

(b)

Before

Overdraft of £1,200,000 × 7% = £84,000
Loans of £4,300,000
    £1,300,000 × 8% (6%+2%) = £104,000
    £1,000,000 × 8% = £80,000
    £2,000,000 × 9% = £180,000
Total loan payments = £364,000
Total repayments = £448,000

After

Overdraft of £1,200,000 × 6% = £72,000 (down £12,000)
Loans of £4,300,000
    £1,300,000 × 7% (5%+2%) = £91,000 (down £13,000)
    £1,000,000 × 8% = £80,000 (same)
    £2,000,000 × 9% = £180,000 (same)
Total loan payments = £351,000 (down £13,000)
Total repayments = £423,000 (down £25,000)
So overhead costs fall by £25,000.

Question 2

(a) Low interest rates perhaps affected Bill's business in two ways. First, Bill was able to borrow money to replace the £250,000 of equipment and stock that were destroyed. Low interest rates were likely to have meant that the repayments were relatively affordable each month by Bill. Second, low interest meant that customers were more likely to borrow money to buy cars and motorcycles. This meant that there was a buoyant market for retreads when Bill relaunched the business.

(b) Previously Bill held £100,000 of stock. After re-launch he only ordered £20 000. There may have been a number of reasons for this. First, Bill probably over-ordered stock. He did not require this much stock for the level of operation. So stock was likely to have been held but not used. Stocks tie up money. This money could have been used to pay off some of the borrowing and reduce his interest payments. Further, Bill borrowed the money to buy the stock. Buying less stock would mean he would have to borrow less and so his interest repayments would be lower.

(c) There are some arguments to suggest that Bill would have struggled to recover had interest rates been high. He had no insurance. So he had to borrow to pay for the stock and equipment that he needed to restart the business. As the case states, he could not have afforded to borrow the money to relaunch if interest rates were not relatively low at 7 per cent. Further, high interest rates were likely to have deterred borrowing for buying vehicles and affected demand. So even though the business had the skills required and the

list of possible customers, Bill may have found it difficult to replace machinery and customers may have been put off borrowing. Perhaps Bill's only chance would have been to rent machinery, keep stocks to an absolute minimum and hope that some customers would still buy retreads.

Case study

(a) Overborrowing takes place where a business borrows so much it leads to other problems in the business. The borrowing of Al's business was influenced by certain factors. One was expanding demand in the mid-1980s. At that time it seemed that borrowing was justified. Both the car and housing markets were growing and even booming. Further, there were relatively low interest rates. This would have helped customers as repayments were low on loans of cars and housing accessories. Al may also have felt justified in taking out a loan of £150,000 to buy equipment in 1988, feeling that his repayments would also have been relatively low.

By 1989, however, he may have regretted his decision to borrow such a large amount. Car sales fell rapidly. Interest rates rose from 7.5 per cent to 14 per cent over a two year period. Sales slumps meant that he had to cut back production and make workers redundant. Machinery lay idle and a loss of £25,000 was forecast with a further loss of £30,000 the next year. However, Al should have realised that economies go through booms and slumps. He had been doing well since the mid-1980s but he should have assessed the risk that the economy would go into recession. Had Al not borrowed so much he would have been in a far better position to ride out the recession.

Overall, then, it could be argued that Al's problems were caused more by failure to assess risk than overborrowing. If he had assessed the risk effectively, he would not have borrowed so much.

(40 marks)

(b) A fall in interest rates from 14 per cent to 6 per cent between 1991 and 1993 would undoubtedly have benefited Al's business. The fall in interest rates is likely to have have significantly reduced the amount of interest he paid on his loans. This will have reduced his overhead costs and improved cash flow. Moreover, a fall in interest rates is likely to have stimulated demand in the economy, including the demand for cars and furniture. If nothing else, this is likely to have halted the fall in sales at Al's company and hopefully will have stimulated some rise. The fall in interest rates was quite large so any benefit in reduced payment and increased demand could have been quite large.

On the other hand, changes in interest rates are not the only factor that can affect the survival of a business. Al lost customers in the period before 1993. They may have gone to other suppliers and Al may not have been able to attract them back to his business. He also had to cut back on his workforce. He may not have been able to hire the same workers or those with similar skills. Further, changes may have taken place in demand and technology so that by the time he wanted to expand again his products and machinery may have been outdated.

In conclusion, therefore, it might be argued that the fall in interest rates might have come too late for Al. The losses he sustained in 1990 and 1991 might have been enough for his bank to call in the overdraft he must have had at the time. This would have been enough to push the company into receivership. The question is whether the fall in interest rates and the consequent rise in demand for Al's products came quickly enough to allow the company to survive. **(40 marks)**

Question 1

(a) A fall in the value of the pound could lead to higher profits for Betteny. First, the business could let the foreign currency price of its products fall. It might then sell more exports if it could offer slightly better prices to overseas customers, which could improve profits. Second, it could keep the foreign currency prices the same and allow a rise in the price in pounds. This means it would earn more in pounds and make more profit. Third, if the value of the pound falls then the value of the US dollar would rise. This could make imports to the UK more expensive if US businesses maintained their foreign currency price. Betteny could increase profit as it might sell more in the UK as US products find it difficult to compete.

Question 2

(a) Rugol and Flynn's has signed a contract to export products in one month's time for 50 000 euros. So the business would earn £35,714 (50 000 ÷ 1.40) if £1 = 1.40 euros. If the value of the pound rose by 5 per cent in one week's time it would now be 1.40 + (1.40 × 5%) = 1.40 + 0.07 = 1.47 euros. If the business had decided not to hedge against exchange rate fluctuations then it would have only earned 50,000 ÷ 1.47 = £34,014 (50,000 ÷ 1.47). So the business gained by hedging, to the amount of £1,700. Overall, whether it gained or not would depend on the cost of administration involved in hedging.

(b) It is argued that adopting the euro will prevent currency fluctuations. This would prevent the uncertainty associated with exchange rate changes and the costs involved in hedging to prevent these fluctuations. A Welsh business trading with a business in another country that has adopted the euro would not have to face uncertainties. It would be the same as trading with a company in Scotland now, where both countries trade in pounds. However, joining the euro would not prevent fluctuations against the dollar, the US currency. The value of the dollar fluctuates on currency markets against the euro in the same way that the dollar fluctuates against the pound. So although joining the euro may help to prevent uncertainties in trade with other countries that have adopted the euro it would not help in trading with the US in this way.

Case study

(a) Joseph Wolff is affected by changes in the value of the pound against other currencies as he trades with businesses in other countries. He imports hot dog sausages from Germany and Denmark. The euro is the currency used in Germany and the krona is used in Denmark. So Wolff has to exchange pounds for these currencies to pay for them. Fluctuations in the rate of exchange between the pound and euro and krona can affect the pricing and profits of Wolff's business. The value of the pound can depreciate against the euro and krona. Assume the value of the pound against the euro fell by 20 per cent, from £1 = 1.5 euros to £1 = 1.2 euros. Before the depreciation, importing 15 euro's worth of sausages would have cost the business £10. But after the depreciation 15 euro's worth of sausages would now cost £12.50 (1.5 ÷ 1.2 × 10). To maintain profit margins Wolff might consider putting up his price to cover for the higher import prices. But he is unable to do this because of the competitive nature of the market in which he operates. So he has to accept that as the value of the pound falls his profit margins will simply be reduced.

If the value of the pound appreciates then the business is in a much better position. Assume the value of the pound against the krona was £1 = 10 krona and the pound appreciated by 20 per cent to £1 = 12 krona. Importing 10 krona's worth of sausages would previously have cost £1. After the appreciation it would have cost just £0.83. If he left his prices at £1 however, his profit margins would improve. So an appreciation of the currency can help the business.

In conclusion, it could be argued that changes in the value of the pound have a great impact on the business. If there are fluctuations in the currency then the cost of imported sausages can change. Given Joseph's position he can not make rapid and large changes to prices of hot dogs. Currency fluctuations can therefore have a great impact on profit as he is not able to alter prices to compensate, for example for a depreciation in the currency.

(40 marks)

(b) There could be certain advantages to Wolff in setting up a manufacturing business in the UK. He would be able to avoid the fluctuations in exchange rates that affect his prices. Fluctuations can affect prices and profits. He faces a difficult position in reacting to rises in import prices. The nature of competition in the hot dog market means that he is not really able in the short run to change prices to prevent reduction in profit levels. If he raises prices too much to compensate for exchange rate changes then customers in the UK will switch to buying products from his rivals. Further, in future if the UK and Denmark join the euro then a common currency will be used between all countries. This will prevent currency fluctuations.

On the other hand switching production to the UK does not necessarily solve his problems. There is the cost of changes in organisation. But also as important is the effect that a change in supply will have. At the moment Wolff may have a competitive advantage over rivals by importing quality sausages. If he changes to buying supplies from the UK he faces a deterioration in quality. UK sausage quality has been disappointing. He may simply find that customers move to rivals and his profits fall anyway.

In conclusion it could be argued that Wolff should continue to import sausages for his hot dog business. He will only suffer higher import prices if the value of the pound falls. He may be able to hedge against this by agreeing contracts before import prices rise. When the pound appreciates he can actually increase profit. The argument for relocating to gain from the euro is also debatable. At the time of writing it did not seem as if the UK would join in the near future. So Wolff's business may be better leaving this decision until when or if the UK did adopt the euro.

(40 marks)

113 | Inflation and deflation

Question 1

(a) Falling prices are a problem for a company such as Zeenat, a small garment manufacturer, because they reduce revenue for the business from each sale that it makes. Prices of clothing had been falling in 2002-2003, for example by 1.8 per cent in December 2002. At the same time, the costs of the business were tending to rise. Hence profits are squeezed unless the company can increase efficiency.

(b) Low levels of deflation can pose problems for a small business. Even small falls in prices can affect revenue, especially if sales are fairly limited. Falling prices encourage greater demand, but in the case of Zeenat it is unlikely to be able to increase sales significantly to take advantage of lower prices. Other businesses will also be cutting prices and Zeenat may find it difficult to compete. High inflation would also cause problems for Zeenat. Periods of inflation are accompanied by rising costs and rapidly increasing costs would place a great pressure on a small business like Zeenat. On the other hand it is suggested that Zeenat, faced with rising costs, was able to cover these by increasing prices in inflationary periods. And even in deflationary periods it might still face rising costs such as government increases in the minimum wage rate. So it could be argued that Zeenat might suffer more from deflation than inflation.

Case study

(a) In periods of inflation prices on average are tending to rise. McGinnel's can be affected by rising prices in a number of ways. One area of price rises that faces most businesses is rises in the prices of raw materials. In the case of McGinnel's, its major material is the cost of oil. It buys oil on the open market and sells to businesses and home owners that use oil fired central heating. As oil prices rise this is likely to have a major effect on a small company such as McGinnel's. Oil is its major material and a sharp rise in oil price is likely to affect the business greatly, cutting its profits. There are likely to be fluctuations in the costs and the uncertainty could be a major problem for McGinnel's. It may be reluctant to take on long term contracts fearing that it might negotiate too high a price. McGinnel's would also have to constantly update its price lists and provide information to customers about changes in prices.

Wage costs also rise in inflationary periods. Workers demand wage rises to retain their relative position in relation to other workers and to be able to pay for rises in costs of living. McGinnel's is likely to be faced with rising wage demands and the added cost of National Insurance contributions. It will also have to take into account the costs of wage negotiations, possible action by employees to further their position and disruption to its operations. To some extent McGinnel's has been able to cope with these rises in costs. They have not increased rapidly, just in line with average increases. Those costs

that have risen, such as tanker drivers' wages, have been offset by rises in productivity. Wage costs have also been controlled by the introduction of new technology and the resulting reductions in staff. Administration costs and the cost of running trucks have also risen over time at slightly above the average rate of inflation.

In conclusion it could be argued that the effects of rising oil prices in inflationary periods are likely to have had the greatest influence on the business. It will have presented the business with the challenge of increasing prices or facing lost profit and uncertainty in periods of fluctuating prices. It has been able to cope with some of the other potential cost increases, such as wage rises, by improving the efficiency of its operations.

(40 marks)

(b) The pricing policy at McGinnel's is affected by the degree of competition in the market in which it operates. Faced with a competitive situation, and the fact that it is a relatively small independent supplier, the business has tended to offer slightly lower prices to customers than the oil majors. It has also tended not to change prices immediately as the prices of its oil supplies have changed. This can be a problem for the business, but sometimes a benefit. For example, if oil prices rise, McGinnel's will not be able to pass these on to customers as oil majors have maintained their prices at the same level. To remain competitive McGinnel's has to keep prices the same and suffer falls in profits. On the other hand, if oil prices fall, oil majors are slow to change their prices, but if McGinnel's maintains its prices, it is able to gain a profit windfall as costs have fallen but prices remain the same.

It has been suggested that the business should change to a policy of immediately passing on any changes in costs to customers. Assume that oil prices rise. If McGinnel's immediately passed these on to customers then it could be charging higher prices or prices equal to those of the oil majors. McGinnel's has always been able to compete by setting its prices at or below those of companies such as BP or Texaco. Raising prices might reduce demand and cause customers to switch to other suppliers. So it could be argued that McGinnel's should not change its prices immediately.

Similarly, it is suggested that if there is a fall in price, McGinnel's should immediately pass this on to customers. There is an argument that if majors are slow to change prices and McGinnel's' reacts first it could win orders. On the other hand, it would lose the profit windfall it currently gains as it waits to change to match the price reductions of majors. Further, McGinnel's customers are not only attracted to buy from the business by prices. They are attracted by the excellent service the business provides and the fact that it is a local company. This loyal base of customers may still be prepared to pay higher prices. So once again it could be argued that the business should not reduce prices immediately.

In conclusion, immediately raising prices could lead to the business being uncompetitive and immediately reducing prices may lose a profit windfall. For these reasons it could be suggested that McGinnel's' should not change prices immediately after a change in oil prices and that its current strategy is suitable for a small business, with a loyal band of customers in a competitive market.

(40 marks)

Question 1

(a) The type of unemployment caused by a downturn in the economy is cyclical unemployment. It is caused by a lack of demand which leads to lower sales by firms and so firms need less labour.

(b) Rising unemployment might lead to certain problems for Gill's. When unemployment increases there is less spending power in the economy as fewer people have jobs. People also face periods of uncertainty, fearing job losses. They tend to spend less on products such as those produced by Gill's. For example, the business has suffered from a lack of 'lunchtime foot traffic' - people visiting to buy their lunch as they pass by in their dinner/lunch hour. As a result of rising unemployment the business may be forced to change its strategy, for example to reduce menu prices in the USA.

(c) It could be argued that closing branches might be a good strategy. It will save costs. It might also reduce unused capacity as shops which are doing poorly could be closed down. The business would be reacting to the market. Falls in demand would tell it that spending is being cut and that customers will demand fewer Gill's products. Market economics would tell a business that it should react to this by reducing supply.

On the other hand closing outlets and reducing capacity can cause problems. When the economy moves into the recovery period of the trade cycle, it may need to expand again. This could be costly if restaurants are closed. So although closing outlets in the short term might give some benefit the business would need to be careful that it did not go 'too far' and cause problems when the economy recovers.

Case study

(a) The closure of textile businesses in the Doncaster area can have a number of effects on manufacturing and service businesses. Unemployed people have less income to spend on the goods and services of manufacturing businesses and service providers. People may have less to spend on clothing, electrical goods and household items produced by manufacturers. They may postpone holidays or have fewer nights out, affecting travel businesses, bars and taxi firms. Their sales may fall and profits may be reduced. The loss of 1 000 textiles jobs in Maggie Rowley's home area for example, as well

as in Doncaster itself, will leave the spending power of families reduced unless they are able to get jobs elsewhere. The problem is compounded by the fact that there is already high unemployment in these areas, where women workers from textiles factories are the only wage earners in the household. These workers do not have transport and may find it difficult to travel to get other jobs.

The region itself may be affected. Regional unemployment is where whole areas are affected by unemployment. If many textile workers lose their jobs and perhaps move to other jobs then vital skills could be lost. If there was a pick up in business then workers may no longer have the skills necessary to be re-employed.

Businesses making workers redundant will also be affected. They will have to make redundancy payments. Government will be affected as lower incomes mean that less is paid in income tax and National Insurance contributions.

Some businesses may actually benefit. For example, when her textile business closed, Maggie Rowley was able to get another job. Unemployment as a result of closures can create a pool of labour which other businesses can draw upon. This can be at lower wages, as in Maggie's case where she was only paid the minimum wage.

In conclusion, it could be argued that although some businesses may benefit from the closure of textile factories in the Doncaster area, many other businesses and the region in general would be adversely affected. So the negative effects are likely to outweigh the positive effects, particularly given the number of people working in the industry in the area.

(40 marks)

(b) Investment, training and planning are vital for almost any business to survive. This is particularly true for firms in the the UK textile industry, which faces ferocious competition from business in the Third World with much lower wage costs, and from firms in Europe and the USA which are at the cutting edge of manufacturing technology and product design. Investment allows firms to buy improved equipment which can lead to better products and lower costs. Training makes workers more productive, improving efficiency. Planning optimises the value of both investment and training for the business.

However, it could be argued that many UK textile companies will never be able to compete against low wage businesses in the Third World. However much they invest in the latest equipment and however well their workers are trained, UK companies can not get their costs down to the level of Third World competitors. Where this is the case, plants will continue to be closed down in the UK and workers made redundant.

(40 marks)

Question 1

(a) Five taxes that Stuart's business might pay are:
- corporation tax, a tax on his company's profits;
- employers' National Insurance contributions, a payment by businesses based on employees' earnings
- Value Added Tax (VAT) paid on ticket prices;
- business rates on the premises it owns or rents;
- capital gains tax, if the business sold property or other assets that it owned for a profit.

(b) (i) A rise in corporation tax will increase the amount that Stuart had to pay to the government on any profit the business makes. This would reduce the profit of the business. Stuart may decide to cut back on any expansion or investment if his profits fall. He may also decide not to pay a dividend to shareholders. He may also decide to cut back on any proposed wage increases.

(ii) Any increase in employers' National Insurance contributions will increase the cost of labour. Stuart may cut back on plans to hire more workers. He may even decide to make some workers unemployed.

Case study

(a) Raising taxes can affect businesses in a number of ways. Changes in taxation have a major effect on investment decisions. For example, if the government raises corporation taxes in the UK, this could affect expansion by UK businesses in the UK. They may decide that higher corporation taxes have reduced profit so much that they do not have the funds to spend on expansion. Also, foreign business will not be attracted to the UK. They will locate in countries with lower rates of corporation tax.

Increases in taxation on airlines could affect what is described as a growing industry. Higher passenger duty could lead to higher prices, if passed on. This could cut demand and revenue and profits could be hit. Increases in business rates could affect expansion plans.. If a business is aiming to locate in an area with high rates, it may decide not to locate there.

On the other hand, increases in taxes do not necessarily lead to

plans being cut. For example, a UK business faced with higher corporation tax in the UK may simply expand abroad. A business faced with high business rates in one local authority in the UK may choose to locate in an area with lower business rates. Further, if the government raises more revenue in taxation, it has more to spend. So, for example, if it decided to spend the money on road building or housing for younger people unable to get onto the property ladder, private businesses such as construction could benefit. They may expand as a result. Also, local authorities will have more funds to spend in regions. They may use these funds to help small businesses, in partnership, to make a 'meaningful contribution' to the local area.

In conclusion, it could be argued that raising taxes may lead some businesses to delay or curtail their expansion plans. However, they may simply change the plans. Further, some businesses may benefit if the government uses the money raised by taxation as part of its government expenditure programme.

(40 marks)

(b) From a business point of view it might be suggested that raising taxes on consumers and workers rather than businesses would be more advantageous. If taxation was not raised on businesses they would have more profit. They could use this for expansion. They could use the money to invest in an attempt to be more competitive against foreign competition. They would have more to pay to shareholders in dividends. Shareholders provide the funds for expansion and will be attracted by dividends. Good profits also raise their share price. Businesses would suggest that taxing consumers and employees rather than businesses themselves gives them freedom of choice. They can decide what to do with their retained profit in the way that best suits their organisation.

On the other hand taxing consumers means that they may not buy goods. Taxing employees means that they have less income to spend. This may therefore reduce the amount of goods they buy. If fewer goods are bought then the revenues and profits of businesses will be reduced.

Whether it is better from a business perspective to tax consumers or businesses will depend on the extent to which the tax will affect the business. For example, some airlines have suggested that imposing a higher rate of passenger duty will have no effect on flights as people will continue to fly. On the other hand, other airlines suggest that increasing passenger taxes will affect sales greatly. Businesses would then have to consider reducing prices to cushion the effect for passengers.

(40 marks)

116 | Population

Question 1

(a) The data show a stark difference in population growth between the developed 'north' of the world and the less developed 'south'. The developed north of Europe, including the former Soviet Union and North America, has population growth rates of less than 1% per annum with the exception of Greenland. The less developed south, with a few exceptions, has higher annual population growth rates than those of the developed north. Population growth in Africa and the Middle East is especially high, with many countries experiencing annual population growth rates in excess of 2 or 3% per annum. Population growth in China is restricted, although this is associated with the government policy on restricting childbirth.

(b) (i) Given the relatively high population growth rate in Africa there are, in theory, likely to be two main possible benefits to African businesses. First, an increased supply of labour for businesses. However, of more importance to businesses in Africa may be the skills levels of this increased pool of labour. The high levels of unemployment which exist in many urban areas of Africa suggest that an increased supply of unskilled labour to businesses will be of little benefit. Second, there may be a greater demand for the goods and services offered in African markets. Again, however, the benefits accruing to African businesses are likely to be slight. The vast majority of Africans have incomes which are low by the standards of even the poorest in the UK. This means that the effect of increased buying power amongst such consumers on African businesses is likely to be modest. In addition, the strain of increased population growth on services, such as education and health, which are traditionally provided by governments, may have indirect negative effects upon African businesses. This is because increased expenditure on these areas may well lead to resources being diverted from development programmes, such as improving transport and telecommunications networks, which can be vital to increasing the efficiency of African businesses.

(ii) Given the relatively low rates of population growth in eastern Europe, this may present two main problems for businesses in eastern Europe. First, there will be a smaller supply of labour for businesses to select from. This may result in businesses not having a sufficient number of workers to employ to produce goods. It would not be as much of a problem if businesses are simply trying to satisfy domestic demand. However, if they are exporting goods as well this may be particularly problematic. The second problem is that if there is a low population, then there may be low demand for goods and services within this area. Businesses may find that domestic demand for goods is low and therefore may find it difficult to sell their goods. However, the income levels of the population within a country may be more important as this will determine whether the customers can afford to purchase these goods. There are benefits for eastern European businesses from the low birth rates. Incomes will generally be higher in low population growth rate countries which will enable businesses to provide a range of goods and services and provide differentiated products. This is beginning to happen more, as eastern Europe moves towards a market economy. There may also be plentiful land as a resource which may benefit agricultural businesses who can exploit this and earn revenue from it.

Question 2

(a) There are two main trends that may be identified in the data. First, the number of divorces has increased over the period of 50 years. The number of divorces rose from below 50,000 in 1955 to nearly 200,000 in the early 1990s. There has been a reduction in the last 10 years in the number of divorces. Table 2 demonstrates that there has been a significant increase in the percentage of households where there is only one person living. There was a rise from 18% of households in 1971 to 29% of households in 2007. There has also been a significant decline in the proportion of households where there are six or more people living in the household.

(b) In terms of the effect these trends may have on businesses, it is clear that businesses should be aiming goods and services at single people. The increase in the divorce rates and the fall in the number of marriages has led to an increase in the number of single people. Businesses need to provide goods and services suited to these people. For food producers this may result in a move away from family sized portions and a movement towards meals for one. Building companies may need to consider reducing the number of four bedroom houses which are built and focus on one/two bedroom flats to suit the single or divorced. As the percentage of households with three people or more is falling then marketing strategies need to have more focus on the single and couples market rather than the family market. For example, discounts could be offered to couples in a gym rather than to family members. Another effect this may have on firms is that as the number of families fall, it is likely that a couple's disposable income will become higher. This will offer opportunities to firms to provide exclusive, select products, which are charged at a premium price, for example Sandals holidays and exclusive gyms. Businesses will be required to change their focus from family strategies to those more suited to singles and couples.

Case study

(a) Certain trends may be identified from the data. The UK population is projected to grow to reach 85 million by 2081. The average age of the whole population will increase, as will the average age of the working population. There will also be more people living longer, beyond retirement age. There will be an increase in the number of births. Part of this will result from young immigrants having children. Net migration is predicted to be positive in future. This will also result in there being more 16 years olds. These predicted changes may have a variety of effects on the supply of labour in the UK.

The growth in the total population will increase the supply of labour to the market. There will be more people looking for work. This will make it easier for businesses to recruit and select from a larger number of candidates. However, this depends on there being enough sufficiently experienced and skilled staff. If there are skills shortages then staff may need to be trained. This may particularly be the case with he growing numbers of 16 year olds entering the market. Of course, if the economy does not expand sufficiently then the large number of potential workers could find that some are unemployed. Again, retraining may be necessary to meet the skills required by businesses. Businesses may also find that an increased supply of labour forces down the wage rate.

The greater number of older people looking for work will also lead to issues in the labour force. Older workers often have more experience. If they remain in work longer then businesses may not have to recruit more staff. Reducing staff turnover cuts costs. Also, it means that businesses do not need to train new workers in skills that could potentially be lost if older workers leave. This may help knowledge management in business.

The rise in net migration can also impact on the workforce and business. Workers arriving from other countries will again increase the choice of businesses from potential applicants for jobs. Workers from other countries may have the skills required by businesses and so training may not be needed. But there may be a need for training in practices with which they are not familiar or the culture of the organisation, or even in English if it is not their second language.

(40 marks)

(b) Businesses may have to change their products and services to take advantage of the trends taking place in the UK population. The ageing population will require businesses to reconsider their target markets, marketing and their product ranges. Businesses which already exist in markets for elderly people may have an advantage as they will already have an established reputation. However they need to be prepared for an increase in the amount of competition which will arise from these changes. Businesses tailored to meet the needs of the older client group may need to consider expansion and greater choice and variety. For example, companies such as Saga, which is already focused on the older client group, may want to consider widening the opportunities they have already and expanding into slightly more niche markets, such as adventure holidays for the over 60s. Businesses operating in residential care, health insurance and mobility products may flourish. However, there is a number of opportunities for firms who are not already focused on the 60+ markets which may require them to change their products and services. Businesses may need to focus their products and services on this older market. Construction companies may need to consider building more bungalows on new housing developments, to meet the demands of the older client group. They may need to consider facilities within the accommodation which could be specifically aimed at that age range, such as special features within the bathroom to help mobility.

Cinema companies may need to reconsider their strategies. Figure 5 shows that only around 30 per cent of people aged 55 and over visit the cinema at least once a year. This compares with over 80 per cent for children aged 7-14 and also younger people aged 15-24. Film makers may therefore target a greater proportion of films at these younger age groups. However, there may also be a potential market aimed at people from other cultures. If net migration is leading to a larger population from other countries then a market for foreign language films may develop. Existing cinemas may show these films or there may be a greater business for cinemas aimed at migrants.

On the other hand the growth in the Internet may mean greater competition for cinemas. More and more people are downloading films to watch. Table 5 shows that this is most prevalent amongst 16-24 years olds and non-existent for those over 65. Again this would suggest targeting a younger market, although it might be argued that in future people who are now young will age and still retain downloading habits. Other areas of Internet activity offer possibilities for certain age groups. For example, a greater percentage of older people than under 24s use travel services over the Internet. Higher percentages of people aged 45-64 shop online than those aged 16-44. This may be because they have more income. They may also have more time to shop. One area that Internet services may target is the market for younger people looking for educational information. This could be particularly attractive given the predicted increased in 16 year olds.

Most businesses will hope that they can respond effectively to changes in the population. However, some may find it more difficult than others. For example a fast food chain may find it difficult to encourage older people to eat in their restaurants. Further, as suggested earlier, trends that exist in 2006 may change. For example, downloading amongst older people may increase as younger people age. If businesses base products on current trends they must be careful to use market research to check that these trends continue.

(40 marks)

Question 1

(a)

No employed	Total revenue annually (£)	Additional revenue from each employee (£)
20	350,000	-
21	390,000	40,000
22	425,000	35,000
23	450,000	25,000
24	470,000	20,000
25	480,000	10,000

(b) (i) 21
(ii) 23
(iii) 25
(c) From the information given in the table the most likely employment level in this business is 25. This is because all of the employees are adding to total revenue. So if Fentons sets a wage at £10,000 per annum it would be able to maximise profits by employing 25 people.

Question 2

(a) Demand for labour at BMW may be affected by a number of factors. First, the demand for Minis will influence the quantity of workers required. Labour is derived demand, (ie the demand arises from the demand for another product) and therefore the quantity of workers required will be determined by the quantity of Minis demanded. BMW is experiencing a rise in the demand for Minis to a high of 165,000 and will therefore increase its demand for workers. Similarly, the increase in the production plans, to 200,000 Minis per year, may also increase the demand for workers. The productivity of workers also affects the demand for workers. The more productive workers become the greater the revenue they bring to the firm. If the workers' productivity rates rise, this will increase the demand for workers. The case study refers to an increase in the productivity rates of 4%. It would be expected that this would increase the demand for workers. Other factors may include the productivity of machinery.
(b) These factors will affect the demand curve for labour in the long term. If the demand for Minis continues to rise in the future, then the demand curve for workers will shift to the right from D to D_1. More workers will be demanded at each and every wage rate.

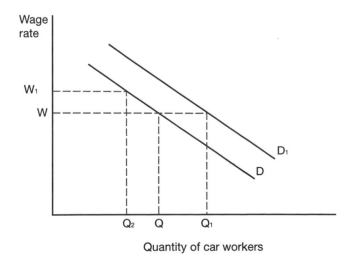

Quantity of car workers

At a wage rate of W, Q_1 number of workers will now be demanded rather than Q workers.

Similarly, this will be the case if there is increased productivity of workers. As the productivity of workers rises, the additional revenue generated by each employee rises, allowing the business to take on workers who previously would not have been employed. The demand for these workers will rise and the demand curve will shift to the right, demanding more workers at each and every wage rate. It does have to be assumed that in this time wages have remained constant.

If wages rise in the future, then the demand for workers will change. Should wage rates rise in the future and not be met with increased productivity, it is likely that there will be a movement along the demand curve and there will be less workers demanded at the new wage rate. At wage rate W, Q workers will be demanded. However, as the wage rate rises to W_1, then the demand for workers falls to Q_2.

Question 3

(a)

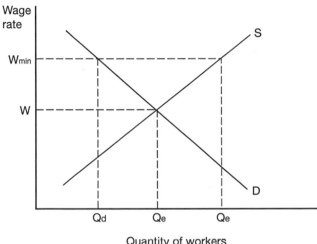

Quantity of workers

With reference to the diagram above, the equilibrium wage is W, with a quantity of workers demanded and supplied at Qe. If the minimum wage is introduced at a wage rate greater than W, then this may lead to a surplus of labour within the market. This means that demand for workers by firms will fall due to the higher wage rate, but at the same time more workers will offer themselves for work due to the higher wage rate. Consequently, there will be a surplus of workers available. According to economic theory, this will lead to a fall in employment within the food industry, as Qe workers were previously demanded and now only Qd are.
(b) It is likely that a café which pays all its workers the same wage regardless of age could be affected by the changes in the minimum wage in a number of ways. The firm is currently paying a wage which is much greater than the minimum wage. Therefore it could be argued that it will not be affected by changes in minimum wages below this level. If it continues to pay higher wages than the minimum then changes below might not affect it.

However, it may find that there is an increase in the number of workers putting themselves forward to work for the firm, as it is paying a far greater wage than the minimum wage. This increases the amount of available labour to the firm and may enable it to recruit better skilled and higher quality staff. In particular, the firm may find that there is a much bigger increase in the quantity of 16 and 17 year olds applying for jobs as the wage differential is greatest at this age range.

Alternatively, in the longer term, the firm may decide to reduce the wage rate for new workers joining the firm. It knows that providing it pays more than £5.73 per hour for 22 year olds and above, it is fulfilling the requirements of the law and may therefore reduce the wage rate for newcomers to the firm, reducing its costs of production.

(a)

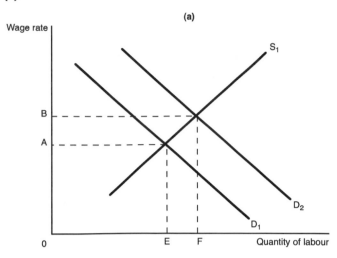

(a)

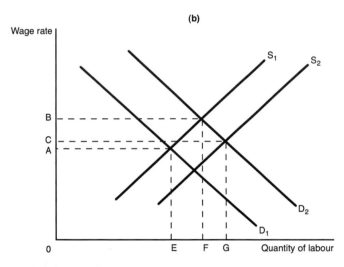

(b)

Demand and supply diagrams can be used to show the effect of demand for and supply of labour in the UK construction industry over the next five years. The downturn in private sector demand for housing has been offset by a surge in demand for other building projects, including spending on transport, schools and projects associated with the London Olympics. The demand for labour is a derived demand. So when the demand for construction work increases, the demand for labour in the construction industry increases. This is shown in the figure. In (a) the demand curve will move to the right from D_1 to D_2. This increase in demand would be met by an extension in the quantity of labour supplied, from OE to OF

In the UK there are skills shortages. One way in which the increase in demand for labour could be met is by the introduction of national skills academies on large building sites. These would train workers to meet the increase in demand. However, another is through the use of migrant labour. This is shown in (b). The influx of workers from abroad has shifted the supply curve to the right from S_1 to S_2.

(40 marks)

(b) It could be argued that wages in the construction industry should rise faster than the national average in future. If there is strong demand in the construction industry then the demand for labour will increase. Given that there are skills shortages, to attract workers business would be expected to pay higher wages. Looking at (a) again, it is clear that a rise in demand has increased the wage rate from OA to OB.

However, there are other factors that could be affecting the wages declared to tax authorities. The influx of labour from abroad has moved the supply curve from S_1 to S_2 as shown in (b). Workers from European countries have entered the UK market. It is suggested that employers are paying these workers relatively lower wages. This is shown in (b). The wage rate has fallen to OC as a result of the influx of workers. Further, it is also suggested that some employers are operating illegally. They are not declaring the wages of workers to save on paying tax and national insurance contributions. Again this would have the effect of lowering the wages in the construction industry compared to the national average. Of course, the actual national average may also need to be taken into consideration. If the economy was in a recession, with wage increases very low, then even the potentially reduced wages in the construction industry may be higher than the average of all industries. Further, some industries may be paying high wages, such as the Olympic projects that may require specialist skills, which could offset the lower wages suggested for migrant workers.

(40 marks)

Question 1

(a) A business that is productively efficient will be operating at its lowest average production costs. If a business improves its productive efficiency it will be reducing its average costs of production. Moving production from Wolverhampton to Eastern Europe helped Goodyear to achieve this. It argued that the move consolidated its 'low-cost sourcing capabilities'. The main reason why costs were lower was because workers in Eastern Europe were paid a fraction of wages paid in the UK. But Goodyear has also invested in modernising production in Eastern Europe, for example the £55 million modernisation at Sava Tires in Slovenia. So when machinery wears out at Wolverhampton, it may be cheaper for the business to move production to Sava rather than replace the machinery at Wolverhampton.

(b) One factor that might persuade Goodyear to retain production at Wolverhampton is if wage costs could be reduced in the UK relative to those in Eastern Europe. This might happen if wage costs rise in Slovenia, as they are forecast to do. This, however, is likely to take a number of years. Alternatively wage costs could fall in the UK. This might happen if alternative methods of working could be introduced, such as flexible working, that could reduce costs.

Alternatively, if the business felt that new machinery could be operated more effectively in Wolverhampton compared to Eastern Europe this could be a factor. It would require machines to be replaced when they wear out. But this might be profitable if production at Wolverhampton was more efficient.

Wolverhampton may have skills as a result of training which cannot be duplicated in Eastern Europe, for example, or Wolverhampton may be able to produce specialist products that cannot be manufactured elsewhere. Goodyear may also consider that training would be more effective in the UK, in which case it might consider spending on training programmes for its staff and leave production in Wolverhampton.

Goodyear may also consider leaving production in the UK if it might experience problems from operating in another country. For example if there were delivery problems, communications problems or other difficulties it might feel that leaving production at Wolverhampton is less risky.

Question 2

(a) Car manufacturing is expensive in many ways. It requires large amounts of capital equipment to manufacture. Production costs are very high. Only by manufacturing in large quantities can economies of scale be exploited and average cost reduced, so that competitive prices that customers can afford can be charged. Car manufacturers also often compete using branding. Prices on similar models are often similar. So manufacturers attempt to differentiate their products using sophisticated promotional techniques aimed at establishing a brand image in the eyes of customers. The manufacture of cars also requires detailed knowledge. Further, it requires constant investment to produce new models to attract customers. For all these reasons, only large manufacturers can be really competitive in the motor industry. This is why large multinationals such as Volkswagen and Toyota tend to be successful.

(b) It is the dream of car manufacturers to produce one model of car and sell this to all markets to gain the cost savings associated with economies of scale. However, car producers now perhaps accept that customers in China and India, for example, might have to be offered different 'solutions' to customers in other countries. These solutions might be needed because of major differences in these markets compared to those in the West. One difference might be in price. Incomes in countries such as China and India may be lower than in the USA for example. Car buyers may only be attracted by lower prices. To set lower prices and still make profits manufacturers either need to make large sales so that revenue is maintained, or cut costs. Large sales in these countries may allow cost savings in economies of scale, but the materials or other features of a car may need to change to accommodate this.

Another difference might be in the tastes of consumers. Consumers in India might want smaller cars. Consumers in China might want larger cars, to reflect growing incomes and status. They may also want features of cars that are different to those in other countries. This might be in the design and look of the car, or it might be in the internal operation.

(c) At the time of the article Toyota was the world's largest car manufacturer by sales volume. VW planned to become the world's most international carmaker. To overtake Toyota it might consider a number of strategies.

Its marketing strategy is likely to be vital in this. It must produce the right product for the market. It currently has weak position in the US market, but is considering the launch of a mid-sized saloon. It would need to make sure that this is what the market demanded. The US market is the world's largest market for cars and it is likely to be vital that it can gain market share. On the other hand emerging markets in China and India could also allow it to gain sales. Again, producing the right product, at the right price and promoting it effectively is likely to be important.

It would also need to consider its production strategy. For example, VW is currently considering building a plant in the US. This would reduce some of its costs of importing, including perhaps import tariffs. But such a large investment would need to be justified. It might only be worthwhile if VW could improve its market share of sales in the US. In countries like India other production issues might arise. For example, such countries restrict the type of operations that can take place. Foreign businesses can only operate in partnership with home companies. This is likely to be the case for both VW and Toyota in these countries. But it is vital that they conform to legislation. If VW expands greatly in China and India it may need to pass some of its products to co-operators.

Question 3

(a) There might be certain advantages to Louis Vuitton in outsourcing production to a country like India. One major advantage could be cost. Many aspects of costs might be lower in a country such as India. In particular wage costs are likely to be lower. The costs involved in production may be lower, including the cost of land and plant. The costs of operation may also be lower. In the EU a French manufacturer may face the costs of complying with EU regulations.

Outsourcing to India may also help as it puts the manufacturing of products close to a growing market. The Asian market is fast growing. Manufacturing close to the market will save on transport costs of the final products. It will also ensure supplies can be delivered with little delay.

However, any benefits of outsourcing must be weighed against potential problems. Louis Vuitton must be careful that its prestige brand image is maintained This means ensuring the quality of its products in India.

(b) (i) Hong Kong might benefit from having a Louis Vuitton store or production facility located in the country. Fashion houses are now opening in Hong Kong, selling fashion products to the very rich. There is likely to be demand for these products. Setting up a production site can increase employment in the area. It may also attract other prestige brands to the area, helping to promote economic growth. If these business pay tax, this will generate extra income in the country. If the business reinvests in the country this will further help to promote development. However, if it repatriates profits back to its home country, without reinvesting, benefits will be reduced. Further, it could be argued that the development of Western style stores selling such fashions may take away the identity of the area. Another problem might be if the business simply employs workers at low wages in order to reduce its manufacturing costs. Multinationals are often accused of exploiting workers in other countries by setting up plants which operate in conditions that are inferior to its other operations to reduce costs.

(ii) Setting up in India may also benefit the country in the same way. There could be employment. Economic growth may be promoted if there is spending as a result of incomes. There are also likely to be similar problems of a loss of identity, repatriation of profits and worker exploitation. However, it could be suggested that the Indian market would be less attracted to the type of prestige product that the business is selling. There is a vast market in India, but it could be suggested that the sales are unlikely to be as great as in Hong Kong.

Case study

(a) The Friends of the Earth website argues that every time people spend money in the supermarket or petrol station, or pay taxes, this helps the growth of multinationals. There is a wide range of stakeholders in multinational businesses. They include the owners, employees, government, customers, suppliers, the society and environment in which they operate and arguably other competitors. Each of these stakeholder groups might be affected in different ways by a break up of multinationals or a reduction in their size.

Owners might suffer. Large companies are able to gain considerable economies of scale that help to cut costs. Without the size required to do this, the costs of the business could increase. Profits may suffer and owners may be paid lower dividends. If these businesses are no longer multinationals, they may not have the political power to influence governments and other bodies that many decisions in their favour. Again, this could affect profits. One issue that may be debatable is the extent to which the share price of the business may be affected. Owners also benefit from higher share prices. The issue then is whether the share price from one large multinational would be higher or lower than a number of smaller operations.

Employees could suffer in the same way as owners. Smaller companies with lower profits may mean lower incomes for employees. There may be less employment opportunities. On the other hand if multinationals are encouraging workers to work in poor conditions at low wages, then reducing their power and influence may mean that they can be controlled more effectively and they may be forced to improve these conditions.

Government can be affected in a number of ways. Friends of the Earth suggests that multinationals are able to threaten governments to get what they want. If this is the case then smaller organisations could have less power to influence governments. Companies like Shell, for example, appeal to governments over environmental issues. They put pressure on governments to introduce environmental policies to manage greenhouse gases, for example.

Suppliers, competitors and consumers may also benefit. Smaller organisations may have less power to influence the market. Suppliers may find that the restrictions placed on them by multinationals are reduced, leaving them with more decision making freedom. They may be able to increase profits if they can raise their prices. Other businesses may find it easier to enter the market, taking market share from the smaller multinational. Suppliers may then have more businesses at which to target their products. This might also suggest that customers may benefit. Competition leads to a greater variety of goods and services available. The question would be whether these goods would be the same quality and price. For example, smaller organisations may not be able to produce the goods at the same quality or price as a larger organisation. On the other hand, competition should force down prices, benefiting the consumer.

There is also perhaps a debate as to whether the break up or reduction in size of multinationals can benefit society and the environment. On the one hand Friends of the Earth suggests that environments are destroyed. They argue, for example, that rainforests are cleared to grow products on supermarket shelves. On the other hand many multinationals are working to control environmental problems such as greenhouse gas emissions and develop sustainable sources. A smaller company may not be able to do this.

In conclusion, smaller businesses are likely to adversely affect owners to some extent. However, any gains to employees, consumers and the environment that may result will be offset by the loss of benefits from large scale activities.

(40 marks)

(b) It could be argued that there are major benefits to the countries in which multinationals operate. Multinationals provide employment opportunities that may not have previously existed. They also bring in FDI into the country. This can lead to greater spending to build premises and infrastructure. They will also bring in knowledge. In some cases this may lead to developments in other areas of the country. Multinationals will pay taxes to the government of the country in which they operate. Taxation will raise revenue that may be spent in areas such as housing or health to raise living standards. In general it is argued that profitable, performing multinationals can bring economic growth to countries in which they operate.

Suppliers may also benefit. If a large organisation moves into an area this presents trading possibilities that may not have previously existed. Existing business may find new business customers fro their products. New businesses may spring up to provide support services. If products are bought from other countries then these countries will benefit from greater trade. The supplies will represent imports to countries in which multinationals operate. If that country has tariffs then revenue may be raised for the government. If suppliers are forced to comply to standards such as the RSPO standard used by Tesco, this can encourage sustainable sources and protect the environment.

On the other hand there are many criticisms of multinationals. It is argued that they can operate poor working conditions. They destroy the environment by using large amounts of scare resources. They influence government. They use lobbies to argue against laws that protect the environment. Their CSR policies, whilst looking good on paper, are failing as they ignore the real problems and there is no enforcement.

Suppliers are also adversely affected. They are forced to comply with the standards set by multinationals which may raise their prices. The prices that multinationals are prepared to pay may not allow them to earn a reasonable living standard.

In conclusion, it could be argued that there are both benefits and problems associated with multinationals operating in a country, for that country and also for suppliers. Whether these problems outweigh the benefits may depend on the extent to which multinationals regard profit as more important than other factors and whether they make good on promises in areas such as sustainable development of sources of materials.

(40 marks)

119 | Government policy

Question 1

(a) The article suggests two changes in taxation that can affect the behaviour of companies on green issues. Before the 2008 Budget companies could 'write-off' 25 per cent of the value of a car emitting more than 160 gm of CO_2 per kilometre. After the budget this would have only been 10 per cent, which would have the effect of increasing the cost of the companies owning cars, as they could not write off as much in their accounts. A second change is the increase in road tax from 2010. For example tax on a Land Rover would rise from £500 to £950. This would increase the costs of car road tax payments to the business. These higher costs might persuade companies to use cars which do not emit as much CO_2 or even to use fewer cars, reducing the effect of emissions on the environment.

(b) (i) If she had decided to make no change then the company would have been faced with increased costs. In both the tax changes in (a) costs have risen.

(ii) Changing the composition of the fleet could have had a positive effect on motivation. Some staff, concerned for the environment, may have supported the decision and been motivated by the environmentally-friendly approach of the business. Other staff may be demotivated, concerned that their rewards and perks were being cut and that they were driving a smaller, perhaps less comfortable car. The net impact on motivation could depend on how environmentally conscious were the staff driving cars. If this was part of the corporate culture of the business then it might motivate staff. On the other hand, many of the 70 staff driving cars might be demotivated unless they were persuaded otherwise.

(c) It could be argued that the Chief Executive might consider switching from a Land Rover to a Vauhall Astra. If he was a particularly committed supporter of the environment, he may decide that changing to a smaller car would be the right thing to do. It might also set a good example to others in the business. It might also send out signals to the market that the business is concerned about its effect on the environment. In some cases this can create a positive marketing image.

On the other hand a large car is often a perk of a senior staff member. The CE may fell that moving to an Astra undermines his position in the business in the eyes of other workers and the business world. It may also suggest that the business is struggling to provide cars for staff. A solution to this might be to suggest that the CE switches to a car that has similar prestige but is less harmful to the environment or to a hybrid car.

Question 2

(a) It is suggested that Wal-Mart could benefit from the one-off tax rebate given to people by the US government, but that other companies such as Starbucks or perhaps a furniture retailer may not. This is because of the type of spending that can take place when such rebates are given. People tend to spend on lower-margin foods, such as ice cream from Wal-Mart. But they do not spend on luxuries, which might include furniture. Nor do they spend on meals and restaurants, which could include spending in Starbucks. Wal-Mart's core customer is the average to below average income earner, the type of customer who may be receiving the rebates.

(b) It could be argued that a retailer in February 2008 might take into account the one-off tax rebate. If it decided that people had more money to spend then it could increase stock. However, the suggestion is that most of the spending will be on low-level food products. If this is the case then it might be unwise for the retailer to increase stock too greatly. It is unlikely that spending on televisions or DVD players would result from the tax rebate. If there was any change in stock it might be a move towards more food orientated products, such as fridges, to take into account that more might be demanded to cope with the increased demand for food.

Case study

(a) Government policy changed in a number of ways during the period described. These changes would have affected Steve Hayne's micro-brewing business in a number of ways. The Smoking ban might have had a positive and negative effect. On the one hand people were now drinking more beer at home, where they could smoke. He may have seen some falls in sales to pubs, but this could have been offset by the 10 per cent rise in sales to retailers, attracted by speciality beers.

Taxation on beer increased. This was justified as a curb on binge drinking. Steve did not agree with this as he suggested that his beers were not the type consumed in such as way. Nevertheless, he would have had to pay higher taxes like all beer producers and this would have hit his profits. Income tax was also increased on low to medium income earners. These were his typical customers. As a result Steve decided to curtail his expansion plans. He must have felt that the rise in tax would have had a major impact on spending for the type of drinker buying his products.

Interest rates were cut. Steve had borrowed £100,000 to fund the purchase of the micro-brewery at a variable rate of interest. A reduction by 1 per cent per annum would have cut his repayments by £1,000.

In conclusion, it could be argued that although there have been some benefits in the changes in government policy, the overall impact has been to ht the development of the business, so much so that Steve had to put off his expansion plans.

(40 marks)

(b) If government cut every tax by 20 per cent and government spending were cut by the same amount, this could have a number of effects on the sales and profits of Steve's business. Cutting income tax and employees' National Insurance contributions would leave people with more of their income. They would therefore have more spending power and aggregate demand may increase. Sales at Steve's business might increase as a result, especially as people who have more income tend to buy more luxuries, such as speciality beers. On the other hand, they might buy other products with their increased income.

Cutting VAT and excise duties on beer by 20 per cent would allow Steve to charge a lower price to customers. On the other hand, VAT would also be cut on other goods and services. The average price of all goods and services would fall. However, because beer is subject to large excise duties, the relative fall in the price of beer is likely to be higher than the average for all goods and services. Therefore, there should be some increase in demand for beer, including Steve's beer.

Cutting other taxes would leave businesses with more profits. For example, a cut of 20 per cent in employers' National Insurance contributions or local council Business Rates will lower Steve's costs. A cut in Corporation Tax, assuming Steve's business is a limited company, would leave him with more profit after tax.

On the other hand, cutting government spending by 20 per cent will have a negative impact on Steve's business. Governments spend on everything from hospitals and schools to roads and welfare benefits. The 20 per cent cut would see a significant fall in total spending in the economy. As a result, average incomes would fall leading to a fall in spending on everything including beer.

Overall, the impact on Steve's business depends on how his customers or potential customers are affected by the cuts in tax and spending and the impact on his cost base. Some of his customers will gain more from the tax cuts than they lose from the fall in government spending. They might buy more beer. Others of his customers will lose more from the fall in government spending than they gain from any tax cut. They will buy less beer. Steve might see falls in the taxes he pays. But he may be forced by tough market conditions to pass these tax cuts on to customers in the form of lower prices, leaving him no better off then before. Cuts in government spending may also impact on his business in the long term. For example, if roads are no longer maintained as well as

197

before and if new road building is cut, travel times may increase leading to a rise in his transport costs. With large cuts in taxes and government spending, there are always winners and losers. It is difficult to assess, without more information, whether Steve's business would be a winner or a loser in this situation.

(40 marks)

Question 1

(a) Businesses in EU countries have the right to appeal against decisions made by national courts or by national bodies. The UK is part of the EU and so it must comply with EU directives and regulations. In this case Marks & Spencer appealed against the UK tax ruling by the Inland Revenue (now HM Revenue and Customs) to the European Court of Justice. The ruling prevented it from offsetting losses made in other countries against its UK tax bill. This, the Court of Justice argued, breached a core EU Treaty of Rome principle.

(b) (i) The Treaty of Rome and the Single European Act prevent member states from stopping businesses setting up in other EU countries. This could benefit Marks & Spencer as it should allow it freedom to set up where it wants. If it decided, for example, that the most potentially profitable location for a new store was France, then the French government could not prevent it from setting up there. The ruling also allowed Marks & Spencer to offset losses in other countries against profits made in the UK. This would help the business as it would have allowed it to pay less corporation tax and keep more of its profit.

(ii) Membership of the EU may also lead to problems for Marks & Spencer. The UK can not prevent businesses from other countries from setting up in the UK. This means that foreign businesses can easily set up retail outlets to compete with Marks & Spencer. In the UK in recent years this has led to a number of clothing competitors establishing businesses, such as Zara from Spain.

Question 2

(a) There may be greater scope for marketing magazines in Poland than, say, the UK over the next 10 years because Poland is one of a number of newly qualified EU countries that is predicted to grow in future years. Such economies are predicted to grow by more than the EU average. Economic growth is likely to lead to greater employment, incomes and spending power. These may also be markets which have few competitors. This may make it easier to establish a new magazine.

(b) Option 1 is to buy an established Polish magazine company and launch magazines that have proved popular in other countries. An advantage of this strategy is that the business will already be established and in operation, with its own editorial team and distribution system. It will have a knowledge of the Polish market. The new magazines will also be new and innovative to the market and could be products that are exciting and appeal to the market. These products also have a track record in other countries. Possible problems may be that the Polish business's existing organisation and systems may not be efficient. Further, just because a magazine has proved popular in one country does not mean it is guaranteed to be popular in another. Tastes may be different in different countries.

Option 2 is to buy a Polish company with an existing strong market share. This option has the same advantages and disadvantages as the first option. However, a possible benefit is that new products can be launched which are geared to the particular needs of the Polish market. This will now be possible with the extra finance provided by BWD.

Option 3 is to set up a company from scratch. This gives the business freedom to set up the exact type of business that it wants. It can organise its structure and distribution in whatever form it considers to be most efficient. It also has freedom to launch whichever magazines it wants. On the other hand this is potentially very risky. BWD is moving into a market in which it has no experience. Any new business is likely to face some initial problems and these may be even greater if the business has little experience of the market.

Overall it could be argued that buying into a Polish publishing business and then reorganising would be the safer option. Launching new products could give BWD the chance to publish whatever magazines it wanted. But perhaps using variations on magazines that have proved popular in a number of other countries might give it a base on which to build, as these magazines seem to have appealed to customers in many different countries. However, the business would need to ensure that tastes in Poland were at least similar to those in these other countries. It would require a knowledge of buying patterns, what prices customers were prepared to pay, and what they wanted to see in magazines, before making a decision. If they were very different, then option 2 might be a better alternative.

Case study

(a) As an EU member, the UK must comply with EU regulations. The details of EU regulations usually then become part of national laws within a period of time. UK businesses are therefore affected by the actions of EU in a number of ways. For example, the suggestion that corporation taxes could be harmonised across EU countries could lead to changes in taxation paid by UK businesses. As the UK has relatively low corporation tax rates compared to those in other EU countries, it is argued that UK businesses would be adversely affected, having to pay higher taxes.

Another factor that can affect UK business is changes in EU regulations regarding health and safety. For example, proposed changes to regulations regarding the industrial use of chemicals could raise costs of UK businesses. They would be faced with costs of as much as £3.4 billion to comply with legislation. Employees in UK businesses, on the other hand will benefit from safer working conditions. The checks would also be put on imported goods. So suppliers of chemicals to UK businesses would face higher costs and might pass these on to UK businesses in higher prices.

The free movement of labour can affect UK businesses. Unlike labour restrictions between the UK and the USA, for example, workers are free to move from one EU country to another. There are also no tariffs placed on the movement of goods within the EU, as there are between certain UK businesses trading with countries outside Europe.

In conclusion, it could be argued that given the eventual conversion of EU regulations into national law, the impact of the UK being an EU member is great for UK businesses. UK businesses are greatly affected, not only in terms of their operations, but also the tax they pay, the prices they charge and the available labour they can make use of.

(40 marks)

(b) It might be argued, as certain EU sceptics do, that UK businesses would benefit from withdrawal from the EU. They argue that there is too much EU red tape. Businesses spend lots of money ensuring they comply with EU standards. Often they are forced to incur extra costs as regulations change. Further, the free movement of goods means that they are open to competition from other EU countries' products. Countries within the EU can not place tariffs on the price of imported goods to force up the price in order to protect home businesses from competition. As a result, it is argued that many go out of businesses when faced with low cost competition.

On the other hand, there are certain aspects of EU membership that can benefit UK businesses. The free movement of labour means that workers who have particular skills, which may be in short supply, in the UK can move here easily. Further, workers who are used to relatively lower wages in other EU countries may take jobs that local workers would not. There are also advantages in not having tariffs placed on goods. Supplies can be brought in from nearby European countries without their prices being artificially raised. These countries also give the advantage of speedy supply, which can lead to lower costs than imported supplies from countries such as China.

A further problem for UK business could be the implications if the UK pulled out. The UK would then have tariffs placed on its exports to the EU, the common external tariff. Its exported goods would then be more highly priced in EU countries and UK businesses would become more competitive. If the UK retaliated and placed its own tariffs on EU imports then its businesses would face the prospect of higher prices for supplies. This would raise costs or force UK businesses to buy from suppliers in Asia, for example, delaying delivery. The EU may even place quotas on UK exports, restricting the amount that can be sold in the EU. This could affect the sales of UK products and products of UK businesses.

In conclusion, it could be argued that there are clear costs for UK businesses in the UK belonging to the EU. A withdrawal would therefore advantage UK business in some areas. However, there are benefits that they would lose. Further, and perhaps most importantly, the imposition of the tariff on UK exports would increase their prices in the EU. So any cost savings that might be made could be offset by loss of sales in EU countries. The overall effect may depend on the extent to which businesses rely on sales abroad and other benefits gained from EU countries, such as the use of low cost labour.

(40 marks)

Question 1

(a) The Consumer Protection Regulations 2008 introduced a duty to ensure that traders act fairly and honestly towards consumers.
(i) It might affect consumers as they could have better knowledge when buying products. For example, they should now know that any reductions in price are due to a business actually closing down. If it did not then this may have been an unfair trading activity designed to encourage consumers to buy products that they would not have previously bought. Also, consumers will be not be able to be coerced to buy services such as psychic readings.
(ii) Businesses will be forced to trade fairly. If they do not they may face prosecution and possibly fines. They would also need to change their marketing. For example, they could not claim a closing down sale if they were not closing. Some businesses could suffer a loss of trade. For example, psychics may find that people no longer use their services.

Question 2

(a) If the recommendation to create the post of ombudsman in the grocery market went ahead certain groups might benefit. Suppliers such as farmers might benefit if decisions were upheld concerning their complaints regarding the prices forced upon them by large supermarkets. They may also have less to fear about contracts being terminated if they complain, as is the case with the current Code of Conduct. Independent grocery stores may also benefit if their claims that supermarkets were forcing them out of business were upheld. Customers may also benefit if there was more competition in the market. They may get more choice. The main losers are likely to be supermarkets. Under the current Codes of Practice they do not have an independent body examining complaints. They fear their costs will rise.
(b) (i) It could be argued that the opening of a new supermarket will benefit consumers. However, any benefits would have to be offset against the losses from the closure of the three independent shops. There may be reduced consumers' choice. There may be reduced convenience if they were closed. The shops may provide products that the supermarket does not.
(ii) A major criticism of the major four supermarket chains in the UK is that they dominate the market. Smaller businesses find it hard to compete against larger supermarkets. Some are forced out of business. However, there are also benefits to customers of large supermarkets. They provide a single shopping area for many of the foods that people want to buy. This saves time shopping around. They also provide parking, which is difficult in main town centres. Their large size means that they are able to exploit economies of scale, which can often mean that some prices are lower than they might be in smaller shops. They also provide employment for many people. Further, the finding of the Competition Commission stated that there were few if any problems in the grocery market. It dismissed the claims of farmers that prices were being controlled and independent stores about unfair competition. For these reasons, it is unlikely that it would recommend that no new stores would be opened.

Question 3

(a) Regulators are needed to control the activities of businesses in the power and telecommunications industries. These industries provide essential services to customers. Formerly they were public utilities, controlled by government. Today the services are provided by private businesses, but controlled by regulators. Regulators ensure that these essential services are available to customers and that the few businesses that dominate these markets are not abusing their market position. For example, Ofgem, which regulates the power

industry, investigated the market tactics used by Npower. Allegedly sales staff misled customers and changed their power supplier without their knowledge. Without regulation, such tactics could have continued at the expense of the consumer.
(b) It could be argued that the actions of regulators such as Ofgem improve competition and consumer service. The regulator is able to investigate unfair practices to the consumer. It is able to fine businesses up to 10 per cent of global income if it finds they are engaging in such practices. This could deter business from such practices. If this is the case then businesses would be able to compete fairly. Also, customers would be in a better position to assess the relative claims of businesses providing power services. However, the extent to which markets may become more competitive may depend on the success of regulators in taking action. If, for example, businesses are able to hide their activities from the regulator, it would be less effective. Further, if regulators do not take action, businesses may see this as a sign that they can consider practices that may benefit the business, perhaps at the expense of consumers.

Case study

(a) A decision to fine airlines can have a variety of effects on businesses and their customers. British Airways, for example, was fined for alleged price fixing by both the Office of Fair Trading in the UK and the US department of justice. This had resulted in higher prices for consumers. It is suggested that the dealings of British Airways, Korean Air and other organisations led to increased charges for passengers and air freight. Consumers and business ended up 'picking up the tab' for the illegal activities. The decision to fine businesses may regulate their activities. As a result both consumers and other business customers may benefit. Prices may be lowered by airline companies, fearing further fines from the regulatory authorities for any illegal activities. This could have a number of effects on the airlines. Lower prices may lead to increased sales to some extent. It may also help them to compete against other airlines. But lower prices may also mean a loss of revenue and possibly profit.

On the other hand, businesses that are fined could attempt to pass on the fine to customers. The extent to which it could do this would depend to some extent on the prices of other airlines. If one airline was fined and tried to raise prices to pass this on, it might only be able to do this if its new higher prices were still competitive against those of other airlines. Further, fines may simply encourage businesses to fined more effective ways to make profit that cannot be detected by the regulatory authorities. In this case consumers may find that there are even more hidden costs in their flights. Or the business may examine legal ways to increase costs, again raising prices to consumers.

In conclusion, it could be argued that both consumers and business customers may benefit from fining airlines for illegal practices. But they will only benefit if these fines do not lead to increased costs in future.

(40 marks)

(b) If there were no laws or regulations covering monopoly or anti-competitive practices then the operations of businesses would not be restricted. In the airline industry, for example, large airlines could operate unfettered by controls. Large organisations could also operate as cartels, agreeing to fix prices or control flight routes. It might be suggested that this could be extremely detrimental to customers. Prices may be fixed very high, raising the cost of flights. There would be no controls over this from a regulatory body. There would be no restrictions on activities to prevent competition. For example, some businesses may agree to lower prices for a period, forcing out low cost airlines, and once they have gone, raise prices again. New businesses will find it very difficult to enter a market, introducing competition on pricing or other services. Markets may be restricted, so that the dominant firms will only operate routes to destinations they feel are profitable.

On the other hand in some businesses there are arguments that monopolies should exist. In some cases only large firms can gain the economies of scale necessary to control costs and sell products at a competitive price. If there were too much legislation and regulations then such businesses would not develop. Further, in markets where large amounts of investment is needed, only large businesses are able to fund the expenditure needed for R&D and other activities. If regulations prevent these businesses developing, such products may not exist. This might be the case for certain life saving drugs, for example.

In conclusion, it could be argued that if there were no laws on monopoly or anti-competitive practices, consumers would be likely to suffer. However, in certain cases too much restriction can be a problem. So any monopoly legislation needs to be set at a level that allows businesses that require large-scale operation, even if they are monopolies, to develop.

(40 marks)

Question 1

(a) The Employment Relations Act, 1999 ensures that every employee who has been with an employer for a year has the right not to be unfairly dismissed. We will assume, for the moment, that John Smart has been employed for this period of time. Certain conditions are set out which stipulate unfair or fair dismissal under the conditions of the Act. Providing an employer acts 'reasonably', an employee can be made redundant if their job has disappeared (for example, if there is not enough work for that person to do). This is arguably a 'fair' reason for dismissal.

In John's case, he could argue that the employers did not act 'reasonably'. There appears to have been no consultation with John or with a worker representative, no reasons given for dismissal and no period of notice. In addition, John's job does not appear to have disappeared. In fact, the business employed another worker the next week, at a far lower salary. John perhaps could conclude that his dismissal was not fair, but a cost-cutting exercise by Jones and Harcourt.

(b) In John's situation, he is likely to feel he has been unfairly dismissed. John and his union representative (if he is a union member) may attempt to negotiate a settlement or reinstatement with Jones and Hadden. If they are unwilling to negotiate satisfactorily, a complaint must be made within a period before the end of contract to an industrial tribunal. Before the case reaches the tribunal, it may be possible for a settlement to be negotiated with the help of ACAS. However, if this is not the case John must attend a pre-hearing assessment to decide if he has a strong enough case to be heard by a tribunal. If the case is referred to a tribunal John is entitled to legal advice.

Question 2

(a) The national minimum wage raises the wages of low paid workers. For example, from October 2008 workers aged 18-21 must be paid a minimum of £4.77 an hour.

(b) A chain of department stores may argue that rises in the national minimum wage could affect the wage costs of businesses. If costs increase, businesses have various alternatives. One is to accept a cut in profits, which they would not want to do. A further option is to cut costs in other areas. It is argued that the rise in the minimum wage could lead to cuts in training costs and overtime. Some employers argue that higher wages mean that fewer workers can be employed. So a department store may suggest that an increase in the minimum wage would lead to job losses.

On the other hand, this does not appear to be supported by evidence. The Low Pay Commission, for example, suggested that job numbers in industries most affected by minimum wages have grown in the past. It is also argued that businesses have been able to absorb the higher wage costs. If this is the case then perhaps other costs have been reduced. Or perhaps the productivity of workers has increased. Alternatively demand may have risen so that the business can afford the higher costs as it has increased revenue. Whether this would be the case in October 2008 and after would remain to be seen.

Question 3

(a) (i) The Data Protection Act sets out principles which businesses must adhere to when dealing with employees' information. However, there are other laws which also protect employees at work. It could be suggested that the use of software by companies such as Black and Decker might help businesses comply with legal requirements in a number of ways. First, by monitoring emails it could prevent employees sending misleading data or misusing data. For example, it might prevent employees sending slanderous details about other employees. It may also prevent employees sending information for which the business could be held vicariously liable, if, for instance, employees sent information which might break copyright. It might also help businesses to ensure that communications conform to legislation in areas such as racial discrimination and follow company policy on areas such as equality of opportunity. Further, software might be used to ensure that all emails are confidential, to prevent access to other people's information. Lastly, it may be possible to monitor the use of computers in other ways. For example, a business may be able to monitor the use of the Internet to prevent access to illegal websites.

(ii) The use of software could however, in certain circumstances, break regulations regarding data protection. For instance, information may be accessed which is then used in other situations. An example might be if a discussion about future work conditions with the personnel department was then used to overlook an employee for promotion on the suggestion that they were looking for work elsewhere. Similarly, monitoring can be excessive, so the checking of every single email by a particular employee may be deemed to be victimisation and may place great stress on the employee in work. Also, keeping information about emails of a worker from an ethnic minority or who was disabled and not those of others might be breaking equal opportunities legislation. Further, keeping details of emails sent years ago which are then used as evidence of breaking conditions of service when conditions have changed may be breaking legislation. An example might be an email sent at 6pm in 2001 when a company policy saying that emails must not be sent after 5pm was introduced in 2005.

Case study

(a) It could be argued that health and safety legislation should be repealed. It might be suggested that health and safety legislation is damaging to businesses. Too much legislation leads to rising costs. Businesses must take steps to comply with legislation and this increases their costs. There is the cost of 'red tape'. One cost is continually assessing risk. Another is taking steps to protect employees to ensure that risks are removed and they are protected. Some businesses have suffered from bad advice from rogue consultants, perhaps incurring costs they did not need to pay. Failure to comply with legislation also has its costs, particularly if firms are found breaching legislation. They can be fined large amounts. For small businesses this can be damaging. Preparing for tribunals to deal with the many claims, some of which are untrue, can be particularly problematic for small businesses.

On the other hand health and safety legislation protects employees and to some extent businesses as well. Protecting key workers prevents them being harmed, taking time off work or even having to leave work. This may affect the productivity and profitability of a business. If key workers are injured then production may be affected. Orders may not be met on time. If they leave work then a business may be unable to replace them. It will also face the extra costs of recruitment and training.

There are also ethical issues associated with protection of employees. A business may feel that this is not really a business issue. But it can be, especially if it affects the image of the business. For example, an important employee may refuse to work for a business with poor health and safety standards. Consumers may refuse to buy the products of a business with poor standards, concerned about the quality of the products.

It is also argued that that the costs associated with health and safety compliance have been artificially inflated by rogue consultants. If this is the case then arguably regulation needs amending and tightening up rather than repealing.

In conclusion, it may be argued that purely from an ethical stance, health and safety legislation should not be repealed. But despite the cost associated with legislation, there are also business reasons why it should not be.

(40 marks)

123 Equal opportunities

Question 1

(a) Discrimination is where people are treated differently. In employment there are some situations where this is unlawful. In each case it might be suggested that discrimination may have taken place. In the first case two workers who are the same age and on the same scale are paid different amounts. When questioned, the employers stated that as the workers did not do exactly the same job, this accounted for the differences in pay. The Equal Pay Act and EU legislation conditions and its amendments may be used to argue that discrimination has taken place. For example, the workers are doing 'broadly similar work'. Also, they appear to be doing work that is of equal value as they make similar decisions and take similar responsibility. Further it could be argued that the terms and demands made on the workers are similar, as they are both on the same scale and again take similar decisions. Therefore it could be argued under the Equal Pay Act that they should be paid the same and discrimination has taken place.

In the second case an employee has taken time off to be a parent. On attempting to return to work the employee was told that she was likely to be unable to carry out her previous duties and that they were using the opportunity of her absence to make some staff redundant. It might be suggested that in this case EU regulations have been broken as they entitle workers to parental leave to have children. It could also be argued that sex discrimination has taken place because a female has been chosen to be made unemployed rather than a male, because of child rearing responsibilities. It is also unlawful in the UK to make employees redundant on grounds of pregnancy.

In the third case staff are being asked to improve the image of the business by wearing smart jackets. These jackets are uncomfortable, but only female staff are being asked to wear them. It is suggested that males do not need to as they can wear neat suit jackets. It might be argued that sex discrimination is taking place in this situation, which might be direct discrimination. Only women are being forced to wear the uncomfortable new uniform. Further, EU regulations state that there should be no discrimination in work conditions. It might be suggested that the uniform is part of the conditions of service and that females are being discriminated against as a result.

Whether any of these cases are actually cases of discrimination or not is likely to depend on rulings by an employment tribunal.

Question 2

(a) Discrimination in business may occur when one person or one group of people is treated differently to another. In some cases this is unlawful as the different treatment is deemed to be unfair. In the UK discrimination on grounds of ethnic grouping is unlawful. It might be suggested that some form of racial discrimination has occurred in the recruitment by public services in the past. Around 6% of the UK population were from ethnic minority groups in 2003. However, only 2% of ethnic minorities were employed in public services. In some parts of the country, notably areas of London, ethnic groups made up a larger part of the population, such as 20%. Further, figures showed that 1 in 10 public bodies had done nothing to comply with the Race Relations Act. These figures might indicate some discrimination in employment. For relative equality, it could be argued that the same percentages of population should be employed in the workforce. If not, it could be argued that 'white' candidates have been favoured in recruitment compared to ethnic minorities.

(b) The London Fire Brigade has made some changes to comply with the Race Relations Act. This sets targets for the employment of ethnic minority workers in public services, such as police forces. So, for example, it might be suggested that a certain percentage of police officers should be from ethnic minority groups. If this was the case, and targets were met which better reflected the proportion of ethnic minorities in the population, it could be argued that discrimination had been reduced.

The London Fire Brigade held open days in mosques and at religious festivals. These are likely to have been attended by a large percentage from ethnic minority groups. They would help to raise the profile of the Fire Brigade, provide information and promote it as an occupation for members of ethnic minorities. Members of ethnic minority groups may be more motivated to apply for jobs in the Fire Brigade as a result. Further, the introduction of mentoring may help to overcome problems of integration when ethnic minority employees first begin. This may be more difficult when integrating with the majority of employees who come from another culture. Again, more members of ethnic minority groups may be more motivated to apply for jobs in the fire service as a result.

In themselves, these changes do not guarantee to remove discrimination. For example, it could be argued that discrimination might still exist if 500 members of ethnic minorities are encouraged to apply for jobs but only one person was employed.

Question 3

(a) A number of trends can be seen from the figures. The first figure shows the percentage of people who feel that their job application was affected by their age, particularly because they were felt to be too old. Between the ages of 45-49 and 50-54 there was an increase in the percentage of people who felt that their application was affected by their age. In particular more women felt this to be the case, increasing from less than 5% to over 7%. For age groups above the age of 54, there is a progressive decline in the proportion of people who think their application was affected by their age. Those who have reached the state retirement age of over 65 tend to feel that their age has relatively no effect.

The second figure shows the percentage of older people who have health problems. Generally older people tend to have more health problems. For example, in the age group 45-49 around 15% of people have health difficulties. In the age group 55-59 this has risen to around 25%. However, in the age group 65-69 men in particular have problems. Around 35% have difficulties, over 10% more than females. There are some figures which buck this trend. For example, a slightly smaller percentage of males aged 50-54 have health problems than those aged 55-59.

(b) The trends illustrated in the figures may give some indications why age discrimination takes place. The first table suggests that less than 10% of older people feel that their applications have been influenced by their age. It could be argued that this shows that age discrimination does not really play a part in job applications. On the other hand some may suggest that this figure is quite high. Even if only a certain amount of these people have actually faced discrimination, this could imply that at least some age discrimination in jobs does exist. Further, the largest proportion is those aged 45-49 and 50-54 and there is a slight increase in the proportion who feel their age may have affected their application in these age groups. This might suggest that people around the age of 50 may face some age discrimination, particularly women. This is the age when people who are made redundant often find it difficult to get employment. Some may have been relatively highly paid managers who may have worked for a business for a number of years. Businesses may not be keen to take on such workers, wishing to employ younger people at lower wages. Also, businesses may suggest that it is more difficult to retrain such workers and that it is harder to 'teach an old dog new tricks'. Some businesses may fear that these workers may be less flexible than younger workers as they have years of experience of working in particular ways. Women in particular may find it hard to get jobs as they may be nearing the retirement age.

The second figure might be used by businesses to argue that older workers are more likely to have health difficulties. There is around a 20% greater chance that men aged 65-69, in particular, will have health problems compared to those aged 45-49. Health problems may cost a business money. Health cover and insurance premiums may be higher. Days at work lost due to illness may be greater. There will also be the cost of lost work and finding replacement staff, perhaps for short periods at high wages or paying overtime to other staff.

Case study

(a) A top City of London financial institution may consider that it is more important to make money than worry about discrimination. Such an organisation is likely to be a private or perhaps a public limited company. It will be owned by shareholders. They will want the business to be successful to make profits and earn dividends. Similarly managers will want the business to make profits. Higher profits for the business could lead to higher salaries. Part of their earnings may be bonuses based on the performance of the business. Alternatively they may be on performance-related pay, which depends on the business making money. Further, being involved in discrimination issues can be expensive. Ensuring that a business complies with legislation can lead to costs. This may be in the form of form filling or training to make sure that employees comply with legislation. It might complicate the recruitment process. Also, time taken up carrying out duties to ensure discrimination does not occur could be time spent earning for the business.

However, discrimination can affect both income and costs of a business. There is evidence that discrimination is still widespread in business. Despite looking as if businesses are recruiting more women, they are 'not following through'. It could be argued that this restricts the potential of the business to make money. Discriminating against women for certain posts may mean that the most suitable candidate is not appointed. It restricts the quality of applicants for new posts. Women might be higher income earners for the business, but would not get a chance to prove this. Further, as the data suggest, ignoring

discrimination issues can be very costly. A business would need to make a lot of money to compensate for the £19 million damages it would have to pay if it lost a tribunal case.

In conclusion, it could be argued that making money is certainly important for City of London financial institutions. But ignoring discrimination legislation could affect their ability to make money.

(40 marks)

(b) It might be argued that equal opportunities legislation is not necessary to prevent discrimination in the workplace. Some argue that businesses are increasingly viewing discrimination as poor business practice and are able to self-regulate. Discrimination can give a business a poor image. This might affect recruitment and sales. Employing a less able candidate could affect profits. Discrimination may also affect the motivation at the business. Employees may lack motivation, particularly female employees. If female employees are not given the same opportunities as male colleagues over flexible work arrangements, for example, they are likely to become disillusioned. But this may also affect the operation of the business, as allowing flexibility may improve productivity.

On the other hand there is strong evidence that legislation is required. Discrimination appears to exist in many areas of UK business. Only 20 per cent of MPs are women. Women in the City are paid 43 per cent less than men. Various cases brought to industrial tribunals highlight the fact that although businesses appear to make statements about the importance of diversity issues, this may just be something that can be used to fight cases and support them against criticism.

In conclusion, therefore, it might be argued that businesses might suggest that discrimination is falling and that self-regulation could be possible. However, in practice there is still evidence of discrimination between sexes, which highlights the need for legislation.

(40 marks)

Case study

(a) The aim of Stop Huntingdon Animal Cruelty (SHAC) is to close the Huntingdon Life Sciences (HLS) animal testing laboratory near Cambridge within three years. SHAC is an animal rights pressure group. In its attempts to further its interests the SHAC pressure group has carried out a variety of pressure group activities. These include traditional campaign techniques, such as picketing the laboratory, lobbying of politicians to close the plant and encouraging the media to represent its views sympathetically. Further, it has targeted suppliers to attempt to prevent other businesses and individuals dealing with HLS and to affect its operations. These have included gas suppliers and shareholders. They faced picketing and demonstrations. The website of the pressure group has also been used to advertise its campaign, using emotive images and language to support its cause.

However, it has also been reported that more extreme measures were carried out. These may have included threats made to staff at HLS, damage to cars, attacks on staff and intimidation of suppliers, such as farmers who supply feed. SHAC however disclaimed all knowledge of these activities.

It could be argued that the promotional activities of SHAC have been effective to some extent. It has certainly raised awareness about animal testing and its problems amongst people in general. Its aggressive campaign techniques have been very effective in highlighting the plight of animals in laboratory testing. Visions of cruelty to animals and their conditions have appeared in the media and make a very powerful argument against animal testing for drug development. Many people are likely to have been shocked by these images, such as the video footage released showing breaches of animal protection laws. As a result support for the pressure group may have increased. It could also be argued that some of the other tactics have been effective, especially those aimed at persuading suppliers to cease dealings with HLS. It is reported that many suppliers pulled out of dealings with HLS as a result of its activities.

On the other hand there is evidence that HLS is still able to operate despite the disruption and any growing concern about its activities. The suppliers that pulled out of dealings with HLS were replaced. So although in the short term there was likely to have been disruption, this could perhaps have only been a short term inconvenience without causing any major problems. For example, when financial transactions became a problem, the Bank of England took over. Further, the UK government appears to have stepped in to solve some of the difficulties. Legislation was introduced to make it illegal to intimidate suppliers dealing with HLS. Police were also given arrest powers in certain circumstances. The new laws are not perhaps as stringent as HLS would like, but they may prevent some of the more extreme actions that allegedly were taken by some in the cause.

In conclusion it could be argued that part of the strategy of SHAC has been very effective. It is likely to have raised awareness of animal testing in general and may have ensured that HLS made more stringent efforts to comply with legislation. When animal rights were breached, staff were sacked. Attempts to disrupt activities may also have been relatively successful. However, the government has introduced legislation to ensure that all protests are within certain limits. Suppliers that have pulled out have been replaced. And at the time of writing the operation was still continuing. So the aim to close the plant has not yet been achieved. Whether it will be in future remains to be seen.

(40 marks)

(b) As a managing director you may feel that you should not accept the contract. There are perhaps reasons why you might not want to provide chemicals to the business. First, you may be concerned with the impact that any protests would have on your own business. Demonstrations and picketing by animal rights activists may slow up delivery, which could be expensive. It may not be possible to make deliveries at certain times, which could cause cash flow problems. Demonstrations at your own plant may affect your own business operation. Some workers may not be prepared to make deliveries and may not wish to cross the picket lines. Staff at your operation may fear possible intimidation from individuals who want to further the cause of animal rights protection.

You may also be concerned about your own image when dealing with the business. Your company may be portrayed in the press in bad light. This could affect your position with other businesses. Some have ethical policies and are not prepared to trade with companies that they consider act in a less than ethical way. As a result you may lose orders or find orders cancelled. A further reason might be your own views. You may be against animal testing on principle. Or your business may have its own ethical policies and any dealings with animal testing businesses may be excluded. In this case you may turn down the contract on ethical grounds.

On the other hand there may be reasons why you might accept the contract. One might be your own views again. For example, you or your business may feel that animal testing is justified. Providing animal conditions meet with legislation regarding protection, you may consider that advances in the field of human medicine justify animal testing. Or you may have a relative or friend who has benefited from developments in medicine that have resulted from animal testing. In either case your views may be influenced by these factors and lead you to accept the contract.

Another view might be that companies are in business to make profit. If a profitable order comes in then you may consider that you should accept this. It will make money for the business which will enable a profit to be made, workers to be employed and a service to be provided to other stakeholders. You may consider that making a profit is the main aim of your business and that the nature of the contract should have little or no influence. You may also consider that protection offered by legislation is adequate and that any disruption to your activities is likely to be minimal. You may also feel that any effect on your image is likely to be minimal.

In conclusion, it could be argued that personal and business views about the nature of HLS's activities and the extent to which profit can be made are likely to be the two major influences on your decision. If you are against the activities of HLS in principle and feel it is unethical or if you feel that there will be so much disruption and bad publicity that your business will suffer, you will not, perhaps, accept the order. If you feel that the prime aim is to make profit above all and that animal testing is justified, you are more likely to accept the order.

(40 marks)

125 | Business ethics

Question 1

(a) Ethical businesses are arguably those businesses that make morally correct decisions. Some, such as animal rights activists, might argue that a business such as Huntingdon Life Sciences can never be an ethical company. They would argue that from their viewpoint it is morally wrong to experiment on animals, no matter what the reason. The business and those who support experiments would counter that whilst experiments may not be ethical they are necessary as they allow the business to develop medicines and drugs that could potentially help benefit humanity by preventing or curing illnesses.

(b) Those who take the view that animal experimentation should not take place under any circumstances would argue that pharmaceuticals companies should not deal with Huntingdon Life Sciences as a matter of principle. They would argue that it is immoral to experiment on animals and that other businesses that deal with the company are perhaps acting in an immoral way by being associated with Huntingdon Life Sciences. Customers of Huntingdon Life Sciences also may decide not to use the company simply because they do not want to be targeted by animal rights protesters. It may be easier simply to use another company which is not so much in the sights of animal rights protesters.

On the other hand, pharmaceutical companies might argue that the law should protect them from illegal protests or threats and that they should be allowed to carry on their businesses. Businesses are in business to make a profit and as long as they can make money by using the services of Huntingdon, they should be allowed to continue. In some cases they might argue that there is no alternative to further scientific and pharmaceutical development than to use the services of Huntingdon.

In conclusion, it could be argued that the main factors that are likely to determine whether a pharmaceuticals company uses the services of Huntingdon are the safety of employees, profits and ethics. If they believe experimentation to be unethical or that protests may affect profit they may stop using the services of Huntingdon Life Sciences.

Question 2

(a) Fairtrade certification is given to products that meet environmental, labour and development standards. It is being given to Tate & Lyle sugar packets sold in the UK but manufactured in Belize. This may have certain benefits for the business. It may attract customers to buy Tate & Lyle sugar and other products sold by the company. Some people are ethically conscious and want to buy products they feel are benefiting growers in less developed countries. Tate & Lyle may see increased sales, higher revenues and greater profits as a result. On the other hand there are possible disadvantages. The main issue is perhaps increasing costs. To gain Fairtrade certification Tate & Lyle will have to pay growers a social premium of around £2 million a year.

The extent to which the advantages will outweigh the

disadvantages may depend on the extent to which sales revenues increase more than the £2 million cost increase per year. As the article states, the impact is difficult to quantify. Sales increases may or may not be greater than costs. The agreement may not cover sales of industrial sugar, a much larger operation. So increases in sales may not be that great. On the other hand, the increases in costs may or may not be a large part of total costs.

Case study

(a) There are arguments that Nike should source its products mainly from low cost locations in the Third World rather than US factories. From an ethical point of view adopting such as stance would benefit suppliers in these countries. Nike would then be seen as an ethical business. There could be a number of benefits for workers in these countries. They could gain higher incomes than if the business did not buy supplies from these countries. They may gain better work conditions if Nike forces suppliers to meet its code of conduct. They may also gain from other initiatives, such as lending programmes.

On the other hand, sourcing products from low cost countries may not always benefit people in those countries. Nike has been accused of employing child labour in countries such as Cambodia for example. Some workers may also work in intimidating conditions. They may also carry our tedious and hard work, repetitively.

In conclusion, from an ethical standpoint Nike should only source its products from low cost locations in Third World countries if it is able to secure acceptable work conditions, similar to those in the USA. It must also avoid using child labour and allow workers to gain from higher earnings. Only then will it be said to be acting ethically.

(40 marks)

(b) There are likely to be certain costs in involving other companies to monitor supply chain conditions. There are likely to be the financial costs involved in the joint operation. This may include things like extra communications. There may need to be extra staff employed to carry out the monitoring and extra paperwork and form filling. There could also be delays caused. Discussions may take place over the exact nature of changes in the work conditions. This takes time and it may affect production. Further, involving another partner may lead to disputes. There could be differences of opinion between Nike and the other company about the level of payments necessary or the extent to which the work conditions need to change. If another company insists on spending on better conditions then costs could rise more than the business might think is acceptable. If this is the case then suppliers may become unprofitable.

On the other hand involving other businesses may have benefits. It may be difficult to monitor all operations. Spreading this task over a number of companies may prevent suppliers slipping through the net and introducing poor work conditions. Other companies may also have different views. This can sometime be helpful. For example, they may have ideas on improving conditions without incurring large costs. The costs of monitoring may also be shared with others.

In conclusion, it could be argued that there are costs involved in working with other companies. But if the arrangements are planned effectively then they may help to prevent the situations that have led to Nike facing criticism. If the business can achieve this, then it will be going a large way to improving conditions for its suppliers. As a result its image, and possibly sales, may benefit.

(40 marks)

126 Business and the environment

Question 1

(a) The private costs to Shell of the disposal of the Brent Spar oil platform were the costs of preparing the platform for sinking and the costs of sinking the platform (if that had actually gone ahead). Such costs would have included labour costs, management costs, raw material costs and transportation costs. The costs of reusing the platform again include all the costs involved in recycling it for an alternative use. For example, the business would have needed to dismantle the platform and was likely to have to alter component parts.

(b) The negative externalities arising out of disposing of Brent Spar in the deep Atlantic would have been the pollution to the sea bed and possibly the ocean itself. The precise nature of negative externalities arising out of this method of disposal were fiercely debated at the time between Shell and Greenpeace. Shell may have argued that disposing in a deep ocean would have caused relatively limited damage. Pressure groups argued that the dumping would cause even further damage to an already overpolluted area. Because the second method of disposal involved the recycling of the oil platform, there would be few negative externalities arising out of this other than those relating to its use as a quay.

(c) The positive externalities arising out of the dumping of the Brent spar oil platform would have been limited. However, they might have included the income earned by tug boat businesses involved in the towing of the platform. The positive externalities arising out of the platform's use as a quay would include the jobs created by such a development and the amenity value of such a development to local residents. They would also have included the reduction of use of natural resources because recycled parts were used instead.

Question 2

(a) There is a number of controls on environmental costs mentioned in the article. First might be the regulation of the quantity of carbon dioxide emissions. The EU set limits on the quantity of carbon dioxide which can be emitted by businesses. Firms which produce and emit more than the legal amount will be fined. This aims to control emissions through increasing the costs of production for businesses which create pollution and setting limits on the legal level permitted. A second method, related to controlling the quantity of carbon dioxide emitted, is the use of permits. Businesses buy permits which enable them to produce a certain amount of carbon dioxide emission. If a business does not produce as much as the permit allows, then it can sell the permit on to firms which produce more than the prescribed amount. In the longer term, the number of permits available to buy is reduced, making it more expensive and more difficult for businesses to pollute and reducing the quantity of pollution which can be created. This encourages firms to find cheaper and cleaner methods of production. Finally, emission limits for power stations have been reduced, preventing them from producing their previous levels of pollution.

(b) It is likely that the competitiveness of the UK industry will be affected by these controls in different ways. The allocation of permits and control of emissions is likely to result in increased costs for firms. Firms will either have to pay for the permits, or they will have to develop cleaner methods of production to remain within the legal limits. This will result in higher costs which may then be passed onto the consumer in the form of higher prices. However, this is unlikely to affect the competitiveness of UK firms within the EU as they are all affected by the same law, but firms who trade outside the EU will find it more difficult to compete as their competitors may not be bound by similar legislation. It is possible that it will not affect all UK firms' competitiveness. Those firms who are already polluting below the legal level will benefit, as they will be able to sell their permits on to other firms at a higher price, reducing their costs. Alternatively, they will not be affected by regulations as their pollution production falls below the legal level anyway. It is likely that in the long term it may benefit most firms, as prior investment into developing cleaner and better production methods may result in reduced costs.

Question 3

(a) Charging for plastic bags might be seen as effective marketing. Marketing can be said to be about four Ps. One of these is promotion. Charging for the bags gives a clear indication that the business is concerned about the effect of the bags on the environment. It is giving any money it earns from the bags to charity, again showing its socially responsible attitude. Some argue that taking an ethical stance in business is attractive to customers.

(b) The banning of plastic carrier bags by government might benefit businesses. Cynics suggest that their profits could increase. This might be because they will no longer need to manufacture bags which are then given away free. Costs will fall and profits will increase.

The environment may also benefit. There will be fewer bags for landfill sites. It will also prevent waste and litter in streets. However, banning plastic bags may not be as beneficial as people might think. If they are replaced with paper bags, then the energy used is greater. This might waste more resources and lead to pollution.

Case study

(a) It could be argued that there are benefits to supermarket chains in reducing the packaging on their products and making the packaging recyclable. Table 1 shows that potentially they have a large amount of packaging that could be recycled. One benefit might be that less packaging means that the production costs of the product may fall. If packages are smaller and weigh less then distribution costs may also fall. If costs fall businesses may be able to reduce prices, leading to increased sales. Recycling may attract customers who are concerned about the environment to buy the products. Reduced packaging may also prevent businesses being fined for dumping, for example.

On the other hand, there are costs associated with both recycling and reducing packaging. Using recyclable packaging may be more expensive then other types of packaging. Further, even if recyclable products are used, there is some debate as to what is deemed recyclable. Some councils will collect cardboard, when others will not, for example.

Reducing the packaging may have implications for the business. It may make the product appear less substantial so it affects the image of the product and the price that can be charged. Less packaging may also lead to damage in transit.

A supermarket chain would need to consider to what extent the benefits outweighed the costs. If the fall in production costs and the improvement in the image of the business in an increasingly environmentally conscious world was of benefit, then reducing packaging and using recyclable packaging might be in its commercial interests. It would need to ensure however that the goods did not suffer as a result.

(40 marks)

127 | Corporate responsibility

Question 1

(a) Lucent was fined $2.5 million by the US Court of Justice under the Foreign Corrupt Practices Act. The fine was for attempting to bribe Chinese officials in the telecommunications market. They were invited to the US, but instead of visiting the facilities for any period the enjoyed sightseeing tours, paid for hotels and spending allowances. It could be argued that the US court saw this as a bribe by the company to encourage Chinese companies to buy telecommunications equipment.

(b) Some might suggest that bribery should be allowed. If a business wants to win a contract then it should be allowed to 'pay' for this if it can afford to do so. The bribe is coming from the funds of the business that is doing the bribing and it is their choice to do so. The people being bribed also have a choice - to accept or not accept the bribe. In some countries, bribery is part of daily business life. For example, in certain countries bribery is simply seen as another cost of production or service provision. Officials may be bribed to allow construction firms to win contracts. Construction businesses may be bribed by suppliers of building materials.

However, in Europe and the US bribery is seen as an anti-competitive, unethical and illegal practice. Offering bribes to win sales in emerging markets, such as China and India, is illegal. Governments create laws to prevent such practices. Without legislation there would be unfair business. Large companies that can afford to bribe would win all the business. They would get larger. Small, potentially profitable and more efficient businesses, may be forced out of business. Consumers may suffer as large businesses force up prices. Businesses are also increasingly responding to concerns about social responsibility. If consumers see that they are acting in a corrupt way, they may boycott their products. Pressure groups may develop to raise awareness of their activities. Sales may suffer. So for both legal, ethical and perhaps profitable reasons, bribery should not be allowed to win contracts in emerging markets.

Case study

(a) British American Tobacco (BAT) is a manufacturer of tobacco products. It could be argued that BAT is making a 'controversial and dangerous' product. The outgoing chairman suggested this in 2004. However, he also argued that this does not mean that the business cannot be socially responsible. He and others may argue that social responsibility takes a variety of forms. These can be illustrated from the activities of BAT.

For example, the business stresses in its social report that its strategies include a focus on responsibility. It sees responsibility as fundamental to building long term stakeholder value. Managing the business responsibly is also vital. In this view the business may consider that it has a responsibility to its overall stakeholders in the business. These might include shareholders. It is the responsibility of a limited company to ensure that the interests of its shareholders are protected. They have invested in the business and expect to see a return. So making a profit and paying them a dividend might be seen as operating responsibly. In 2003 the company made a profit of £788 million after tax. The holders are also concerned about their share value. A company that continues to make profits is likely to have shares with a relatively high value, which is likely to make

shareholders satisfied. In 2006 the number of employees rose to over 97,000 and taxation paid increased to over £16 billion.

Other stakeholders in the business may also consider its activities to be responsible. Employees, for example, may benefit if the business does well and hires extra staff. In 2003 BAT employed nearly 87,000 workers and had 87 factories in 66 countries. In 2006 it employed over 97,000. Some of the factories may be in less developed countries, providing vital employment and income, and helping economic growth. Governments may also benefit from the activities of the business. In 2003 it paid £14 billion in tax worldwide. In 2006 this was £16 billion. This vast payment will have provided large amounts of revenue to fund government activities in areas such as health and social services.

There are certain other areas of BAT's operations that might be considered socially responsible. In 2003 it gave £12.7 million and in 2006 £17.6 million in charitable and community donations. It supports charity work in any area of the world. For example, it was involved in poverty relief in Vietnam and helped to develop businesses and social projects such as water pump stations. In 2003 it spent £34.8 million and in 2006 £23.6 million on environmental projects and health and safety. This might suggest that it is making efforts to improve not only the work conditions of employees but also the environments in which its factories operate. Further, BAT appears to have made real efforts to reduce the amount of waste it produces. Over the period 2002-2006 the amount of non-hazardous waste and hazardous waste it produced fell by 14 per cent. This was also a 5.9 per cent reduction per million cigarettes produced. The business could argue that waste management is an important criterion in assessing social responsibility and that it has been relatively successful in cutting the amount of waste it produces.

On the other hand, there is evidence to suggest that the business is not operating as socially responsibly as it might want. One factor could be the relationship between male and female employees at the business. At all levels the percentages of males employed is far higher than females. Perhaps also important, the higher up the hierarchy of the business the worse the ratio of female to male employees. Only 6 per cent in 2003 and 7 per cent in 2006 of female employees were senior managers.

A survey named BAT as the worst of Britain's top 50 companies for social responsibility. Perhaps the argument here is that BAT will always be reflected poorly in such surveys as it is the nature of the product that may be the major influence on people's view of social responsibility. On this argument it will never be possible for a company selling 'a controversial and dangerous' product to operate in a socially responsible way. No matter what other efforts it makes, it will always be producing a product which warnings on packets show can be damaging to heath.

It could also be argued that BAT's efforts to be socially responsible are insignificant and largely there for public relations reasons. For example, its £12.7m spending in 2003 for community and charitable projects was just 0.05 per cent of sales turnover and 1.6 per cent of profit after tax.

In conclusion, a business that produces a 'controversial and dangerous product' can act in a socially responsible way if a variety of factors is taken into account and they are all given similar weightings of importance. It is then a case of assessing whether the performance of these criteria means that the positives outweigh the negatives. However, if the one major factor is the nature of the product and this outweighs all other factors, then it might be suggested that tobacco manufacturers can only operate in a socially responsible manner to a limited extent.

(40 marks)

Question 1

(a) Automation is the replacing of employees with machines in the production process. Robots are machines used in the assembly of car parts to make the final vehicle. Robot arms, for example, can carry parts to other production points in the assembly process or be used in dangerous jobs such as welding parts together.

(b) There are certain advantages to car manufacturers in using robots. Robots do not join trade unions so there is no industrial unrest. They do not demand pay rises so there are no regular increases in costs. They can carry out dangerous jobs safely which might lead to difficulties for employees. They also avoid human errors in production, which can lead to delays or costly errors for a business. They are accurate every time and can carry out detailed and complex tasks with precision.

(c) There are reasons why car manufacturers have started to use less technology and rely on human resources. First, robots can prove expensive. The initial cost is high and they are costly to replace, especially as new technology changes rapidly and robots need updating. Breakdowns prove costly as well, as production has to stop until robots are replaced. Second, robots are inflexible. They are suited to making a standard product in large quantities, but changing production techniques for different parts or products can be time consuming and costly. This is the case not only in the final assembly process, such as installing windows, but in the manufacturing system where businesses often need to change to another product to react to changes in demand.

Case study

(a) Technological change is important in new products. In the case of electrical goods, for example, the technical nature of the product must change to keep pace with the latest developments in technology. But it is also important in new production processes. As technology develops it changes the way in which products are designed and manufactured.

Kesslers makes display stands for retailers. There are many types of display available. Kesslers makes 1,000 types a year. They use a variety of machines. The designs of these machine change rapidly and each year about 80 per cent of display styles change. Display stands are likely to involve some technology. Developments in stands might incorporate the latest lighting or moving parts. As technology develops then the product is likely to become more sophisticated and incorporate the latest technological applications.

However, it could be argued that developments in technology are far more important to the production process for Kesslers. There is a number of reasons for this. First, the many different designs and the fact that they change every year means that Kesslers will need design and production software that is adaptable and flexible, easy to change to react to different styles. Customers often want to change designs at a late stage, so machines also need to be able to react to this quickly and cost effectively. It will also need machinery that is accurate and can handle complex cutting processes, such as the cutting of metal on the shop floor. Further, instructions need to be passed effectively from one machine to another quickly, as in the situation where digital instructions from the designer are sent via computer within 20 minutes to the production process.

In conclusion, it could be argued that although changes in technology will have some effect on the product made by Kesslers, it is changes in the technological nature of the business process that are more important. Given the requirements of the design and production processes at Kesslers, technological change is essential for the business to operate effectively and meet the needs of customers.

(40 marks)

(b) There are many advantages to Kesslers of using new technology.

Using computer aided design and manufacturing processes, often referred to as computer integrated manufacturing, can help a business design quickly and accurately. Designs can also be changed easily to meet customers' needs. This flexibility is attractive to customers of the business.

However, the introduction and use of technology may not be without its problems. There is a major cost of investment. Machinery is expensive to buy and it will need maintaining and constantly updating, costing around £500,000 a year. There is also the cost of training staff. Staff will need initial training and constant updates as new machinery is bought. Training costs are £80,000 a year. There will also be training in new techniques, such as lean production methods. Further, there will need to be reorganisation after new technology is introduced. There may need to be changes in job roles or responsibilities. There is also the need to constantly update customers about the latest developments so that sales can be increased to justify the expenditure.

In conclusion, there are always likely to be some problems with introducing new technology. But it could be argued that given the success of Kesslers this is a price worth paying for the business. It is a successful company and Europe's largest maker of display stands. It has good relations with customers and it is able to meet their needs effectively. It might even be suggested that without introducing new technology into the design and production process the business would not be able to cope effectively with the changing needs of this market.

(40 marks)

Question 1

(a) Competitive markets are markets where there are many businesses, perhaps of similar sizes, all of which have little market power. To some extent businesses are price takers. Oligopolistic markets are where there may be many businesses, but only a few dominate the market. Businesses are affected by the actions of others. There is also strong branding and competition often takes place on this basis, rather than on price, although there may be short price wars.

To some extent UK manufacturing companies have been moving from competitive markets to oligopolistic markets. They are moving into fields where 'price competition is less important'. They are competing on factors such as quality and customer service. These are features of more oligopolistic markets.

(b) There might be certain advantages to businesses in moving to oligopolistic markets. They can to some extent set a price. Businesses in this market can often set premium prices. They can charge a higher price because of the branding and quality of products. They may therefore earn higher profits. Also, these markets have higher barriers to entry. The costs of entry to be able to compete with existing producers can be higher, preventing businesses joining the markets. This prevents new businesses joining the market and taking the profits of existing businesses.

(c) JCB might use a number of strategies to become dominant. One is to target market niches. The business has introduced specialist trucks and telescopic handlers into its product range. These are made by few other businesses. If it can get into the market early and set a relatively high price, it can make profits. But it can also achieve brand loyalty as these products are likely to be bought by the military or other businesses. Once contracts have been set in place, this may prevent others entering the market.

Question 2

(a) Business or generic strategies can be used by companies to gain a competitive advantage over their rivals. One strategy used by Fudges is differentiation. This is where a business makes a product that is different to those of competitors, with a unique selling point. Fudges makes high quality wafers, crackers and seasonal offerings, including cakes. It has a local brand image, from Dorset. Some of its products are still made by hand. It might also be argued that part of its strategy is differentiation focus. For example, it is working with companies such as Unilever and Tate & Lyle to produce products for smaller markets, such as Marmite biscuits.

(b) Fudges started as a bread making operation. In the late 1980s it was struggling as sales of bread fell. After moving out of bread making for a period, the business returned when there was spare capacity in larger premises. This too proved to be a problem. It could be argued that the business would not be able to achieve a competitive advantage in bread making unless it was also to establish a very differentiated product, perhaps in a small niche market. It might be able to sell speciality breads, for example. However, selling to a mass market, faced with competition from companies such as Warburtons and Premier Foods, it is unlikely to be able to gain a major competitive advantage.

Case study

(a) Car manufacturing is sometimes argued to be an oligopolistic market. It is dominated by a few very large companies. These include manufacturers such as Volkswagen and Ford. Many car producers sell worldwide, into many countries. The cars are often standard versions or versions with slight changes. There is strong branding of products. Within a product line there is often little price competition. Instead, features of the car that differentiate it from others are stressed in the marketing. It is difficult for new entrants to set up in competition. There are very high entry costs, such as the cost of manufacturing machinery and the cost of marketing.

The Nano has arguably introduced a greater element of competition into the market. It is a car that will sell at a lower price, $2,500, instead of the usual $7,000 price for cars with similar features. Low cost cars have been developed but nothing with such a low price. It is estimated that low cost vehicles could achieve a 13 per cent market share by 2010. This may encourage other manufacturers to produce similar cars and enter the market.

Whether the competitive environment will change could depend on the extent to which Tata can maintain the price and competitive nature of the car. For example, it is suggested that the Nano in its current version does not pass EU safety standards. If changes need to be made then the price might increase. So although competition might be greater in India, this might not be the case in other parts of the world.

(40 marks)

(b) A multinational car company such as Ford, could respond to the Nano in a number of ways. It could attempt to undercut the price of the Nano by introducing its own range of low cost cars. This is cost leadership according to Porter's business strategies. It would need to be careful when choosing this strategy. For example, it would need to make sure that if it introduced a car in India at such a low price, it could cover its costs. Large businesses can gain economies of scale, perhaps more so than a small manufacturer. And the Indian market is very large. So it may be able to produce a car in competition. However, if the price of the Nano had to rise to accommodate changes for the EU market, it might be able to charge a higher price than the $2,500 suggested, but still undercut the price of the Nano.

Another cost strategy could simply be to ignore the low cost market. The Chinese market is predicted to grow in future. Demand for cars is likely to be high. However, demand for small cars is limited, as people prefer larger vehicles to show status. Another strategy could therefore be to produce larger cars for the Chinese market but to make sure that costs are lower than the copycat products of Chinese producers.

Porter's analysis also suggests that a multinational could attempt to differentiate its products. For example it could use differentiation strategies, such as looking at energy saving vehicles. Or it could use differentiation focus strategies. This migth involve producing small vehicles for the Indian market that save on energy. Or it might involve concentrating on the Chinese market, selling larger, high value products with many features.

(40 marks)

Question 1

(a) The information in Figure 6 is presented using percentage component bar charts.
(b) The first chart shows the revenue contribution by product for confectionery. In the confectionery market Cadbury's generates revenue from the sale of chocolate, gum and candy. In 1997, more than 60 per cent of revenue was generated from the sale of chocolate. Also, only a very small proportion of revenue came from gum sales - less than 10 per cent. However, in 2006, the contribution to revenue made by chocolate sales fell sharply to under 50 per cent. There was a huge increase in the contribution made by gum. It rose from under 10 per cent in 1997 to over 40 per cent in 2006. The contribution made by candy fell slightly over the time period.

The second chart shows the contribution to confectionery revenue made by each region. In 1997, most of Cadbury's revenue, over 70 per cent, was generated in EMEA. However, by 2006, a much larger contribution was made by emerging markets in the Americas. It rose from about 13 per cent to over 25 per cent. The contribution from Asia Pacific did not change very much over the time period.
(c) Component bar charts allow more information to be shown when presenting information. Each bar in the charts is divided into a number of components. This method allows readers to make immediate comparisons between the components in the chart. For example, in the first chart it is clear that more revenue was generated from chocolate sales in 1997 than in 2006. The growth in gum sales is also shown very clearly. The main disadvantage of this method is that values are not shown. For example, the first chart does not show the total revenue generated from confectionery sales at Cadburys.

Question 2

(a)

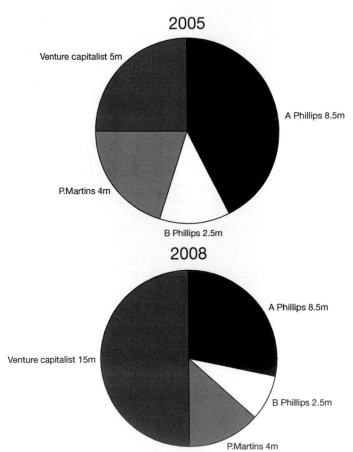

Question 2 continued

(b) Pie charts are an effective way of presenting certain types of data. They are particularly useful when showing a set of data made up of different parts. The relative importance of each part can be seen. For example, in this case, in 2005 Tony Phillips is clearly the largest shareholder in gamesroom.com. He has more shares than any other shareholder. It can also be seen that the company is under the control of the Phillips family. This is because they own more than half the company's shares between them. However, in 2008 it is clear from the chart that the venture capitalist is now the largest shareholder. Indeed, the venture capitalist now owns enough shares to control the company.

Unfortunately there are drawbacks with pie charts. Quite often, they do not allow precise comparisons to be made. For example, in this case in 2005, it is not easy to see that the venture capitalist has more shares than Paul Martins. It is also difficult to show changes in the size of the total pie. This is because it is difficult to compare the areas of two circles accurately. In this case the number of shares held in the company has risen from 20 million to 30 million. It is difficult to deduce the exact change when looking at these two pie charts.
(c) The pie charts show that the control of gamesroom.com has changed between 2005 and 2008. In 2008, Tony Phillips had the largest shareholding and along with Mrs B Phillips, completely controlled the company. However, in 2008 the venture capitalist owned the majority of shares and therefore took control.

Question 3

(a) The first graph shows the number of users the three companies has. Google has around 530 million unique users globally compared with slightly fewer for Microsoft and only around 480 million for Yahoo. All three companies have enjoyed a surge in visitors in February and March of 2007. Increases of around 20 million unique visitors were recorded. The second graph shows the global market shares for Microsoft, Google and Yahoo. The graphs show that Google has been the clear market leader over the time period and has increased its share from around 60 per cent to about 67 per cent over the time period. This increase in market share has been at the expense of both Yahoo and Microsoft. Microsoft has the smallest market share with less than 10 per cent.
(b) Using line graphs is an effective way of presenting certain types of data, particularly data that is linked by two variables. Line graphs are probably the most common type of method used to present data. The main advantage of line graphs is the way in which the reader can get an immediate picture of the relationship between the two variables. For example, when looking at the first graph in this case it is clear that all three search engines enjoy an increase in the number of visitors in February and March of 2007. It is also possible to take measurements from the graphs. For example, in the second graph you can see that Google has exactly 60 per cent share of the market at the end of 2006. Finally, as in this case, it is possible to show more than one line on a line graph. In both graphs there are three lines - one for each company. This allows comparisons to be made which is useful.

Case study

Note: in the first impression of the 4th edition there is a misprint. This has been corrected in reprints. (d) Should be 'What methods of presentation are being used in Figures 15 and 16.
(a) Businesses like BP generate huge quantities of data during their normal trading activities. Data can be stored on computer, manipulated, called up on screen at any time and presented in a wide variety of ways. Businesses use graphs, charts, tables and other pictorial methods of communicating data. Data is presented in these ways because information is often easier to understand, it takes less time to interpret, trends can be identified more easily, comparisons can be made and it may be possible to create an impact or image. BP presents data for a number of reasons. The main reason is to communicate information to its stakeholders such as shareholders, employees, customers, environmentalists, the Inland Revenue and managers. For example, shareholders will be concerned about the

performance of BP and may be interested in the data shown in Table 11 and Figure 15. On the other hand, employees and environmentalists may be interested in the data shown in Figure 16. Information is also likely to be used by the media. TV companies, newspapers, magazines and others may use data in their programmes and reports. Much of the data generated by BP is presented every year in the Annual Report and Accounts. This is sent to all shareholders but can be accessed online. **(6 marks)**

(b) The information is in the form of a table. A table is probably the best way to present this information. This is because it contains a mixture of both qualitative and quantitative information. There is also a wide range of variables being presented. These include sales, profit before tax and interest, profit for the year, capital expenditure, profit per share and so on. Other methods of presentation may not be suitable for this type of information. **(4 marks)**

(c) (i) The information in Figure 14 is presented using a line graph. A line graph shows the relationship between two variables, in this case time and the hypothetical £100 holding in shares. **(2 marks)**

(ii) Line graphs are probably the most common type of method used to present data. Line graphs show the relationship between two variables. The main advantage of line graphs is the way in which the reader can get an immediate picture of the relationship between the two variables. For example, when looking at the line graph, it is clear that the FTSE All World Oil and Gas Index has risen sharply over the time period. It has risen far more quickly than the other two variables. **(4 marks)**

(iii) The information in Figure 2 shows the TSR (total shareholder return) for BP compared with the FTSE 100 and the FTSE All World Oil and Gas Index. Plcs have to publish TSR by law. TSR shows how well BP has performed in relation to the dividends paid to shareholders and movements in the share price. In this case the TSR is shown along with two other performance indicators which are relevant to BP. In this case BP is both a constituent of the FTSE 100 and the FTSE All World Oil and Gas Index. The graph shows that BP's TSR has improved over the time period from £100 to about £125. This was slightly better than the FTSE 100 over the time period although it finished slightly below right at the end. However, BP did not perform very well compared with the FTSE All World Oil and Gas Index. This rose much more sharply than BP's TSR. At the end of the time period the FTSE All World Oil and Gas Index was over £250 - over £100 better than BP. **(6 marks)**

(d) (i) Figures 15 and 16 use bar charts to present data. The bar charts are parallel bar charts. Bar charts present information in the form of blocks or bars. The length of the bar or block illustrates a value and its importance. **(3 marks)**

(ii) The parallel bar charts show a variety of data about the performance of the business. Bar charts are an effective way to see how variable have changed. This can be shown using examples from

Figures 15 and 16. Figure 15 shows performance data. A bar chart in Figure 15 shows information about the dividends paid to shareholders. It shows that in pence, this has increased each year from 15p in 2004 to 21p in 2006. Figure 16 shows information that may reflect the social responsibility of the business to both its employees and the outside community. For example, a bar chart in Figure 16 shows the contribution made by BP to communities. This illustrates that the amount in $million has increased from 87.7 to 106.7. This could imply that the business is taking its social responsibility seriously. **(8 marks)**

(e) Some information suggests that BP has improved its financial performance over the last four years. For example, sales and other operating revenues have increased from $164,653 million in 2003 to $265,906 million in 2006. This is a 61 per cent increase over the time period. Profit before tax and interest has increased by a larger amount from $18,776 million to $35,158 million. This is an 87 per cent increase. This improvement is supported by the increase in profit per share for BP shareholders. It has risen from 56.14 cents in 2003 to 109.84 cents per share in 2006. This is a 95 per cent increase.

This is supported by the information relating to BP's financial performance. Between 2001 and 2006, the TSR (total shareholder return) has risen from £100 to about £125. This is a 25 per cent increase. However, this increase is not as good as the increase shown by the FTSE All World Gas & Oil Index. This has risen to well over £250 - significantly better than BP. Compared with the FTSE 100 Index, of which BP is also a constituent, the performance is about the same over the time period.

Figure 15 shows the return on capital employed (ROCE) for BP for the last three years. ROCE has increased every year from 16 per cent to 22 per cent. This appears quite good considering money placed in a bank would only generate between 5 and 6 per cent over this time period. It also shows the dividends per share between 2004 and 2006. This has also increased in every single year from 15.25p to 21.1p. The amount spent on capital expenditure by BP has also increased in every year from $13.8 billion to $16.9 billion. This suggests that BP has been able to sustain heavy investment over the time period.

Data in Figure 16 illustrates the corporate responsibility of the business. In each case there has been an improvement. The frequency of recordable injuries has fallen over the period. One bar chart shows greenhouse gas emissions by BP over a five year period. It shows clearly that CO_2 emissions have fallen between 2002 and 2006 from 82.4 million tonnes to 64.4 million tonnes. This suggests that BP has improved its environmental performance.

The data shown here suggest that BP's financial performance has improved over the time period. In some respects the improvements seem significant. For example, the profit per share has nearly doubled. However, to make a final judgement it would be prudent to compare BP's financial performance with that of other companies in the same industry. **(16 marks)**

Question 1

(a) (i) Mean = 220 ÷ 40 = £5.50.
(ii) Mode = £6 largest (18).
(iii) Median = 40 ÷ 2 = 20th item = £6.

x	f	fx	cf
£2	4	8	4
£4	10	40	14
£6	18	108	32
£8	8	64	40
	Σf=40	Σfx=220	

(b) (i) Mean = 320 ÷ 50 = £6.40, an increase of 90p.
(ii) Mode = £6 largest (18), so no change.
(iii) Median = 40 ÷ 2 = 20th item = £6, so no change.

x	f	fx	cf
£2	4	8	4
£4	10	40	14
£6	18	108	32
£8	8	64	40
10	10	100	50
	Σf=50	Σfx=320	

Question 2

(a) The modal group is the salary group with the largest number of employees, £10,001 - £11,000.

(b)

Salary range(£)	Number of employees(f)	Centre (x)	fx
8,001 - 9,000	6	8,500	51,000
9,001 - 10,000	15	9,500	142,500
10,001 - 11,000	40	10,500	420,000
11,001 - 12,000	25	11,500	287,500
12,001 - 13,000	10	12,500	125,000
13,001 - 14,000	4	13,500	54,000
	Σf=100		Σfx=1,080,000

$$\bar{x} = \frac{£1,080,000}{£100} = £10,800$$

(c)

Salary range (£)	Cumulative frequency
9,000 or less	6
10,000 or less	21
11,000 or less	61
12,000 or less	86
13,000 or less	96
14,000 or less	100

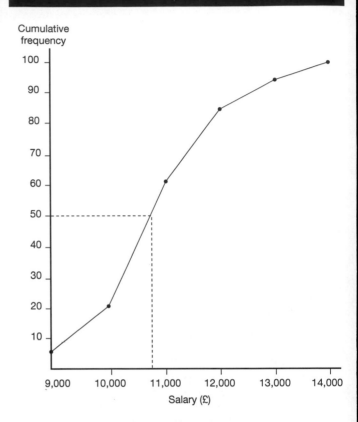

The median value can be found by looking at the salary level of the 50th worker shown in the figure below. The estimated median salary would be £10,700. This can be found by drawing the figure accurately on graph paper.

Question 3

(a) Mean = $\dfrac{\text{Total petrol consumption per annum}}{\text{Number of sales representatives}}$

= $\dfrac{10,400}{8}$ = 1,300 gallons per annum.

	NW	NE	SW	SE	WM	EM	WAL	SCOT
No. of gallons	1,200	1,360	1,140	1,000	1,150	1,300	1,250	2,000
Deviation from 1,300	-100	+60	-160	-300	-150	0	-50	+700
Sum (Σ) of deviations (ignoring signs) = 1,520.								

So, the mean deviation = $\dfrac{1,520}{8}$ = 190gpa.

(b) (i) 2,000 - 1,000 = 1,000gpa.
(ii) Figures in order are 1,000, 1,140, ,1150, 1,200, 1,250, 1,300, 1,360, 2,000. So:

Quartile 1 $= \dfrac{8}{4} = 2$ Second figure is 1,140gpa

Quartile 3 $= \dfrac{3 \times 8}{4} = \dfrac{24}{4} = 6$ Sixth figure is 1,300gpa

Interquartile range is 1,300 - 1,140 = 160gpa.

(c) Quantex PLC might want to analyse these figures in order to place tighter control over this item of expenditure of their sales representatives. It might therefore decide that using the range will be less useful, as it includes the extreme figures for consumption of petrol. The interquartile range ignores any extreme figures and should provide a better basis for judging the normal range of mileage that sales representatives are allowed. At the same time, however, the business would need to take into account the different distances between customers in the various areas. The representatives in Scotland might be provided with a higher target range than those in other areas because of this.

Question 4

(a)

	2005	2006	2007	2008
Managers	100	120	128	140
Administration	100	105	110	120
Production	100	125	140	150

Example: calculation of index for managers.
2005 £25,000 pay is given a value of 100.
2006 is calculated by 30,000 ÷ 25,000 x 100 = 120
2007 is calculated by 32,000 ÷ 25,000 x 100 = 128
2008 is calculated by 35,000 ÷ 25,000 x 100 = 140

(b) *(Note: There is a printing error in early editions of the book. The text should state (the other 15% being cleaners). This will be corrected in reprints. It does not effect the answer.)*

Employee	Employees x 2003 wage	Wage cost
Managers	5 x £35,000	£175,000
Administration	25 x £12,000	£300,000
Production	55 x £18,000	£990,000

(c) The index shows that production workers have seen their average wages rising most rapidly of these three groups of workers, ie there has been a 50% increase in the period 2000 to 2003. For managers there has been a 40 per cent increase, whilst for administration staff the increase has only been 20 per cent. The company will be able to use these figures in negotiations with representatives of the various groups over future pay. They can compare the increases which they have given with increases in other businesses or with national pay increases in manufacturing. This will help them to decide if their workforce has been well treated in recent years, and if their future pay increases should be reduced. Pay increases of 40-50 per cent in the last 3 years do appear to be generous. Only with the administrative workers do they not appear to have evidence to support pay restraint. The index might also be used by the management as a basis for productivity negotiations. They might wish to tie future increases in average pay to future increases in productivity. Using index figures to represent such changes facilitates comparison because the same units are employed. For every one point increase in the wage index, they might expect to see a one point increase in output.

Quantity	Mid point	Before		After	
	x	f	fx	f	fx
1-10	5	16	80	36	180
11-20	15	44	660	44	66
21-30	25	84	2,100	112	2,800
31-40	35	142	4,970	162	5,670
41-50	45	204	9,180	182	8,190
51-60	55	160	8,800	184	10,120
61-70	65	138	8,970	136	8,840
71-80	75	114	8,550	92	6,900
81-90	85	62	5,270	30	2,550
91-100	95	36	3,420	22	2,090
		Σf=1,000	Σfx=52,000	Σf=1,000	Σfx=48,000

Case study

(a) (i) The mean quantity purchased is an average amount which is bought. EcoFibre is concerned about the average amount bought by consumers in a year of its low sugar grain bar, Nutrafibre, both before and after a marketing campaign.

(3 marks)

(ii) The standard deviation is the average deviation or difference from the mean. In the case of EcoFibre, it is the amount by which spending on Nutrafibre differs, on average, from the average amount bought by consumers, both before and after the marketing campaign.

(3 marks)

(iii) An index shows how a series of figures changes in relation to an initial or 'base' figure. Weighting adjusts these figures to take into account the relative importance of variables. In the case of EcoFibre, an index is calculated showing how expenditure on different products in a cereal bar range changes over four years, taking into account the relative importance of the expenditure on each of these products.

(3 marks)

(b) (i) The modal group is the group which appears most frequently.
The modal group before the marketing campaign is 41-50 purchases a year. This appears most frequently. 204 out of the 1,000 customers bought this number a year.
The modal group after the marketing campaign is now 51-60 purchases a year. This appears most frequently. 184 out of the 1,000 customers bought this number a year.

(2 marks)

(ii)
Mean before = 52,000 ÷ 1,000 = 52.
Mean after = 48,000 ÷ 1,000 = 48.

(8 marks)

Q'ty	Mid-p	Before (mean = 52)						After (mean = 48)				
	x	f	fx	x-x̄	(x-x̄)²	f(x-x̄)²	f	fx	x-x̄	(x-x̄)²	f(x-x̄)²
1-10	5	16	80	-47	2,209	35,344	36	180	-43	1,849	66,564
11-20	15	44	660	-37	1,369	60,236	44	660	-33	1,089	47,916
21-30	25	84	2,100	-27	729	61,236	112	2,800	-23	529	59,248
31-40	35	142	4,970	-17	289	41,038	162	5,670	-13	169	27,378
41-50	45	204	9,180	-7	49	9,996	182	8,190	-3	9	1,638
51-60	55	160	8,800	3	9	1,440	184	10,120	7	49	9,016
61-70	65	138	8,970	13	169	23,322	136	8,840	17	289	39,304
71-80	75	114	8,550	23	529	60,306	92	6,900	27	729	67,068
81-90	85	62	5,270	33	1,089	67,518	30	2,550	37	1,369	41,070
91-100	95	36	3,420	43	1,849	66,564	22	2,090	47	2,209	48,598
		Σf= 1,000	Σfx= 52,000			Σf(x-x̄)² = 427,000	Σf= 1,000	Σfx= 48,000			Σf(x-x̄)² = 407,800

(c) (i) Standard deviation before = square root of f(x-x) ÷ Σf
= square root of 427,000 ÷ 1,000 = 20.66.
Standard deviation after = square root of f(x-x̄) ÷ Σf
= square root of 407,800 ÷ 1,000 = 20.19.

(8 marks)

(ii) Before the promotional campaign, on average, customers of Nutrafibre purchased 52 products a year, about one every week. This is based on the sample of market research results of 1,000 customers. The standard deviation was 20.66. After the promotional campaign the average spending on Nutrafibre was 48 and the standard deviation was 20.19.

The business might conclude from these results that the promotional campaign had not been a success. The average number of Nutrafibre products bought each year has in fact fallen by 4 products per annum. Also, the standard deviation has fallen. So for example, if a business expected 3 standard deviations at the top end of the range of purchases, before the promotional campaign this could have been 52 + (3 x 20.66) = 111. After the promotional campaign this could have been 48 + (3 x 20.19) = 108. Both these figures might suggest that the promotional campaign has been unsuccessful.

However, care must be taken interpreting results from a sample. The business may question to what extent the sample is representative of the population of customers who purchase the product. If a sample of a different 1,000 customer were taken or if a larger sample was taken different results might be found. For example, if 1 million customers bought the product each year then a sample of just 0.1% might be unrepresentative of the population. The business might also question whether the population was normally distributed above and below the mean and whether it was able to apply statistical analysis relating to a normal

distribution. For example, if most of its customers bought amounts below the mean, then assessing the top of the range at 3 standard deviations above the mean may be misleading.

(8 marks)

(d) (ii) EcoFibre is concerned generally about customer spending on cereal bars. It might use the results of its weighted average calculations to assess whether this concern is justified. It appears from the index that expenditure on certain products has increased, such as products A, B, D and F. In the case of product A, for example, expenditure has doubled over the four year period, so that a simple index calculation in year four gives an index of 200. The other products, products C and E, have seen a fall in expenditure. In each case a simple index shows a fall in the index number, from 100 to 70 and 80 respectively.

It is the fall in expenditure on these relatively important products over the four years which may lead the business to be concerned. Product C accounts for 30% of all expenditure. Product E accounts for 25%. So between them they account for over half of all expenditure on cereal products and revenue from these products. When a weighted index is calculated expenditure on these products has a major effect on the index of spending on all cereal products. In year 2 the stable spending on product C and the rise in spending on product E leads to a rise in the index of expenditure on cereal products. After four years, however, the index of spending has fallen, despite increases in spending on four of the six products. This is likely to indicate a fall in revenue for the business. Unless it is able to reduce costs in some way this is likely to lead to reduced profits from the cereal bar range and is a major concern for EcoFibre.

(12 marks)

(d) (i)

	Weight	Yr 1	Yr 1 Index	Yr 2	Yr 2 Index	Yr 2 WI	Yr 3	Yr 3 Index	Yr 3 WI	Yr 4	Yr 4 Index	Yr 4 WI
A	15	30	100	45	150	22.5	45	150	22.5	60	200	30
B	5	10	100	22	220	11	24	240	12	22	220	11
C	30	60	100	60	100	30	45	75	22.5	42	70	21
D	5	10	100	12	120	6	14	140	7	16	160	8
E	25	50	100	55	110	27.5	50	100	25	40	80	20
F	20	40	100	48	120	24	50	125	25	44	110	22
	200	100				Yr2 WI=121			Yr3 WI=114			Yr4 WI=112

Units		OCR	IB	EDEXCEL Business/ Economics and business	SQA (Higher)
1	The nature of business	F291	1.1		Business and contemporary society
2	Enterprise	F291	1.2	1.3.1	Business and contemporary society
3	Business ideas		1.2, 1.7	1.3.3	Business and contemporary society
4	Business plans		1.2	1.3.7	Business and contemporary society
5	Evaluating business start-ups		1.2	1.3.6	Business and contemporary society
6	Stakeholders	F291	1.4, 1.5	1.3.3	Business and contemporary society
7	Legal structure - sole traders and partnerships	F291	1.2	1.3.5	Business and contemporary society
8	Legal structure - limited companies	F291	1.2	1.3.5	Business and contemporary society
9	Legal structure - not for profit organisations	F291	1.2		Business and contemporary society
10	Legal structure - public sector organisations	F291	1.2		Business and contemporary society
11	The nature of marketing	F291, F292, F293	4.1	1.3.2, 1.3.3	Internal organisation
12	Market research	F291, F293	4.1	1.3.3	Marketing
13	Sampling	F292, F293	4.1	1.3.3	Marketing
14	Market segmentation	F292, F293	4.1	1.3.3	Marketing
15	Market size, share and growth	F292, F293	4.1	1.3.3	Marketing
16	The marketing mix	F292	4.1, 4.2	2.3.1a	Marketing
17	The product life cycle	F292, F293	4.3	2.3.1a	Marketing
18	New product development and product portfolio analysis	F292, F293, F297	4.3	2.3.1a	
19	Price - influencing the market	F292, F293	4.4	1.3.6, 2.3.1b	Marketing
20	Price - the influence of demand	F292, F293	4.4	2.3.1a, 2.3.1b	
21	Promotion	F292, F293	4.5		Marketing
22	Place	F292, F293	4.6		Marketing
23	Branding	F292, F293	4.3		
24	The market	F291	4.4	1.3.2	
25	Competition and business	F291	1.7	2.3.2b	
26	Marketing objectives	F292	4.1	2.3.1a	
27	Marketing budgets	F293	4.1	2.3.1a	
28	Marketing planning	F292, F293	4.1	2.3.1a	
29	Marketing strategies	F292, F293, F297	1.7, 4.1	4.3.2a	Marketing
30	International marketing	F293	4.7	3.3.1, 3.3.5	
31	E-commerce		4.8	2.3.2b	
32	Interpreting sampling results	F293	4.1		
33	Forecasting and analysis	F297	4.1		
34	Sources of finance	F291, 294	3.1	1.3.5	
35	Costs, revenue and profit	F292	5.2	1.3.6	
36	Contribution	F292	5.2	1.3.6, 4.3.2a	
37	Break-even analysis	F292, F296	5.3	1.3.6	
38	Applications of break-even analysis	F292, F294, F296	5.3	1.3.6	
39	Cash flow	F291, F292, F294	3.3	2.3.3a	Financial management
40	Improving cash flow	F292, F294	3.3	2.3.3a	Financial management
41	Setting budgets	F292, F294	3.4	2.3.3a	Financial management
42	Using budgets	F292, F294, F297	3.4	2.3.3a	Financial management
43	The role and objectives of accounting	F294			Internal organisation
44	Balance sheets	F292, F294	3.5	4.3.3a	Financial management
45	Business assets and depreciation	F294	3.5		
46	Calculating depreciation and stock values	F294	3.5, 3.6		
47	Working capital	F294	3.3	2.3.3a	
48	Profit and loss accounts and income statements	F292, F294	3.5	4.3.3a	Financial management
49	Measuring and increasing profit	F294	3.5	1.3.6, 2.3.3a	
50	Financial data and performance	F294			
51	Accounting concepts	F294			
52	Costing methods	F294, F296	5.2	4.3.2a	
53	Investment appraisal	F292, F294	3.2	4.3.2a	
54	Selecting financial strategies	F294	5.2		Financial management
55	Interpreting published accounts - ratio analysis	F294, F297	3.6	4.3.3a	Financial management
56	The value and limitations of ratio analysis	F294	3.6	4.3.3a	Financial management
57	Constructing accounts	F294	3.5		
58	The valuation of businesses				
59	Organisational structures	F291	2.2	2.3.4a	Internal organisation
60	Business organisation		2.2		Internal organisation
61	Measuring the effectiveness of the workforce	F295, F297		4.3.3a	
62	Recruitment	F291	2.1	2.3.4a	Human resource management
63	Selection	F291	2.1	2.3.4a	Human resource management
64	Appointment and termination	F291, F295	2.1	2.3.4a	Human resource management
65	Training and appraisal	F291, F295	2.1	2.3.4a	Human resource management
66	Motivation theories	F292, F295	2.5	2.3.4a	
67	Financial methods of motivation	F292, F295	2.5	2.3.4a	
68	Non-financial methods of motivation	F292	2.5	2.3.4a	
69	Management	F291, F295	2.4	2.3.4a	Internal organisation

Units	OCR	IB	EDEXCEL Business/ Economics and business	SQA (Higher)
70 Leadership	F292, F295	2.4	1.3.1	
71 Individuals in business				
72 Groups and teams in business	F295			
73 Competitive workforce structures	F295, F297	2.1, 2.2	2.3.4a	Human resource management
74 Workforce planning	F291, F292	2.1	4.3.3a	
75 Human resources management	F295, F295	2.1	4.3.3a	Human resource management
76 Communication	F295	2.3		
77 Representation at work	F295, F297	2.7		Human resource management
78 Industrial democracy, bargaining, consultation and participation	F295, F297	2.7		Human resource management
79 Industrial disputes	F295, F297	2.7		Human resource management
80 The nature of production	F296	5.1		Operations
81 Types of production	F292, F296	5.1		Operations
82 Capacity utilisation	F292, F296	5.7		Operations
83 Stock control	F292	5.7	2.3.2a	Operations
84 Quality	F292	5.4	2.3.2a	Operations
85 Customer service				
86 Purchasing				Operations
87 Using technology in operations	F296			Business and contemporary society
88 Business size	F291, F296	1.7	2.3.3b	
89 Economies of scale and resource mix	F291, F296	1.7	2.3.2a, 2.3.3b, 4.3.4a	Business and contemporary society
90 Mergers and takeovers	F296	1.7	4.3.4a	Business and contemporary society
91 Innovation, research and development	F296	5.6		Internal organisation
92 Product design		5.6	2.3.2a	
93 Factors affecting location	F296	5.5		
94 Location strategies	F296, F297	5.5		
95 Lean production	F292, F296	5.1, 5.4	2.3.2a	Operations
96 Resources and waste management	F296			
97 Efficiency and strategy	F296	5.7		
98 Critical path analysis	F297	5.8	4.3.2a	
99 Operations management techniques				
100 Aims and vision	F297	1.3	4.3.1a	Business and contemporary society
101 Objectives and mission	F291, F297	1.3	4.3.1a	Business and contemporary society
102 Strategy	F297		4.3.1a	Business and contemporary society
103 Planning	F297	1.5, 1.6	2.3.4b	Business and contemporary society
104 Decision making	F297	1.6	4.3.2a	Business and contemporary society
105 Decision trees	F297	1.6	4.3.2a	Business and contemporary society
106 Fishbone diagrams and force field analysis		1.6		
107 Contingency planning	F297	2.8	2.3.4b, 4.3.2a	
108 Organisational culture	F297	2.6	4.3.1a	
109 Implementing and managing change	F297	1.8	2.3.4b	
110 Growth and the business cycle	F297		1.3.4, 2.3.5b	Business and contemporary society
111 Interest rates	F297		1.3.4	Business and contemporary society
112 Exchange rates	F297		1.3.4, 2.3.4b	Business and contemporary society
113 Inflation and deflation	F297		1.3.4, 2.3.5b	Business and contemporary society
114 Unemployment	F297		1.3.4, 2.3.5b	Business and contemporary society
115 Taxation	F297		1.3.4	Business and contemporary society
116 Population	F291			Business and contemporary society
117 Labour markets and business	F297			Business and contemporary society
118 Globalisation and multinational companies	F297	1.9	3.3.4, 3.3.5, 3.3.6	Business and contemporary society
119 Government policy	F297		1.3.4, 2.3.4b, 4.3.3b	Business and contemporary society
120 The EU and other international trading blocs	F297	1.9	3.3.1	Business and contemporary society
121 Consumer protection	F293, F297		2.3.2a, 4.3.4a, 4.3.2b	Business and contemporary society
122 Protection at work	F295, F296, F297			Human resource management
123 Equal opportunities legislation	F295, F297			Human resource management
124 Pressure groups	F297			Business and contemporary society
125 Business ethics	F291, F296, F297	1.3	3.3.4	Business and contemporary society
126 Business and the environment	F296, 297		3.3.4, 4.3.1b	Business and contemporary society
127 Corporate responsibility	F297	1.3	3.3.4, 4.3.1a	Business and contemporary society
128 Technology	F291, F297			Business and contemporary society
129 Competition and business strategies	F297	1.7	2.3.3b	Business and contemporary society
130 Collecting and presenting data	F297			Business and contemporary society
131 Analysing data	F297			Business and contemporary society

Units		CCEA	WJEC
I	The nature of business	3.1 Adding value	BS1 What is business?
2	Enterprise	3.1 Forms of business organisation	BS1 Producing goods and services
3	Business ideas		
4	Business plans		
5	Evaluating business start-ups		
6	Stakeholders	3.3 Business objectives	BS1 External influences
7	Legal structure - sole traders and partnerships	3.1 Forms of business organisation	BS1 Business organisation
8	Legal structure - limited companies	3.1 Forms of business organisation	BS1 Business organisation
9	Legal structure - not for profit organisations	3.1 Forms of business organisation	BS1 Business organisation
10	Legal structure - public sector organisations	3.1 Forms of business organisation	BS1 Business organisation
11	The nature of marketing	3.1 Markets and market forces	BS1 Marketing
12	Market research	3.1 Market research	BS1 Marketing
13	Sampling	3.1 Market research	BS1 Marketing
14	Market segmentation	3.1 Marketing planning and strategy	BS1 Marketing
15	Market size, share and growth	3.1 Spectrum of competition	BS1 Marketing
16	The marketing mix	3.1 Marketing mix	BS2 Marketing
17	The product life cycle	3.1 Product life cycle	BS2 Marketing
18	New product development and product portfolio analysis	3.1 Product life cycle	BS2 Marketing
19	Price - influencing the market	3.1 Marketing mix	
20	Price - the influence of demand	3.1 Markets and market forces	BS4 Business analysis:marketing
21	Promotion	3.1 Marketing mix	
22	Place	3.1 Marketing mix	
23	Branding		BS2 Marketing
24	The market	3.1 Markets and market forces	BS1 External influences
25	Competition and business	3.1 Spectrum of competition	BS1 External influences
26	Marketing objectives	3.1 Marketing planning and strategy	
27	Marketing budgets	3.1 Marketing planning and strategy	
28	Marketing planning	3.1, 3.3 Marketing planning and strategy	BS4 Business analysis:marketing
29	Marketing strategies	3.1, 3.3 Marketing planning and strategy	BS4 Business analysis:marketing
30	International marketing		BS2 Marketing
31	E-commerce	3.1 Marketing mix	
32	Interpreting sampling results		
33	Forecasting and analysis		BS4 Business analysis:marketing
34	Sources of finance		BS1 Producing goods and services
35	Costs, revenue and profit		BS2 Accounting and finance
36	Contribution	3.2 Break-even analysis	BS2 Accounting and finance
37	Break-even analysis	3.2 Break-even analysis	BS2 Accounting and finance
38	Applications of break-even analysis	3.2 Break-even analysis	BS2 Accounting and finance
39	Cash flow	3.2 Cash flow	BS2 Accounting and finance
40	Improving cash flow	3.2 Cash flow	BS2 Accounting and finance
41	Setting budgets	3.2 Budgets	BS2 Accounting and finance
42	Using budgets	3.2 Variance analysis	BS4 Business analysis: accounting and finance
43	The role and objectives of accounting		
44	Balance sheets	3.2 Final accounts, 3.3 Company accounts	BS2 Accounting and finance
45	Business assets and depreciation	3.2 Depreciation	BS4 Business analysis: accounting and finance
46	Calculating depreciation and stock values	3.2 Depreciation	BS4 Business analysis: accounting and finance
47	Working capital		
48	Profit and loss accounts and income statements	3.2 Final accounts, 3.3 Company accounts	BS2 Accounting and finance
49	Measuring and increasing profit	3.2 Cash flow	BS4 Business analysis: accounting and finance
50	Financial data and performance		BS3 Business analysis
51	Accounting concepts		
52	Costing methods		BS4 Business analysis: accounting and finance
53	Investment appraisal	3.3 Investment appraisal	BS4 Business analysis: accounting and finance
54	Selecting financial strategies		
55	Interpreting published accounts - ratio analysis	3.3 Ratio analysis	BS3 Business analysis
56	The value and limitations of ratio analysis	3.3 Ratio analysis	BS3 Business analysis
57	Constructing accounts		
58	The valuation of businesses		
59	Organisational structures	3.2 Organisational design	BS2 People in organisations
60	Business organisation		
61	Measuring the effectiveness of the workforce		BS4 Business analysis: people in organisations
62	Recruitment	3.2 Investing in people	
63	Selection	3.2 Investing in people	
64	Appointment and termination		
65	Training and appraisal	3.2 Investing in people	
66	Motivation theories	3.2 Motivation	BS2 People in organisations
67	Financial methods of motivation	3.2 Motivation	BS2 People in organisations
68	Non-financial methods of motivation	3.2 Motivation	BS2 People in organisations
69	Management	3.2 Management and leadership	BS2 People in organisations
70	Leadership	3.2 Management and leadership	BS2 People in organisations
71	Individuals in business		

Units	CCEA	WJEC
72 Groups and teams in business		
73 Competitive workforce structures	3.2 Organisational design	BS4 Business analysis: people in organisations
74 Workforce planning	3.2 Investing in people	BS2 People in organisations
75 Human resources management		BS4 Business analysis: people in organisations
76 Communication	3.2 Communication	
77 Representation at work		BS4 Business analysis: people in organisations
78 Industrial democracy, bargaining, consultation and participation		BS4 Business analysis: people in organisations
79 Industrial disputes		BS4 Business analysis: people in organisations
80 The nature of production		BS1 Producing goods and services
81 Types of production	3.1 Investment and productivity	BS1 Producing goods and services
82 Capacity utilisation	3.1 Investment and productivity	BS2 Operations management
83 Stock control		BS2 Operations management
84 Quality	3.1 Quality	BS2 Operations management
85 Customer service		
86 Purchasing		BS2 Operations management
87 Using technology in operations	3.2 Organisational design	BS2 Operations management
88 Business size		
89 Economies of scale and resource mix	3.1 Investment and productivity	BS1 Producing goods and services
90 Mergers and takeovers	3.4 Change	BS3 Business objectives and strategy
91 Innovation, research and development		BS2 Operations management
92 Product design		BS2 Operations management
93 Factors affecting location		BS1 Producing goods and services
94 Location strategies		BS1 Producing goods and services
95 Lean production	3.1 Quality	BS2 Operations management
96 Resources and waste management	3.4 Change	BS4 Business analysis: operations management
97 Efficiency and strategy	3.1 Investment and productivity, 3.4 Change	BS2 Operations management
98 Critical path analysis		BS4 Business analysis: operations management
99 Operations management techniques		
100 Aims and vision	3.3 Business objectives	BS1 Business organisation
101 Objectives and mission	3.3 Business objectives	BS3 Business objectives and strategy
102 Strategy	3.3 Business strategy and planning	BS3 Business objectives and strategy
103 Planning	3.3 Business strategy and planning	BS3 Business objectives and strategy
104 Decision making		
105 Decision trees	3.3 Decision tree analysis	BS4 Business analysis: operations management
106 Fishbone diagrams and force field analysis		
107 Contingency planning	3.3 Contingency planning	BS4 Business objectives and strategy
108 Organisational culture	3.4 Corporate culture	BS3 Business objectives and strategy
109 Implementing and managing change	3.4 Change	BS3 Business objectives and strategy
110 Growth and the business cycle	3.4 Macroeconomic framework	BS3 External influences
111 Interest rates	3.4 Macroeconomic framework	BS3 External influences
112 Exchange rates	3.4 Macroeconomic framework	BS3 External influences
113 Inflation and deflation	3.4 Macroeconomic framework	BS3 External influences
114 Unemployment	3.4 Macroeconomic framework	BS3 External influences
115 Taxation	3.4 Macroeconomic framework	BS3 External influences
116 Population	3.4 Change	BS3 External influences
117 Labour markets and business	3.1 Spectrum of competition	BS3 External influences
118 Globalisation and multinational companies	3.4 Globalisation	BS3 External influences
119 Government policy	3.4 Macroeconomic framework	BS3 External influences
120 The EU and other international trading blocs	3.4 Change	BS3 External influences
121 Consumer protection	3.4 Change	BS3 External influences
122 Protection at work	3.4 Change	BS3 External influences
123 Equal opportunities legislation	3.4 Change	BS3 External influences
124 Pressure groups	3.4 Change	BS3 External influences
125 Business ethics	3.4 Business ethics and corporate social responsibility	BS3 External influences
126 Business and the environment	3.4 Change	BS3 External influences
127 Corporate responsibility	3.4 Business ethics and corporate social responsibility	BS3 External influences
128 Technology	3.4 Change	BS1 External influences
129 Competition and business strategies	3.4 Change	BS3 Business objectives and strategy
130 Collecting and presenting data		BS4 Business objectives and strategy
131 Analysing data		BS4 Business objectives and strategy